SEX AND DESIRE IN MUSLIM CULTURES

Gender and Islam Series

Published and Forthcoming Titles

Mainstreaming the Headscarf: Islamist Politics and Women in the Turkish Media, Ezra Ozcan

Masculinities and Displacement in the Middle East: Syrian Refugees in Egypt, Magdalena Suerbaum

Queer Muslims in Europe: Sexuality, Religion and Migration in Belgium, Wim Peumans

SEX AND DESIRE IN MUSLIM CULTURES

Beyond Norms and Transgression from the Abbasids to the Present Day

Edited by Aymon Kreil, Lucia Sorbera and Serena Tolino

I.B.TAURIS
LONDON • NEW YORK • OXFORD • NEW DELHI • SYDNEY

I.B. TAURIS
Bloomsbury Publishing Plc
50 Bedford Square, London, WC1B 3DP, UK
1385 Broadway, New York, NY 10018, USA
29 Earlsfort Terrace, Dublin 2, Ireland

First published in Great Britain 2021
This paperback edition published in 2022

Series cover design: Adriana Brioso
Cover image: © Huda Lutfi

A catalogue record for this book is available from the British Library.

A catalog record for this book is available from the Library of Congress.

ISBN: HB: 978-1-8386-0408-0
PB: 978-0-7556-3713-3
ePDF: 978-1-8386-0409-7
eBook: 978-1-8386-0410-3

Series: Gender and Islam

Typeset by Integra Software Services Pvt. Ltd.

CONTENTS

Part II
SUBVERTING THE SEXUAL NORM IN MODERN ARAB CULTURAL PRODUCTIONS

Part III
SEXUALITY, POWER AND RESILIENCE IN THE MIDDLE EAST AND NORTH AFRICA TODAY

ILLUSTRATIONS

LIST OF CONTRIBUTORS

Nadia Al-Bagdadi is Director of the Institute of Advanced Studies and Professor of History at Central European University, Budapest and Vienna. She received her doctoral degree from the Free University, Berlin, in 1996, in the field of Islamic Studies. She has held positions at the Free University, Berlin and the American University of Beirut, and has received a number of international fellowships. Among her publications are *Vorgestellte Öffentlichkeit: Zur Genese moderner Prosa in Ägypten 1860–1908* (2010) and *Striking from the Margins: State, Religion and Devolution of Authority in the Middle East* (2020), which she co-edited with Aziz Alazme and Harout Akdedian.

İrvin Cemil Schick holds a PhD from the Massachusetts Institute of Technology (MIT) and has taught at Harvard University, MIT and İstanbul Şehir University, as well as holding guest positions at Boston University, Sabancı University and Boğaziçi University. He is the author, editor or co-editor of twelve books including *The Erotic Margin: Sexuality and Spatiality in Alteritist Discourse* (1999) and *Writing the Body, Society, and the Universe: On Islam, Gender, and Culture* (in Turkish, 2011). He is currently working on a second doctorate at the Ecole des Hautes Etudes en Sciences Sociales; his thesis concerns occult practices in Islam, with special emphasis on their legitimation.

Mériam Cheikh is Lecturer in Anthropology at the Institut national des langues et civilisations orientales (Inalco), Paris. She is an anthropologist specializing in the study of the moral dissent of young people from the working classes in Morocco. Her work focuses on the transformation processes of sexuality, intimacy and gender relations at work in juvenile counter cultures. She was a Marie Skłodowska-Curie Fellow in the Department of Islamic and Middle Eastern Studies at the University of Edinburgh and a research fellow at OpenEdition-CNRS. She recently published *Les filles qui sortent: Jeunesse, sexualité et prostitution au Maroc* (2020).

Nijmi Edres is Postdoctoral Research Fellow at the Georg-Eckert Institute in Braunschweig, Germany. She was awarded a PhD in 'Islamic civilization' from the University of Rome 'Sapienza'. Before moving to Braunschweig, she held positions at Göttingen University and Exeter University. Among her recent publications are *Donne palestinesi in Israele: L'evoluzione del diritto musulmano all'ombra del conflitto* (2019) and *Uses of the Past: Sharīʿa and Gender in Legal Theory and Practice in Palestine and Israel* (2018), which she co-edited with Irene Schneider.

Aymon Kreil is Assistant Professor at the Department of Languages and Cultures and co-director of the Centre for Anthropological Research on Affect and

Materiality (CARAM) at Ghent University. He has conducted most of his research on love, sex and desire in Egypt. His work has been published in the *Journal of Middle East Women Studies*, *Arab Studies Journal*, *Critique internationale*, *Archives de Sciences sociales des religions* and *La Ricerca folklorica*. Recently, he has co-edited the books *Reinventing Love: Gender, Intimacy and Romance in the Arab World* (2018) and *Making Sense of Change: Methodological Approaches to Societies in Transformation* (forthcoming).

Erica Li Lundqvist is Senior Lecturer in Comparative Religions at the University of Malmö, Sweden. She has a PhD in Islamic studies and her doctoral thesis, 'Gayted Communities: Marginalized Sexualities in Lebanon', opened up virgin territory with extensive empirical material. Her recent publications include research on the intersection of sexuality and religion, attempting to put queer theory in dialogue with the study of leaving religion. She recently published 'Leaving Islam from a Queer Perspective', in the *Handbook of Leaving Religion* (2020) and 'Den skeva vägen: Queera strategier bland homosexuella muslimska män', in *i Levd Religion: Det heliga i vardagen* (2018).

Danilo Marino received his PhD in 2015 from both Università degli Studi di Napoli 'L'Orientale' and INALCO in Paris. From 2018 to 2019, he was a postdoctoral fellow at the Berlin Graduate School Muslim Cultures and Societies. His current research is devoted to the evolution of the notion of *muruwwa* in pre-modern Arabic and Islamic sources and models of masculinities as portrayed in Medieval Arabic historiography and literature. His publications include 'Hashish and Food: Arabic and European Medieval Dreams of Edible Paradises', in *Insatiable Appetite* (2019) and 'Raconter l'ivresse à l'époque mamelouke: Les mangeurs de haschich comme motif littéraire', in *Annales Islamologiques* (2015).

Achim Rohde is a Middle East historian and the academic coordinator of Academy in Exile's Critical Thinking Residency Program at the Free University, Berlin. Academy in Exile is a joint institutional platform for supporting scholars at risk from across the globe, supported by the Turkish Studies Department at the University of Duisburg-Essen, the Kulturwissenschaftliches Institut (Institute for Advanced Study in the Humanities, KWI) in Essen, the Berlin-based Forum Transregionale Studien and the Free University, Berlin. Rohde's research focuses on the modern and contemporary history of the Middle East and North Africa. He recently co-edited *Nationalism and Sexualities in Transregional Perspective: The Homophobic Argument* (2018).

Johannes Thomann gained his PhD in 1992 from the University of Zurich. He is now retired. His main interest lies in the history of science in the Islamic world. Among his publications are *Studien zum 'Speculum physionomie' des Michele Savonarola* (1997) and, with Mattias Vogel, *Schattenspur: Sonnenfinsternisse in Wissenschaft, Kunst und Mythos* (1999). In recent years, his main occupation had been the editing of Arabic astronomical documents, but he has also published on Arabic and Turkish folk literature.

Lucia Sorbera is Chair of the Department of Arabic Language and Cultures at the University of Sydney. A historian, she specializes in modern and contemporary Egyptian history, with a focus on women and gender. Her works have been published in *The Routledge Handbook of Middle East Politics* (2020), *Alphaville: Journal of Film and Screen Media* (2019), *Global Discourse: An Interdisciplinary Journal of Current Affairs and Applied Contemporary Thought* (2016), *Post-Colonial Studies* (2014) and *Genesis: The Journal of the Italian Society of Women's Historians* (2013).

Serena Tolino is Associate Professor of Islamic and Middle Eastern Studies at the University of Bern and co-director of the Institute for Islamic and Middle Eastern Studies. She specializes in the history of gender and sexuality in modern and pre-modern Islamicate societies and in Islamic law. She recently edited a special issue of *Oriente Moderno* on *Gender Equality and Women's Rights in the Constitutions of the Middle Eastern and North African Countries* (2018) and co-edited a special issue of the *Journal of Islamic and Arabic Studies* on *Minorities and Islamic Law* (2017) and a book on *Ambiguous Masculinity and Power: Ruling Bishops and Eunuchs in the Pre-modern World* (2018).

Koen Van Eynde worked for over five years at the Netherlands-Flemish Institute in Cairo, teaching Arabic and working on his PhD research, entitled 'Men in the Picture', awarded by the Katholieke Universiteit Leuven in 2015. He is an independent researcher, writing on women and gender representations in Arab cinema. His publications include a chapter on Egypt in *Women Screenwriters: An International Guide* (2015) and, with Mona Abdel-Fadil, *Golden Age Divas on the Silver Screen* (2016).

ACKNOWLEDGEMENTS

Every book is always both the terminal station of a shared journey and the point of departure for new ones. It is definitively a collective enterprise. This is even more true if the book is an edited volume. With these few words, we would like to acknowledge the contribution of all the colleagues, family and friends who made the writing of this book possible.

The project that inspired us kicked off in 2015 in Venice, where Serena and Lucia organized a panel titled 'Constructing and Subverting Gender Norms in the Middle East: History, Politics and Narratives of Non-Normative Sexualities', for the 12th Conference of the Italian Society for Middle East Studies, SeSaMO, which was held at Ca' Foscari University in Venice, on 16 and 17 January 2015.

We would like to thank the then President of SeSaMO Matteo Legrenzi and the board of the society who hosted the conference, as well as the participants of our panel for their insights and the productive debates during these days: Ashraf Hassan, Hans-Peter Pökel, Mirella Cassarino, Johannes Thomann, Achim Rohde, Martina Censi, Francesca Biancani, Federica Fedeli, Almut Höfert and Jolanda Guardi for starting the conversation that allowed this book to be conceived. However, none of the contributions collected in this book are the papers presented in the conference. When we first approached I.B.Tauris with the book proposal, we conceived a new project. It was a lucky circumstance that Aymon accepted Lucia and Serena's invitation to join the editorial team and, together, we reached out to new contributors. We would like to thank them all for agreeing to be part of this project and for being so patient, humble and generous in incorporating both our suggestions and those of the anonymous peer reviewers.

The editors of the I.B.Tauris series on Gender and Islam have gone far beyond their duties, guiding us through the whole process of conceiving and curating the manuscript. Heartfelt thanks to Bettina Dennerlein, Nadia Al-Bagdadi and Randi Deguilhem for their overwhelming support during the process of preparing the book proposal, collecting and editing the contributions, as well as Sophie Rudland and Yasmin Garcha for always being close to us during all the phases of the work. The anonymous peer reviewers gave us very generous and insightful feedback, as did our colleagues and friends. We are most indebted to the intellectual generosity of Hülya Çelik, Ashraf Hassan, Petr Kučera, Lana Tatour, Marco Lauri and Mark LeVine. Thank you!

We have been lucky to receive help from our graduate students and research assistants in several phases of the work: Rosemary Hancock, Shima Shahbazi, Paul Esber, Jennifer McLean and Ella Topolnicki at the University of Sydney; Lovisa Schau at the University of Hamburg for her support with revising the transliteration; Laura Emunds at the University of Bern for preparing the index; and Pat FitzGerald for her careful copyediting.

This book provides an unconventional history of the Arab and Muslim world by trying to bridge the gap between women and feminist and gender and sexuality scholarship, and between discipline and areas studies, philosophy and fieldwork-based research, while covering a long chronology from an interdisciplinary perspective. It is not straightforward to obtain institutional support for projects of this kind. We are grateful to our home institutions for supporting our work with travel grants that allowed us to work together, even if we are based in two different continents: the Faculty of Arts and Social Sciences and the School of Languages and Cultures at the University of Sydney; the Swiss National Foundation; the History Department and the Institute of Asian and Oriental Studies at the University of Zurich; the Asia and Africa Institute at the University of Hamburg; the Faculty of Humanities and the Institute for Islamic and Middle Eastern Studies at the University of Bern; and the Department of Languages and Cultures at Ghent University.

It was not easy to find a cover for this book. It was a further exercise of negotiation between norms and desires … special thanks go to the historian and artist Huda Lutfi for allowing us to use one of her works to illustrate the book cover. We feel humbled by her generosity, and we consider it one of the texts in the collection, which, we regret, does not include a contribution on visual arts and their role in shaping the past and contemporary Arab and Islamic cultural and intellectual sphere.

We are grateful to our friends and family for supporting and bearing with us during the journey. You know who you are.

Last but not least, we would like to thank each other for the mutual generosity, patience and care that we experienced during this long journey. A lot happened in our personal and professional lives, and it is with pride that we say that we have always been capable of backing each other up and giving each other empathic and active listening, as well as intellectual and emotional support, without which this book would never have come to fruition.

We learned a lot from each other, and a lot remains to be learned.

We like to think of this book as a tool through which we have learned something, and we are now passing it to the readers, with a dedication to Sofia, Francesco and Elias, with the wish that their desires will never know borders.

Aymon, Lucia and Serena

NOTE ON TEXT

For the transliteration of Arab, Ottoman and Persian terms, we followed the *International Journal of Middle East Studies* (IJMES) transliteration rules. Our only departure from IJMES is that we also retained the diacritics for book and film titles. In the ethnographic chapters, the authors have occasionally decided to maintain a transcription that is closer to the spoken language, as is common practice in their disciplines. We respected this decision, while also trying to keep consistency across the chapters. For pre-modern periods, dates given first are according to the *hijrī* calendar and second, to the Gregorian. All translations are by the authors, unless otherwise stated.

INTRODUCTION: THE MANY NAMES OF DESIRE

On the Study of Sexual Practices, Norms and Binaries in the Middle East

Aymon Kreil, Lucia Sorbera and Serena Tolino

The south and the east of the Mediterranean have long been the inverted mirror of Europe's fears and longings,[1] and as such, a defining place to try to circumvent by contrast the very idea of Europe in appreciative or critical fashion. Sexuality in this region has piqued the curiosity of Europeans and North Americans for a long time, either because it appears to be a place with fewer constraints on sexual practices, inducing desire or repulsion, or on the contrary, to condemn the rigidity and violence of its patriarchal norms and the ensuing sexual repression.[2] These clichés show concrete effects when North American and European governments justify the wars they launch in the Middle East by referring to the oppression of women, for instance, or when political parties of North American and European countries agitate in favour of exclusory politics against Muslim minorities using similar assertions.

Thus, the path to studying sex practices in the Middle East is littered with obstacles. Postcolonial feminist scholars have been the most vocal in challenging clichés, unveiling the imperial agendas hidden behind the 'white man's burden' and asserting that, indeed, Muslim women do not need the West to save them.[3] One of the risks in the endeavour of studying sexualities in Middle Eastern contexts is of othering the inhabitants of the region, a risk that has lain at the core of contemporary critiques of orientalism since Edward Said's foundational work.[4] The issue starts with the very assumption that there is a region called the 'Middle East' whose different parts bear enough commonalities to consider it as a relevant whole. The category of Middle East was created by colonial adventurers and entrepreneurs, initially to write about regions commanding access to India, with Persia and Afghanistan at its centre.[5] This geographical category has always been ill defined, but the term has nevertheless survived, despite its lack of precision, notably due to its use in international policy institutions and, concomitantly, to the expansion of area studies research and teaching programmes developed in the United States of America and later spreading all around the world, including the region designated as the Middle East itself.[6]

In this regard, what is most significant for us is the existence of a scholarly community engaging in a discussion on related topics, which makes a volume such as this possible. Thus, we accept the partial arbitrariness of the geographical framework behind this collection of essays. For us, problems start when the attempt to describe what the Middle East is, or even what sexuality in this ill-defined region is, leads to one form or another of cultural essentialisation. Yet, such an approach should not prevent us from exploring common genealogies around gender and sexualities, acknowledging the existence of common referents over the whole area and drawing comparisons between the different case studies assembled here.[7]

Among the commonalities between the different parts of the region, the strong presence of the Islamic referent all over its extent features prominently. Nevertheless, is this enough to link the sexual arousal of hashish smokers in Mamluk Cairo to the self-identified gay men wishing to marry in contemporary Beirut, or female slaves dressed as men in the time of the Abbasids, to women writers in Saddam Hussein's Iraq employing family metaphors to reflect about the situation of their society, to name a few examples taken from this volume?

Stressing the influence of Islam as a common feature of all the settings described in this book inevitably leads to the question of the reach of the norms bound to its teachings. How far can the practices mentioned above be described as Islamic even if they sometimes openly contradict rulings of major *ʿulamāʾ*? The notion of 'Islamicate' reflects this concern. It gave its name to a book on sexuality to which this volume owes much.[8] Coined by Marshall G. S. Hodgson to refer to 'the social and cultural complex historically associated with Islam and the Muslims, both among Muslims themselves and even when found among 'non-Muslims', in contrast to 'Islamic', which is instead used to refer to what has to do specifically with Islam as a religion,[9] the notion of Islamicate reflects this concern. Later, Shahab Ahmed criticized Hodgson's approach for narrowing down Islam to its prescriptive dimension. For Ahmed, such an understanding of Islam rests on its translation as a 'religion', a category whose modern definition originates in European secularism.[10] As a counterproposal, he suggests labelling as Islamic all aspects of experience that can become meaningful to Muslims in regard to Islam. This includes, for instance, drinking wine as a means to attain a state of knowledge and felicity, which allows exploration of the divine rule,[11] a position whose proponents were influential for many centuries.

In regard to gender and sexuality, both a prescriptive and a more expansive and open-ended approach to Islam are worth scrutinizing, as the chapters in this volume show. Beyond, it is also important to reflect on the existence of settings that people do not frame in relation to Islam, or at least not primarily, even if they could. Certain texts aim, for instance, mainly at literary entertainment[12] and certain situations, such as partying, do not foreground the relationship with God.[13] In certain instances, references to the divine seem out of place[14] as a result of the plurality of aspirations people hold, and this occurs even when they make no normative claims about secularism, as this book shows through its transhistorical scope.

To address the epistemic challenges facing empirical approaches to gender normativity in the Middle East, we propose in this introduction to rely on four core sociological insights that are valid for the whole period under consideration in this book: (1) the variability of hierarchies shaping norms; (2) the multiplicity of sources of authority on gender and sexuality that always coexist; (3) the existence of realms of activity in which the quest for pleasure seems to take precedence over dominant ethical goal setting, sometimes producing its own framework of normative expectations; and (4) the limits of our capacity as historians and social-science researchers to give a full account of the experience of sexuality. Before getting into the detail of these four premises, we first need to address a major issue of research on gender and sexuality: how sexuality outside Europe and North America is used in debates which are mainly shaped in the West and how the overbearing role of philosophy in contemporary gender studies influences the way it is done.

Conscription, philosophy and social sciences

As Andrew and Harriett Lyons have suggested, 'conscription' into the politics of home countries best defines the scholarly and literary approach of most authors interested in the topic of sexuality outside of Europe and North America.[15] As the Lyons underline, 'conscription' can be part of oppressive and emancipatory discourses alike. There are for instance racist depictions of oversexed Africans and undersexed Native Americans aimed at underpinning white superiority. However, attempts to present Pacific Islanders as models for sexual and educational reform, as in Bronislaw Malinowski's and Margaret Mead's accounts, are another instance of conscription. In all these cases it is accompanied by important distortions of ethnographical facts and should make us aware of the multivalence of the politics of representation. It highlights how problems can arise from a progressive agenda engaging in the critique of the configurations of power, of which sexualities are part, as well as from conservative research goals.

For instance, there has been a broad critical discussion of the limits of the categories of gay and lesbian in other historical and cultural contexts due to their North American and European origin, albeit research on the topic was originally triggered by emancipatory intentions. Homosexuality and heterosexuality are not self-evident categories. Concerning the Middle East, historians showed that sexual categories and the very place of sexuality for purposes of self-identification changed over time. Khaled El-Rouayheb, Dror Ze'evi, Kathryn Babayan and Afsaneh Najmabadi have written some of the most influential contributions, showing the diversity of meaning attached to sexual practices depending on the historical period under scrutiny.[16] Historically, poetry, medicine and juridical scholarship did not address sexuality in the same way, for instance, sometimes with opposite criteria of good involved, and limits between love, desire and friendship were always tangential, no matter the gender of those involved.

Joseph Massad wrote a harsh criticism of what he labelled the 'gay international' trying to impose Western sexual categories on Arab countries and triggering in reaction a conservative backlash on same-sex practices.[17] At the same time, for example, Lebanese exponents of Massad's 'gay international' directly engaged with his critique and underlined that they do not see themselves as 'agents of the West'.[18] Most of the chapters in this volume engage with this issue directly, in both past and present societies. For this volume, following Valerie Traub's discussion of Massad and Stephen Murray and Will Roscoe's works, we consider it important not to overstate the difference between identities and practices but to show how they intersect differently according to the period[19] by focusing more on processes of subjectivation than on the movement of abstract categories. This permits us to account for the new meanings acquired by transnational sexual categories through the process of their circulation and the manner in which they reshape aspirations, which consequently cannot be simply equated to some form of projection of epistemic imperialism.[20]

This leads us to an issue of possible conscription about which this edited volume invites a discussion, as not all its authors share the same approach to it: the relation of feminist history and sexuality studies with philosophy. Considerable attention has been paid to sexuality in the four last decades, notably since Michel Foucault paved the way in the early 1980s for new approaches that put an emphasis on the historical trends in which sexualities participate,[21] and since the success of Judith Butler's approach to the performativity of gender and heteronormativity as an organizing principle of society, which she developed in the mid-1990s.[22]

These two founding figures are among the few authors whose encounter was often experienced by readers as life changing. The radical questioning of the position of the subject they triggered by embedding knowledge in microphysics of power and the strength of sexual binaries in their performative reiteration remain at the core of contemporary studies on gender and sexuality. It is not our purpose to question the importance of power relations in the process of subjectivation, nor the historical contingency of gender binaries. Nor do we deny the appeal of the conceptual apparatus they developed, which had a deep influence on our reflections at different stages, right up to the present day. Our concern is more about certain uses of the references to Foucault and Butler, which in part probably result from the liberating effect their work can have, and which lead to neglect of the fact that their researches are primarily anchored in the field of philosophy before being applied to the exploration of social realities.

Pierre Bourdieu's biting criticism of Jacques Donzelot's work on family assistance in France as a means of disciplining the working class[23] should clarify our point. Bourdieu attacks overall what he sees as Donzelot's research dilettantism and opportunism:

> This overflight history gathers all conditions for a high symbolic return on the market of cultural products: the incessant back-and-forth between complicit allusions to the present – likely to produce the effect of 'high criticism' – and disjointed and disconnected references to the past – well suited to give the

> appearance of 'high culture' – and the resulting crossover of requirements which exempts both from any systematic investigation into the present – which would only remove its philosophical height from the discourse – and from any in-depth research in the past – which by placing institutions and practices back into the system from which they receive their meaning and their sociological necessity, would constitute the past as the past and cancel out the object of retrospective indignation.[24]

Bourdieu later expanded this critique to certain aspects of Foucault's approach, despite their friendship at the Collège de France. For Bourdieu, Foucault plays a 'double-game',[25] reinforcing the symbolic pre-eminence of philosophy over social sciences by refusing to engage with their own epistemology and methods while claiming authority from knowledge derived from historical and sociological data.[26]

This shows, for instance, in the periodization and spatial divide Foucault proposes to sustain his philosophical argument, which historians and researchers specializing in the Middle East have questioned since, most notably his distinction between *ars erotica* and *scientia sexualis*, the latter paving the way, according to him, for the regime of modernity.[27] Classical Islamic sources do indeed not explicitly categorize sexual norms as a specific realm of knowledge. For example, Classical Arabic dictionaries, such as the thirteenth-century *Lisān al-ʿArab* by Ibn Manẓūr, the treaties of *fiqh* and the manuals of medicine produced in the medieval context, do not explicitly attempt at disciplining the different forms of desire and sexualities, as discussed in the first part of the book. Nevertheless, we tend to agree with Valerie Traub when she writes that: 'disciplinary apparatuses and taxonomic classifications regulated sexuality long before the nineteenth century' and, moreover, that 'the anxiety for regulation goes well beyond the so-called "West"'.[28] Likewise, Lucia Sorbera's contribution to this volume invites us to nuance Foucauldian approaches to psychiatry, which have traditionally focused on it as a form of disciplinary power, by highlighting how feminist activists have made it an important vector of critical political engagement in Egypt.

In some regards, Judith Butler's work shows the same ambivalent positioning towards social sciences as do Foucault's researches. In contemporary studies on sexuality, this becomes clear with the category of norm, for instance, and more specifically of the non-normative, the use of which elicited discussions among the editors of this volume. Following Butler's decisive influence, the non-normative seems to be both an interpretative lens of interpreting sexual practices and an emancipatory promise. By contrast, the normative almost always refers to the binarism of heteronormativity, which needs to be overcome for emancipatory perspectives to become true. Traub has already warned of the possible dangers of dehistoricizing heteronormativity, as the meanings associated with heterosexual relations change through time, along with the sense of conformity and transgression.[29] Tom Boellstorff likewise pointed to the contextual variability of the meaning of sameness and difference when associated with sexual relations, as they could also apply to religion and ethnicity, for instance.[30] There is indeed something slightly anti-sociological in a definition of norms that seems to equate them solely to one model of hegemonic rule, heteronormativity, which explains the singular 'the norm' that was taken up by some of Butler's followers. The 'non-normative', by contrast, seems to be a word for replacing the derogatory notion of the 'abnormal' by fuelling it with positive connotations, a choice that is in many ways unfortunate as it maintains the notion of a monolithic and exclusive centre of hegemony in society.

Indeed, the underlying question is the coherency and cohesiveness of social orders, if there is only one reference model with which to agree, or which to question or oppose. This conception is problematic as paradoxically it leads back to what looks like a functionalist understanding of domination, with which every element would simultaneously concur. Defining elements defying this central norm as non-normative further denies them the possibility of articulating counter-norms and imposes them in restricted spaces. Advocating the 'non-normative' as a project of emancipation leads to calls for relationships devoid of any constraints of power, which is paradoxically anti-political as a utopia, if we consider that politics starts with struggle. A norm, we would rather say, starts when people begin to express expectations about each other's behaviour, even in dominated groups. Advocating such a position does not mean denying that social domination exists and that some norms are stronger than others. It simply accounts for the fact that there exist multiple competing attempts to establish hegemony, and each of these attempts produces its own effects of power.

Nowadays, as 'the moral absolutism of their informants may present a strong challenge for anthropologists who believe in sexual relativism', according to the Lyons,[31] it is possible to reasonably ask: are the subalterns Foucauldians? Are the repressed and invisibilized Butlerians? Too often, the philosophical concerns of social researchers are transposed into the reality of their interlocutors and described as moulding their own preoccupations.[32] It is difficult not to see here another form of conscription of the sexuality of others, based on emancipatory ideals many of us would agree with at least morally even if not historically and sociologically, or even of 'puppeteering', to use John Borneman and Abdellah Hammoudi's expression.[33] The appeal of approaches presenting the study of sexuality as a tool to overcome heteronormativity by historicizing it; by exploring ancient and contemporary queer positions towards sex, repressive strategies and regimes of sexuality; and by supporting queer livings by making this knowledge available is strong, legitimate and useful. However, acknowledging this need for alternative narratives should not make us abide by wishful thinking based on philosophical assumptions, which would by consequence just represent another means of confiscating the others' words, but in the name of progressive ideals.

To counter such risks, the answer cannot be a low-brow empiricism, denying the tacit assumptions necessarily shaping its interpretations.[34] Therefore, we would like to argue, in line with Tom Boellstorff, for 'critical empiricism', an approach he defines as follows:

> An approach that although not fetishizing 'data' nevertheless demands that theorizations be accountable to their subjects of study. To those in the academy

> who wish to speak about the actual lives of persons embodied in specific historical, cultural and material contexts, this critical empiricism asks between the relation of adequation between any theorization and the discursive realities they claim to interpret.[35]

The contribution of philosophy to shaping our understanding of the world, through providing us with concepts and questioning common-sense conceptions, is vital. Our own work testifies to the inspiration of such philosophers as Foucault, Butler and Gilles Deleuze, for instance, on our understanding of reality.[36] To become a dialogue, however, the relationship between philosophy and social sciences needs to recognize the more speculative character of the former and the need for the latter in the last resort to remain true to the interlocutors with whom it engages through research in archives, literary exploration and ethnography, to quote just the inquiry methods employed by the contributors to this edited volume.

The many names of desire

As mentioned above, we identified four premises on which to build a meaningful dialogue between philosophy and social sciences around gender and sexuality, of which the contributions to this volume give examples. First, to explore the ways power games, hierarchies and fluidity resonate with each other, beyond the mere ethnocartography of instances of gender fluidity or subversive sexual practices,[37] for a better understanding of historically situated configurations of power in which sexualities partake. To embed hierarchies into practices that North Americans and Europeans would define as sexual is not restricted to the West.[38] Therefore, it is necessary to pay close attention to the diversity of configurations commanding hierarchies, their enforcement and subversion. Serena Tolino's chapter in this volume is a good example of such an approach.

Second, to reflect on the multiplicity of competing institutional realms claiming authority over gender and sexualities, and the ways people accommodate this plurality in their ethical reflections and for practical purposes. Are sexual categories constructed as 'general' norms or are they constructed in different ways when looking at different fields of knowledge? For instance, was the 'sexual norm' in the legal discourse, which developed between the ninth and the thirteenth centuries, conceived in the same way as in the coeval medical discourse or in *adab*, namely that part of literature that included mostly prose or poetry of a non-religious nature? How were social practices developed in relation to these discourses? Stressing the importance of understanding which kinds of knowledge can simultaneously claim access to the truth about sexuality – for instance, poetry, religious science and medicine – should lead us to critically reassess the knowledge–power nexus by showing a plurality of discourses competing to describe reality.[39] Instead of reducing the formulation of norms to a single coherency, recognizing this plurality of discourses on sexuality will allow us to offer a better account of the many names of desire, which is one of the core ambitions of this book.

Third, to discuss the variety of settings in which people do not aim at conformity with dominant norms, even when they do not openly antagonize them. It is, for instance, fully possible to both recognize the general validity of contemporary Salafi interpretations when it comes to Islam and to celebrate the enjoyment of hashish or to recount bold sexual adventures to friends at gatherings.[40] Marino's depiction of bawdy literature from the Mamluk time evokes similar settings in which it is less about reinterpreting a large array of practices in the light of Islam than simply enjoying a good time, even if he shows the links commentators at the time drew between hashish and certain Sufi orders. These are the stances Ahmed defines as 'para-nomian' rather than anti-nomian, i.e. beside the law rather than against it.[41] Such settings are productive of their own normativity for those involved. There is often a strong link, for instance, between pleasure excess and masculinity, in a way that is not necessarily congruent with shared conceptions of the common good in a given period. Total indifference to dominant norms is impossible, though, and creates ambivalence towards alternative normativities. Silence about certain sexual practices, for example, reflects this ambivalence. Avoiding open discussion about certain practices can be both a way to mute the existence of certain desires and a strategy for avoiding conflict with dominant social expectations and carving out spaces of liberty,[42] as Erica Li Lundqvist emphasizes in this volume. However, when it comes to subjectivation, it is important not to presume that dominant rules always gain the upper hand, as contrary discourses can be as decisive in the process of shaping the self.

Fourth, any research on gender and sexuality needs a 'recognition of the impossibility of our ever fully knowing what [material sex] acts might mean' due to the inadequacy of words to express certain dimensions of sexual experience and of desire.[43] Traub considers that it is our role as scholars to make such an acknowledgement productive. Desire, pleasure, the 'event' of the body happening all of a sudden 'randomly in an embrace',[44] all these are experiences that escape their formalization into coherent meaning and to which explanation by context will never do justice. Hence, the recognition of the existence of aspects of experience we cannot know should make us aware of the limits of all knowledge,[45] even if it should not, however, lead to a mysticism of sexuality as a reflection of some hidden truth about the self, thus unduly overstating its importance without regard for differences between social and historical settings.

Summary of the book

The book is composed of three parts, each one addressing the discussion about sexuality and desire from different disciplinary perspectives and with different historical and geographical focuses. All together the eleven chapters question sexual categories by historicizing the notion of masculinity, femininity and what is in between, shifting the focus from the construction of identity to subjectivity, and showing how sexuality contributes to shape subjectivities.

The first part of the book includes four chapters that look, using different sources and approaches, at how gender categories were constructed, discussed and challenged from the Abbasid to the Ottoman period. Serena Tolino's chapter looks at how the concepts of masculinity and femininity were understood in different genres in the so-called classical period of Islamic history, namely the period from the third/ninth to the seventh/thirteenth century AH/CE. The chapter addresses the question of whether a gender binary, constructed in terms of men/women, male/female, makes sense at all with reference to Islamic pre-modern societies. Looking at how lexicography, medicine, legal sources and *adab* (particularly through al-Jāḥiẓ's work) defined and categorized who is a male and who is a female, and how they approached intermediate categories, the chapter argues that if, on the one hand, the fluidity of categories was certainly relevant when looking at the construction of gender in pre-modern sources, on the other hand, gender was clearly constructed into a hierarchical system. Categories were probably more fluid than the modern gender binary is, but still there was a clear difference between being a man and not being a man: the adult male, 'the man', however defined, was still the only person to be at the top of this hierarchical categorization. This also had an impact on which kinds of sexual acts were socially accepted, even when deemed morally reprehensible, and which were completely rejected: if an adult man could have sex with a boy, something that was still prohibited according to prevailing interpretations of Islamic jurisprudence, it would not have been acceptable for the same man to express the desire to be penetrated, because a man had to be the active partner of a sexual intercourse, while all the other possible gender categories were supposed to take a passive role. Here, the tension between legal sources and other genres deserves to be underscored again, and it confirms Thomas Bauer's point on 'the culture of ambiguity'.[46] In the pre-modern period in Islamic societies there was not one single register of truth but many 'truths' that coexisted, that should not be understood as 'norms' and 'deviation' from the norm, but more as a coexistence of different norms, all of them considered as such by the same group of people at the same moment. In this sense, literary sources do not 'contradict' legal sources: they simply shape another kind of discourse.

The fluidity of the gender categories is also the object of Johannes Thomann's chapter, which focuses on women dressing up and adorning themselves or being adorned as men with the intention of producing desire. The chapter argues that there are basically two categories of these women, the *ghulāmiyyāt*, who were slaves, and the *shāṭirāt*, who were free women who voluntarily cross-dressed. When jurists started to perceive them as a widespread challenge to Islamic morals, they put the *ghulāmiyyāt* and the *shāṭirāt* together and coined the term *mutarajjilāt* (masculine women) for both. Thomann shows that while in the Umayyad time *mutarajjilāt* were not a topic in *ḥadīth*, they became so later, probably when they became a widespread phenomenon in Abbasid Bagdad that worried the local *ʿulamāʾ*, who felt the need to put into circulation *ḥadīth*-s attributed to the Prophet Muḥammad, where not only feminine men (*mukhannathūn*) but also *mutarajjilāt* were blamed. Interestingly, this is similar to what happened with *ḥadīth*-s on *liwāṭ* (sodomy),[47] and this obviously confirms the centrality of social and historical circumstances in the making of what would later become the canonical corpus of the Sunna.

Danilo Marino's chapter looks at masculinity during the Mamluk period, and in particular at the role that intoxication (*sukr*) had in the definition of masculinity in comparison to drunkenness. Marino's chapter sheds light on the tensions between legal and literary narratives on the topic: while Muslim jurists were mostly concerned to assess the difference in effects that the two substances had on sexual desire and masculinity, literary sources tend to borrow from the repertoire of wine literature with the aim of entertaining the reader. Further, as in Tolino's contribution, in this chapter, the binary active/passive seems central to the definition of sexuality: while Muslim jurists created an analogy between deviant dervishes, hashish eaters and men who practised passive sodomy, as they consider that all of them challenged the accepted ideas of masculinity, literary sources seem to point out that the use of hashish was connected to the active penetration of beardless boys, which did not affect the masculinity of an adult man at all. The tension between these two typologies of texts hints once again at Thomas Bauer's point on the coexistence of norms.

Finally, İrvin Cemil Schick's chapter allows us once again to question the suitability and the historicity of a binary representation of gender and sexuality: focusing on Ottoman erotic terminology from the mid-fourteenth to the mid-nineteenth century, Cemil Schick argues that the Ottomans had three and not two main genders: indeed, even though boys shared some characteristics with women, they were considered another gender, and this allows him to theorize a model including men, women and boys. In regard to sexuality, Cemil Schick argues, in concordance with research on Arabic-speaking sources from previous periods, and as Tolino's chapter does, that pre-modern sources from Islamic societies allow recognition of two main categories: those who penetrate (active) and those who are penetrated (passive).

Overall, this first section of the book aims at building the foundation of the discourse on sexuality in pre-modern and early modern Arab and Islamic sources, contributing to the discussion on how to historically study sexual norms and categories before the 'invention' of modern sexuality.[48]

The second part of the book crosses the borders between the pre-modern and the modern age. As it has been argued already by a number of authors (most notably Najmabadi and Massad),[49] in the nineteenth century, attitudes on sexuality began to change fundamentally, in particular under European influence, and the modernization project put at its centre new conceptions of gender and sexuality that included, for example, a less fluid gender binary, now strictly constructed in terms of man and woman, a stronger disapproval of homoerotic practices, the emergence of the companionate marriage and the centrality of the nuclear family.

As one of the consequences of this shift, an entire literary genre inevitably disappeared. This genre included different typologies of text: obscene poetry (*mujūn*), love poetry (*ghazal*), erotic handbooks, philosophical treatises that dealt with both physical and spiritual love, and the works of *adab* that included discussions on eros, sexuality and social etiquette. Nadia Al-Bagdadi's chapter tackles this shift, discussing how, in the nineteenth century, while the *ars erotica* disappeared, the novel was adapted to discuss forms of sexuality more in line with the new moral and sexual standards. Al-Bagdadi focuses in particular on the novels of the Egyptian author ʿAlī Mubārak, and in particular on his *ʿAlam al-Dīn* (1882), whose title refers to the name of its main character, and of the Lebanese author Aḥmad Fāris al-Shidyāq, namely his *al-Sāq ʿalā al-Sāq* (*Leg over Leg*) (1855).

The centrality of literature and its poietic function is also at the centre of Achim Rohde's contribution, which looks at the relation between literature, sexuality and war in Baʿthist Iraq. Rohde focuses on the genre of 'war literature' during the 1980s and particularly on the work of one prominent female author, Luṭfiyya al-Dulaymī (b.1943). Al-Dulaymī's work shows subversive dimensions that become particularly evident when applying a gender perspective to its reading. This allows Rohde to problematize the construction of gender relations even in a totalitarian dictatorship, challenging the 'masculinity' rhetoric expressed by the Baʿthist regime, but also the ideal of the companionate marriage, which was so central to the modernist project but reached a critical point in the context of war.

Finally, Koen Van Eynde's chapter discusses the representations of male homosexuality in Egyptian cinema, trying to answer the question of how films assert, challenge and reframe gender norms. Van Eynde analyses two films produced in the 1970s: *Ḥammām al-Malaṭīlī* (Malatili Bath)[50] and *Qiṭṭa ʿalā Nār* (Cat on Fire).[51] Van Eynde decides to focus on these two films, as they seem to depart from the common practice of simply showing the existence of same-sex sexual acts and, rather, make a case for the possibility of gay identities. The analysis of the two films allows Van Eynde to question the equation of normalcy with heteronormativity in representations of homosexuality in Egyptian cinema, arguing for a more nuanced approach that takes into consideration the dialectic between the international and the local debate. This approach allows the author to take into consideration multiple factors influencing the representation of homosexuality in cinema, including political factors. In the case of Egypt, the theme of 'indigeneity' and 'cultural authenticity' has been used by conservative political actors – both religious and secular – and the current backlash against gay people confirms the inherent link between gender representations, the governing of sexuality and authoritarianism.

Overall, this section illustrates how modern and contemporary Arabic cultural production is a site of construction, transgression and reformulation of gender norms. It also bridges the gap between pre-modern and modern cultural studies, generally conceived as discontinuous fields, showing that continuities between the pre-modern and the modern world are as relevant as fractures. Literature and the arts are the fields where these continuities are more visible, especially in the readaptation of classical genres to illustrate new themes.

The third part of the book contributes to the debate from the perspective of the social sciences with four contributions that, building on feminist historiography and social anthropology, question simplistic dichotomies and binaries, and emphasize the necessity to situate the debates about sexuality and the emergence of subjectivities in their specific contexts, taking into consideration the mutual constitutive relationship between gender and political power.

Lucia Sorbera's chapter illustrates the bond between feminists and the human rights communities in Egypt, and the revolutionary potential of this link. Drawing on some critical insights of the feminist oral historian Luisa Passerini,[52] especially her emphasis on memory as a mode of subjectivity and the mutual constitutional relationship between memory and the present, Sorbera focuses on the political biography of Aida Seif al-Dawla, a veteran of both second-wave feminism and the human rights movement in Egypt. Central to the analysis in this chapter is the relationship between psychiatry, feminism and human rights activism. Feminist psychiatrists, explains Sorbera, have conceived psychiatry as a politics of care, and in so doing they bridged the gap between psychiatry and politics, showing that mental health care intersects the critique of political authoritarianism and socio-economic injustice. Charting a feminist genealogy of the human rights movement, Sorbera questions both Western-centred histories of human rights activism and male-centred narratives of the history of Egyptian political dissidence. She asserts that feminist human rights defenders have been crucial both in inscribing gender and sexuality at the centre of the human rights agenda in Egypt and in opening a discussion about the necessity to decolonize the international history of human rights.

Mériam Cheikh's ethnographic study on young women engaging in sexual relations in return for money in Tangier questions the notion of 'prostitution' that is commonly adopted by social commentators and suggests that trajectories and pathways of young women experiencing transactional sex have a plurality of horizons. Grounding her analysis on women's accounts about their own practices, and on the observation of intimate spaces where new collective subjectivities are constructed, Cheikh recognizes the triple dimension of *khrīj* (going out): prostitution, date and fun. Fostering the understanding of the formation of young women's subjectivities, Cheikh's ethnography highlights changes of norms and transformations, and questions the binary that opposes sexual financial transaction to morality by showing that, among women who practise *khrīj* in Tangier, asserting youthfulness attenuates the sense of transgression otherwise bound to practices going against common-sense morality.

Personal narratives (and silences) are also at the centre of the last two chapters of this book, written by Erica Li Lundqvist and Nijmi Edres, respectively. Lundqvist's chapter is also the result of a long ethnographic research, this time in Lebanon among young gay men, and it discusses the strategy of silence, not only as a mechanism for controlling what is seen as diverting from the norm but also as a useful tactic for personal liberation. Silence is seen not only as oppressive or as a consequence of fear, shame and guilt, or as an approval of the heteronormative way of life but as a navigating tool and a useful tactic among young men in Lebanon who self-identified as Muslim and gay. This analysis breaks the normative binary between coming out and being in the closet by introducing new nuances in the debate and explaining how opacity can be a conscious strategy to live a gay life without addressing issues of sexuality in a conservative environment.

Edres looks at how religion is configured and reconfigured by Palestinian queers in Israel, and how this discussion can offer some useful insights into the debate on the relationship between religious normativity and sexual subjectivity. Edres observes that the Palestinian debate on sexuality does not engage with religious normativity. The relationship between religious normativity and sexual identity is tackled at the individual level or in the restricted circle of intimates. Similarly to what happens for women and feminism, debates on lesbian, gay, bisexual, transgender and queer (LGBTQ) rights in this specific context intersect nationalism and the discrimination that Palestinians experience as Israeli citizens towards their Jewish counterparts, their claims for equality getting bound to those of the Palestinian minority as a whole.

Overall, the four chapters contribute to bridging the gap between speculative and fieldwork-based approaches to the study of gender and sexuality, shifting the focus from the theme of identity to subjectivity, as mentioned above, by narrating history from the perspective of their subjects. What is central to all these chapters is indeed how the subjects define themselves and their experiences. The biographical method adopted in these chapters allow subjectivities to emerge through the processes of self-definition and self-narration, and this contributes to understanding the formation of subjectivities beyond gender binaries.

Sex and desire beyond norm and transgression: From the Abbasids to the present day

This book endeavours to shed light on how sexual norms and the categories underpinning them are constructed and challenged, and how multiple subjectivities emerge in the process of their construction. Based on rich evidence of interdisciplinary enquiry, and applying a *longue durée* perspective, it shows the way the formulation of norms, their boundaries and their subversion are interconnected. In addition, this book contributes to confirm that their meaning cannot be grasped without taking into account their specific social and historical context. Acknowledging the plurality of discourses on desires, instead of reducing the formulation of norms to a single source – as for example Islamic jurisprudence – nor reducing norms to a single instance – as heteronormativity, for example – allows us to go beyond the dichotomy of norm and transgression, in multipolar social environments. However, this volume does not aim to provide an exhaustive perspective on sexuality in the Middle East across time. Such an endeavour would be illusory, in any case, and would produce the fallacious impression of the possibility of an overarching gaze on sexual practices in the region, which would necessarily be arbitrary and reductive. Therefore, as editors, our aim with this book is to present evidence of different ways to engage with sexuality by trying to stay true to the words of those we portray, and to show the plurality of meaning attached to sexual practices. If we managed to convey at least a glimpse of desire in the Middle East as its inhabitants experience it, and some of the many names they use to approach it, we have, in our perspective, fulfilled our goal.

Notes

1 François Hartog, *The Mirror of Herodotus: The Representation of the Other in the Writing of History* (Berkeley, CA: University of California Press, 1988).
2 Frédéric Lagrange, *Islam d'interdits, islam de jouissance* (Paris: Téraèdre, 2008); Julia Ann Clancy Smith, *Domesticating the Empire: Race, Gender, and Family Life in French and Dutch Colonialism* (Charlottesville, VA: University Press of Virginia, 1998); Malek Alloula, *The Colonial Harem* (Minneapolis, MN: University of Minnesota Press, 1986).
3 Lila Abu-Lughod, *Do Muslim Women Need Saving?* (Cambridge, MA: Harvard University Press, 2013).
4 Edward W. Said, *Orientalism* (New York: Pantheon Books, 1978).
5 Its first known mention appears in an article of 1900 by General Thomas E. Gordon. In 1902, in an article by the American naval strategist Alfred Thayer Mahan, it was used to designate the area around the sea route between Suez and Singapore. Soon after, *The Times* published a series of articles by Valentine Ignatius Chirol devoted to 'The Middle Eastern Question', where the term Middle East referred to the Persian (or Arab) Gulf and the lands and sea close to India, which at that time was the strategic core of the Middle East. Later, during the First World War, it came to designate what was formerly known as the Near East on the Asian remains of the Ottoman Empire. See Roderic H. Davison, 'Where is the Middle East?' *Foreign Affairs*, 38 (4) (1960): 665–75; Clayton R. Koppes, 'Captain Mahan, General Gordon, and the Origins of the Term "Middle East"', *Middle Eastern Studies*, 12 (1) (1976): 95–8; James Renton, 'Changing Languages of Empire and the Orient: Britain and the Invention of the Middle East, 1917–1918', *Historical Journal*, 50 (3) (2006): 645–67.
6 For an exhaustive analysis of the development of area studies in the United States between the 1920s and the 1980s with reference to the Middle East, see Zachary Lockman, *Field Notes: The Making of Middle East Studies in the United States* (Stanford, CA: Stanford University Press, 2016).
7 Nevertheless, we need to remain conscious that other commonalities and *tertium comparationis* could be found if we chose to focus on an area including Europe, China or South Asia, for instance.
8 Kathryn Babayan and Afsaneh Najmabadi (eds), *Islamicate Sexualities: Translations across Temporal Geographies of Desire* (Cambridge, MA: Harvard University Press, 2008).
9 Marshall G. S. Hodgson, *The Venture of Islam. Conscience and History in a World Civilization*, vol. 1, *The Classical Age of Islam* (Chicago, IL: University of Chicago Press, 1977), 59.
10 Shahab Ahmed, *What Is Islam? The Importance of Being Islamic* (Princeton, NJ: Princeton University Press, 2015), 157–75. On the topic of secularization, see also Talal Asad, *Genealogies of Religion: Discipline and Reasons of Power in Christianity and Islam* (Baltimore, MD: Johns Hopkins University Press, 1993).
11 Ahmed, *What Is Islam?*, 417–22.
12 See Marino and Al-Bagdadi, in this volume.
13 See Cheikh, in this volume. See also Asef Bayat, 'Islamism and the Politics of Fun', *Public Culture*, 19 (3) (2007): 433–59.
14 Aymon Kreil, 'Se faire cheikh au Caire: Exemplarité et intériorité religieuse', *Archives de Sciences sociales des religions*, 149 (2010): 255–72
15 Andrew P. Lyons and Harriet Lyons, *Irregular Connections: A History of Anthropology and Sexuality* (Lincoln, NE: University of Nebraska Press, 2004), 18–19.

16 Dror Ze'evi, *Producing Desire: Changing Sexual Discourse in the Ottoman Middle East, 1500–1900* (Berkeley, CA: University of California Press, 2006); Khaled El-Rouayheb, *Before Homosexuality in the Arab-Islamic World: 1500–1800* (Chicago, IL: University of Chicago Press. 2005); Babayan and Najmabadi, *Islamicate Sexualities.*

17 Joseph Andoni Massad, *Desiring Arabs* (Chicago, IL: University of Chicago Press, 2008).

18 See Joseph Massad and Ernesto Pagano, 'The West and the Orientalism of Sexuality: Joseph Massad (Columbia University) talks to Ernesto Pagano' (*Reset Dialogues*, 14 December 2009). Available online: https://www.resetdoc.org/story/the-west-and-the-orientalism-of-sexuality/(accessed 1 February 2020); Ghassan Makarem, 'We Are Not Agents of the West: Ghassan Makarem Replies to Joseph Massad' (*Reset Dialogues*, 14 December 2009). Available online: https://www.resetdoc.org/story/we-are-not-agents-of-the-west/ (accessed 1 February 2020); and Joseph Massad, 'I Criticize Gay Internationalists, not Gays: Joseph Massad Counter-replies to Ghassan Makarem' (*Reset Dialogues*, 14 December 2009). Available online: https://www.resetdoc.org/story/i-criticize-gay-internationalists-not-gays/(accessed 1 February 2020).

19 Valerie Traub, 'The Past Is a Foreign Country? The Times and Spaces of Islamicate Sexuality Studies', in Kathryn Babayan and Afsaneh Najmabadi (eds), *Islamicate Sexualities: Translations across Temporal Geographies of Desire*, 1–40 (Cambridge, MA: Harvard University Press, 2008); Stephen O. Murray and Will Roscoe (eds), *Islamic Homosexualities: Culture, History, and Literature* (New York: New York University Press, 1997).

20 Dennis Altman, 'Global Gaze/Global Gays', *GLQ: A Journal of Lesbian and Gay Studies*, 3 (4) (1997): 417–36.

21 Michel Foucault, *Histoire de la sexualité* (Paris: Gallimard, 2011).

22 Judith Butler, *Gender Trouble: Feminism and the Subversion of Identity* (New York: Routledge, 1990); Judith Butler, *Bodies That Matter: On the Discursive Limits of Sex* (New York: Routledge, 1994).

23 Jacques Donzelot, *La police des familles* (Paris: Minuit, 1977).

24 Pierre Bourdieu, *Le bal des célibataires: Crise de la société paysanne en Béarn* (Paris: Seuil, 2002), 293 (our translation).

25 Pierre Bourdieu, *Science de la science et réflexivité: Cours du Collège de France 2000–2001; Cours et travaux* (Paris: Raisons d'Agir, 2001), 201.

26 Staf Callewaert, 'Bourdieu, Critic of Foucault: The Case of Empirical Social Science against Double-Game-Philosophy', *Theory, Culture and Society*, 23 (6) (2006): 73–98.

27 Traub, 'The Past Is a Foreign Country?', 17–18.

28 Ibid., 17.

29 Ibid., 23.

30 Tom Boellstorff, 'Queer Studies in the House of Anthropology', *Annual Review of Anthropology*, 36 (2007): 27.

31 Lyons and Lyons, *Irregular Connections*, 330.

32 Jean Bazin, Des *clous dans la Joconde: L'anthropologie autrement* (Toulouse: Anacharsis, 2008), 85–7.

33 John Borneman and Abdellah Hammoudi, 'The Fieldwork Encounter, Experience, and the Making of Truth: An Introduction', in John Borneman and Abdellah Hammoudi (eds), *Being There: The Fieldwork Encounter and the Making of Truth*, 1–24 (Berkeley, CA: California University Press, 2009), 11.

34 Margot Weiss, 'The Epistemology of Ethnography: Method in Queer Anthropology', *GLQ: A Journal of Lesbian and Gay Studies*, 17 (4) (2011): 649–64.

35 Boellstorff, 'Queer Studies in the House of Anthropology', 19.
36 Aymon Kreil, 'Love Scales: Class and Expression of Feelings in Cairo', *La Ricerca Folklorica*, 69 (2014): 83–91; Aymon Kreil, 'Territories of Desire: A Geography of Competing Intimacies in Cairo', *Journal of Middle East Women's Studies*, 12 (2) (2016): 166–80; Serena Tolino, *Atti omosessuali e omosessualità fra diritto islamico e diritto positivo: il caso egiziano con alcuni cenni all'esperienza libanese* (Naples: Edizioni Scientifiche Italiane, 2013); Serena Tolino, 'Homosexuality in the Middle East: An Analysis of Dominant and Competitive Discourses', *DEP: Deportate, Esule, Profughe*, 25 (2014): 72–91.
37 Kath Weston, 'Lesbian/Gay Studies in the House of Anthropology', *Annual Review of Anthropology*, 22 (1993): 341; Boellstorff, 'Queer Studies in the House of Anthropology', 18–19.
38 Lyons and Lyons, *Irregular Connections*, 14; Maurice Godelier, *The Making of Great Men: Male Domination and Power among the New Guinea Baruya*, trans. Rupert Swyer (Cambridge: Cambridge University Press, 1996).
39 Paul Veyne, *Les Grecs ont-ils cru à leurs mythes? Essai sur l'imagination constituante* (Paris: Seuil, 1983); El-Rouayheb, *Before Homosexuality in the Arab-Islamic World*; Thomas Bauer, *Die Kultur der Ambiguität: Eine andere Geschichte des Islams* (Berlin: Verlag der Weltreligionen, 2011).
40 Kreil, 'Se faire cheikh au Caire'.
41 Ahmed, *What Is Islam?*, 454.
42 Aymon Kreil, 'Pudeur des corps, impudeurs des mots en Égypte : Formes et usages de la "rhétorique du bris de silence" sur la sexualité', in Yasmina Foehr-Janssens, Silvia Naef and Aline Schlaepfer (eds), *Voile, corps et pudeur: Approches historiques et anthropologiques*, 155–68 (Geneva: Labor et Fides, 2015); Matthew Carey, '"The Rules" in Morocco? Pragmatic Approaches to Flirtation and Lying', *HAU: Journal of Ethnographic Theory*, 2 (2) (2012): 188–204.
43 Valerie Traub, 'Making Sexual Knowledge', *Early Modern Women*, 5 (2010): 257.
44 François Cusset, 'Intérieur *queer*: Plaisir sans corps, politique sans sujet', *Rue Descartes*, 40 (2003): 8–17.
45 Traub, 'Making Sexual Knowledge'.
46 Bauer, *Die Kultur der Ambiguität*.
47 Arno Schmitt, 'Liwāṭ im fiqh: Männliche Homosexualität?', *Journal of Arabic and Islamic Studies*, 4 (2001–2002): 49–110; Scott Siraj al-Haqq Kugle, *Homosexuality in Islam: Islamic Reflections on Gay, Lesbian, and Transgender Muslims* (Oxford: Oneworld Publications: 2010); Tolino, *Atti omosessuali e omosessualità;* Serena Tolino, 'Homosexual Acts in Islamic Law: Siḥāq and Liwāṭ in the Legal Debate', *GAIR-Mitteilungen*, 6 (2014): 187–205.
48 Kim M. Phillips and Barry Rea, *Sex Before Sexuality: A Premodern History* (Malden, MA: Polity Press, 2011).
49 Afsaneh Najmabadi, *Women with Mustaches and Men without Beards: Gender and Sexual Anxieties of Iranian Modernity* (Berkeley, CA: University of California Press 2005); Massad, *Desiring Arabs*.
50 *Ḥammām al-Malaṭīlī* (Malatili Bath) (1973), [Film] Dir. Ṣalāḥ Abū Sayf, Wrs Ismāʿīl Walī al-Dīn and Muḥsin Zayyid (Egypt: Ṣalāḥ Abū Sayf), 93 minutes.
51 *Qiṭṭa ʿalā Nār* (Cat on Fire) (1977), [Film] Dir. Samīr Sayf, Wrs Hānī Muṭāwiʿ and Rafīq al-Ṣabbān (Egypt: N. B. Films), 108 minutes.
52 Luisa Passerini, *Fascism in Popular Memory: The Cultural Experience of the Turin Working Class* (Cambridge: Cambridge University Press, 1987); Luisa Passerini, *Autobiography of a Generation: Italy, 1968* (Middletown, CN: Wesleyan University Press, 2003).

References

Abu-Lughod, Lila (2013), *Do Muslim Women Need Saving?*, Cambridge, MA: Harvard University Press.
Ahmed, Shahab (2015), *What Is Islam? The Importance of Being Islamic*, Princeton, NJ: Princeton University Press.
Alloula, Malek (1986), *The Colonial Harem*, Minneapolis, MN: University of Minnesota Press.
Altman, Dennis (1997), 'Global Gaze/Global Gays', *GLQ: A Journal of Lesbian and Gay Studies*, 3 (4): 417–36.
Asad, Talal (1993), *Genealogies of Religion: Discipline and Reasons of Power in Christianity and Islam*, Baltimore, MD: Johns Hopkins University Press.
Babayan, Kathryn and Afsaneh Najmabadi (eds) (2008), *Islamicate Sexualities: Translations across Temporal Geographies of Desire*, Cambridge, MA: Harvard University Press.
Bauer, Thomas (2011), *Die Kultur der Ambiguität: Eine andere Geschichte des Islams*, Berlin: Verlag der Weltreligionen.
Bayat, Asef (2007), 'Islamism and the Politics of Fun', *Public Culture*, 19 (3): 433–59.
Bazin, Jean (2008), *Des clous dans la Joconde: L'anthropologie autrement*, Toulouse: Anacharsis.
Boellstorff, Tom (2007), 'Queer Studies in the House of Anthropology', *Annual Review of Anthropology*, 36: 17–35.
Borneman, John and Abdellah Hammoudi (2009), 'The Fieldwork Encounter, Experience, and the Making of Truth: An Introduction', in John Borneman and Abdellah Hammoudi (eds), *Being There: The Fieldwork Encounter and the Making of Truth*, 1–24, Berkeley, CA: California University Press.
Bourdieu, Pierre (2001), *Science de la science et réflexivité: Cours du Collège de France 2000–2001; Cours et travaux*, Paris: Raisons d'Agir.
Bourdieu, Pierre (2002), *Le bal des célibataires: Crise de la société paysanne en Béarn*, Paris: Seuil.
Butler, Judith (1990), *Gender Trouble: Feminism and the Subversion of Identity*, New York: Routledge.
Butler, Judith (1993), *Bodies that Matter: On the Discursive Limits of Sex*, New York: Routledge.
Callewaert, Staf (2006), 'Bourdieu, Critic of Foucault: The Case of Empirical Social Science against Double-Game-Philosophy', *Theory, Culture and Society*, 23 (6): 73–98.
Carey, Matthew (2012), '"The Rules" in Morocco? Pragmatic Approaches to Flirtation and Lying', *HAU: Journal of Ethnographic Theory*, 2 (2): 188–204.
Clancy-Smith, Julia Ann (1998), *Domesticating the Empire: Race, Gender, and Family Life in French and Dutch Colonialism*, Charlottesville, VA: University Press of Virginia.
Cusset, François (2003), 'Intérieur *queer*: Plaisir sans corps, politique sans sujet', *Rue Descartes*, 40: 8–17.
Davison, Roderic H. (1960), 'Where is the Middle East?', *Foreign Affairs*, 38 (4): 665–75.
Donzelot, Jacques (1977), *La police des familles*, Paris: Minuit.
El-Rouayheb, Khaled (2005), *Before Homosexuality in the Arab-islamic World: 1500–1800*, Chicago, IL: University of Chicago Press.
Foucault, Michel [1984] (2011), *Histoire de la sexualité*, Paris: Gallimard.
Godelier, Maurice (1996), *The Making of Great Men: Male Domination and Power among the New Guinea Baruya*, trans. Rupert Swyer, Cambridge: Cambridge University Press.

Ḥammām al-Malaṭīlī (Malatili Bath) (1973), [Film] Dir. Ṣalāḥ Abū Sayf, Wrs Ismā'īl Walī al-Dīn and Muḥsin Zayyid, Egypt: Ṣalāḥ Abū Sayf, 93 minutes.
Hartog, François (1988), *The Mirror of Herodotus: The Representation of the Other in the Writing of History*, Berkeley, CA: University of California Press.
Hodgson, Marshall G. S. (1977), *The Venture of Islam. Conscience and History in a World Civilization*, vol. 1, *The Classical Age of Islam*, Chicago, IL: University of Chicago Press.
Koppes, Clayton R. (1976), 'Captain Mahan, General Gordon, and the Origins of the Term "Middle East"', *Middle Eastern Studies*, 12 (1): 95–8.
Kreil, Aymon (2010), 'Se faire cheikh au Caire: Exemplarité et intériorité religieuse', *Archives de Sciences sociales des religions*, 149: 255–72.
Kreil, Aymon (2014), 'Love Scales: Class and Expression of Feelings in Cairo', *La Ricerca Folklorica*, 69: 83–91.
Kreil, Aymon (2015), 'Pudeur des corps, impudeurs des mots en Égypte: Formes et usages de la "rhétorique du bris de silence" sur la sexualité', in Yasmina Foehr-Janssens, Silvia Naef and Aline Schlaepfer (eds), *Voile, corps et pudeur: Approches historiques et anthropologiques*, 155–68, Geneva: Labor et Fides.
Kreil, Aymon (2016), 'Territories of Desire: A Geography of Competing Intimacies in Cairo', *Journal of Middle East Women's Studies*, 12 (2): 166–80.
Kugle, Scott Siraj al-Haqq (2010), *Homosexuality in Islam: Islamic Reflections on Gay, Lesbian, and Transgender Muslims*, Oxford: Oneworld Publications.
Lagrange, Frédéric (2008), *Islam d'interdits, islam de jouissance*, Paris: Téraèdre.
Lockman, Zachary (2016), *Field Notes: The Making of Middle East Studies in the United States*, Stanford, CA: Stanford University Press.
Lyons, Andrew P. and Harriet Lyons (2004), *Irregular Connections: A History of Anthropology and Sexuality*, Lincoln, NE: University of Nebraska Press.
Makarem, Ghassan (2009), 'We Are Not Agents of the West: Ghassan Makarem Replies to Joseph Massad', *Reset Dialogues*, 14 December 2009. Available online: https://www.resetdoc.org/story/we-are-not-agents-of-the-west/ (accessed 1 February 2020).
Massad, Joseph (2008), *Desiring Arabs*, Chicago, IL: University of Chicago Press.
Massad, Joseph (2009), 'I Criticize Gay Internationalists, not Gays: Joseph Massad Counter-replies to Ghassan Makarem', *Reset Dialogues*, 14 December 2009. Available online: https://www.resetdoc.org/story/i-criticize-gay-internationalists-not-gays/(accessed 1 February 2020).
Massad, Joseph and Ernesto Pagano (2009), 'The West and the Orientalism of Sexuality: Joseph Massad (Columbia University) talks to Ernesto Pagano', *Reset Dialogues*, 14 December 2009. Available online: https://www.resetdoc.org/story/the-west-and-the-orientalism-of-sexuality/(accessed 1 February 2020).
Murray, Stephen O. and Will Roscoe (eds) (1997), *Islamic Homosexualities: Culture, History, and Literature*, New York: New York University Press.
Najmabadi, Afsaneh (2005), *Women with Mustaches and Men without Beards: Gender and Sexual Anxieties of Iranian Modernity*, Berkeley, CA: University of California Press.
Passerini, Luisa (1987), *Fascism in Popular Memory: The Cultural Experience of the Turin Working Class*, Cambridge: Cambridge University Press.
Passerini, Luisa (1996), *Autobiography of a Generation: Italy, 1968*, Middletown, CN: Wesleyan University Press.
Phillips, Kim M. and Barry Rea (2011), *Sex Before Sexuality: A Premodern History*, Malden, MA: Polity Press.
Qiṭṭa 'alā Nār (Cat on Fire) (1977), [Film] Dir. Samīr Sayf, Egypt: Samīr Sayf, Wrs Hānī Muṭāwi and Rafīq al-Ṣabbān, Egypt: N. B. Film, 108 minutes.

Renton, James (2007), 'Changing Languages of Empire and the Orient: Britain and the Invention of the Middle East, 1917–1918', *Historical Journal*, 50 (3): 645–67.
Said, Edward W. (1978), *Orientalism*, New York: Pantheon Books.
Schick, İrvin Cemil (1999), *The Erotic Margin: Sexuality and Spatiality in Alteritist Discourse*, London: Verso.
Schmitt, Arno (2001–2002), 'Liwāṭ im fiqh: Männliche Homosexualität?', *Journal of Arabic and Islamic Studies*, 4: 49–110.
Tolino, Serena (2013), *Atti omosessuali e omosessualità fra diritto islamico e diritto positivo: il caso egiziano con alcuni cenni all'esperienza libanese*, Naples: Edizioni Scientifiche Italiane.
Tolino, Serena (2014), 'Homosexual Acts in Islamic Law: *Siḥāq* and *Liwāṭ* in the Legal Debate', *GAIR-Mitteilungen*, 6: 187–205.
Tolino, Serena (2014), 'Homosexuality in the Middle East: An Analysis of Dominant and Competitive Discourses', *DEP: Deportate, Esule, Profughe*, 25: 72–91.
Traub, Valerie (2008), 'The Past Is a Foreign Country? The Times and Spaces of Islamicate Sexuality Studies', in Kathryn Babayan and Afsaneh Najmabadi (eds), *Islamicate Sexualities: Translations across Temporal Geographies of Desire*, 1–40, Cambridge, MA: Harvard University Press.
Traub, Valerie (2010), 'Making Sexual Knowledge', *Early Modern Women*, 5: 251–59.
Veyne, Paul (1983), *Les Grecs ont-ils cru à leurs mythes? Essai sur l'imagination constituante*, Paris: Seuil.
Weiss, Margot (2011), 'The Epistemology of Ethnography: Method in Queer Anthropology', *GLQ: A Journal of Lesbian and Gay Studies*, 17 (4): 649–64.
Weston, Kath (1993), 'Lesbian/Gay Studies in the House of Anthropology', *Annual Review of Anthropology*, 22: 339–67.
Ze'evi, Dror (2006), *Producing Desire: Changing Sexual Discourse in the Ottoman Middle East, 1500–1900*, Berkeley, CA: University of California Press.

Part I

WHO'S WHO: BEYOND THE GENDER BINARY

Chapter 1

LOCATING DISCOURSES ON THE GENDER BINARY (AND BEYOND) IN PRE-MODERN ISLAMICATE SOCIETIES

Serena Tolino

> Women are more inclined to be tender, ready to cry, envious, polemic, insulter, wrong-doer, impatient, rude, liar, deceiver and deceivable, to recall the worse things, to be inactive and lazy; this can be corrected only with patience. They are also less capable of defending the vulnerable.[1]

With these words the well-known polymath Ibn Sīnā (d.428/1037), also known by his Latinized name Avicenna, summarizes what are for him the differences between masculinity (*dhukūra*) and femininity (*unūtha*) in reference to human beings. This difference in degrees but not in kind (women are something less or something more but not something different than men) lies at the core of the relation between the genders in pre-modern Islamicate societies, which is characterized by the continuous tension between two main principles: on the one hand fluidity, on the other hierarchy, as I will show in this chapter.

Notwithstanding the rapid growth of research on gender, sex and sexuality in Islamicate societies over the last two decades, we still do not know much about what masculinity and femininity meant in pre-modern Islamicate contexts. Research on the topic is certainly mushrooming; however, while scholars working on sex and sexuality in pre-modern Islamicate societies particularly focused on homoeroticism from a historical, literary or legal perspective,[2] scholars working on gender mostly focused on women's histories.[3] This means that, if much has been written on women's agency, on what women achieved and on how they moved in a patriarchal society, less has been produced on how they were defined and how their femininity was socially and historically constructed: what did it mean to be a woman in a certain period and in a certain place? What characteristics were attributed to femininity?[4]

Even less research has been devoted to masculinity, especially from a historical perspective.[5] Few scholars have worked on sex difference in Islamic medicine. Inspired by Thomas Laqueur's theory of the 'one-sex model', according to which, in pre-modern medical thinking, male and female anatomies were understood as belonging to the same sex, with the woman being considered to be an imperfect version of the man, Dror Ze'evi's book *Producing Desire* tested this paradigm with reference to the Ottoman Empire,[6] while Sherry Sayed Gadelrab's did the same for the Arab-Islamic medieval culture.[7]

This relative paucity of scholarship is surprising if we consider that it has already been demonstrated that not only gender but also sex is historically and socially constructed. If we start from this assumption, then it is probably necessary to try to deconstruct the categories of female and male and, with Joan Scott, to consider that '"man" and "woman" are at once empty and overflowing categories. Empty because they have no ultimate, transcendent meaning. Overflowing because even when they appear to be fixed, they still contain within them alternative, denied, or suppressed definitions.'[8]

This chapter is an attempt to understand how these empty concepts were 'filled' with meanings in different genres in the pre-modern period and, moreover, to see whether the gender binary, constructed in terms of men/women; male/female, makes sense at all with reference to Islamicate pre-modern societies. In this sense I am building here on Abdallah Cheikh-Moussa's approach. In an article he published in 1982 under the title 'Ǧāḥiẓ et les eunuques ou la confusion du même et de l'autre',[9] he demonstrated how, in al-Jāḥiẓ's (d.255/868) writings on eunuchs, the most convincing analytical binary we have at our disposal is not the 'men/women' binary, but the 'men/the other' binary. The first term of the binary is defined by Cheikh-Moussa as such: 'Est homme, celui qui est adulte, en pleine possession de la raison, des moyens de procréer et de se reproduire, et qui se plie aux normes de la Cité' (A man is the one who is an adult, in full possession of his reason, able of procreation and reproduction, and who knows the norms of urban life).[10] The second term includes, for him, eunuchs, children and women, but we could add also other categories.

Al-Jāḥiẓ, who was one of the most influential scholars of the Islamic Middle Ages, lived at the Abbasid Court of Baghdad, and composed many works of profane prose (*adab*), that were clearly addressed to the cosmopolitan urban elite of which he was part. The aim of this chapter is to verify whether this scheme (man/the other) can be applied also to sources that go beyond al-Jāḥiẓ, presenting an overview of gender and sex differences in lexicography, medicine and Islamic law.

The typologies of texts were selected for the key role they played in shaping medieval Islamicate cultures. The sources analysed here range from the ninth to the eleventh century, with the exception of lexicography, where I analyse sources from the period, but also later sources, as some of the most important Arabic dictionaries have been composed after this period.

The Islamic empire in this period was huge, and simple generalizations do not help to understand the reality. However, most of the written sources we have at our disposal for this period allow us to reconstruct only the vision of one specific layer of the society (namely the well-educated urban elite) on masculinity and femininity, and basically only the masculine perspective, as they were written by male authors for a male public. All the research that we do with these sources is thus necessarily a generalization. This is even more the case if we restrict ourselves to one single kind of source. Following Khaled El-Rouayheb's approach,[11] the idea is that it is necessary to look at a wider range of genres to get a wider perspective on gender relations in the pre-modern Islamicate world. While El-Rouayheb mostly focused on how homoerotic behaviours were perceived and represented in pre-modern Islamicate societies, I build here on his approach and his findings to try to get a picture of how the two genders were understood and represented.

For this reason I will bring into focus different categories of sources in an attempt to reconstruct a picture that, far from being exhaustive, would at least be more inclusive and help us to understand what were the characteristics of what was considered to be the 'hegemonic masculinity' and the 'hegemonic femininity' of that time.[12] Interestingly enough, as we will see, even though men and women were often defined in opposition to each other, it is often easier to understand what was really meant by these two concepts when we look at those figures that challenged this strict binary, particularly figures such as effeminates, eunuchs and intersex. While on the one hand these figures challenged a sharp 'traditional' gender binary (man/woman), on the other they somehow reinforced it: as a reaction to their presence, scholars writing on them had to reflect and articulate the (perceived) differences between being a man and being a woman, contributing to the crystallization of these categories.

The presence of ambiguous figures has often been seen as a demonstration that there was a certain fluidity between the genders in pre-modern Islamicate societies. While I agree with Dror Ze'evi[13] that a certain fluidity between the genders existed, I also show that this fluidity was structured around the dominance of a particular masculine model, and that the gender system, even though not based on the male/female binary, was in any case a hierarchical system, with male at the top.

The chapter is divided into four sections: the first is devoted to lexicography; the second to medicine and the third to Islamic law. In the fourth and final section I will come back to al-Jāḥiẓ's and Cheick-Moussa's approach to the gender binary in terms of a 'man/non-man' binary.

Historicizing masculinity and femininity: What about language?

In order to historicize what masculinity and femininity meant in a given period, a good starting point is lexicography. By their nature, lexicographical sources can be understood as reflecting the collective perception on a given concept in a given period. They allow us to get a 'picture' of the language, which is a continuously changing phenomenon.

It is important to mention here that words in Arabic, as in all Semitic languages, are mostly derived by a sequence of consonantal letters called 'roots'. In Semitic languages these roots usually consists of three consonants, but they can also consist of two or four. Nouns, adjectives and verbs are formed from these consonantal skeletons with different strategies, such as inserting vowels, inserting long vowels, doubling consonants or adding prefixes, infixes or suffixes. For the specific needs of this chapter, I have decided to analyse the roots *dh-k-r*, *f-ḥ-l* and *r-j-l*, which, with different shades, refer to the concepts of masculinity, and *ʾ-n-th*, *m-r-ʾ*, *n-s-w* and *kh-n-th*, which are related to the concepts of femininity.

I focus on three dictionaries, respectively the tenth-century lexicon *Tāj al-Lugha wa-Ṣiḥāḥ al-ʿArabiyya*[14] by al-Jawharī (d. *c.* 393–400/1002–1003 to 1009–1010); the thirteen-century lexicon *Lisān al-ʿArab*[15] (the tongue of the Arabs), by Ibn Manẓūr (d.711/1312), the most well-known and comprehensive dictionary of classical Arabic language; and the fourteenth-century lexicon *Qāmūs al-Muḥīṭ*[16] by al-Fīrūzābādī (d.817/1415). Given their temporal range, these three lexicons allow us to get a good overview of how concepts referring to masculinity and femininity were linguistically understood from the tenth to the fourteenth centuries. Furthermore, Arabic lexicographical sources work by accumulation: they do not only show us how a given lexicographer understood a given concept in a specific moment but also what former lexicographers said on that concept up to the moment the lexicon was compiled, allowing us to get an overview of what it meant in former periods as well as in a much larger number of sources than the one we are analysing. For example, the *Lisān al-ʿArab*, notwithstanding its being a thirteenth-century lexicon, is based on five earlier works; therefore, it gives us access not only to linguistic meanings before its compilation but also to a greater number of lexicographers' works.[17]

Al-Jawharī, Ibn Manẓūr and al-Fīrūzābādī tend to define the male (*dhakar*) and the female (*unthā*) as two categories which both oppose and define each other: 'the male is the opposite of the female', say, for example, al-Jawharī[18] and al-Fīrūzābādī.[19] 'To become masculine [*tadhkīr*] is the opposite of to become feminine [*taʾnīth*], and the male is the opposite of the female', says Ibn Manẓūr.[20]

The root *dhkr* is linked on the one hand to the meaning of 'remembering'. On the other, it is linked to the meaning of hardness: for example, the stronger sword is called *sayf dhakar*, the male sword.[21] Also the hardest, strongest and the higher quality metal is called *dhakar* (or *dhakīr*) *al-ḥadīd*, the male of the metal, which is contrary to *anīth* metal, which comes from the same root as the term *unthā*, female.[22] Ibn Manẓūr and al-Fīrūzābādī also mention that *al-dhikr*, coming from the same root, is honour (Ar. *sharaf*).[23]

Another element is worth mentioning: the same term used to refer to the 'male' is also used to refer to the 'penis', as mentioned by the three authors. Ibn Manẓūr even says that 'the *dhakar* (in this case the penis) is well known',[24] taking for granted what it is. The centrality of the penis is also confirmed when looking at the term *faḥl*, which is used to refer to the 'complete' and 'perfect' man. Ibn Manẓūr says, for example, that the *faḥl* is 'the male in all living creatures', 'the contrary of the female (*unthā*)', but also 'the contrary of the *khaṣī*', the eunuch. Moreover, a *faḥl faḥīl*, the maximum grade of the *faḥl*, is noble and a procreator,[25] which demonstrates the centrality of procreation for the definition of hegemonic masculinity at that time, as pointed out by Cheikh-Moussa. Moreover, and confirming Cheikh-Moussa's point, we see here that a line is traced not only between the male and the female, but more generally between the male and the incomplete male, which is in this case the *khaṣī*, the eunuch.

When looking at the root ʾ*-n-th*, we find again the opposition to the root *dh-k-r*. Al-Jawharī starts by saying that 'the female is the opposite of the male'.[26] Ibn Manẓūr adds that 'the female is the opposite of the male in everything'.[27] According to the opinion of Ibn al-Aʿrābī (d. *c*. 231/846), a former Kufan lexicographer and philologist quoted by Ibn Manẓūr,[28] the female has been called so from the meaning of *anīth*, which is a place where it is easy to live and that is easy to cultivate.[29] A land that is *anīth* is a fertile land, which seems to point out a link between femininity and fertility. Ibn Manẓūr also explains that, compared to the male, the female is softer (but the term here used, *alyan*, a comparative of *layyin*, could also mean gentle, tender, submissive, weak).[30] Interestingly, a comparative is used here: the difference then is not so much a qualitative difference but, if anything, a difference of degrees; the female is softer than a male, and this entails that also the male must be 'soft' (or whatever we want to understand with *layyin*).

Similarly, the adjective *anīth*, when used in reference to a metal, is the opposite of the 'male' metal,[31] that is, as we have seen, the metal of highest quality. Ibn Manẓūr also mentions that a *sayf anīth*, a feminine sword, is the opposite of a strong and sharp sword.[32]

We find a similar binary also under the root *r-j-l*. The first meaning of the root is 'to walk', and the term *rajul* is first and foremost used to refer to the human being, who usually walks, in opposition to the horseman.[33] Al-Jawharī also says that '*al-rajul* is the opposite of the *marʾa*', the woman.[34] Ibn Manẓūr adds that '*al-rajul* is a concept to refer to the male of the human being in opposition to the woman'.[35] Both Ibn Manẓūr[36] and al-Fīrūzābādī[37] mention that a *rajul* is as such after puberty, but also that the term can be used to refer to a male from the moment he is born.

The concept *marʾa* is slightly different. Indeed, the root *m-r-*ʾ refers to the 'completeness of the human being', but also to the 'complete virility' (*kamāl al-rujūliyya*), as Ibn Manẓūr makes it clear.[38] Generally speaking though, *al-mar*ʾ is simply the human being,[39] whose regular feminine form *marʾa* became the standard word to denote 'woman'.[40] It is also said that there are masculine females and feminine males, therefore confirming that a certain continuity exists: if a female is defined as masculine (*dhākira* or *mutadhākira*), this means that she resembles males, while a woman who is *mutarajjila* resembles men.[41] Instead, if a man is said to be a *rajul dhakar*, a 'masculine man', then he is strong, brave, generous and proud.[42]

The root *kh-n-th*, which Everett Rowson explained as originally meaning 'to fold back the mouth of a waterskin for drinking',[43] is associated with weakness and flaccidness. From this root derives the term *mukhannath*, the effeminate man, which lexicographers define as a man 'who resembles a woman in behaviour, posture, voice and dressing',[44] and the term *khunthā*, which refers to intersex people. The concept is explained as referring to a person who is missing some organs of his/her prevalent sex or a person who has the sexual organs of the male and those of the female together.[45] Not surprisingly, effeminacy, intersexuality and femininity all come from the same root, and they are all somehow associated.

From this short overview we can conclude that for lexicographers the penis is a fundamental element of the masculinity of the man. Its absence is considered relevant also for all those categories of men who are considered incomplete, like eunuchs. Other characteristics that are considered attributes of masculinity are the ability to reproduce, hardness, honour and courage, which are certainly considered characteristics of the 'perfect' man but could also be characteristics of women who come 'closer' to the masculine sphere, namely 'masculine women'. Finally, there is a perceived connection between femininity and 'weakness' and 'flaccidness', which are connected to females, effeminates (*mukhannath*) and intersex (*khunthā*).

This seems to confirm Cheikh-Moussa's binary: on the one side the man, the complete and the perfect one. If something is missing, then the perfection of the man is no longer guaranteed, and the person enters into the realm of 'the other'. In the next section we will see whether this also applies to medical sources.

Masculinity and femininity in the medical discourse

Thomas Laqueur suggested that in pre-modern times the so-called 'one-sex model' was dominant. According to this model, male and female anatomy were considered to be basically the same sex, with females considered to be an imperfect version of males rather than a sex per se.[46] Even though Laqueur has been criticized for having overgeneralized pre-modern discussions, his main argument remains valid, as we will see also in reference to the Islamicate world.

It would be impossible to understand the pre-modern Islamic vision of the body without taking into account the Greco-Roman medical and natural philosophical knowledge. Indeed, starting from the third/ninth century, Greek sources were widely translated in Arabic and were accessible by the cultural elite. The debate concerning sex differences was particularly shaped by the reception and re-elaboration of the opinions of the two leading authorities in pre-modern medicine, Hippocrates (*c.* 460–375 BCE) and Galen (*c.* 129–201 CE), and by the opinions of the leading figure in natural philosophy, Aristotle (*c.* 384–322 BCE).

A basic tenet of Greco-Roman and later Islamic medicine was the theory of 'humoral balance'. According to this theory, the world is composed of four elements: fire, air, water and earth. Each of these elements corresponds to a bodily humour. The four humours were: yellow bile (associated with fire, hot and dry); blood (associated with air, hot and moist); phlegm (associated with water, moist and cold); and black bile (associated with earth, cold and dry). The humours were believed to govern the complexion of a given person and their physical and behavioural characteristics: for example, men were considered to be of hot and dry complexion, women of cold and moist complexion. Illness was supposedly caused by the imbalance of these humours, and the role of the physician was to restore the balance.[47]

This theory should be understood in connection with another relevant topic of debate, which was about whether there were one or two semens.[48] While Hippocrates and Galen maintained that there existed a male and a female semen, and that both contributed to the formation of the embryo, Aristotle supported the view that males produced semen while females offered the matter, which was passive and which the male semen would transform into an embryo. Aristotle assumed that the semen was the residual of fully digested blood. The process of digestion could be completed only by males, due to their vital heat, while women could only produce menstrual blood, because the lack of internal heat did not allow them to complete this digestive process. With the discovery of ovaries (which Galen called 'female testicles'), the theory of Hippocrates regained importance.

These theories greatly influenced Arab-Islamic discussions: Muslim authors knew these sources, discussed and reinterpreted them. Some of them also explicitly tried to connect these theories to the Quranic verses related to conception,[49] or to the prophetic *ḥadīth*-s that mention the presence of two semens. This was, for example, the case of Ibn Qayyim al-Jawziyya (d.751/1350), who made reference to the Quranic verses 86.5–7 – 'So let man observe from what he was created. He was created from a fluid, ejected, emerging from between the backbone [Ar. *ṣulb*] and the ribs [Ar. *tarāʾib*]' – to support the two-semen theory, arguing that *ṣulb* refers to the male semen and *tarāʾib* to the female one.[50]

Abū Bakr Muḥammad b. Zakariyyā al-Rāzī (d.313/925 or 323/935), a Persian physician, alchemist and philosopher, also supported the two-semen theory. He believed that to be a male or to be a female was first of all an issue of conception: when the male sperm was prevalent during conception, then the foetus was going to be a male; when the female sperm was prevalent, the foetus was going to be a female.[51] According to him, 'the organs of reproduction in the female are placed inside the belly and conditioned to tend in that direction, while in males, they are outside the belly and are by nature disposed to tend in that direction',[52] something that resonates very much with Laqueur's one-sex model.

This distinction, based on a lack of heat that did not allow the female organs to come outside, also had consequences on sexual preferences. Danilo Marino's chapter in this volume shows, for example, how wine, for its heat, was considered to stimulate men's sexual power, as opposed to dry and cold substances, such as hashish, which were considered a danger to that power. Heat also has a prominent place in a treatise by al-Rāzī on the so-called 'hidden illness', the *ubna*, or passive sodomy.[53] In this work, al-Rāzī describes what are, according to him, the characteristics of masculinity: 'limbs hard, dry and large, much hair, a strong pulse and breath, prominent joints, thick bones and similar properties peculiar to persons of a hot and dry temper, such as courage, quickness of speech and anger, and the like'.[54] Femininity is simply described as the opposite.

In the same work al-Rāzī also discusses the reasons for the desire to be penetrated, which he considers pathological. Indeed, he starts from the assumption that penetration and penetrability, that is to say, activity and passivity, are respectively characteristics of masculinity and femininity. Al-Rāzī considers that a physical imperfection is the reason of such a desire, which he considers to be the consequence of an incomplete process of 'masculinization' of the sexual organs, which happens when 'the male newborn child is feminine because of the weak degree of prevalence of the sperm of the male over the sperm of the female'.[55]

This is particularly interesting when one thinks that we do not find in the Islamic medical tradition a book devoted to *liwāṭ*, active sodomy, the punishment for which was instead a topic of discussion in books of Islamic jurisprudence (*fiqh*). Even though *liwāṭ* was considered a sin by Muslim jurists, the desire to penetrate was considered perfectly normal for a man. Only if an adult man desired to be penetrated was his desire considered pathological and attracted the attention of the physician.

Ibn Sīnā tried to reconcile the Galenic theory of the two semens with the Aristotelian view of form and matter.[56] He did so by stating that the female semen was thin in comparison to the male semen, due to the incompleteness of the cooking process, which was a consequence of the lack of heat in the female.[57] Ibn Sīnā dealt with sex differences in two of his works, *al-Qānūn*, which was considered the reference book for physicians in the Islamicate world and beyond for centuries, and *al-Shifā'*, a philosophical compendium that also includes a specific book devoted to animals, the *Kitāb al-Ḥayawān*, on the model of Aristotle's *De animalibus*. This book also includes a discussion about the human being and sex differences.[58] In *al-Qānūn*, Ibn Sīnā stated that the sex of the foetus depended on the 'male's sperm, its warmth and its quantity, on the fact that the intercourse took place when the female was pure, and the fact that the sperm flows from the right testicle, because in this case it is warmer and thicker [...] and ends up on the right side of the uterus'.[59] Again, we see the relevance of the 'heat', as only warm sperm can create a male. Nevertheless, this is not always the case: 'If it comes from the left side to the right side of the uterus then the result is a masculine female and if it comes from the right side to the left side of the uterus then the result will be an effeminate male.' Finally, 'if the sperm comes from the left testicle to the left side of the uterus then she is female'.[60] We see here that the 'perfect' case is the one of the sperm coming from the right testicle and going into the right side of the uterus (not coincidentally, both on the right, that is traditionally perceived as the favourite side, especially in religious contexts),[61] which is the only case when a man will be generated, but we also see a range of other possibilities that go well beyond the 'pure' male and the 'pure' female.

Ibn Sīnā described the female reproductive organs as similar to the male ones, being different only in the completeness, which was caused by the hotter temperament of men. He also added that 'not every male is masculine in the extreme and not every female is feminine in the extreme and [...] there exist masculine women and feminine men'.[62] An imperfect man, which means, a 'feminine man', because of his disposition has organs which 'do not fully tend outward and do not hang down low', but that are 'withdrawn inward into the cavity of the belly and are drawn toward the hypogastric and pubic regions'.[63]

In his *Kitāb al-Ḥayawān*, Ibn Sīnā focuses on the differences between males and females from the behavioural point of view. He writes for example that 'animals of the same species differ in some respects with reference to sex [*jins*], masculinity [*dhukūra*] and femininity [*unūtha*], and for differences in habitat'.[64] He also adds that these differences are particularly evident, both 'in nature' and 'in behaviour', in the human species. As mentioned at the beginning, for him, 'women are more inclined to be tender, ready to cry, envious, polemic, insulter, wrong-doer, impatient, rude, liar, deceiver and deceivable, to recall the worse things, to be inactive and lazy; this can be corrected only with patience. They are also less capable of defending the vulnerable.'[65] These elements could probably be classified under the modern category of (a stereotyped) gender. Yet Ibn Sīnā considers them to be very much linked to an issue of complexion: he believed that the moist and cold complexion of the female caused them.[66] Moreover, once again we see here that the difference is not a qualitative one, but one of degrees.

Ibn Rushd (d.595/1198), known as Averroes in the West, a theologian, philosopher and scholar of natural sciences, who composed *al-Kulliyyāt fī al-Ṭibb* (Generalities in Medicine), theorized instead a model according to which males and females had specific sexual organs. According to him, all these differences are derived from a basic difference in the internal heat,[67] which does not allow females to produce seed. He believed that women could not provide anything more than matter, and depicted females as 'passive vessels who play no role in conception'.[68] Also, physical differences were explained by him as related to differences in the internal heat: this is why, for example, usually men have abundant and thick hair (a sign of heat), while women have little hair.

To sum up these three authors' approaches we can say that, notwithstanding their differences, they all seemed to agree on one point, as Gadelrab also points out: the inferiority of the female. Moreover, there are a number of elements that are relevant for our understanding of 'hegemonic masculinity' and 'hegemonic femininity' in this period: the relation between masculinity and activity on one side, and femininity and passivity on the other; the representation of the 'proper' man as the one who penetrates; the heat of the masculine complexion, which is what makes a man 'courageous', 'quick in speech and anger', with 'thick air', able to produce the most powerful semen. Conversely, this lack of heat, apart from 'trapping' the female sexual organs within her body, makes females incapable of dominating their feelings and following their intellect.

Once again, the two genders were not represented in strict opposition but there were a number of intermediary positions between them: effeminate men, masculine women and intersex. To quote Ze'evi's words: 'This view also envisioned man and woman as part of a continuum of perfection, leading from the basest creatures to the celestial. Man in this scheme of things was the crowning achievement of terrestrial creatures, whereas woman was regarded as a less-developed version of man, physically and mentally.'[69] Even if it is clear that a continuum in medical sources existed, it is also clear that this continuum was constructed in a hierarchical system, where one gender, the masculine, was clearly considered superior.

The gender binary in Islamic law

Muslim jurists, notwithstanding the many differences concerning rights and duties between men and women, did not feel the need to explicitly discuss how to distinguish them. This is quite surprising for the contemporary reader and becomes even more so if we consider that Islamic law did not aim at being an egalitarian system of law. On the contrary, it assumed several differences between its subjects: male and female is one but other significant differences are between adult and child, *muḥṣan* (the person which consummated a valid marriage) and non *muḥṣan*, Muslim and non-Muslim, free and slave. The 'perfect' and 'complete' subject of Islamic law is a free adult married Muslim man. The other variations intersect to create a complex system of hierarchies and of duties and rights that affect the entire legal system.[70]

In this scheme, ambiguity was hardly tolerated, at least in theory, as the rich discourse on 'gendering' the *khunthā*, shows.[71] We can certainly argue about whether the long discussions on the gender of the *khunthā* served the solution of 'real cases' or represented intellectual exercises aimed at solving disputes between scholars. Recently, Sara Scalenghe has used the statistics on the number of intersex in the contemporary Arab world to show that, due to the high number of inter-family marriages, the percentage of intersex was also quite remarkable in Islamicate societies in the past.[72] At the same time, we cannot dismiss the importance of creating a system of law that, being religion-based, aimed at being as comprehensive as possible.

However, what is relevant for our purposes is that it is exactly here, where the ambiguity needs to be solved, that we can infer something about the definition of the male and the female for jurists. For example, the Ḥanafī jurist al-Sarakhsī (d. *c.* 438–500/1046–1106) states that a *khunthā* is an individual who either has 'both the apparatus of the male and the female' or has 'neither the apparatus of the male nor that of the female'.[73] The Ḥanbalī jurist Ibn Qudāma (d.620/1223) is more explicit and describes the *khunthā* as the individual who either has 'the penis [*dhakar*] of the male and the vagina [*farj*] of the female' or 'has a hole instead of the vagina from which urine comes'.[74]

The discussion on the *khunthā* teaches us a number of things. In order to determine whether the *khunthā* was a male or a female, jurists first of all looked from which sexual organ they urinated. For example, if they urinated from one of the sexual organs, then according to some jurists the sexual organ from which the urine came before should determine the sex of the *khunthā*. If they urinated from both the sexual organs, for some jurists the last organ that stops urinating is the one determining the sex of the *khunthā*, for others the one from which the urine comes more abundantly.[75] If this was not sufficient to define the sex of the *khunthā*, jurists waited for the appearance of the so-called 'signs of puberty'. For men these were the growing of a beard or of a moustache, seminal emissions and/or the ability to penetrate a female.[76] For women they included menstruation, pregnancy, the development of breasts, secretion of milk and/or the possibility of being penetrated.[77] Moreover, the attraction of an ambiguous *khunthā* towards men was considered a sign of their femininity, and towards women, a sign of masculinity: this was clearly based on the assumption that men should feel attracted by women and vice versa. If the sex of the *khunthā* could not be clarified even after puberty, or if the *khunthā* died before reaching puberty, then they were defined as a *khunthā mushkil*, a problematic ambiguous *khunthā*, with a special legal status. The jurists were still convinced that the *khunthā* had a 'real' sex, but they were not able to identify it. In this case, the application of specific legal solutions was intended to prevent the violation of appropriate gender roles and legal rules.[78]

So, the difference was first of all a biological one, one that in modern terms we would define as 'sex'. The ability to penetrate or to be penetrated, which are mentioned as identifying respectively a man or a woman, are also relevant, and they become particularly important in reference to another figure that somehow challenged the male/female binary: the eunuch.

Indeed, the case of the eunuch is a tricky one: most eunuchs in Islamicate societies did not have a *dhakar*, a penis, or not any more, at least. Moreover, they could not be gendered as a *khunthā*: in the case of the *khunthā*, the duty of the jurist was basically that of discovering their true but hidden sex, as the assumption was that they had one. Clearly this did not apply to the eunuch, who had supposedly been created by God as a man but had then been changed by human intervention.

Interestingly enough, Muslim jurists did not explicitly discuss the eunuch's gender. Looking at legal discussions on marriage, divorce and the attribution of maternity/paternity, though, it is still possible to infer something about what jurists thought about their gender. Eunuchs were usually gendered as men: for example, they were allowed to perform the call to prayer, something that a woman could not do, to act as *imām* in congregational prayers and to repudiate their wives (via the *ṭalāq* and other forms of divorce reserved to men). Also, paternity could be attributed to a eunuch if at least one testicle was still present.[79] Still, a woman could easily apply for divorce if her husband was castrated and she was not informed about it or if he was not able to penetrate her.[80] Moreover, it is well known that one of the main functions of eunuchs was that of acting as harem guardians: certainly, if they were considered 'complete' men, they would have not been allowed to do that. So even though from a legal perspective they were classified closer to men than *khunthā*-s (and certainly closer than to women), they were still far from being 'perfect' and 'complete' men.

The sexual norm

This understanding of the sexes also had an impact on what was considered sexual 'normativity': if we understand the normative as the 'ideal standard' or as the 'model', then from a legal perspective the only legally accepted intercourse was between a male and a female. Moreover, this intercourse had to be 'legalized' by a relation of *mulk*, of possession, or marriage. *Zinā*ʾ (which means both fornication and adultery), sodomy (Ar. *liwāṭ*),[81] tribadism (Ar. *siḥāq*), bestiality, necrophilia and so on were all prohibited, even though different degrees of prohibition applied.

But if we go beyond the legal discourse, things tend to change. Indeed, pre-modern Arabic sources, both literary and historical, show us that legal prescriptions and social practices were in this regard far apart, and point out that, with regard to sexuality, the main binary was not man/woman, but active/passive. While a man was supposed to be the active partner, the passive partner could change: it could certainly be a woman, either a wife or a concubine, but also a young boy or a slave. This last option was completely reprehensible from a moral and a religious standpoint, as it would constitute *liwāṭ*, a serious crime in Islamic law. Even so, while jurists all agreed on the illicitness of *liwāṭ*, there is a wide range of sources that shows how social practices were far removed from the legal discourse. This becomes particularly evident when looking at poetry and *adab*, and can be explained by what Thomas Bauer defined as 'Die Kultur der Ambiguität', the culture of ambiguity.[82] According to him, Islamicate pre-modern societies were characterized by an extreme tolerance for what he calls 'cultural ambiguity': there was not one single register of truth, but many 'truths' coexisted. This 'ambiguity' should not be intended simply as 'Norm und Abweichung', 'norm' and 'deviation' from the norm, but more as a coexistence of different norms, all of them considered as such by the same group of people at the same moment. There are many examples that we could mention to substantiate that: we can think of the prohibition of drinking wine or having same-sex intercourse and the importance that both had in literature in the same historical moment. This could seem a contradiction, but clearly it was not: simply, Islamic law and poetry were two different registers.[83]

I am going to quote here from two of these sources, both by al-Jāḥiẓ, to come back to our point of departure and to Cheikh-Moussa's theory. In an essay entitled *Tafḍīl al-Baṭn ʿalā al-Ẓahr*, translated into English as 'The Superiority of the Belly over the Back', in which al-Jāḥiẓ uses the literary artifice of writing to a nephew to invite him to abandon anal sex, he writes:

> What a difference between the one who faces the war and the one who gives to it his back, between the one who couples and the one who is coupled [*al-nākiḥ wa-l-mankūḥ*], the rider and the mounted, the active and the passive, the one who penetrates and the one who is penetrated, the lower and the higher, the one who visits and the one who is visited, the one who conquers and the one who is conquered.[84]

The dichotomy here is not between a 'male' and a 'female', nor between a 'man' and a 'woman': what it counts here is who is active and who is passive, who penetrates and who is penetrated, which is not necessarily the woman[85] but any 'non-man' who accepts that.

This can be seen also in another work by al-Jāḥiẓ, the *Kitāb Mufākharat al-Jawārī wa-l-Ghilmān*, translated into English as 'Boasting Match over Maids and Youths'.[86] In this essay al-Jāḥiẓ presents a controversy between a man who prefers to have intercourse with maids and a man who prefers to have intercourse with boys, analysing both the pros and the cons of their positions. The boys' supporter says, for example: 'when a girl is described with complete beauty it is said: "She's just like a *ghulām* [a boy] or she has the characteristics of a *ghulām*"'.[87] The maids' supporter answers that 'the scent of the girl is better, her clothing more perfumed, her walk better, her voice more delicate and the hearts tend to her'.[88] The maids' supporter also says:

> The enjoyment with a maid is greater and longer, because the minimum it can last is forty years. And you do not find anything in the boy that you cannot find double in the maid. If you want thighs, then she has soft and prominent buttocks that you cannot find in a boy. If you want the hug, then she has turgid breasts which a boy does not have. If you want a good place to penetrate, there is enough, and a boy does not have it. And if you penetrate him in the back, there is dirt and filth that disgust anyone and spoils every pleasure.[89]

The maids' supporter adds that:

> A boy's beauty and the purity of his cheeks can last maximum ten years, then his beard arrives and he goes out from the condition of being beardless. When he is incredibly shameless, he removes his beard. At other times, he cut it to attract men's passion.[90]

In both the positions we see an adult man who is having intercourse with a 'non-man'. The discussion is completely androcentric: it is only about what is better for the man. Moreover, the comparison is not constructed presenting two antithetical figures: the difference between 'maids' and 'boys' is one of degree and not of kind. The comparison does not seem to be a construction of a gender binary but, instead, of different degrees and shadows of softness, beauty, enjoyment, pleasure, penetrability. The reference to the beard is also interesting: indeed, even though we cannot say to what extent the entire literary canon on homoerotic pederasty was a representation of social reality or a matter of literary topos, still the idealized male lover was described as a beardless boy and not as an adult man. It is not a case that in poetry and prose the most often used term to refer to the boy as subject of love and passion is *amrad*, beardless. It is exactly the appearance of the beard that represents the key of access to the masculine world.[91] When the beard appears, the non-man (and in this case man-to-be) becomes a man: therefore, he can no longer be penetrated, otherwise he would be considered affected by *ubna*. He clearly has a privilege over the female: he will become a man and ascend to the last degree of perfection, while a female will never achieve that.[92]

Conclusion

In this chapter I have been inspired on the one hand by Joan W. Scott's invitation to question the stability and fixity of the categories 'man' and 'woman', which are historically and socially constructed and that, as such, do not always mean the same thing in different contexts and in different periods. On the other, I have been inspired by Cheikh-Moussa's suggestion that in al-Jāḥiẓ's writings on eunuchs one could speak, instead of a 'traditional' gender binary (men/women; male/female), of a system based on a dichotomy 'man/the other', with 'man' referring to the adult urban man, in possession of reason and the ability and means to procreate, and 'the other', including eunuchs, effeminates, women and children. Therefore, on the one hand, I examined how the categories man and woman, male and female were constructed in medieval Islamic sources; on the other, whether this binary made sense at all and, if not, whether Cheikh-Moussa's binary would be a valid alternative for sources beyond al-Jāḥiẓ. To do so, I looked at lexicographical, medical and legal sources, before coming back to *adab*, and particularly to al-Jāḥiẓ himself.

Lexicographical sources define the concepts of male/man and female/woman as opposing categories. However, when defining the content of this opposition, they often use comparatives, showing that the difference is not so much a qualitative or an essential one, but one of degrees of whatever adjectives they decide to use. Moreover, they recognize the presence of intermediate categories (the masculine woman, the effeminate man). Medical sources seem to suggest the presence of a continuum of perfection, to mention Ze'evi, with the man on top of this perfection and the woman on an inferior position. They also recognize the presence of intermediate categories: masculine women, effeminate men, intersex. Legal sources also consider the woman as 'incomplete' in comparison to the man, but they do not intend the woman as the only 'other', as the discussion on a number of 'other others' showed.

To go back to our question, whether a gender binary existed in pre-modern Islamicate societies and, if so, whether it was constructed on the two poles of the male and the female, I would suggest that it is important to consider fluidity and hierarchy as the two main principles in the understanding of the relation between the genders. These two principles were in a continuous tension. On the one hand, in line with Ze'evi, I tend to say that we should imagine the two genders as a continuum on a scale of perfection, on top of which we find the free adult Muslim man. It is difficult to make a proper classification on who we find below him on the ladder, but certainly we do not only find women, as a proper gender binary would suppose: we also find all the other possible categories of non-(complete)men, such as eunuchs, intersex, boys, but also non-Muslim men, non-Muslim eunuchs, non-Muslim *khunthā*-s. Then, certainly, we also find women, Muslim and non-Muslim, free and slave, etc. But still we cannot say that there was no binary at all: it made a lot of difference whether one was born as a male or not. But then, if we want to think in binary terms, certainly Cheikh-Moussa's proposed binary is more accurate than the male/female binary: the main point in pre-modern Islamicate societies was not being a man or being a woman. The point was much more being included in the category of the 'man' or not. All the others could come more or less close to 'perfection', but could never aspire to it, with the only exception being a young boy who could, with the appearance of the beard, move from the category of the 'non-man' to the category of 'the man'.

Notes

1 Abū ʿAlī al-Ḥusayn Ibn Sīnā, b. ʿAbd Allāh, *al-Shifāʾ, al-Ṭabīʿiyyāt*, vol. 8, *al-Ḥayawān*, ed. Saʿīd Zāʾid ʿAbd al-Ḥalīm Muntaṣir and ʿAbd Allāh Ismāʿīl (Cairo: al-Hayʾa al-Miṣriyya al-ʿĀmma li-l-Taʾlīf wa-l-Nashr, 1970), 111.

2 For an overview of what has been published on sexuality, see Leslie Pierce, 'Writing Histories of Sexuality in the Middle East', *American Historical Review*, 114 (5) (2009): 1325–339. For historical and literary studies, see also the pioneering collection edited by al-Sayyid-Marsot Afaf Lutfi, *Society and the Sexes in Medieval Islam* (Malibu, CA: Undena Publications, 1979). For works on homoeroticism, see also Everett K. Rowson's contributions, and particularly 'The Traffic in Boys: Slavery and Homoerotic Liaisons in Elite ʿAbbāsids Society', *Middle Eastern Literatures*, 11 (2) (2008): 193–204 and 'The Effeminates of Early Medina', *Journal of the American Oriental Society*, 111 (1) (1991): 671–93; J. W. Wright Jr and Everett K. Rowson (eds), *Homoeroticism in Classical Arabic Literature* (New York: Columbia University Press, 1991); Samar Habib, *Female Homosexuality in the Middle East: Histories and Representations* (London: Routledge, 2007); Samar Habib (ed.), *Islam and Homosexuality* (Santa Barbara, CA: ABC Clio, 2009); Kathryn Babayan and Afsaneh Najmabadi (eds), *Islamicate Sexualities: Translations across Temporal Geographies of Desire* (Cambridge, MA: Harvard University Press, 2008); Khaled El-Rouayheb, *Before Homosexuality in the Arab-islamic World: 1500–1800* (Chicago, IL: Chicago University Press, 2005); Stephen O. Murray and Will Roscoe (eds), *Islamic Homosexualities: Culture, History, and Literature* (New York: New York University Press, 1997). For religious and legal aspects, see Scott Siraj al-Haqq Kugle, *Homosexuality in Islam: Islamic Reflections on Gay, Lesbian, and Transgender Muslims* (Oxford: Oneworld Publications, 2010); Arno Schmitt, 'Liwāṭ im fiqh: Männliche Homosexualität?', *Journal of Arabic and Islamic Studies*, 4 (2001–2002): 49–110; Camilla Adang, 'Ibn Ḥazm on Homosexuality: A Case-study of Ẓāhiri Legal Methodology', *Al-Qanṭara*, 24 (1) (2003): 5–31; Mohammed Mezziane, 'Sodomie et masculinité chez les jurists musulmans du IXᵉ au XIᵉ siècle', *Arabica*, 55 (2008): 276–306; Amr A. Shalakany, 'Islamic Legal Histories', *Berkeley Journal of Middle Eastern and Islamic Law*, 1 (2008): 1–82; Sara Omar, 'From Semantics to Normative Law: Perceptions of *Liwāṭ* (Sodomy) and *Siḥāq* (Tribadism) in Islamic Jurisprudence (8th–15th Century CE)', *Islamic Law and Society*, 19 (2012): 222–56; Serena Tolino, 'Homosexual Acts in Islamic Law: *Siḥāq* and *Liwāṭ* in the Legal Debate', *GAIR-Mitteilungen*, 6 (2014): 187–205.

3 The literature on the topic is vast. See, for example, Nikki R. Keddie and Beth Baron (eds), *Women in Middle Eastern History: Shifting Boundaries in Sex and Gender* (New Haven, CT: Yale University Press, 1991); Leila Ahmed, *Women and Gender in Islam: Historical Roots of a Modern Debate* (New Haven, CT: Yale University Press, 1992); Amina Wadud, *Qur'an and Woman: Rereading the Sacred Text from a Woman's Perspective* (New York: Oxford University Press, 1999); Barbara Stowasser, *Women in the Qur'an, Traditions, and Interpretations* (New York: Oxford University Press, 1994); Manuela Marín and Randi Deguilhem (eds), *Writing the Feminine: Women in Arab Sources* (London: I.B.Tauris, 2002); Asifa Quraishi and Frank Vogel (eds), *The Islamic Marriage Contract: Case Studies in Islamic Family Law* (Cambridge, MA: Harvard Law School, 2008); Amira el-Azhari Sonbol (ed.), *Beyond the Exotic: Women's Histories in Islamic Societies* (Cairo: American University Press, 2005); Fedwa Malti-Douglas, *Woman's Body, Woman's Word: Gender and Discourse in Arabo-Islamic Writing* (Princeton, NJ: Princeton University Press, 1991).

4 There are of course exceptions, the most prominent being Kathryin M. Kueny, *Conceiving Identities: Maternity in Medieval Muslim Discourse and Practice* (New York: State University of New York, 2013), which focuses on how maternity was seen a constitutive part of femininity.
5 Mai Ghoussoub and Emma Sinclair-Webb (eds), *Imagined Masculinities: Male Identity and Culture in the Modern Middle East* (London: Saqi Books, 2000); Paul Amar, 'Middle East Masculinity Studies: Discourses of "Men in Crisis", Industries of Gender in Revolution', *Journal of Middle East Women's Studies*, 7 (3) (2011): 36–70; Lahoucine Ouzgane (ed.), *Islamic Masculinities* (London: Zed Books, 2006); Amanullah De Sondy, *The Crisis of Islamic Masculinities* (London: Bloomsbury, 2013).
6 Dror Ze'evi, *Producing Desire: Changing Sexual Discourse in the Ottoman Middle East, 1500–1900* (Berkeley, CA: University of California Press, 2006). This approach is also followed by Sara Scalenghe in her chapter on 'Intersex'; see Sara Scalanghe, *Disability in the Ottoman World, 1500–1800* (New York: Cambridge University Press, 2014), 124–62.
7 Sherry Sayed Gadelrab, 'Discourses on Sex Differences in Medieval Scholarly Islamic Thought', in *Medicine and Morality in Egypt: Gender and Sexuality in the Nineteenth and Early Twentieth Centuries* (London: I.B.Tauris, 2016), 5–44, also published in the *Journal of the History of Medicine*, 66 (1) (2011): 40–81.
8 Joan W. Scott, 'Gender: A Useful Category of Historical Analysis', *American Historical Review*, 91 (5) (1986): 1053–75, 1074.
9 A. Cheikh-Moussa, 'Ǧāḥiẓ et les eunuques ou la confusion du même et de l'autre', *Arabica*, 29 (2) (1982): 184–214.
10 Ibid., 211.
11 El-Rouayheb, *Before Homosexuality*.
12 With this concept I am building on R. W. Connell's definition of 'hegemonic masculinity' as the one embodying 'the currently most honored way of being a man, [it] which required all other men to position themselves in relation to it', that, *mutatis mutandis*, I extend here also to femininity. See Raewyn W. Connell and James W. Messerchmidt, 'Hegemonic Masculinity: Rethinking the Concept', *Gender and Society*, 19 (6) (2005): 829–59, 832. See also Raewyn W. Connell, *Masculinities* (Cambridge: Polity Press, 1995).
13 Ze'evi, *Producing Desire*.
14 Abū Naṣr Ismāʿīl b. Ḥamād al-Jawharī, *al-Ṣiḥāḥ. Tāj al-Lugha wa-Ṣiḥāḥ al-ʿArabiyya*, ed. Muḥammad Muḥammad Tāmir, Anas Muḥammad Shāmī and Zakariyyā Jābir Aḥmad (Cairo: Dār al-Ḥadīth, 2009).
15 Muḥammad b. Mukarram b. ʿAlī b. Aḥmad b. Manẓūr, *Lisān al-ʿArab*, 15 vols (Beirut: Dār al-Ṣādir, n.d.).
16 Majd al-Dīn al-Fīrūzābādī, *al-Qāmūs al-Muḥīṭ*, ed. Muḥammad Naʿīm al-ʿArqūsī (Beirut: Muʾassasat al-Risāla, 2005).
17 These are al-Azharī's (d.370/980–981) *Tahdhīb al-Lugha*, Ibn Sīda's (d.458/1066) *al-Muḥkam*, al-Jawharī's (d. *c.* 400/1010) *al-Ṣiḥāḥ*, Ibn Barrī's (d.582/1186–1187) *al-Ḥawāshī* and Majd al-Dīn ibn al-Athīr's (d.606/1210) *al-Nihāya fī Gharīb al-Ḥadīth wa-l-Athar*. See Ramzi Baalbaki, 'Ibn Manẓūr', in Kate Fleet, Gudrun Krämer, Denis Matringe, John Nawas and Everett Rowson (eds), *Encyclopaedia of Islam*, 3rd edn. (Leiden: Brill, 2016). http://dx.doi.org/10.1163/1573-3912_ei3_COM_30632.
18 al-Jawharī, *al-Ṣiḥāḥ*, s.v. 'ḏ-k-r', 406.
19 al-Fīrūzābādī, *al-Qāmūs al-Muḥīṭ*, s.v. 'ḏ-k-r', 396.

20 Ibn Manẓūr, *Lisān al-ʿArab*, s.v. 'ḏ-k-r', 4:309.
21 Ibid., 311.
22 Ibid.
23 Ibid., 310; al-Fīrūzābādī, *al-Qāmūs al-Muḥīṭ*, s.v. 'ḏ-k-r', 396.
24 Ibn Manẓūr, *Lisān al-ʿArab*, s.v. 'ḏ-k-r', 4:311.
25 Ibn Manẓūr, *Lisān al-ʿArab*, s.v. 'f-ḥ-l', 11:516.
26 Al-Jawharī, *al-Ṣiḥāḥ*, s.v. 'ʾ-n-th', 57.
27 Ibn Manẓūr, *Lisān al-ʿArab*, s.v. 'ʾ-n-th', 2:112.
28 Not to be confused with the renowned Sufi Ibn al-ʿArabī, who died in 638/1240.
29 Ibn Manẓūr, *Lisān al-ʿArab*, s.v. 'ʾ-n-th', 2:113.
30 Ibid.
31 Ibid.
32 Ibid.
33 Al-Jawharī, *al-Ṣiḥāḥ*, s.v. 'r-j-l', 430.
34 Ibid.
35 Ibn Manẓūr, *Lisān al-ʿArab*, s.v. 'r-j-l', 11:625.
36 Ibid.
37 al-Fīrūzābādī, *al-Qāmūs al-Muḥīṭ*, s.v. 'r-j-l', 1003.
38 Ibn Manẓūr, *Lisān al-ʿArab*, s.v. 'm-r-'', 1:154.
39 Ibid., 155.
40 Ibid.
41 See Thomann, in this volume.
42 al-Fīrūzābādī, *al-Qāmūs al-Muḥīṭ*, s.v. '*ḏ-k-r*', 396.
43 Rowson, 'The Effeminates of Early Medina', 672.
44 Ibid.
45 Ibn Manẓūr, *Lisān al-ʿArab*, s.v. 'kh-n-th', 2:145.
46 Thomas Laqueur, *Making Sex: Body and Gender from the Greeks to Freud* (Cambridge, MA: Harvard University Press, 1990).
47 See Gadelrab, 'Discourses on Sex Differences' and Ursula Weisser, *Zeugung, Vererbung und Pränatale Entwicklung in der Medizin des arabisch-islamischen Mittelalters* (Erlangen: Verlagsbuchhandlung Hannelore Lüling, 1983). See also Hans-Peter Pökel, *Der unmännliche Mann: Zur Figuration des Eunuchen im Werk von al-Ǧāḥiẓ (gest. 869)* (Würzburg: Ergon-Verlag, 2014), 109–32, for the representation of the masculine body in the humoral theory.
48 Ibid., 114–28; Kueny, *Conceiving Identities*, esp. 53–61.
49 The most relevant Quranic verses on conception are 22.5 ('O People, if you should be in doubt about the Resurrection, then [consider that] indeed, We created you from dust, then from a sperm-drop, then from a clinging clot, and then from a lump of flesh, formed and unformed – that We may show you. And We settle in the wombs whom We will for a specified term, then We bring you out as a child, and then [We develop you] that you may reach your [time of] maturity. And among you is he who is taken in [early] death, and among you is he who is returned to the most decrepit [old] age so that he knows, after [once having] knowledge, nothing. And you see the earth barren, but when We send down upon it rain, it quivers and swells and grows [something] of every beautiful kind'); 23.12–14 ('And certainly did We create man from an extract of clay. Then We placed him as a sperm-drop in a firm lodging. Then We made the sperm-drop into a clinging clot, and We made the clot into a lump [of flesh], and We made [from] the lump, bones, and We covered the bones with

flesh; then We developed him into another creation. So blessed is Allah, the best of creators'). For more details, see Serena Tolino, 'Pregnancy', in *Encyclopaedia of Islamic Bioethics* (Oxford: Oxford University Press, 2019).For more details on how medical authorities tried to connect these verses with their medical knowledge, see Julia Bummel, 'Zeugung und pränatale Entwicklung des Menschen nach Schriften mittelalterlicher muslimischer Religionsgelehrter über die "Medizin des Propheten"', PhD dissertation (University of Hamburg, 1999), esp. 76–86.

50 Ibid., 77.

51 Franz Rosenthal, 'Ar-Rāzī on the Hidden Illness', *Bulletin of the History of Medicine*, 52 (1978): 45–60, 54–5.

52 Ibid., 55.

53 More generally on the desire to be penetrated in Islamic medicine, see Hans-Peter Pökel, 'Der sexualpathologische Diskurs über den penetrierten Mann in der arabisch-islamischen Medizin des 10. und 11. Jahrhunderts', in Roswitha Badry, Maria Rohrer and Karin Steiner (eds), *Liebe, Sexualität, Partnerschaft: Paradigmen im Wandel. Beiträge zur orientalistischen Gender-Forschung*, 65–79 (Freiburg: fwpf, 2009).

54 Rosenthal, 'Ar-Rāzī', 54.

55 Ibid., 55.

56 Bummel, 'Zeugung und pränatale Entwicklung des Menschen', 85.

57 Weisser, *Zeugung, Vererbung und Pränatale Entwicklung*, 122–24.

58 Gadelrab, 'Discourses on Sex Differences', 24–5

59 Abū ʿAlī al-Ḥusayn ibn ʿAbd Allāh ibn Sīnā, *al-Qānūn fī al-Ṭibb*, ed. Muḥammad Amīn al-Ḍannāwī (Bayrūt: Dār al-Kutub al-ʿIlmiyya, 1999), 1:766–67.

60 Ibid., 767. Nevertheless, this is not always the case: 'If it comes from the left side to the right side of the uterus than the result is a masculine female and if it comes from the right side to the left side of the uterus then the result will be an effeminate male.' Ibid.

61 On the primacy of the right side, see the classical article by Robert Hertz, 'La Prééminence de la main droite: étude sur la polarité religieuse', *Revue Philosophique de la France et de l'Étranger*, 68 (1909): 553–80.

62 Ibn Sīnā, *al-Qānūn fī al-Ṭibb*, 1:766–67.

63 Ibid.

64 Ibn Sīnā, *al-Shifāʾ, al-Ṭabīʿiyyāt*, 111.

65 Ibid.

66 Ibid., 179.

67 Abū al-Walīd Muḥammad b. Aḥmad ibn Rushd, *Kitāb al-Kulliyyāt fī al-Ṭibb*, ed. J. M. Fórneas Besteiro and C. Alvarez de Morales (Madrid: Consejo Superior de Investigaciones Científicas, Escuela de Estudios Árabes de Granada, 1987), 204.

68 Gadelrab, 'Discourses on Sex Differences', 32.

69 Ze'evi, *Producing Desire*, 22.

70 For more details on this topic, see Marion Katz, 'Gender and Law', in *Encyclopaedia of Islam*, 3rd edn. (Leiden: Brill, 2017). http://dx.doi.org/10.1163/1573-3912_ei3_COM_27397.

71 On this discussion, see Peter Freimark, 'Zur Stellung des Zwitters im rabbinischen und islamischen Recht', *Zeitschrift der Deutschen Morgenländischen Gesellschaft*, 120 (1970): 85–102; Agostino Cilardo, 'Historical Development of the Legal Doctrine Relative to the Position of the Hermaphrodite in the Islamic Law', *Search: Journal for Arab and Islamic Studies*, 7 (1986): 128–70; Paula Sanders, 'Gendering the Ungendered Body: Hermaphrodites in Medieval Islamic Law', in Nikki R. Keddie and Beth Baron (eds), *Women in Middle Eastern History: Shifting Boundaries in Sex and*

Gender, 74–95 (New Haven, CT: Yale University Press, 1991); Vardit Rispler-Chaim, *Disability in Islamic Law* (Dordrecht: Springer, 2007), 69–74. For the Ottoman period, see also Scalenghe, *Disability in the Ottoman World*, 124–62.

72 Ibid., 125–29.

73 Shams al-Aʾimma Abū Bakr al-Sarakhsī, *Kitāb al-Mabsūṭ fī al-Fiqh al-Ḥanafī* (Beirut: Dār Maʿarifa, 1989), 30:92.

74 Muwaffaq al-Dīn ibn Qudāma al-Maqdisī, *al-Mughnī*, ed. ʿAbd Allāh b. ʿAbd al-Muḥsin al-Turkī and ʿAbd al-Fattāḥ Muḥammad al-Ḥulw (Riyadh: Dār ʿĀlam al-Kutub, 1997), 9:108.

75 See Cilardo, 'Historical Development of the Legal Doctrine', 129–34.

76 Ibn Qudāma, *al-Mughnī*, 9:110; al-Sarakhsī, *Kitāb al-Mabsūṭ*, 30:104–05.

77 Cilardo, 'Historical Development of the Legal Doctrine', 133. See also Ibn Qudāma, *al-Mughnī*, 9:110.

78 For more details, see Katz, 'Gender and law' and Sanders, 'Gendering the Ungendered Body'.

79 For more details, see Serena Tolino, 'Eunuchs in the Fatimid Empire: Ambiguities, Gender and Sacredness', in Almut Höfert, Matthew M. Mesley and Serena Tolino (eds), *Celibate and Childless Men in Power: Ruling Eunuchs and Bishops in the Pre-modern World*, 246–66 (London: Routledge, 2018), esp. 251–52.

80 See, for example, Ibn ʿAbd al-Barr, *al-Istidhkār*, ed. Sālim Muḥammad ʿAṭā and Muḥammad ʿAlī Muʿawwaḍ, 9 vols (Beirut: Dār al-Kutub al-ʿIlmiyya, 2000), 6:192; al-Marghīnānī, *al-Hidāya, Sharḥ Bidāyat al-Mubtadī*, 4 vols (Cairo: Dār al-Salām, 2000), 2:619.

81 See Schmitt, 'Liwāṭ im fiqh'; Omar: 'From Semantics to Normative Law'; Tolino: 'Homosexual Acts in Islamic Law'.

82 Thomas Bauer, *Die Kultur der Ambiguität. Eine andere Geschichte des Islams* (Suhrkamp: Verlag der Weltreligionen im Insel Verlag, 2011).

83 See ibid. and El-Rouayheb, *Before Homosexuality*.

84 al-Jāḥiẓ, 'Tafḍīl al-Baṭn ʿalā al-Ẓahr', in ʿAlī Abū Mulḥam (ed.), *Rasāʾil al-Jāḥiẓ. al-Rasāʾil al-Adabiyya*, 147–60 (Beirut: Dār wa-Maktaba al-Hilāl, 2002), 153. The essay has been translated into English by William M. Hutchins, *Nine Essays of al-Jahiz* (New York: Peter Lang, 1989), 167–73. The translation used here is my own.

85 This is even evident by the fact that the form used for the 'penetrated', *mankūḥ*, is not a feminine but a masculine one that could refer to both males and females.

86 For an analysis of this work and the wider genre of the 'Rangstreit literature', see Franz Rosenthal, 'Male and Female: Described and Compared', in J. W. Wright Jr and Everett K. Rowson (eds), *Homoeroticism in Classical Arabic Literature*', 24–54 (New York: Columbia University Press, 1997). See also Pökel, *Der unmännliche Mann*, 245–48.

87 Al-Jāḥiẓ, 'Kitāb Mufākharat al-Jawārī wa-l-Ghilmān', in Mulḥam (ed.), *Rasāʾil al-Jāḥiẓ*, 147–60, 161–96, 166. The essay has also been translated by Hutchins, *Nine Essays of al-Jahiz*, 139–66. The translation used here is my own.

88 Al-Jāḥiẓ, 'Kitāb Mufākharat al-Jawārī wa-l-Ghilmān', 167.

89 Ibid., 182.

90 Ibid.

91 This is quite similar to what Afsaneh Najmabadi observed for the Persianate world, namely that 'the growth of a full beard marked adult manhood, the adolescent male's transition from an object of desire to a desiring subject'. Afsaneh Najmabadi, *Women with Mustaches and Men without Beards: Gender and Sexual Anxieties of Iranian Modernity* (Berkeley, CA: University of California Press, 2005), 15.

92 On the centrality of the beard, see al-Rouayheb, *Before Homosexuality*, 26; Faegheh Shirazi, 'Men's Facial Hair in Islam: A Matter of Interpretation', in Geraldine Biddle-Perry and Sarah Cheang (eds), *Hair: Styling, Culture and Fashion*, 111–22 (Oxford: Berg, 2008).

References

Adang, Camilla (2003), 'Ibn Ḥazm on Homosexuality: A Case-study of Ẓāhiri Legal Methodology', *Al-Qanṭara*, 24 (1): 5–31.

Ahmed, Leila (1992), *Women and Gender in Islam: Historical Roots of a Modern Debate*, New Haven, CT: Yale University Press.

Al-Barr, Ibn ʿAbd (2000), *al-Istidhkār*, ed. Sālim Muḥammad ʿAṭā and Muḥammad ʿAlī Muʿawwaḍ, 9 vols, Cairo: Dār al-Kutub al-ʿIlmiyya.

Al-Fīrūzābādī, Majd al-Dīn (2005), *al-Qāmūs al-Muḥīṭ*, ed. Muḥammad Naʿīm al-ʿArqūsī, Beirut: Muʾassasat al-risāla.

Al-Jāḥiẓ (2002), 'Tafḍīl al-Baṭn ʿalā al-Ẓahr', in ʿAlī Abū Mulḥam (ed.), *Rasāʾil al-Jāḥiẓ. al-Rasāʾil al-Adabiyya*, 147–60, Beirut: Dār wa-Maktaba al-Hilāl.

Al-Jawharī, Abū Naṣr Ismāʿīl b. Ḥamād (2009), *al-Ṣiḥāḥ. Tāj al-Lugha wa-Ṣiḥāḥ al-ʿArabiyya*, ed. Muḥammad Muḥammad Tāmir, Anas Muḥammad Shāmī and Zakariyyā Jābir Aḥmad, Cairo: Dār al-Ḥadīth.

Al-Maqdisī, Muwaffaq al-Dīn ibn Qudāma (1997), *al-Mughnī*, ed. ʿAbd Allāh b. ʿabd al-Muḥsin al-Turkī and ʿAbd al-Fattāḥ Muḥammad al-Ḥulw, Riyadh: Dār ʿĀlam al-Kutub.

Al-Sarakhsī, Shams al-Aʾimma Abū Bakr (1989), *Kitāb al-Mabsūṭ fī al-Fiqh al-Ḥanafī*, Beirut: Dār Maʿarifa.

Al-Sayyid-Marsot, Afaf Lutfi (1979), *Society and the Sexes in Medieval Islam*, Malibu, CA: Undena Publications.

Amar, Paul (2011), 'Middle East Masculinity Studies: Discourses of "Men in Crisis", Industries of Gender in Revolution', *Journal of Middle East Women's Studies*, 7 (3): 36–70.

Baalbaki, Ramzi (2016), 'Ibn Manẓūr', in Kate Fleet, Gudrun Krämer, Denis Matringe, John Nawas and Everett Rowson (eds), *Encyclopaedia of Islam*, 3rd edn. http://dx.doi.org/10.1163/1573-3912_ei3_COM_30632.

Babayan, Kathryn and Afsaneh Najmabadi (eds) (2008), *Islamicate Sexualities: Translations across Temporal Geographies of Desire*, Cambridge, MA: Harvard University Press.

Bauer, Thomas (2011), *Die Kultur der Ambiguität. Eine andere Geschichte des Islams*, Suhrkamp: Verlag der Weltreligionen im Insel Verlag.

Bummel, Julia (1999), 'Zeugung und pränatale Entwicklung des Menschen nach Schriften mittelalterlicher muslimischer Religionsgelehrter über die "Medizin des Propheten"', PhD dissertation, University of Hamburg.

Cheikh-Moussa, Abdallah (1982), 'Ǧāḥiẓ et les eunuques ou la confusion du même et de l'autre', *Arabica*, 29 (2): 184–214.

Cilardo, Agostino (1986), 'Historical Development of the Legal Doctrine Relative to the Position of the Hermaphrodite in the Islamic Law', *Search: Journal for Arab and Islamic Studies*, 7: 128–70.

Connell, Raewyn W. (1995), *Masculinities*, Cambridge: Polity Press.

Connell, Raewyn W. and James W. Messerchmidt (2005), 'Hegemonic Masculinity: Rethinking the Concept', *Gender and Society*, 19 (6): 829–59.
De Sondy, Amanullah (2013), *The Crisis of Islamic Masculinities*, London: Bloomsbury.
El-Rouayheb, Khaled (2005), *Before Homosexuality in the Arab-islamic World: 1500–1800*, Chicago, IL: University of Chicago Press.
Freimark, Peter (1970), 'Zur Stellung des Zwitters im rabbinischen und islamischen Recht', *Zeitschrift der Deutschen Morgenländischen Gesellschaft*, 120: 85–102.
Gadelrab, Sherry Sayed (2011), 'Discourses on Sex Differences in Medieval Scholarly Islamic Thought', *Journal of the History of Medicine*, 66 (1): 40–81.
Gadelrab, Sherry Sayed (2016), *Medicine and Morality in Egypt. Gender and Sexuality in the Nineteenth and Early Twentieth Centuries*, London: I.B.Tauris.
Ghoussoub, Mai and Emma Sinclair-Webb (eds) (2000), *Imagined Masculinities: Male Identity and Culture in the Modern Middle East*, London: Saqi Books.
Habib, Samar (2007), *Female Homosexuality in the Middle East: Histories and Representations*, London: Routledge.
Habib, Samar (ed.) (2009), *Islam and Homosexuality*, Santa Barbara, CA: ABC Clio.
Hertz, Robert (1909), 'La Prééminence de la main droite: étude sur la polarité religieuse', *Revue Philosophique de la France et de l'Étranger*, 68: 553–80.
Hutchins, William M. (1989), *Nine Essays of al-Jahiz*, New York: Peter Lang.
Katz, Marion (2017), 'Gender and Law', in Kate Fleet, Gudrun Krämer, Denis Matringe, John Nawas and Everett Rowson (eds), *Encyclopaedia of Islam*, 3rd edn. (Leiden: Brill). http://dx.doi.org/10.1163/1573-3912_ei3_COM_27397.
Keddie, Nikki R. and Beth Baron (eds) (1991), *Women in Middle Eastern History: Shifting Boundaries in Sex and Gender*, New Haven, CT: Yale University Press.
Kueny, Kathryin M. (2013), *Conceiving Identities: Maternity in Medieval Muslim Discourse and Practice*, New York: State University of New York.
Ibn Manẓūr, Muḥammad b. Mukarram b. ʿAlī b. Aḥmad (n.d.), *Lisān al-ʿArab*, 15 vols, Beirut: Dār al-Ṣādir.
Kugle, Scott Siraj al-Haqq (2010), *Homosexuality in Islam: Critical Reflections on Gay, Lesbian, and Transgender Muslims*, Oxford: Oneworld Publications.
Ibn Rushd, Abū al-Walīd Muḥammad b. Aḥmad (1987), *Kitāb al-Kulliyyāt fī al-Ṭibb*, ed. J. M. Fórneas Besteiro and C. Alvarez de Morales, Madrid: Consejo Superior de Investigaciones Científicas, Escuela de Estudios Árabes de Granada.
Ibn Sīnā, Abū ʿAlī al-Ḥusayn, b. ʿAbd Allāh (1970), *al-Shifāʾ*, *al-Ṭabīʿiyyāt*, vol. 8, *al-Ḥayawān*, ed. Saʿīd Zāʾid ʿAbd al-Ḥalīm Muntaṣir and ʿAbd Allāh Ismāʿīl, Cairo: al-Hayʾa al-Miṣriyya al-ʿĀmma li-l-Taʾlīf wa-l-Nashr.
Ibn Sīnā, Abū ʿAlī al-Ḥusayn, b. ʿAbd Allāh (1999), *al-Qānūn fī al-Ṭibb*, ed. Muḥammad Amīn al-Ḍannāwī, Beirut: Dār al-Kutub al-ʿIlmiyya.
Laqueur, Thomas (1990), *Making Sex: Body and Gender from the Greeks to Freud*, Cambridge, MA: Harvard University Press.
Malti-Douglas, Fedwa (1991), *Woman's Body, Woman's Word: Gender and Discourse in Arabo-Islamic Writing*, Princeton, NJ: Princeton University Press.
Marín, Manuela and Randi Deguilhem (eds) (2002), *Writing the Feminine: Women in Arab Sources*, London: I.B.Tauris.
Mezziane, Mohammed (2008), 'Sodomie et masculinité chez les jurists musulmans du IXe au XIe siècle', *Arabica*, 55: 276–306.
Murray, Stephen O. and Will Roscoe (eds) (1997), *Islamic Homosexualities: Culture, History, and Literature*, New York: New York University Press.

Najmabadi, Afsaneh (2005), *Women with Mustaches and Men without Beards: Gender and Sexual Anxeities of Iranian Modernity*, Berkeley, CA: University of California Press.
Omar, Sara (2012), 'From Semantics to Normative Law: Perceptions of *Liwāṭ* (Sodomy) and *Siḥāq* (Tribadism) in Islamic Jurisprudence (8th–15th Century CE)', *Islamic Law and Society*, 19: 222–56.
Ouzgane, Lahoucine (ed.) (2006), *Islamic Masculinities*, London: Zed Books.
Pierce, Leslie (2009), 'Writing Histories of Sexuality in the Middle East', *The American Historical Review*, 114 (5): 1325–339.
Pökel, Hans-Peter (2009), 'Der sexualpathologische Diskurs über den penetrierten Mann in der arabisch-islamischen Medizin des 10. und 11. Jahrhunderts', in Roswitha Badry, Maria Rohrer and Karin Steiner (eds), *Liebe, Sexualität, Partnerschaft: Paradigmen im Wandel; Beiträge zur orientalistischen Gender-Forschung*, 65–79, Freiburg: fwpf.
Pökel, Hans-Peter (2014), *Der unmännliche Mann: Zur Figuration des Eunuchen im Werk von al-Ǧāḥiẓ (gest. 869)*, Würzburg: Ergon-Verlag.
Quraishi, Asifa and Frank Vogel (eds) (2008), *The Islamic Marriage Contract: Case Studies in Islamic Family Law*, Cambridge, MA: Harvard Law School.
Rispler-Chaim, Vardit (2007), *Disability in Islamic Law*, Dordrecht: Springer.
Rosenthal, Franz (1978), 'Ar-Rāzī on the Hidden Illness', *Bulletin of the History of Medicine*, 52: 45–60.
Rosenthal, Franz (1997), 'Male and Female: Described and Compared', in J. W. Wright Jr and Everett K. Rowson (eds), *Homoeroticism in Classical Arabic Literature*, 24–54, New York: Columbia University Press.
Rowson, Everett K. (1991), 'The Effeminates of Early Medina', *Journal of the American Oriental Society*, 111 (1): 671–93.
Rowson, Everett K. (2008), 'The Traffic in Boys: Slavery and Homoerotic Liaisons in Elite ʿAbbāsids Society', *Middle Eastern Literatures*, 11 (2): 193–204.
Sanders, Paula (1991), 'Gendering the Ungendered Body: Hermaphrodites in Medieval Islamic Law', in Nikki R. Keddie and Beth Baron (eds), *Women in Middle Eastern History: Shifting Boundaries in Sex and Gender*, 74–95, New Haven, CT: Yale University Press.
Scalanghe, Sara (2014), *Disability in the Ottoman World, 1500–1800*, New York: Cambridge University Press.
Schmitt, Arno (2001–2002), 'Liwāṭ im fiqh: Männliche Homosexualität?', *Journal of Arabic and Islamic Studies*, 4: 49–110.
Scott, Joan W. (1986), 'Gender: A Useful Category of Historical Analysis', *American Historical Review*, 91 (5): 1053–75.
Shalakany, Amr A. (2008), 'Islamic Legal Histories', *Berkeley Journal of Middle Eastern and Islamic Law*, 1: 1–82.
Shirazi, Faegheh (2008), 'Men's Facial Hair in Islam: A Matter of Interpretation', in Geraldine Biddle-Perry and Sarah Cheang (eds), *Hair: Styling, Culture and Fashion*, 111–22, Oxford: Berg.
Sonbol, Amira el-Azhari (ed.) (2005), *Beyond the Exotic: Women's Histories in Islamic Societies*, Cairo: American University Press.
Stowasser, Barbara (1994), *Women in the Qur'an, Traditions, and Interpretations*, New York: Oxford University Press.
Tolino, Serena (2014), 'Homosexual Acts in Islamic Law: *Siḥāq* and *Liwāṭ* in the Legal Debate', *GAIR-Mitteilungen*, 6: 187–205.
Tolino, Serena (2018), 'Eunuchs in the Fatimid Empire: Ambiguities, Gender and Sacredness', in Almut Höfert, Matthew M. Mesley and Serena Tolino (eds), *Celibate*

and Childless Men in Power: Ruling Eunuchs and Bishops in the Pre-modern World, 246–66, London: Routledge.

Tolino, Serena (2019), 'Pregnancy', in *Encyclopaedia of Islamic Bioethics*, Oxford: Oxford University Press.

Wadud, Amina (1999), *Qur'an and Woman: Rereading the Sacred Text from a Woman's Perspective*, New York: Oxford University Press.

Weisser, Ursula (1983), *Zeugung, Vererbung und Pränatale Entwicklung in der Medizin des arabisch-islamischen Mittelalters*, Erlangen: Verlagsbuchhandlung Hannelore Lüling.

Wright, J. W. Jr and Everett K. Rowson (eds) (1991), *Homoeroticism in Classical Arabic Literature*, New York: Columbia University Press.

Ze'evi, Dror (2006), *Producing Desire: Changing Sexual Discourse in the Ottoman Middle East, 1500–1900*, Berkeley, CA: University of California Press.

Chapter 2

ILLUSIONS OF ANDROGYNY: CROSS-DRESSING WOMEN (*GHULĀMIYYĀT*) IN ABBASID SOCIETY

Johannes Thomann

The name *ghulāmiyya* (pl. *ghulāmiyyāt*) is derived from *ghulām*, originally with the general meaning 'boy, male adolescent', but in early Abbasid times, 'young male slave', especially 'military slave of Turkish origin'.[1] Thus, *ghulāmiyya* literally means a female being with the look and the attributes of a *ghulām*. Historical sources describe the *ghulāmiyyāt* as young female slaves dressed as young men serving at the court of the early Abbasids. They seem to have been a fashion restricted to the first Abbasid century (750–850 CE), even if there was also an occasional revival in the Mamluk epoch, both in literature and in everyday life.[2] In recent scholarship the *ghulāmiyyāt* were put into the context of lesbianism.[3] This chapter will demonstrate that this cannot be substantiated by looking at the sources.[4]

At the outset, the topic of this chapter will be the construction of desire. The topic involves different social techniques: techniques of power and of the self, to name only two.[5] The focus is on a critical case: women dressed up and adorned as men with the intention to produce desire. It will be shown that in the epoch under consideration, this procedure was by no means tied to a homogenous agenda. Most notably, there is a strong contrast between *ghulāmiyyāt*, who were slaves, as already mentioned, and *shāṭirāt*, who were free women voluntarily cross-dressing. Thus, the chapter starts with a survey on slavery in general and on the role of slaves as partners for sexual intercourse. Next, I present examples from poetry evoking the phenomenon. After that, I argue that the discussions on cross-dressing women in Muslim tradition and jurisprudence arose at the beginning of the Abbasid epoch, at the same time as the *ghulāmiyyāt* became a topic in poetry. Poetry and jurisprudence reveal contrasting attitudes towards female cross-dressing, balancing the praise for the women's charms and the blame for the blurring of differences between women and men that it causes. Later historians also discussed the *ghulāmiyyāt* as an ideal of beauty. Finally, the phenomenon of the *ghulāmiyyāt* is discussed through the lens of spatiality, further underlying the sublime associated with the desire triggered by these androgynes.

The status of slaves

Slavery as a legal concept and a social phenomenon has a long history. In the oldest surviving law book, the Codex Hammurabi, 'free men' (sg. *awīlum*) and 'slaves' (sg. *wardum*) have a different legal status. The same holds for ancient Jewish, Greek, Roman and Persian law. In the Qur'an, slavery is presented as a legitimate social practice. In particular, social inequality between master and slave is recognized.[6] However, the liberation of slaves is recommended as a pious act.[7] In Islamic law, slaves (sg. *ʿabd*, pl. *ʿabīd*) were regarded as being the property of their masters and they could be sold.[8] In theory it was forbidden to enslave Muslims, but there were cases in which rebels were denounced as infidels and reduced to slavery.[9] Conversion to Islam by a non-Muslim slave did not require his/her liberation, and Muslim children born to slave parents were not free.[10]

In Abbasid society, slaves fulfilled diverse purposes. At the top of society were the military slaves. Eventually they could rise to great power and wealth, and were normally liberated at some stage of their career.[11] A particular group among them were eunuchs, who served as military trainers of boys and young men but could also, more rarely, become important military commanders.[12] Many slaves were servants in private households[13] or in the palace of the ruler.[14] At the bottom of the society were working slaves, both men and women, labouring under the harshest of conditions in the marches or in gold, copper and salt mines.[15]

The price of slaves varied enormously, according to their origin, individual physical constitution and education. White slaves were usually more expensive than black slaves. Bodily strength in the case of adult men and bodily beauty in the case of women and adolescent young men were in demand. The highest prices were paid for female singers and male champions in the martial arts, as for example al-Manṣūr Qalāwūn al-Alfī (active 1280–1290; purchase price 1,000 dinars).[16]

Slaves could also be partners for sexual intercourse. According to Islamic law there were two forms of licit sexual intercourse: between married partners and between a male master and a female slave. It has been shown that both legal forms had much in common, even if the legal status of a female slave was lower than that of a married woman.[17] In both cases, licit sexual intercourse was linked to a transaction in which a man gains domination (*mulk*) over a woman in exchange for paying a sum of money, either to the woman or to the former owner.[18] Sexual relations with slaves of the same sex were declared forbidden by most jurists, but intercourse between a male owner with his male slave was permitted by a few later Mālikī jurists. In any case, the application of a *ḥadd* punishment was excluded by most jurists because of *shubha*, the 'semblance' between these relations and lawful relations with female slaves.[19]

According to the available sources, sometimes love relations could also happen between owners and their slaves. This seems particularly the case with a special high class of female slave, the singers, called *qiyān*,[20] at least according to the ninth-century Iraqi polymath al-Jāḥiẓ (d.255/868–869).[21] Al-Jāḥiẓ wrote a treatise on them, in which he gave a detailed description of their techniques to produce passion in eventual future owners. He identified three stages of affection, namely love (*ḥubb*), passion (*ʿishq*) and infatuation (*hawā*). Love is the starting point of passion, and passion is followed by infatuation. Passion is characterized by the admission of carnal instinct, a natural affinity (*mushākilat al-ṭabīʿa*), similar to that found in the animal world.[22] According to al-Jāḥiẓ, slave singers were producing passions but in most cases were not affected themselves. Instead, they only pretended to have fallen in love with their male targets, and they were hardly ever sincere. There are exceptions to this, when 'this pretence leads her to turning into reality' (*qādahā al-tamwīh ilā al-taṣḥīḥ*).[23] In such cases 'they may renounce their crafts, in order to be cheaper for [the men they love]'.[24] As I show below, similar kinds of infatuation of owners for *ghulāmiyyāt* appear in the Abbasid literature. However, our source represents the owners' perspectives, and there is no evidence of the feelings of the enslaved women, as we do not have sources written by them.

The ghulāmiyyāt *in poetry*

The motif of the *ghulāmiyyāt* appeared first in the poems of Abū Nuwās (d.198–200/813–815):[25]

Here you have images [*ṣuwar*], females [*muʾannathāt*]
    in coquetry [*dall*], and in the costumes of males [*dhukūr*],
With bare extremities,
    at the places of the buttons and the cleavages,
They are slim like reins,
    like suspensions of swords and like belts
But their buttocks are bouffant
    in the tunics, and daggers are at their hips,
Their cheeks [have] scorpion-like curls,
    and their whiskers are made out of perfume.

With the term *ṣūra*, 'image', in the first line Abū Nuwās emphasizes the virtual status of the *ghulāmiyyāt*. They have a likeness to something different from them. However, the object of which they are an image is ambiguous. In their elegant coquetry they mirror femininity, in their costume they mirror masculinity. In the subsequent lines, male attributes dominate. These are partly natural features of their bodies, partly artificial attributes created by hairdressing and makeup.

Addressees of the performance of *ghulāmiyyāt* are always men. Abū Nuwās, who preferred young men as sexual partners, as he declared in many poems, confesses to have once fallen in love with a *ghulāmiyya*:[26]

The full bosomed among the servants of the castle,
    with ringlets on their cheeks and desirable hair,
A *ghulāmiyya*, whose clothes are fragrant from *barmakī* essence,
    whose girdles have disappeared in the thinness of her waist,
I fell in love [*kaliftu*] when I saw the beauty of her face, [only]
    for a while, since love of starlets [*kawākib*] is not my thing.

Again, the attractiveness of the *ghulāmiyya* is described as a combination of male and female attributes. She has an ample bosom but a slim waist and her hair is dressed like that of a male youth.

In another poem of Abū Nuwās, a *ghulāmiyya* is described as equally attractive to men generally preferring male sexual partners and to men generally preferring female sexual partners:[27]

> [Wine] from the hand of someone with a vagina [*dhāt ḥir*] in the costume of someone with a penis [*dhū dhakar*],
> she has two lovers, a pederast [*lūṭī*] and a fornicator [*zannāʾ*].

Here the ambiguity includes the sexual organs, at least for the eye of the spectator.

The ambiguity is further extended to the nature of sexual intercourse with the *ghulāmiyya*:[28]

> Eye and ear hold me back from a masculine [*mudhakkara*] [female youth],
> who has relationship in desire with the pederast [*lūṭī*] and the womanizer [*ghazil*].
> Both are behind her, ambitious in their endeavour
> despite their dissent on the position of [sexual] act.

Abū Nuwās implies that a pederast would practice anal intercourse, while a womanizer would prefer vaginal penetration. He played with this motif in a verse that became famous:

> He is called Maʿn but if you turn him round
> then it is as if you call his sister, for his name, when you invert it, is Nuʿm.

The expression 'to turn him round' is ambiguous. The obvious sense is to read the name 'Maʿn' (a male name) backwards, which yields 'Nuʿm' (a female name; short vowels are not written in Arabic and do not count), but there is an underlying sense. This connotation becomes clear if one understands that with brother and sister, Abū Nuwās is referring to one person, a *ghulāmiyya*. From behind she can be penetrated like a young male slave (*ghulām*), and turned around she can be penetrated like a young female slave (*jāriya*).

At first, *ghulāmiyyāt* were slaves in the household of the caliph, as historical accounts indicate. But they were imitated by free women with a libertine lifestyle. Abū Nuwās uses the term *shāṭira* in this context. They adopted a fashion *à la ghulāmiyya*:[29]

> Oh hussy, who boasts of the beauty of the face,
> like a lightning in the obscurity of the darkness,
> She looks upon the costume of the youth as perfection of beauty,
> and most suitable for obscenity [*furūq*] and sin [*āthām*]

She does not stop to behave like that, until
    she resembles him [i.e. *ghulām*] in action and speech
She goes as far as to claim over the female youths [*al-jawārī*]
    precedence in libertinism and ferventness [...]
She goes out to play polo every day,
    and shoots with bowls and arrows.

It seems that this *shāṭira* adopted an entirely male lifestyle, participating in what were considered typically male sports such as riding and shooting.

Muslim tradition and jurisprudence on cross-dressing

Theologians and jurists of the early Abbasid epoch seem to have judged such phenomena as cross-dressing differently than did poets. They put the *ghulāmiyyāt* and the *shāṭirāt* together and coined the term *mutarajjilāt* for both of them. In doing so they applied the juridical device of *qiyās* (analogy) and compared them with cross-dressing men, called *mukhannathūn* (effeminate), who in Umayyad time were already a topic in *ḥadīth* tradition, where they were negatively judged. This judgement was now transferred to the *mutarajjilāt*.

In the form it was conceived by al-Shāfiʿī (d.204/820), Islamic jurisprudence was based on the Qurʾan on the one hand and on Muslim tradition (*ḥadīth*, pl. *aḥādīth*) on the other. Even though the complete process of canonization of the Qurʾan took several generations, it soon became a canonical text for which only minor variant readings existed. The textual tradition of *ḥadīth* material was far more dynamic, and its history was and is highly controversial. It consists of reports on actions or utterances of the Prophet or his companions.[30] It is characteristic of *ḥadīth* reports that they are composed of two parts. The first part, the *isnād* (pl. *asānīd*), contains a list of those who supposedly handed down the report from the time of the prophet to the time the collector included the report in his work. The second part, the *matn* (pl. *mutūn*), contains the report itself, mostly in a brief form of only a few lines of text.

There exists a tradition saying: 'that the Messenger of God cursed those men who sought to resemble women and those women who sought to resemble men' (T1).[31] In another version this is expressed more specifically: 'the man who dresses like a woman, and the woman who dresses like a man' (T2).[32] There is a more general version: 'effeminate men and manly women' (T3).[33] In the case of men the expression 'effeminate' (*mukhannath*) leaves it open if natural bodily characteristics are meant for intentional dressing and adornment. The expression 'behaving like men' (*mutarajjil*, active participle) points to an active intentional practice. There is a version that presents both sets of expressions (T1 and T3) side by side. In yet another version, the words of the Prophet Muḥammad (T3) are followed by an imperative statement by the Prophet: 'Put them out of the house' (T4). After that two actions are reported: 'The messenger of God did put somebody out of the house', and 'ʿUmar did put somebody out of the house' (T5).[34] This seems to indicate that cross-dressing was not regarded as a severe crime.

However, female cross-dressing appears in another context as an unforgivable sin: 'The messenger of God said: Three will not enter paradise and God will not look at them at the day of resurrection: who is disobedient to his parents, the manly woman who sought to resemble men, and the pimp' (T6).[35] It is conspicuous that men who sought to resemble women are not mentioned here. Later jurists held the opinion that female and male cross-dressers should be punished more severely than with an order to stay away from the house, as indicated in canonical *ḥadīth* (T4 and T5).

In which historical context the different versions of the narrative concerning cross-dressing men and women were put into the form they are found in the ninth-century CE *ḥadīth* collections is a question that remains. The leading method of dating *ḥadīth* is the so-called *isnād-cum-matn* analysis, analysing both chains of transmitters and the content of *ḥadīth*-s. Some of the results of such an analysis of *ḥadīth*-s referring to cross-dressing are important for our topic, as they allow us to link them all to the early Abbasid period.

The *asānīd* of the two main textual versions (T1 and T3) on which I am going to focus show a neatly separate pattern. In the first case (T1), five collections trace it back to one transmitter of the fourth generation after the prophecy of Muḥammad (see Diagram 2.1). From him there is a single line of transmitters

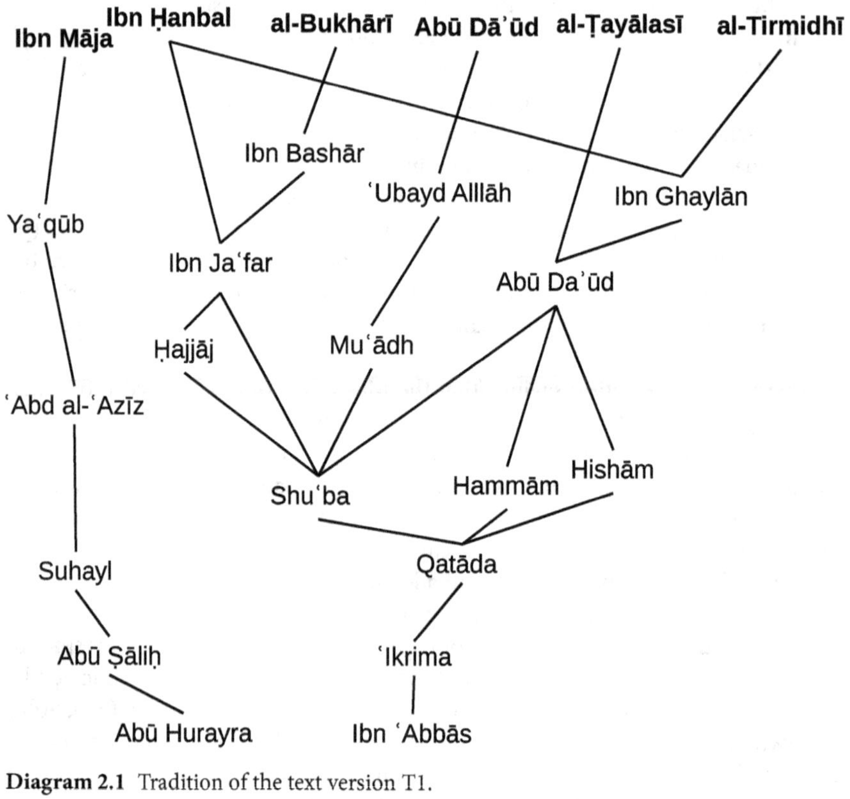

Diagram 2.1 Tradition of the text version T1.

to the Prophet Muḥammad himself. The transmitter from whom the tradition later spreads is Shuʿba ibn al-Ḥajjāj (d.160/777), who lived in Basra. Most later transmitters praised Shuʿba as a reliable source but there were also divergent voices. Abū Ḥanīfa (d.150/767) called him 'stuffing of the town' (*ḥashw al-miṣr*), pointing to the incredibly high number of *ḥadīth* teachers from whom Shuʿba claims to have transmitted *ḥadīth* material with which he 'stuffed the town'. Shuʿba mentioned three hundred names of his immediate informers. Many of them are otherwise unknown and are in all probability fictitious, as are the *ḥadīth*-s allegedly transmitted by him. The *ḥadīth* on the 'women who sought to resemble men' (T1) most probably belongs to them too. The historical context of this *ḥadīth* can be summarized as follows: it is most likely to have been conceived by a scholar in southern Iraq who visited Baghdad between 762 and 776 CE.

In the case of the other main version of the *ḥadīth* (T3), Diagram 2.2 shows a different structure. The transmitters of the first four generations produce a single line. Then follows a bifurcation to two transmitters. The first, Hishām ibn Abī ʿAbdallāh al-Dastawāʾī (also Dastuwāʾī or al-Dustuwāʾī d.152–154/769–771), was a major figure among the *ḥadīth* collectors of his generation. He lived in Basra.[36] The second, Maʿmar ibn Rāshid al-Azdī (d.153/770), lived in Basra and later went to Yemen. A whole collection of *ḥadīth*-s ascribed to him was fabricated later. The most probable interpretation of the bifurcation in Diagram 2.2 is that

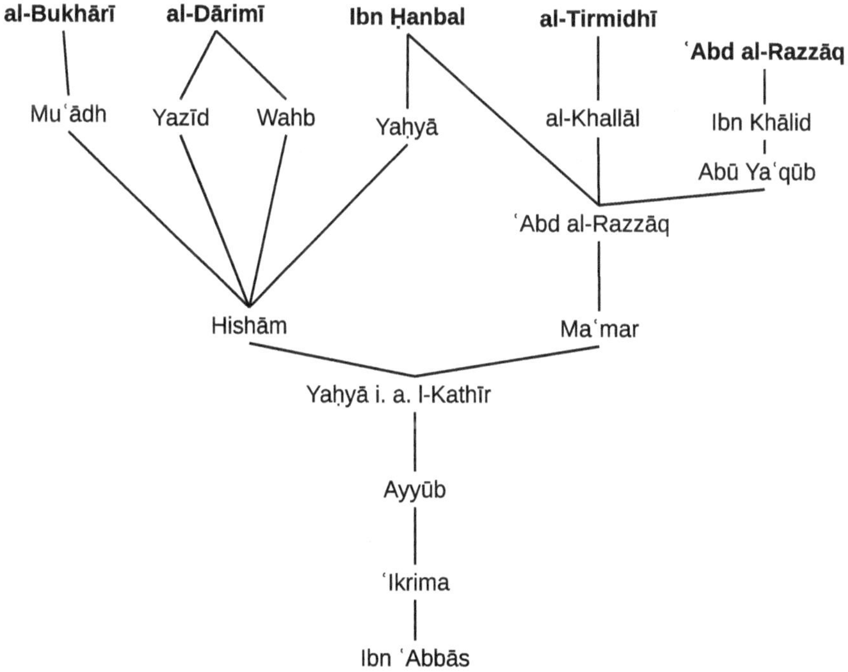

Diagram 2.2 Tradition of the text version T3.

Hishām al-Dastawāʾī was the 'common link' from which the report spread, and that the name of Maʿmar was introduced later. Maʿmar might have heard the shorter version (T3) from Hishām al-Dastawāʾī and transmitted it to another *ḥadīth* scholar, and Hishām might have transmitted the longer version (T3+T4) to two scholars and the extended (T3+T4+T5) to another two scholars. But it cannot be excluded that even greater manipulation was involved.

Consequently, the emergence of both versions can be historically situated within a narrow time frame. They came into circulation in the first two decades of the Abbasid era (*c.* 750–770 CE) in Basra. The three scholars involved then lived in the same town and all were non-Arabs, most probably Iranians. Thus, it is likely they knew each other. The evidence suggesting that the formulation of the *ḥadīth*-s condemning female cross-dressing is almost contemporary with the first evocations of the *ghulāmiyyāt* and *shāṭirāt* in the poems of Abū Nuwās hints at a possible link between these condemnations and the spread of a new phenomenon linked to the newly established Abbasid court. Scott Kugle demonstrated that a very similar contemporary case is the condemnation of males who practised anal intercourse, which was received as a cultural transformation.[37]

Historical accounts of the ghulāmiyyāt *of the Abbasid period*

Lexcographers of the Abbasid period referred to the phenomenon of *ghulāmiyyāt*. In Khalīl ibn Aḥmad's (d.175, 170 or 160/791, 786 or 776) *Kitāb al-ʿAyn*, the basic verbal meaning of the root *gh-l-m* is explained as 'to be defeated by desire' (*ghuliba shahwatan*). Accordingly, the derivate noun *al-mighlīm* designates someone 'in whom the male and the female are equal' (*yastawī fī-hi al-dhakar wa-l-unthā*), and it was said *jāriya mughlīm* (a young woman being equally male and female).[38] It seems that *ghulāmiyyāt* became a generally accepted model of female beauty.

Al-Jāḥiẓ wrote an essay on the 'Competition of Male Youths [*ghilmān*] and Female Youths [*al-jawārī*]'. He argued that when a *jāriya* excels in beauty, she is said to be like a *ghulām*, that she has 'characteristics of a *ghulām*' (*waṣīfa ghulāmiyya*).[39] Further, al-Jāḥiẓ cites verses in which a *jāriya* is praised as having the 'shape of a *ghulām*' (*qadd al-ghulām*), or is described as 'having the appearance of a *ghulām*' (*ziyy al-ghulām*).[40]

A century later, historians reported anecdotes about the first *ghulāmiyyāt* at the caliphal court in Baghdad. One of these anecdotes, reported by al-Masʿūdī (d.345/956), tries to explain the origin of the *ghulāmiyya*:

> When Zubayda's son [al-Amīn] succeeded to the caliphate [in the year 809], he favored the eunuchs and advanced their standing, notably Kawthar [his favourite], but others as well. When Zubayda saw how entranced he was by the eunuchs, and how he spent all his time with them, she took some of the slave girls who were well-built and had beautiful faces, and put turbans on their heads, arranged their hair in bangs and sidecurls, and cut short at the back, and

> dressed them in *qabā*-s [a close-fitting robe], *qurṭaq*-s [a close-fitting tunic], and *minṭaqa*-s [a sash]; this attire gave them a svelte carriage, and emphasized their buttocks. Zubayda then sent them to al-Amīn, and they took turns serving him. He was pleased with them, and attracted by them, and brought them into public view, before both the elite and the commons. Then both elite and commons began to have slave girls with bobbed hair, whom they dressed in *qabā*-s and *minṭaqa*-s; and they called them *ghulāmiyyāt*.[41]

Another anecdote, reported by al-Qālī (d.356/967), describes the love of the young al-Maʾmūn (Rajab 218/August 833) and a *ghulāmiyya* who was a slave of the caliph Hārūn al-Rashīd (d.193/809).[42]

> Hārūn al-Rashīd had a *ghulāmiyya* slave – this means a female slave with the shape of a young man – and al-Maʾmūn had a predilection towards her. He was still beardless. [Sometimes] she was about to pour [water] from a pitcher on to the hand of al-Rashīd. Al-Maʾmūn was sitting behind al-Rashīd and made a sign as if he would kiss her, but she did not react to it with her eyes but slowed down in her pouring [the water] in order to show herself to al-Maʾmūn and to make a sign towards him. Al-Rashīd said: 'What is that? Put this pitcher out of your hand.' – She made it. He said: 'By God! If you don't tell me the truth, they should kill you.' – She said: 'O my master! ʿAbdallāh made a sign as if he would kiss me, but I did not react to it against him.' – Al-Rashīd turned himself towards al-Maʾmūn, and he saw him as if he would be dead because of what befell him of anxiety and shyness. Al-Rashīd had mercy with him, embraced him and said: 'Do you love her?' – Al-Maʾmūn said: 'Yes, Commander of the Faithfuls.' – Al-Rashīd said: 'She is yours. Go and enter in that [chamber with a] cupola!' – and he did it.

These sources, even if written much later, seem to confirm the strong link existing between the *ghulāmiyyāt* and the new Abbasid court. What is striking in the narrative of al-Masʿūdī is the way the *ghulāmiyyāt* are depicted each time as a substitute for young men, while in al-Qālī's story, they are credited with possessing a sexual attraction of their own. This shift is strongly reminiscent of Khalīl ibn Aḥmad's insistence on gender ambivalence when describing the *ghulām*, al-Jāḥiẓ's praising of the beauty of female androgyny and the dynamics of desire built around ambivalence in the poems of Abū Nuwās on the *ghulāmiyyāt*.

Shaking gender boundaries in early Abbasid times

Ḥabīb Zayyāt (1871–1954) dedicated a treatise to the *ghulāmiyyāt*. His sources allow us to understand better the debates on cross-dressing in early Abbasid times, and what distinguishes the phenomenon of the *ghulāmiyyāt* from other forms of transgressing gender boundaries sometimes implying cross-dressing. Since historical works of that time are scarce, later sources will be used as well.

In the two anecdotes quoted above, the *ghulāmiyyāt* were subaltern persons, probably slaves, who played their role according the instructions of their masters. But there are accounts of women of a higher status wearing men's clothes. For instance, the first historical person who is mentioned in Zayyāt's study to have been a *ghulāmiyya* is the famous female singer ʿAzza al-Maylāʾ (d. *c.* before the end of the first/seventh century or the beginning of second/eighth century).[43] She lived in Medina and worked as a singer and composer.[44] The reported fact that she was a *mawlāt* of the clan al-Anṣār could indicate that she was a liberated slave of non-Muslim origin. Zayyāt's reason for categorizing her as a *ghulāmiyya* is based on a single sentence in the *Kitāb al-Aghānī* where different explanations of her *laqab* al-Maylāʾ are given. In one of them, 'Maylāʾ' is said to have been derived from *mulāʾ*, the name of a male dress.[45] In this line of reasoning she might have had this nickname because she imitated men (*tashabbihu bi-l-rijāl*).[46] However, Abū al-Faraj considered another explanation to be the right one. According to him, the nickname was derived from her swinging gait (*li-maylihā fī mishyatihā*).[47] This explanation was accepted in most studies on her. Her role as a *ghulāmiyya* was probably an artefact created by a philologist in Abbasid time who was familiar with that figure. Zayyāt referred only to that explanation of 'Maylāʾ' and concealed Abū al-Faraj's rejection of it.[48]

There are two more singers who were referred to by Zayyāt: Umm Saʿīd al-Islāmiyya and Bint Layḥī ibn al-Ḥakam ibn Abī al-ʿĀṣī (both d. *c.* 150/767). They are said to have been companions of the well-known effeminate (*mukhannath*) poet al-Dalāl (d. *c.* 145/767).[49] It is reported that they were riding horses and raced against each other, on which occasion their foot rings (*khalākhīl*) became visible. Further, they are described as 'extremely shameless' (*amjan*). Even if these reports share some elements of descriptions of the *ghulāmiyyāt*, they do not explicitly state that they were dressed in male clothes. As in the case of ʿAzza al-Maylāʾ, the source does not seem to provide conclusive evidence for the existence of *ghulāmiyyāt* or women dressed like men in pre-Abbasid time.

However, besides the cases discussed by Zayyāt, there is at least one exception in Umayyad time of the case of a woman of high social rank practising cross-dressing. According to a later report, ʿĀtika bint ʿAbdallāh ibn Yazīd (d. after 36/656), granddaughter of the caliph Yazīd ibn Muʿāwiya (d.64/683) and wife of Khālid ibn Yazīd (d.85/709 or 90/709), used to wear men's clothes and it provoked her divorce.[50] The short note does not mentions ʿĀtika's motives. Her divorce makes clear that her actions were regarded as inadmissible according to the moral standards of their time.

It seems that the *Taʾrīkh Madīnat Dimashq* is the only source in which this episode is found (except for the abridged version of the same work). Ibn ʿAsākir (d.571/1175), its compiler, lived in the twelfth century CE, but he gave a long list of transmitters of the report on ʿĀtika's cross-dressing, which was the method of historiographical critique at that time. A full transmission analysis cannot be carried out in this case, since no textual variants exist. However, it appears that at one point ʿAbd al-ʿAzīz al-Kitānī (d.466/1073)[51] is mentioned as the unique transmitter, and he is mentioned by Ibn ʿAsākir himself in another case as unreliable.[52] It is likely that cross-dressing was introduced as a fictional element in the report on ʿĀtika.

There is a reported case of exactly the opposite situation in Abbasid time. The caliph al-Mutawakkil (d.247/861) had chosen Rayṭa bint al-ʿAbbās ibn ʿAlī to be his wife and married her. He then asked her to cut off her hair and to imitate the male military slaves (*an taṭimma shaʿarahā wa-tatashabbiha al-mamālīka*). She refused, but he explained to her that if she would not do it, he would divorce her. She chose the divorce and he divorced her.[53] In this case, the husband's desire was the motive for the wish for cross-dressing, and he even tried to blackmail her to achieve it. Obviously, the story was meant as an exemplum of a virtuous noble woman, maybe with a hint of ethnic prejudice by presenting her with a pure Arab name.

In the tenth century the othering of cross-dressing became manifest in literary sources. In the *ʿIqd al-Farīd* of Ibn ʿAbd Rabbih (d.328/940) a scene of *ghulāmiyyāt* acting as singers takes place in Constantinople. It forms part of the story of Jabala, the last king of the Ghassānid dynasty.[54] He first came to the caliph ʿUmar in order to become Muslim, after which he went to the court of the emperor Heraclius in Constantinople in order to become Christian. A cousin of Jabala came to Constantinople as a messenger of ʿUmar and visited him in his luxurious house. After dinner, twenty female slaves with short hair wearing silk clothes came. A very beautiful female slave singer followed, wearing a crown similar to the one Jabala was wearing.[55] The story is presented by Ibn ʿAbd Rabbih as a historical account with a chain of transmitters. But its content is full of fictional exoticism. The female slaves played the lute and sang lyrics of the Christian Arabic poet Ḥassān ibn Thābit (d. *c.* 40/661); they combine the appearance of the *ghulāmiyyāt* and the performance of the *qiyān*. However, there seems to be no equivalent of the *ghulāmiyyāt* in Byzantine sources. There are descriptions of men-like women, but they are not referred to as an ideal of beauty.

Spaces and places

The social geography of the Islamic world was and still is characterized in many aspects by gender segregation. The veil and proper clothing, including gloves, were requirements for women to safely enter public spaces. Women showing their bodies 'as men do', as the legal scholar Ibn Taymiyya (d.728/1328) would put it later, referring to the *mutarajjilūn*, must have been considered as obscene by large parts of society. If the scenes of cross-dressing women as they were described in the sources are considered, they were in most cases in private parts of a palace or house. One gets the impression that the *ghulāmiyyāt* were not present in public places, and that their living space was confined to palaces and the houses of the wealthy men who owned them. This might not have been the case of the *shāṭirāt*, the free women who adopted a male lifestyle. In their case, considering the kind of physical activities Abū Nuwās ascribes to them, one can easily gain the impression they were claiming their liberty by explicitly transgressing boundaries in public spaces, in a similar way to certain examples described in Zayyāt's treatise.

However, there is something more in the anecdote quoted above on the young al-Maʾmūn falling in love with his father's *ghulāmiyya*. The scene itself is staged in the private dining room of Hārūn al-Rashīd, but at the end Hārūn advises his son to go with the beloved *ghulāmiyya* to a *qubba*, which could be either a round tent, a pavilion or a room with a dome. The last seems the most likely in the caliph's palace. In the palace in the centre of Baghdad, the central hall with a cupola was the most prestigious and most lavishly decorated room. This detail could emphasize the generosity of Hārūn, but it is conspicuous that the union of al-Maʾmūn and the *ghulāmiyya* occurs at a place where otherwise the highest ceremonies and negotiations of the Abbasid empire were carried out. This narrative element shows an intention to ennoble the most refined and perfect production of desire and its fulfilment.

In one report – the abovementioned story of Jabala – the *ghulāmiyyāt* are placed into an exotic scene taking place in Constantinople in a remote time during the rulership of Emperor Heraclius (d.641). Moreover, they appear in a Christian house and perform lyrics containing Christian motifs written by a Christian poet, and all in the presence of a Muslim. This threefold contrast of place, time and religion puts them in line with the tables of gold and silver dishes, equipment forbidden to Muslims.[56] At the end, religious space is opened. The enjoyable elements of this world are set in contrast to the sinister fate to be expected in the hereafter.

Conclusion

The cross-dressing of the *ghulāmiyyāt* was not self-determined. They got their role by a process of selection by their owner, and they were trained and shaped by their owner too. Their stages were spaces reserved for the male section of society, either the private rooms of their owner or the official meeting room of a palace or house. It seems that they did not appear in the public realm. They were shaped to fit the company of men and to evoke amusement and desire among them. They probably did not live in the women's space, and therefore they could hardly have been the object of women's desire. Thus their association with lesbianism is most likely an anachronism.

Evidence has been provided that another group of cross-dressing women, different in social status, existed. They were free women who deliberately adopted a male lifestyle, dressed like men and preferring men's occupations. However, nothing is said in the historical sources about their sexual preferences. It is only later that juridical texts state that some of them imitated men in their sexual behaviour, both with male and with female partners. To sum up again in other words, the two groups of cross-dressing women can be characterized as: (1) women forced to be desired by men as non-women; and (2) women deciding to be not desired as women but being accepted on equal terms among men as non-women.

It could be argued that the enslaved *ghulāmiyya* and the free *shāṭira* were independent phenomena. However, they both appear first in the poems of Abū Nuwās.[57] Possibly, the *ghulāmiyyāt* acted as a trigger in early Abbasid society, showing that the device of cross-dressing could enable women to enter space restricted to males and to join a wider male company other than the close family.

The accounts in historiography and poems have shown that the *ghulāmiyyāt* were seen as refined aesthetic objects. They fulfilled the ideal of erotic beauty in a society that was in a process of cultural change. Illusions of androgyny met the taste of men's desire in that epoch.

Notes

1 Hugh Kennedy, 'Al-Jāḥiẓ and the Construction of Homosexuality at the Abbasid Court', in April Harper and Caroline Proctor (eds), *Medieval Sexuality: A Casebook*, 175–88 (New York: Routledge, 2008), 178.

2 Johannes Thomann, 'The End of the Arabian Nights in Early MS Tradition', in Jaako Hämeen-Anttila, Petteri Koskikallio and Ilkka Lindstedt (eds), *Contacts and Interaction: Proceedings of the 27th Congress of the Union Européenne des Arabisants et Islamisants, Helsinki 2014*, 477–85 (Leuven: Brill, 2016), 483–84; Johannes Thomann, 'Reshaping the Frame Story of the Thousand and One Nights: The Coherence of Prologue and Epilogue in the Earliest Existing Arabic Mss', in Ibrahim Akel and William Granara (eds), *The Thousand and One Nights Sources and Transformations in Literature, Art, and Science*, 22–38 (Leiden: Brill, 2020), 32–3.

3 Sahar Amer, *Crossing Borders: Love Between Women in Medieval French and Arabic Literatures* (Philadelphia, PA: University of Pennsylvania Press, 2008), 152; Sahar Amer, 'Medieval Arab Lesbians and Lesbian-Like Women', *Journal of the History of Sexuality*, 17 (2) (2009): 215–36, 227.

4 See Everett K. Rowson, 'Gender Irregularities as Entertainment: Institutionalized Transvestism at the Caliphal Court in Medieval Baghdad', in Sharon A. Farmer and Carol Braun Pasternack (eds), *Gender and Difference in the Middle Ages*, 45–72 (Minneapolis, MN: University of Minnesota Press, 2003), 51.

5 Michel Foucault, *Technologies of the Self: A Seminar with Michel Foucault*, ed. Luther H. Martin, Patrick H. Hutton and Huck Gutman (London: Tavistock Press, 1988), 18, quoted in İrvin Cemil Schick, *The Erotic Margin: Sexuality and Spatiality in Alteritist Discourse* (London: Verso, 1999), 9.

6 Bernard Lewis, *Race and Slavery in the Middle East: An Historical Enquiry* (New York: Oxford University Press, 1990), 6; Qurʾan 4.3, 23.6, 33.50–2; Kecia Ali, *Sexual Ethics and Islam: Feminist Reflections on Qurʾan, Hadith and Jurisprudence* (Oxford: Oneworld Publications, 2006), 44; Bernard K. Freamon, *Possessed by the Right Hand: The Problem of Slavery in Islamic Law and Muslim Cultures*, Studies in Global Slavery 8 (Leiden: Brill, 2019), 116–22.

7 Lewis, *Race and Slavery*, 6; Qurʾan 4.92, 5.92, 58.3; Ali, *Sexual Ethics*, 44; Freamon, *Possessed by the Right Hand*, 135.

8 For an overview on Islamic law (with a focus on Mālikī law) and slavery, see Rainer Oßwald, *Das islamische Sklavenrecht*, Mitteilungen zur Sozial- und Kulturgeschichte der islamischen Welt, vol. 40 (Würzburg: Ergon Verlag, 2017).

9 Lewis, *Race and Slavery*, 6.

10 Ibid., 9; Ali, *Sexual Ethics*, 45–6; Freamon, *Possessed by the Right Hand*, 75–6.

11 Lewis, *Race and Slavery*, 10; Ali, *Sexual Ethics*, 41; Freamon, *Possessed by the Right Hand*, 286–93.

12 See, for example, Hugh Kennedy, 'Muʾnis al-Muẓaffar: An Exceptional Eunuch', in Almut Höfert, Matthew M. Mesley and Serena Tolino (eds), *Celibate and Childless Men in Power. Ruling Eunuchs and Bishops in the Pre-Modern World*, 79–91 (London: Routledge, 2018).
13 Lewis, *Slavery*, 56; Freamon, *Possessed by the Right Hand*, 284–86.
14 Freamon, *Possessed by the Right Hand*, 302–06.
15 Lewis, *Race and Slavery*, 56; Freamon, *Possessed by the Right Hand*, 300–02. For an overview over the different kinds of slavery, see also Franz Kurt, 'Slavery in Islam: Legal Norms and Social Practice', in Reuven Amitai and Christoph Cluse (eds), *Slavery and the Slave Trade in the Eastern Mediterranean (c. 1000–1500 CE)*, 51–141 (Turnhot: Brepols, 2017).
16 Daniel Pipes, *Slave Soldiers and Islam: The Genesis of a Military System* (New Haven, CT: Yale University Press, 1981), 7.
17 Oßwald, *Das islamische Sklavenrecht*, 53–5; Freamon, *Possessed by the Right Hand*, 300–02.
18 Kecia Ali, *Marriage and Slavery in Early Islam* (Cambridge, MA: Harvard University Press, 2010), 12.
19 Ibid., 182.
20 Mika Paraskeva, *Entre la música y el eros: Artes y vida de las cantoras en el Oriente medieval según El libro de las canciones (Kitab al-agani)* (Granada: Editorial Universidad de Granada, 2017), 57–104.
21 al-Jāḥiẓ, *The Epistle on Singing-Girls of Jāḥiẓ*, ed. A. F. L. Beeston (Warminster: Aris and Phillips, 1980).
22 ʿAmr b. Baḥr al-Jāḥiẓ (1980), *The Epistle on Singing-Girls of Jāḥiẓ* (*Risalat al-Qiyān*), ed. and trans. A. F. L. Beeston, Warminster: Aris and Phillips, 15–16 (Arabic text), 28–9 (English translation).
23 al-Jāḥiẓ, *Qiyān*, 20; al-Jāḥiẓ, *The Epistle on Singing-Girls*, 33.
24 al-Jāḥiẓ, *Qiyān* 20; al-Jāḥiẓ, *The Epistle on Singing-Girls*, 33. In another treatise, al-Jāḥiẓ goes on to explain why men prefer female slaves to their legal wives: 'Some who argue on the reason why most female slaves are more preferred [*aḥẓā*] among men then most legal wives, [say] that before a man becomes the owner of a female slave he can inspect everything of her and learns to know everything about her, except favor and intimacy. After it has occurred that she is fitting [his needs] he dares to buy her. In the case of a free woman he must consult [other] women concerning her beauty. But women do not have an eye for the beauty of women and understand absolutely nothing of the needs [*ḥājāt*] of men and if the women are fitting [men's needs]. Men have a better eye for women. A woman only learns to know the superficial appearance of a woman. She does not learn to know the properties which matter in [the question of] fitting [the needs of] men. A woman is only capable to say things like "her nose is a sword", "her eye is like the eye of a gazelle", "her neck is a silvery pitcher", "her leg is like heart of palm", "her hair is like a bunch of grapes", "her extremities are like the axis [of the firmament]", and more the like. This way she has other motifs which are [expressions of] love and hate.' Al-Jāḥiẓ, *Rasāʾil al-Jāḥiẓ*, ed. ʿAbd al-S. M. Hārūn (Cairo: Maktabat al-Khānjī, 1964–1979), 3:157–58.
25 Unless stated otherwise, the translations are by the author. Abū Nuwās, *Dīwān*, ed. Ewald Wagner and Gregor Schoeler (Wiesbaden: Steiner and Schwarz, 1958–2006), 1:174; Ewald Wagner (ed.), *Abū Nuwās: Eine Studie zur arabischen Literatur der frühen Abbasidenzeit* (Wiesbaden: Franz Steiner, 1965), 177; on Abū Nuwās and the *ghulāmiyyāt* in general, see Kennedy, *Abu Nuwas*, 18, 47–8.
26 Abū Nuwās, *Dīwān*, 5:101; Wagner, *Abū Nuwās*, 177.

27 Abū Nuwās, *Dīwān*, 3:3; Wagner, *Abū Nuwās*, 178.
28 Abū Nuwās, *Dīwān*, 1:184; Wagner, *Abū Nuwās*, 176.
29 Abū Nuwās, *Dīwān*, 5:92; Wagner, *Abū Nuwās*, 177; Ḥabīb Zayyāt, 'al-Mar'a al-ghulāmiyya fī al-islām', *Al-Machriq*, l (1956): 153–92, 174.
30 In research on *ḥadīth* material as historical, extreme positions were taken, ranging from full acceptance of the judgements found in the classical collections to total rejection of any historical value in *ḥadīth*. Neither position will be adopted here. There exists an increasing number of specialists in *ḥadīth* studies who believe in the possibility of dating reports on this material if a rigorous methodic approach is applied, see, for example, Harald Motzki, Nicolet Boekhoff-van der voort and Sean W. Anthony, *Analysing Muslim Traditions: Studies in Legal, Exegetical and Maghāzī Ḥadīth*, Islamic History and Civilization, vol. 78 (Leiden: Brill, 2010); Jens J. Scheiner, *Die Eroberung von Damaskus: Quellenkritische Untersuchung zur Historiographie in klassisch-islamischer Zeit*, Islamic History and Civilization, vol. 76 (Leiden: Brill, 2010).
31 al-Bukhārī, *al-Ṣaḥīḥ* (Damascus: Dār Ibn Kathīr, 2002), no. 5585; Abū Dāwūd, *Sunan*, ed. Sh. al-Arna'ūṭ and M. K. Q. Balilī (Beirut: Dār al-Risāla al-'Ālimiyya, 2009), no. 4097; al-Tirmidhī, *Jāmi' al-Kabīr*, ed. B. 'A. Ma'rūf (Beirut: Dār al-Gharb al-Islāmī, 1996), no. 2784, 3151; Ibn Māja, *Musnad*, ed. M. F. 'Abd al-Bāqī (Cairo: 'Īsā al-Bābī al-Ḥalabī, 1952–1953), no. 1904; al-Ṭayālisī, *Musnad*, ed. M. 'A. al-Turkī (Cairo: Dār Hajar, 1999), no. 2801; Ibn Ḥanbal, *Musnad*, ed. Sh. Al-Arna'ūṭ and 'A. Murshid (Beirut: Mu'assasat al-Risāla, 1995), no. 3059.
32 Abū Dāwūd, *Sunan*, no. 4098; Ibn Māja, *Musnad*, no. 1903.
33 al-Bukhārī, *al-Ṣaḥīḥ*, nos 5586, 6834; al-Tirmidhī, *Jāmi'*, no. 2785; al-Dārimī, *al-Musnad al-Jāmi'*, ed. N. b. H. v. 'A. al-Bā'alawī (Beirut: Dār al-Bashā'ir al-Islāmiyya, 2013), no. 2853; 'Abd al-Razzāq, *Muṣannaf* no. 21357; Ibn Ḥanbal, *Musnad*, nos 1982, 2123, 2291, 2328, 3458, 5649.
34 al-Bukhārī, *al-Ṣaḥīḥ*, no. 5586, 6834; al-Dārimī, *al-Musnad*, no. 2853; Ibn Ḥanbal, *Musnad*, nos 1982, 2006, 2123, 2263.
35 Ibid., no. 6180.
36 Gautier H. A. Juynboll, *Encyclopedia of Canonical Ḥadīth* (Leiden: Brill, 2007), 177–82.
37 Scott Siraj al-Haqq Kugle, *Homosexuality in Islam: Critical Reflections on Gay, Lesbian, and Transgender Muslims* (Oxford: Oneworld Publications, 2010), 87.
38 Khalīl ibn Aḥmad, *Kitāb al-'Ayn*, ed. M. al-Makhzūmī and I. al-Sāmirrā'ī (Beirut: Maktabah Al Hilal, 1988), 4, 422.
39 al-Jāḥiẓ, *Rasā'il*, 2:95.
40 Ibid., 95–6.
41 al-Mas'ūdī, *Murūj al-Dhahab*, ed. Charles Pellat, trans. Everett K. Rowson (Beirut: Université Libanaise, 1966–1979), 3451–453; al-Mas'ūdī, *The Meadows of Gold: The Abbasids*, trans. Paul Lunde and Caroline Stone (London: Kegan Paul, 1989), 390–91; Amer, 'Medieval Arab Lesbians and Lesbian-Like Women', 227–28.
42 Ismā'īl Ibn al-Qāsim al-Qālī, *al-Amālī*, ed. M. 'A. al-Aṣmā'ī (Cairo: Dār al-Kutub al-Miṣriyya, 1926), 225; translations without a reference to an English translation are made by the present author.
43 Zayyāt, 'al-Mar'a al-ghulāmiyya fī al-islām', 153; followed by Amer, *Crossing Borders*, 188n6.
44 Suzanne M. Meyers Sawa, 'Azza al-Maylā'', in Kate Fleet, Gudrun Krämer, Denis Matringe, John Nawas and Everett Rowson (eds), *Encyclopaedia of Islam*, 3rd edn. (Leiden: Brill, 2013).

45 Reinhart Pieter Anne Dozy, *Supplément aux dictionnaires arabes* (Leiden: Brill, 1881), 2:609b; Reinhart Pieter Anne Dozy, *Dictionnaire détaillé des noms des vétements chez les Arabes* (Amsterdam: J. Müller, 1845), 408–11.
46 Abū al-Faraj ʿAlī b. al-Ḥusayn al-Iṣbahānī, *al-Aghānī*, ed. A. Z. Ṣafwat et al. (Cairo: Dār al-Kutub al-Miṣriyya, 1927–1974), 17:162, lines 4–5.
47 Ibid., 17:162, line 8.
48 Zayyāt, 'al-Marʾa al-ghulāmiyya fī al-islām', 157.
49 Ibid.; Everett K. Rowson, 'The Effeminates of Early Medina', *Journal of the American Oriental Society*, 111 (1) (1991): 671–93, 681–82.
50 Abū al-Qāsim ʿAlī Ibn ʿAsākir, *Taʾrīkh Madinat Dimashq*, ed. ʿUmar al-ʿAmrawī and ʿAlī Shīrī (Beirut: Dār al-Fikr, 1995–2001), 69: 234, no. 9376; cf. Monika Winet, 'Female Presence in Biographical Dictionaries: Ibn ʿAsākir's Selection Criteria for Women in his *Taʾrīkh Madīnat Dimashq*', in Steven Judd and Jens Scheiner (eds), *New Perspectives on Ibn ʿAsākir in Islamic Historiography*, 93–138 (Leiden: Brill, 2017), 131.
51 Steven Judd and Jens Scheiner (eds), *New Perspectives on Ibn ʿAsakir in Islamic Historiography* (Leiden: Brill, 2017), appendix 259.
52 Scheiner, *Die Eroberung von Damaskus*, 35.
53 ʿAmr b. Baḥr al-Jāḥiẓ, *al-Kitāb al-Musammāh bi al-Maḥāsin wa-l-Aḍdād*. ed. G. van Vloten (Leiden: Brill, 1898), 234, line 10; cf. Zayyāt, 'al-Marʾa al-ghulāmiyya fī al-islām', 162.
54 Ibn ʿAbd Rabbih, *al-ʿIqd al-Farīd* (*The Unique Necklace*), trans. Issa J. Boullata (Reading: Garnet, 2006), 310–15; Ibn ʿAbd Rabbih, *Necklace*, 1:255–59.
55 Ibn ʿAbd Rabbih, *ʿIqd*, 313; Ibn ʿAbd Rabbih, *Necklace*, 1: 257.
56 Arent Jan Wensinck, *A Handbook of Early Muhammadan Tradition: Alphabetically Arranged* (Leiden: Brill, 1927), 241.
57 Everett K. Rowson, 'Gender Irregularities as Entertainment: Institutionalized Transvestism at the Caliphal Court in Medieval Baghdad', in Sharon A. Farmer and Carol Braun Pasternack (eds), *Gender and Difference in the Middle Ages*, 45–72 (Minneapolis, MN: University of Minnesota Press, 2003), 49–50.

References

Primary sources

ʿAbd al-Razzāq b. Hammām al-Ṣannānī, Abū Bakr (2015), *al-Musannaf*, ed. Markaz al-Buḥūth wa-l-Taqdhīr al-Maʿlūmāt, Cairo: Dār al-Taʾṣīl.

Abū Dāwūd al-Sijistānī, Sulaymān b. al-Ashʿath (2009), *Sunan*, ed. Sh. al-Arnaʾūṭ and M. K. Q. Balilī, Beirut: Dār al-Risāla al-ʿĀlimiyya.

Abū al-Faraj al-Iṣbahānī, ʿAlī b. al-Ḥusayn (1927-74), *al-Aghānī*, ed. Aḥmad Zakī Ṣafwat, ʿAbd al-Salām Muḥammad Hārūn, Muṣṭafā al-Saqqā, ʿAlī Muḥammad al-Bajāwī, ʿAbd al-Karīm Ibrāhīm al-ʿAzbāwī, ʿAlī al-Najdī Nāṣif, ʿAlī al-Sibāʿī, ʿAbd al-ʿAzīz Maṭar, and Maḥmūd Muḥammad Ghanīm, Cairo: Dār al-Kutub al-Miṣriyya and al-Hayʾa al-Miṣriyya al-ʿĀmma li-l-Kitāb.

Abū Nuwās al-Ḥasan b. Hāniʾ (1958–2006), *Dīwān*, ed. Ewald Wagner and Gregor Schoeler, Wiesbaden: Steiner and Schwarz.

Abū Nuwās al-Ḥasan b. Hāniʾ (1979), *Le vin, le vent, la vie: Poèmes traduits*, trans. V. Monteil, Paris: Sindbad.

al-Bukhārī, Muḥammad b. Ismāʿīl (2002), *al-Ṣaḥīḥ*, Damascus: Dār Ibn Kathīr.
al-Dārimī, ʿAbdallāh b. ʿAbd al-Raḥmān (2013), *al-Musnad al-Jāmiʿ*, ed. N. b. H. v. ʿA. al-Bāʿalawī, Beirut: Dār al-Bashāʾir al-Islāmiyya.
Ibn ʿAbd Rabbih, Aḥmad b. Muḥammad (1983), *al-ʿIqd al-Farīd*, ed. M. M. Qumayḥa, Bayrūt: Dār al-Kutub al-ʿIlmiyya.
Ibn ʿAbd Rabbih, Aḥmad b. Muḥammad (2006), *al-ʿIqd al-Farīd* (*The Unique Necklace*), trans. Issa J. Boullata, Reading: Garnet.
Ibn ʿAsākir, Abū al-Qāsim ʿAlī (1995–2001), *Taʾrīkh Madinat Dimashq*, ed. ʿUmar al-ʿAmrawī and ʿAlī Shīrī, Beirut: Dār al-Fikr.
Ibn Ḥanbal, Aḥmad b. Muḥammad (1995), *Musnad*, ed. Sh. Al-Arnaʾūṭ and ʿA. Murshid, Beirut: Muʾassasat al-Risāla.
Ibn Māja, Muḥammad b. Yazīd (1952–1953), *Musnad*, ed. M. F. ʿAbd al-Bāqī, Cairo: ʿĪsā al-Bābī al-Ḥalabī.
al-Jāḥiẓ, ʿAmr b. Baḥr (1893–1894), *Kitāb al-Bayān wa-l-Tabyīn*, Cairo: al-Maṭbaʿa al-ʿIlmiyya
al-Jāḥiẓ, ʿAmr b. Baḥr (1898), *al-Kitāb al-Musammāh bi-l-Maḥāsin wa-l-Aḍdād*. ed. G. van Vloten, Leiden: Brill.
al-Jāḥiẓ, ʿAmr b. Baḥr (1964–1979), *Rasāʾil*, ed. ʿAbd al-S. M. Hārūn, Cairo: Maktabat al-Khānjī.
al-Jāḥiẓ, ʿAmr b. Baḥr (1980), *The Epistle on Singing-Girls of Jāḥiẓ (Risalat al-Qiyān)*, ed. and trans. A. F. L. Beeston, Warminster: Aris and Phillips.
Khalīl, b. Aḥmad (1988), *Kitāb al-ʿAyn*, ed. M. al-Makhzūmī and I. al-Sāmirrāʾī, Beirut: Maktabat al-Hilāl.
al-Masʿūdī, ʿAlī b. al-Ḥusayn (1966–1979), *Murūj al-Dhahab*, ed. Charles Pellat, trans. Everett K. Rowson, Beirut: Université Libanaise.
al-Masʿūdī, ʿAlī b. al-Ḥusayn (1989), *The Meadows of Gold: The Abbasids*, trans. Paul Lunde and Caroline Stone, London: Kegan Paul.
al-Qālī, Ismāʿīl b. al-Qāsim (1926), *al-Amālī*, ed. M. ʿA. al-Aṣmāʿī, Cairo: Dār al-Kutub al-Miṣriyya.
al-Ṭayālisī, Abū Dāwūd Sulaymān b al-Jārūd (1999), *Musnad*, ed. M. ʿA. al-Turkī, Cairo: Dār Hajar.
al-Tirmidhī, Muḥammad b. ʿĪsā (1996), *al-Jāmiʿ al-Kabīr*, ed. B. ʿA. Maʿrūf, Beirut: Dār al-Gharb al-Islāmī.

Secondary literature

Ali, Kecia (2006), *Sexual Ethics and Islam: Feminist Reflections on Qurʾan, Ḥadith and Jurisprudence*, Oxford: Oneworld Publications.
Ali, Kecia (2010), *Marriage and Slavery in Early Islam*, Cambridge, MA: Harvard University Press.
Amer, Sahar (2008), *Crossing Borders: Love Between Women in Medieval French and Arabic Literatures*, Philadelphia, PA: University of Pennsylvania Press.
Amer, Sahar (2009), 'Medieval Arab Lesbians and Lesbian-Like Women', *Journal of the History of Sexuality*, 17 (2): 215–36.
Dozy, Reinhart Pieter Anne (1845), *Dictionnaire détaillé des noms des vétements chez les Arabes*, Amsterdam: J. Müller.
Dozy, Reinhart Pieter Anne (1881), *Supplément aux dictionnaires arabes*, Leiden: Brill.
Foucault, Michel (1988), *Technologies of the Self: A Seminar with Michel Foucault*, ed. Luther H. Martin, Patrick H. Hutton and Huck Gutman, London: Tavistock Press.

Freamon, Bernard K. (2019), *Possessed by the Right Hand: The Problem of Slavery in Islamic Law and Muslim Cultures*, Studies in Global Slavery 8, Leiden: Brill.
Judd, Steven and Jens Scheiner (eds) (2017), *New Perspectives on Ibn ʻAsakir in Islamic Historiography*, Islamic History and Civilization, vol. 145, Leiden: Brill.
Juynboll, Gautier H. A. (2007), *Encyclopedia of Canonical Ḥadīth*, Leiden: Brill.
Kennedy, Hugh (2008), 'Al-Jāḥiẓ and the Construction of Homosexuality at the Abbasid Court', in April Harper and Caroline Proctor (eds), *Medieval Sexuality: A Casebook*, 175–88, New York: Routledge.
Kennedy, Hugh (2018), 'Mu'nis al-Muẓaffar: An Exceptional Eunuch', in Almut Höfert, Matthew M. Mesley and Serena Tolino (eds), *Celibate and Childless Men in Power: Ruling Eunuchs and Bishops in the Pre-modern World*, 79–91, London: Routledge.
Kennedy, Philipp F. (2005), *Abu Nuwas: A Genius of Poetry*, Oxford: Oneworld Publications.
Kugle, Scott Siraj al-Haqq (2010), *Homosexuality in Islam: Critical reflections on Gay, Lesbian, and Transgender Muslims*, Oxford: Oneworld Publications.
Kurt, Franz (2017), 'Slavery in Islam: Legal norms and Social Practice', in Reuven Amitai and Christoph Cluse (eds), *Slavery and the Slave Trade in the Eastern Mediterranean (c. 1000–1500 CE)*, 51–141, Turnhot: Brepols.
Lewis, Bernard (1990), *Race and Slavery in the Middle East: An Historical Enquiry*, New York: Oxford University Press.
Motzki, Harald, Nicolet Boekhoff-van der voort and Sean W. Anthony (2010), *Analysing Muslim Traditions: Studies in Legal, Exegetical and Maghāzī Ḥadīth*, Islamic History and Civilization, vol. 78, Leiden: Brill.
Oßwald, Rainer (2017), *Das islamische Sklavenrecht*, Mitteilungen zur Sozial- und Kulturgeschichte der islamischen Welt, vol. 40, Würzburg: Ergon Verlag.
Paraskeva, Mika (2017), *Entre la música y el eros: Artes y vida de las cantoras en el Oriente medieval según El libro de las canciones (Kitab al-agani)*, Granada: Editorial Universidad de Granada.
Pellat, Charles (1967), *Arabische Geisteswelt: Ausgewählte und übersetzte Texte von al-Ǧāḥiẓ (777–869)*, Zurich: Artemis Verlag.
Pipes, Daniel (1981), *Slave Soldiers and Islam: The Genesis of a Military System*, New Haven, CT: Yale University Press.
Rowson, Everett K. (1991), 'The Effeminates of Early Medina', *Journal of the American Oriental Society*, 111 (1): 671–93.
Rowson, Everett K. (2003), 'Gender Irregularities as Entertainment: Institutionalized Transvestism at the Caliphal Court in Medieval Baghdad', in Sharon A. Farmer and Carol Braun Pasternack (eds), *Gender and Difference in the Middle Ages*, 45–72, Minneapolis, MN: University of Minnesota Press.
Sawa, Suzanne M. Meyers (2013), 'Azza al-Maylā'', in Kate Fleet, Gudrun Krämer, Denis Matringe, John Nawas and Everett Rowson (eds), *Encyclopaedia of Islam*, 3rd edn., Leiden: Brill. http://dx.doi.org/10.1163/1573-3912_ei3_COM_23983.
Scheiner, Jens J. (2010), *Die Eroberung von Damaskus: Quellenkritische Untersuchung zur Historiographie in klassisch-islamischer Zeit*, Islamic History and Civilization, vol. 76, Leiden: Brill.
Schick, İrvin Cemil (1999), *The Erotic Margin: Sexuality and Spatiality in Alteritist Discourse*, London: Verso.
Thomann, Johannes (2016), 'The End of the Arabian Nights in Early MS Tradition', in Jaako Hämeen-Anttila, Petteri Koskikallio and Ilkka Lindstedt (eds), *Contacts and*

Interaction: Proceedings of the 27th Congress of the Union Européenne des Arabisants et Islamisants, Helsinki 2014, 477–85, Leuven: Peeters.

Thomann, Johannes (2016), 'Reshaping the Frame Story of the Thousand and One Nights: The Coherence of Prologue and Epilogue in the Earliest Existing Arabic Mss', in Ibrahim Akel and William Granara (eds), *The Thousand and One Nights Sources and Transformations in Literature, Art, and Science*, 22–38, Leiden: Brill.

Wagner, Ewald (1965), *Abū Nuwās: Eine Studie zur arabischen Literatur der frühen Abbasidenzeit*, Wiesbaden: Franz Steiner.

Wensinck, Arent Jan (1927), *A Handbook of Early Muhammadan Tradition: Alphabetically Arranged*, Leiden: Brill.

Winet, Monika (2017), 'Female Presence in Biographical Dictionaries: Ibn ʿAsākir's Selection Criteria for Women in his *Taʾrīkh Madīnat Dimashq*', in Steven Judd and Jens Scheiner (eds), *New Perspectives on Ibn ʿAsākir in Islamic Historiography*, 93–138, Leiden: Brill.

Zayyāt, Ḥabīb (1956), 'al-Marʾa al-ghulāmiyya fī al-islām', *Al-Machriq*, l: 153–92.

Chapter 3

Contesting Masculinity in Pre-Modern Arab Societies: Intoxication, Desire and Antinomian Mysticism

Danilo Marino

In a short poem Fatḥ al-Dīn ibn Sayyid al-Nās (d.734/1334) lists the six habits of the Sufi:

> In our time, the conditions for being a Sufi
> are no more than six:
> the penetration of young boys [*nīk al-ʿulūq*], [wine] intoxication [*al-sukr*], [hashish] inebriation [*al-saṭla*]
> dancing, singing and piping [*al-qiyyāda*].
> Whoever does all of these, and has also expressed openly [the doctrine of] the unity of existence [*ittiḥād*]
> and of incarnation [*ḥulūl*], does it either because of ignorance or by imitation.
> Whenever he has indulged in reprehensible acts [*al-munkarāt*], either consciously or following the habit,
> he would still be the master of sheikhs carrying the prayer-rug.[1]

These verses offer a satirical portrait of Sufis, highlighting certain of their practices and two basic tenets of their faith, the unity of existence (*ittiḥād*) and the incarnation (*ḥulūl*).[2] Accounts portraying deviant mystics as libertines, hashish addicts and active sodomites are frequent during the Mamlūk period (648–922/1250–1517) and beyond. In this chapter, I examine ideas of masculinity conveyed through the relation between antinomian Sufism and hashish consumption in sources from the thirteenth to the fifteenth century and see if this link can be used as a pattern.

The use of hashish, which at that period was eaten in the form of pills, electuaries (*maʿjūn*) or confectionaries based on a paste made of grains or leaves of hemp mixed with spices and honey,[3] was considered by many as a dubious and potentially dangerous form of recreation. Studying hashish in pre-modern Arab-Islamic societies leads to considering the role of intoxication (*sukr*) in the definition of masculinity, especially because being high on hashish rather than wine apparently conveyed other images of manliness.

In this regard, I show that legal and literary narratives are sometimes contradictory. While experts on Islamic law were much more concerned with the different effects in terms of sexual desire produced by the two substances, literary descriptions of hashish addicts tend to borrow from the longstanding repertoire of wine literature for the purpose of entertainment.

A useful theoretic frame for discussing the issue at stake here is Julia Kristeva's notion of *abjection*. For Kristeva, 'it is [...] not lack of cleanliness or health that causes abjection but what disturbs identity, system, order. What does not respect borders, positions, rules. The in-between, the ambiguous, the composite.'[4] Kristeva goes even further, considering abjection as part the mystical experience:

> Abjection will not be designated as such, that is as other, as something to be ejected, or separated, but as the most propitious place for communication – as the point where the scales are tipped towards pure spirituality. The mystic's familiarity with abjection is fount of infinite jouissance.[5]

Interestingly, Kristeva suggests that excrement and menstrual blood both derive from 'the *maternal* and/or the feminine, of which the maternal is the real support'.[6] In other words, in her view 'defilement is accompanied by a strong concern for separating the sexes, and this means giving men rights over women'.[7] Also, since women and defilement are both put in the position of passive objects, Kristeva continues, they threaten the borders of the symbolic (male) law. In other words, hashish and mysticism, with their uncontrollable and irrational features, seem to be opposed to the dominant *masculine*. Therefore, I assume that both hashish and deviant mysticism represent some form of abjection because both raise questions related to cleanness, defilement and amorality but they also challenge the identity of the male body in the public space.

In what follows, I will first review the sources that describe the habit of hashish consumption within some mystic communities or even postulate their involvement in the discovery of the mind-altering effects of this herb. Then, I will briefly consider other devotional practices of these 'deviant' dervishes deemed equally scandalous, as they were a deliberate challenge to gender boundaries. Finally, through the analysis of legal and literary discourses on the herb, I will try to understand which ideas of masculinity are carried out by hashish consumption in the medieval Arabic normative and fictional fields.

Hashish and mysticism

The Arabic term *ḥashīsh* is attested in association with the mystics in numerous sources,[8] including moral treatises and literary texts as early as the seventh/thirteenth century. Two long poems (*qaṣīda*-s) by al-Nūr al-Isʿirdī (d.656/1258), for example, allude to the use of hemp during 'the nights of pious devotion' (*layālī al-taʿabbud*)[9] and his contemporary Ibn al-Ḥaddād (d. after 673/1275) compiled three *maqāma*-s – narratives written in non-metrical rhymed prose – where he describes a group of people including adepts of the *qalandarīyya* sect debating about the virtues and damages of cannabis consumption.[10]

Hashish is also listed among the deviant practices of the antinomian Sufis in the tenth chapter of the book *Deception of the Devil* (*Talbīs Iblīs*) by Ibn al-Jawzī (d.597/1200). The Ḥanbalī scholar denounces the scandalous behaviour and the indecent aspect of these mystics. He criticizes the singing, dancing and gazing at beardless boys (*al-aḥdāth*) during the so-called *samāʿ* sessions where, in order to reach trance (*al-wajd*) through music and dance, the Sufis 'replaced the [temporary] loss of consciousness [*izālat al-ʿaql*] entailed by wine with something they called *al-ḥashīsh* and the electuary [*al-maʿjūn*]'.[11]

One of the outcomes of this correlation between hashish use and antinomian mysticism was the popularization of the story according to which renunciants discovered the hallucinogenic effects of hashish. Al-Qasṭallānī (d.686/1287), al-Zarkashī (d.794/1392), al-Maqrīzī (d.845/1442) and al-Badrī (d.894/1489), all drawing upon an earlier source apparently lost – *The Literary Good Omens in the Poems Praising Cannabis* (*al-Sawāniḥ al-Adabiyya fī al-Madāʾiḥ al-Qinnabiyya*), written in the second half of the seventh/thirteenth century by the Shāfiʿī scholar Ḥasan al-ʿUkbarī (d. *c.* 690/1291) – report the opinion that hashish was discovered either by the sheikh Quṭb al-Dīn Ḥaydar (d. *c.* 618/1221–1222), from Zāwa in Khurāsān, or by Jamāl al-Dīn (active seventh/thirteenth century), from Sāva in Persia, who later moved to Syria and Egypt.[12] According to this account, the sheikh Ḥaydar describes to his companions his first experience with hashish as follows:

> In my isolation, I suddenly got an urge to go out into the countryside all by myself. When I came out, I noticed that every plant was completely quiet and showed not the slightest motion because there was no wind and the summer (heat) was oppressive. But then, I passed by a plant with leaves and noticed that in this weather it was gently swaying and moving without any force (being exercised upon it from the outside), like someone who is inebriated. I started to pick a few of the leaves and eat them. Thus it happened that I was filled with this restful joy you have observed in me. Now let us go, and I shall show you the plant, so that you can recognize its shape.

Then, one of his fellows continued the story:

> We went out into the countryside, and he showed us the plant. When we saw it, we said that it was the plant known as hemp [*qinnab*]. He told us to take a leaf and eat it, which we did. Then, we returned to the monastery, finding in our hearts an irrepressible joy and gladness. When the Shaykh saw us in this condition, he told us to guard this drug, and he made us take an oath not to tell anyone of the common people about it.[13]

Eventually, the secret of the herb rapidly spread to the Khurāsān and Fārs regions then to ʿIrāq, and by the first quarter of the seventh/thirteenth century it had reached the Shām region (nowadays Syria, Lebanon, Jordan and Israel/Palestine), Egypt and Anatolia.

Some sources condemn this story, presenting evidences that the two sheikhs, considered the masters of the Ḥaydariyya and Qalandariyya movements respectively, never consumed hashish. Al-Maqrīzī and al-Badrī in particular argued that the origin of the eating of this plant is much older and can be placed in India where a certain Pīr Ranṭan, while worshipping one of his gods, received the revelation of the secrets of this herb from Satan (*al-Shayṭān*) from inside a statue.[14]

The motif of the diabolic origin of hashish recurs in different sources and in particular in the *The Merciful's Exhortations to Forbid the Devil's Herb* (*Zawājir al-Raḥmān fī Taḥrīm Ḥashīshat al-Shayṭān*) of the Shāfiʿī scholar Shams al-Dīn ibn al-Najjār, who also lived in the ninth/fifteenth century. This work, apparently lost, was extensively quoted in al-Badrī's *The Delight of the Soul in Hashish and Wine* (*Rāḥat al-Arwāḥ fī al-Ḥashīsh wa-l-Rāḥ*), which I will describe more thoroughly later in the chapter. Al-Najjār suggests that hashish is ritually impure (*nājis*) because the herb was watered with the Devil's urine.[15] Similarly, al-Badrī also relates the opinion of the Ḥanbalī scholar Ibn Taymiyya (d.728/1328), who states that if the fermented drink (*khamr*) is an unclean liquid such as urine, then hashish – which is as intoxicating as *khamr* but was consumed in solid form – is as impure as faeces.[16] Moreover, in another passage, al-Badrī also reports a recipe for the preparation of hashish products that involves another ritually impure substance: menstrual blood.[17] Thus, for many authors, hashish falls under the category of an unclean, abject and potentially dangerous substance. As such, it should be subject to general prohibition.

It seems that as early as the first half of the seventh/thirteenth century these deviant forms of piety were considered as a corruption of the real Sufism to the extent that these 'would-be Sufi libertines', as Karamustafa called them, were looked upon with a certain suspicion. As a result, Jamāl al-Dīn ʿAbd al-Raḥmān al-Jawbarī (d. after 646/1248–1249) wrote a whole chapter of his *Unveiling of the Secrets* (*Kashf al-Asrār*) to 'those who pretend to be Sufi'. According to al-Jawbarī, purported Sufis such as the followers of the *ḥaydarīyya* sect, an antinomian group who used to shave their beards and wear iron rings and chains, considered hashish legal and, after consuming it, satisfied the strong sexual arousal produced by the herb with teenage boys.[18]

Deviant practices of antinomian Sufism

A close reading of the legal discussions surrounding hashish consumption between the thirteenth and fifteenth centuries shows a shared concern with the rapid spread of this substance[19] by dervishes, whose aspects and conduct intentionally challenged preconceived models of masculinity. Among their practices, I will briefly deal with celibacy and the shaving of facial and bodily hair, as they are both central elements of hegemonic medieval images of the Muslim masculinity.

Renouncing marriage, as many of these mystics did, was an extreme form of rejection of the conventionally gendered role of men as husbands and fathers. Abstinence (*jūʿ*) was not a deplorable attitude in itself, as Islamic religion prescribes self-restraint from sexual activity on particular occasions, such as the month of Ramaḍān, for instance. However, celibacy as a total disregard of the male generative role was apparently judged by scholars as a lack of the male's *murūʾa* or ethics.[20] This form of renunciation was taken to the extreme by the Ḥaydarī adepts who had their penis transpierced with iron rings in order to avoid any penetrative act.

The fourfold shave (*chahār ẓarb* in Persian), consisting of completely removing hair, beard, moustache and eyebrows, was a particularly shocking practice of both the Qalandarīs and dervishes. The shaving of bodily hair may have referred to the idea that a renunciant should act as if he were 'dead before his death', following the prophetical saying 'die before dying' (*mūtū qabla an tamūtū*).[21] Nevertheless, the particular symbology attached to the beard in Arab-Islamic societies also suggests that, by shaving facial hair, the mystics' transgressive bodies showed a deliberate rejection of established models of masculinity.[22] The beard, as the most visible of male sex features, was considered a symbol of virility and honour, to the point that one would even swear by the beard.[23] Clean-shaven faces may be identified as belonging to a teenage boy (*amrad*), whose manliness is still incomplete, to women or to eunuchs. Therefore, the act of intentionally shaving one's own beard or being shaved by force as a sort of punishment was considered an insult to the dignity of adult men and a threat to gender distinctions[24] by a *feminization* of the face. Moreover, some 'deviant' *dervishes* even went so far as to invert the prevalent gender hierarchy, adopting the feminine grammatical gender to address male interlocutors or even choosing female names for them.[25]

Consequently, if for Heghnar Watenpaugh the antinomian Sufi's deliberate demeaning of masculinity 'was only shocking, and therefore effective, in a context in which the hierarchies were securely anchored and ultimately served to reinforce the gendered construction of society',[26] for Durre S. Ahmed, instead, mysticism and Sufism in particular, considered in their 'inner', 'private' and 'hidden' dimension, can be regarded as the *feminine* expression of religion and as such a counterpart to the more 'public', 'outer', 'moralistic' and 'cerebral' expression of *masculine* performances of Islam:

> The 'feminine' nature of mysticism aims psychologically to 'de-masculinize' human consciousness, feminizing it to the extent that the heroic attitudes such as mastery, control, action and a narrow material notion of rationality must take a back seat to a more contemplative, passive-receptive attitude.[27]

At any rate, one would assume that the antinomian practices of these ascetics were hardly understood by their contemporaries, to such an extent that their presence in the public space would result in a polarization of opinions, especially among members of the political elites. Some, for instance al-Mālik al-Ẓāhir (r.658–676/1260–1277), bestowed gifts and even a yearly stipend to the Qalandars, others, such as the Mongol Hülegü (r.654–663/1256–1265), showed hostility towards them. As a result, these mystics were accused of all possible crimes and vices to discredit their doctrines and rituals.[28] Interestingly, the scholar Naṣīr al-Dīn al-Ṭūsī (d.672/1274) considered the Qalandars to be 'the excess of this world',[29] thus putting them on the margins, outside of morals and society.

Wine, hashish and competitive images of virtues and masculinity in legal writings

What were the images of masculinity that the hashish-eating mystics were openly challenging? Further, how were wine and hashish involved in defining or contesting male identities?

Most of the values attached to men's roles in pre-modern Arab society were inherited from the Bedouin pre-Islamic concept of *murū'a*, also spelled *muruwwa*. This term conveys complex meanings that evolved throughout history. Some of the experiences, attitudes and values it encompasses are inherited, for instance having an honourable lineage (*nasab*), while others are praiseworthy moral qualities, such as generosity, fidelity, modesty, self-control, chastity, honour, respectability, compassion and observance of the law. Finally, there are other features of *murū'a* accentuating heroism, for example, courage, proudness, engagement in physical violence, combativeness, etc.[30]

However, from the fourth/tenth to the fifth/eleventh century onwards, following what Julia Bray calls the 'post-Ummayyad detribalisation of society', leading to a 'demilitarisation' of Abbasid men and a 'diversification of male roles, and of the self, in response to the diversification of career opportunities',[31] the meaning of *murū'a* comes closer to signifying good manners (*maḥāsin al-akhlāq*), even if traces of the former understanding were still circulating.[32]

The status of wine seemed more problematic, revealing the tension inherent in the notion of *murū'a* itself. Joseph Sadan has argued that the dialectic between wine and milk was a central component in the definition of the idea of *murū'a*. At the beginning of the spread of Islam, drinking wine was considered a Bedouin habit, and consequently tantamount to paganism, whereas milk was indicative of the new Muslim ethic. However, in a second phase, wine became a symbol of the Muslim sedentary society while the nomadic habits were so much idealized that abstention from wine became a Bedouin habit and virtue associated with early Islamic ideas of *murū'a*.[33]

In works such as the *Branches of Descriptions for the Transmission of Happiness* (*Fuṣūl al-Tamāthīl fī Tabāshīr al-Surūr*), the author, prince and poet Ibn al-Mu'tazz (d.296/908), lists the merits of wine (*faḍā'il al-sharāb*) as follow:

> They said that [wine] is the most sought-after thing bringing full happiness, the most effective to attain immediate joy, it interacts with the bodily forms and gives rest to the souls. It causes the improvement of strength and the intensification of desire. It relieves from being always on one's guard and anxiety, from the excessive heat and the trouble provoked by it. It makes one love wit and humor and hate stinginess and enmity. He will then cease to be parsimonious for the drinking [expenses] and more acquainted with the desired quantity [of wine] suitable for him to attain his pleasure, lose the shyness and affirm *murū'a*.[34]

In a similar vein, al-Jāḥiẓ (d.255/868) also praises wine as a means to 'fully satisfy pleasures and complete virtues' (*bihi tamām al-ladhdhāt wa-kamāl al-murū ʾāt*).[35] For his part, Ibn Qutayba (d. *c.* 276/889) wrote in his *Book of Drinks* (*Kitāb al-Ashriba*) that *al-aḥmarān*, or the two reds, meaning wine and red meat, are more appropriate to men, whereas *al-aṣfarān*, or the two yellows, meaning gold and saffron, are more suitable for women.[36] Although Ibn Qutayba's classification can be seen as an attempt to 'genderize' wine consumption, the author considers *khamr* a source of decadence and debauchery because it leads to unlawful sexual intercourse between men and women (*zinā ʾ*).[37] Moreover, in a brief though meaningful paragraph consecrated to *murū ʾa* in the *Book of Princeship* (*Kitāb al-Su ʾdad*), the third book of *The Sources of Knowledge* (*ʿUyūn al-Akhbār*), Ibn Qutayba mentions the well-known saying according to which *murū ʾa* is temperance or chastity and the occupation by which one gains subsistence (*al-ʿiffa wa-l-ḥirfa*). Therefore, laziness and wasting time in unfruitful activities such as drinking alcohol is considered harmful for *murū ʾa*, as this verse clearly shows:

> Sleeping in the morning and drinking in the evenings,
> these two are responsible for the destruction of the virtues [*al-murū ʾāt*].[38]

A similar pattern of contradictory interpretations of the question of whether wine reinforces or destroys *murū ʾa* also emerges in later sources.[39]

A different pattern occurs, however, about hashish consumption. This plant, which is not mentioned in the Qur ʾan, *Sunna* and other *fiqh* books, was nevertheless from the very beginning assimilated to *khamr* and labelled as an intoxicant (*muskir*).[40] However, there was a difference, at least terminologically, between *sukr* and *saṭla*: while the former usually indicates the intoxication produced by fermented liquids, the latter seems to concern hashish inebriation.[41] Accordingly, a central issue was to know what differentiates the effects of the two substances on the body and the mind.

The Mālikī scholar al-Qarāfī (d.684/1285), for instance, gives his formulation of the legal category to which the herb belongs. *Khamr* and the other intoxicants (*muskirāt*) are a source of intoxication (*nashwa*) and enjoyment (*surūr*), but also courage (*shajā ʿ*), happiness (*masarra*), confidence (*quwwat al-nafs*), inclination towards violence (*al-mīl ilā al-baṭsh*), revenge (*al-intiqām*), rivalry (*al-munāfasa*) and *akhlāq al-kuramā ʾ*, the manners of the (ancient) nobles. According to al-Qarāfī, these manners are perfectly described by the following well-known verse of Ḥassān ibn Thābit ibn al-Mundhir (d. *c.* 40/659), a poet belonging to the companions of the Prophet:

> When we drink it [wine], it leaves us kings
> And lions. Battle action does not repel us.[42]

By contrast, al-Qarāfī sees hashish as simply a corruptive substance (*mufsid*) because it 'bewilders the mind without procuring any enjoyment' (*huwa al-mushawwish li-l-ʿaql ma ʿa ʿadam al-surūr*).[43]

Al-Qarāfī's attempt to dissociate hashish from *khamr* on the basis of the difference in their effects received strong criticism from members of other schools of law. Shāfiʿī authorities almost unanimously considered hashish as an intoxicant (*muskir*); however, they also seemed perfectly aware of the issue raised by al-Qarāfī. The Egyptian Shāfiʿī scholar Ibn Ḥajar al-Haytamī (d.974/1567), for instance, considered hashish *mufattir*, that is, 'everything that provokes languor and weakens the extremities'[44] and, although 'it does not give to the body neither a feeling of energy and joy [*nashāṭ*] nor a quarrelsome behavior [*ʿarbada*]'[45] like *khamr*, yet hashish is illegal on the basis of the *ḥadīth*: 'the Prophet has forbidden everything that intoxicates [*muskir*] and weakens [*mufattir*]'.[46]

Considering the effects of hashish on *murūʾa*, Ibn Ghānim al-Maqdisī (d. *c.* 678/1279) is to my knowledge the first to clearly refer to hashish as a threat to it. He was a preacher and the author of several treatises, among which *The Assembly in Blaming Hashish* (*Majlis fī Dhamm al-Ḥashīsh*). In this text, he states that:

> Among its blameworthy properties, [hashish] encourages laziness [*al-kasal*] to its eater, causes weakness [*al-fashal*], turns the lion into a beetle, the noble into a miserable, healthy into sick. Eating it doesn't satiate the appetite, possessing it doesn't satisfy and if someone speaks to the hashish eater, he doesn't listen. It turns the eloquent into an idiot and the trustworthy person into a fool. It decreases *murūʾa* and diminishes *futuwwa*. It also corrupts the rational activity [*al-fikra*], weakens the natural disposition [*al-fiṭra*], freezes the intelligence [*al-fiṭna*], causes indigestion [*al-biṭna*], prolongs the affliction [*al-miḥna*], makes someone give in to the natural temperament [*al-fitna*] and changes the facial expression [*al-siḥna*].[47]

Ibn Ghānim's description of the harms of hashish echoes the idea that the consumption of hemp-based products results in cowardice. His depiction of hashish as turning 'the lion into a beetle' stands in stark contrast to what Ḥassān ibn Thābit is reported to have said about *khamr* turning its drinkers into 'kings and lions'. Thus, the herb damages both *murūʾa* and *futuwwa*.

This concern was also raised by the famous Syrian legal scholar Ibn Taymiyya. He constantly reiterates that hashish either threatens the man's honour, diminishing his control over his womenfolk, or leads to *ubna*, the desire to be anally penetrated:

> Where do these misguided persons [*al-ḍullāl*] fit into the fact that this abhorred substance induces a loss of jealousy [*al-ghayra*] and a disappearance of honor [*al-ḥamiyya*], so much that its eater becomes either a man who knows of his wife's infidelity and tolerates it [*dayyūth*] or a catamite [*maʾbūn*] or both.[48]

And:

> Beside the fact that [hashish] intoxicates so much that its eater becomes high [*maṣṭūl*], it also leads to effeminacy [*takhnīth*] and makes [the husband] a cuckold [*al-dayyūtha*].[49]

In another passage, the Ḥanbalī sheikh elaborates further on the difference between wine and hashish:

> The trustworthy scholars know that it is an intoxicant and that the debauchees consume it because they find in it drunkenness and delight. This is what [hashish] shares with the intoxicating drinks. While wine [*al-khamr*] provokes motion [*al-ḥaraka*] and hostility [*al-khuṣūma*], [hashish] induces instead laxity [*al-futūr*] and submission [*al-dhilla*]. Beside the fact that it corrupts the complexion [*al-mizāj*] and the mind, opens the door of passion [*al-shahwa*] and leads to cuckoldry, it also brings all the bad things related to the intoxicating drink.[50]

The *maʾbūn* and the *mukhannath* – the man who desires to be anally penetrated and the effeminate man, respectively – were both considered abnormal types because they were seen as antitheses of desirable masculinity and a challenge to gender boundaries.[51]

The legal discussion about hashish shows the *feminization* of the hashish eater, who loses his virility by becoming passive, failing to safeguard his family reputation and indulging in being penetrated.[52] In other words, according to these legal texts, the hashish eater is an antithesis of *murūʾa*, becoming a threat to masculinity like the deviant dervishes.

Most of the sources at our disposal on hashish were either overtly polemic – the case of Ibn Taymiyya's aversion vis-à-vis Sufism is emblematic – or were written by advocates of what their authors considered the real Sufism (Ibn Ghānim, for instance). However, whether or not these deviant dervishes made use of psychoactive substances and intoxicants – a thesis that for Ahmet Karamustafa 'cannot be substantiated due to lack of detailed information on this subject'[53] – and whether or not they were practising sodomy, the stereotype of the Sufi hashish addict and pederast is a constant of the legal sources of this period to such an extent that it also influenced the literary imaginary. However, as I show in the following section, the urge to entertain the readers often gained priority over moral concerns.

Literary renditions of hashish consumption: Between transgression and entertainment

The Delight of the Souls in Hashish and Wine (*Rāḥat al-Arwāḥ fī al-Ḥashīsh wa-l-Rāḥ*), is an anthology of poetic texts and anecdotes about wine and hashish, as the title suggests, written in the second half of the ninth/fifteenth century by Taqī al-Dīn Abū l-Tuqā al-Badrī.[54] In the introduction of the sixth chapter of the *Rāḥa*, al-Badrī clearly formulates his ideas on the effects of hashish as follows:

> I say that what pushed the mass to consume hashish is the attraction of the supposed pleasure intended to give relief to the body: hashish relaxes from working activities, makes people eat the food that stimulates their appetite and

> enhances the intercourse with women. However, to the majority of its users, hashish provokes instead so much laziness that people delay in delivering their crafts and fail to meet the agreement. It increases inactivity because one is so occupied by eating hashish, that if he takes up a loan he doesn't repay it. He spends his time hanging around in some pleasant places and his head is so subjugated by desire that if he sees a beardless boy [*amrad*], he starts following him as if he was from the people of Lot.[55]

Al-Badrī reports the widespread idea that hashish relaxes the body, increases the appetite and works as an aphrodisiac enhancing male sexual stamina, a belief that certainly betrays an anxiety over male virility and sexual performance. However, al-Badrī himself notes that this is a mere illusion, because hashish leads instead to laziness and inactivity. The author of the *Rāḥa* seems indeed very much aware of this unfounded conviction and in the third chapter of his book, devoted to the medical discussions concerning hashish, he lists several opinions indicating that the herb provokes male impotence (*qaṭ ʿ al-bāh*) and the loss of sperm production (*qaṭ ʿ al-manī*).[56]

However, the link between hashish, deviant Sufism and a lack of masculinity is far from evident. Instead, there are constant allusions to the alleged power of the plant for stimulating sexual drives, as it is clear in the following claim:

> You won't find a hashish eater who wouldn't be driven more by the desire to penetrate passive sodomites [*ṭalab al-ʿulūq wa-l-liwāṭ bi-him*] rather than by having extramarital intercourse with a woman [*al-zinā ʾ*]. Rather, the wine drinker would be driven more by the desire to have extramarital relations with a woman [*al-zinā ʾ*] than by having anal intercourse with a man [*al-liwāṭ*].[57]

Al-Badrī tends to transfer to the two substances the *liwāṭ/zinā ʾ* legal classification, linking the desire for women or men contrastingly either to wine or to hashish. Yet, the general idea behind all of this is that both hashish and wine work as creators of an erotic atmosphere or, as Michel Foucault would call it, *des régions de haute saturation sexuelle*.[58]

However, al-Badrī also relates stories in which both hashish and wine are used to stimulate desire as in the following story:

> It has been reported about Ibn al-Tarbalī that he couldn't stop consuming hashish. One day he met a beardless boy who accepted his invitation: 'But on the condition that we drink wine' [he said] and [Ibn al-Tarbalī] consented. Thus they came together and got so intoxicated that their heads couldn't stay upright anymore.[59]

In another anecdote, wine and hashish appear as equivalents, one easily replacing the other:

> He narrated: On a rainy day, when the drug has made effect, I knocked at his door and he asked 'Is it so-and-so?', I answered: 'Yes' and he said: 'Today I have a guest', and I replied: 'And I am the one inclined to him'.[60] When I entered,

I found close to him a beautiful beardless boy and in front of them the rest of some wine that they have been drinking until it was finished. Then I asked [the beardless boy]: 'Take this dirham and bring us some wine', and he said: 'Yes'. He disappeared and later he brought to us some hashish and I said: 'What is that?', he replied: 'The governors have forbidden to buy wine and to drink it openly, so I couldn't find anything else to continue our intoxication than that'. Thus we took [hashish], played and laughed:

We replaced wine with hashish [*zīh*]
when all the strangers (or those who don't know us) started to be spies:
we abandoned what was immoral
and replace it with something that is more harmful.[61]

A closer look at the different versions of some anecdotes reported in the two manuscripts of the *Rāḥa* reveals that wine and hashish could also work narratively as equivalents. This is the case, for instance, in the following anecdote, where in one of the two manuscripts, wine and hashish are both offered to the young boy whereas in the other only wine consumption is described:

A preacher, when hashish went up to his eyes, headed towards the channel where he found a beardless boy wallowing in the dust and then going to the water. The preacher asked: 'Do you want to walk with me to my place, we will eat the fishes you have taken' and he agreed. When he arrived at his place, the preacher gave the boy something to eat, wine and [hashish], but the boy didn't want to be penetrated and left. After some days, the boy went to the Friday mosque and, when the preacher, who was sitting on the chair, saw him, he turned his face towards the women and said, knocking on the chair: 'Where are those that we pulled out from water and dust, that we fed with the better food and to whom we gave the most delicious drink and they didn't fulfil their duty, they didn't want and they have lost their patience? These will be punished by God with the severest of punishment.' A lady screamed: 'Sir, what did we not want to do?' and the boy breaking his silence answered: 'Damned lady, this one is blaming me because I didn't let him penetrate me, there is no need for you to scream.'[62]

However, if hashish can function as an ersatz wine, hashish alone is the preferred aid to stimulate male–male sensual pleasure, as this anecdote shows:

It has been narrated that Sharīf ibn al-Barīdī was a regular consumer of pills of hashish, which he used to offer to beardless boys so much that, in a day and a night he could get his hands on no more than ten boys. He didn't drink wine unless the boys convinced him; otherwise his daily dose of hashish confectionaries was an Egyptian *waqiyya* (37 g).[63]

Al-Barīdī is indeed prototypical of most of the protagonists of the *Rāḥa*: a drug addict, one of these *promeneurs aux impulsions étranges* in Foucauldian terms,[64] who is erotically attracted by male adolescents, even when they turn out to be young girls, as in the following anecdote:

> Someone whose name I don't remember narrated: It was the night when the *maḥmal* is brought in the streets; I consumed some hashish and left my house to have a look to the lights and the decorations. When I met a Turkish boy, beautiful like a gazelle, who has lowered his veil to rub the sleep out of his eyes, I invited him and he accepted to follow me. I also took with me a paper bag with some sweets. When we entered the house and he had eaten from the sweets and had found some delight in it, I desired him so much that I laid on him. Then, he turned on his back, spread his legs and when I wanted to penetrate him in his hole, he pointed his finger: it was a vagina. And I said: 'What is that?' he replied: 'Do your work!' and I said: 'I get excited only by the anus' and she said: 'I want to give you a taste of a loaf of bread from Asyut and you eat a mush of something?' At the end, I satisfied my desire by anally penetrating being afraid that she was still a virgin. She said: 'You didn't see us and we didn't see you'. Nothing but the *khalqa* [the typical Sufi's dress] and eating drug can provoke something like that.[65]

That hashish is involved in the flirting and 'hunting' is made clear in this other story, where we find also the jocular figure of the old pederast:

> The sheikh Qawwām al-ʿAjamī, after eating hashish and having left his place, used to sit at Bāb Zuweyla in order to hunt beardless boys and al-Miʿmār composed a poem on this man:
> Never have we ever seen someone like the sheikh:
>   if he sees a beardless boy, falls in love,
> but if [he sees] a bearded man,
>   he runs towards him because he is sheikh Qawwām/the master of the procurers.[66]

The appearance of beard-down (ʿ*idhār*) on a teenage boy's face was abundantly celebrated in Arabic poetry as early as the ninth century and was largely exploited in the post-Abbasid period.[67] Moreover, by the thirteenth century, following the spread of the consumption of hemp-based products as a recreational substance, hashish was also used as a metaphor for the sprouting of a beard,[68] as in the following three poems:

> The dark-green hashish of your cheek awakens a desire in creatures
> And the amber-scented beauty spot on your cheek refreshes those who smell (it)
> How many toasted (hashish) pills have intoxicated your delicate eyes
> And in your hair lock how many lovers have stumbled over you.[69]

> A beautiful boy said in public:
>   Oh souls of the people, my whole existence

is made of my cheek and my saliva
that is to say between my wine and my hashish.[70]

When around my beloved's mouth appeared
a dark-green beard-down, they blamed.
And I answered: What's the matter with you? Probably you ignore
that this one is hashish and that one is wine?[71]

Although most of these narratives clearly belong to the longstanding tradition of the Arabic *mujūn* literature, where jocular effects are attained through descriptions of sexually explicit situations and provocative behaviours defying both social norms and a set of cultural and religious assumptions,[72] they also reveal how hashish was believed to facilitate the sexualization of the other.

According to legal writings, deviant dervishes, hashish eaters and men enjoying passive sodomy share similar characteristics: they are all challenging common ideas of masculinity and the set of virtues related to *murūʾa*. However, the literary material put together by al-Badrī in his *Rāḥa* displays instead images of active and vigorous hashish eaters trying to get the favours of beardless boys. Despite the legal discourse of a 'less-man-hashish eater' argument, in this jocular literature hashish shapes the equally masculine desire to penetrate male adolescents and, as such, neither affects virility nor the masculine gender. In other words, if for the normative texts of medieval legal scholarship abjection is a way to reject what does not conform to custom and the law, literary texts, far from any moral concern, imply instead a sublimating elaboration of the uncanny from the uncomfortably strange to humour and entertainment.

Notes

1 Taqī al-Dīn Abū al-ʿAbbās Aḥmad al-Maqrizī, *Kitāb al-Mawāʿiẓ wa-l-Iʿtibār bi-Dhikr al-Khiṭaṭ wa-l-Āthār*, 2 vols (Beirut: Dār Ṣādir, 1970), 2:414. Unless otherwise stated, all translations are by the author of this chapter.

2 Khaled al-Rouayheb has demonstrated that ritual sessions of *samāʿ*, improper conduct with beardless teenage novices, but also *ḥulūl* and *ittiḥād* were problematic and liable to be misunderstood as heretical doctrines in the Ottoman period. Khaled al-Rouayheb, 'Heresy and Sufism in the Arab-Islamic World, 1550–1750: Some Preliminary Observations', *Bulletin of the School of Oriental and African Studies*, 73 (3) (2010): 359–80.

3 Taqī al-Dīn Abū al-Tuqā al-Badrī, *Rāḥat al-Arwāḥ fī al-Ḥashīsh wa-l-Rạḥ* (hereafter *Rāḥa*), Ms Dār al-Kutub al-Ẓāhiriyya of Damascus, *adab ʿarabī* 7855, *majmūʿ* 210 (Ms D), ff58a–b; Ms Bibliothéque nationale de France, *arabe* 3544 (Ms P), ff8a–b.

4 Julia Kristeva, *Powers of Horror: An Essay on Abjection*, trans. Leon S. Roudiez, (New York: Columbia University Press. 1982), 4.

5 Ibid., 127.

6 If the latter is easily understandable, the former's link to the *maternal/feminine* is based on the idea that the anus is in general associated with the feminine sex, see Kristeva, *Powers of Horror*, 71, emphasis in the original.

7 Ibid., 70. See also 90–1 and 100–06, where Kristeva reads the biblical semiotics of defilement, impurity and abomination in the 'cathexis of maternal function/mother, women, reproduction'.

8 The Andalusian botanist Ibn al-Bayṭār (d.646/1248) writes in his *Jāmiʿ* that *ḥashīsh* is the name that the Egyptians give to *qinnab* (or *qunnab*, from the Greek *κάνναβις*) and it is widespread among the *fuqarāʾ*, at this period a term designating the Sufis, Abū Muḥammad ʿAbd Allāh ibn al-Bayṭār, *Kitāb al-Jāmiʿ li-Mufradāt al-Adwiyya wa-l-Aghdiyya*, 4 vols (Būlāq: Maktabat al-Āmira, 1874), 4:39, and the Spanish translation in Indalecio Lozano Cámara, *Solaz del espíritu en el hachís y el vino: y otros textos árabes sobre drogas* (Granada: Editorial Universidad de Granada 1999), 43–4.

9 Abū ʿAbd Allāh Muḥammad al-Kutubī, *Fawāt al-Wafiyāt*, ed. Iḥsān ʿAbbās, 4 vols (Beirut: Dār Ṣādir, 1973), 3:272–73. For the English translation see Franz Rosenthal, *The Herb: Hashish versus Medieval Muslim Society* (Leiden: Brill, 1971), 163–64.

10 Ibrahim Geries, 'Débat sur le Haschich dans les *maqāmas* d'Ibn al-Ḥaddād', in Mirella Cassarino and Antonella Ghersetti (eds), *Il dialogo nella cultura araba: strutture, funzioni, significati (VIII-XIII secolo)*, Giornate internazionali di studio, IX Colloquio internazionale Medioevo romanzo e orientale (Catania, 14–15 June 2012) (Soveria Mannelli: Rubbettino, 2015), 107–21.

11 Jamāl al-Dīn ibn al-Jawzī, *Talbīs Iblīs* (Beirut: Dār al-Fikr li-l-Ṭibāʿa wa-l-Nashr, 2001), 329.

12 For the biographies of both sheikhs, see Ahmet Karamustafa, *God's Unruly Friends. Dervish Groups in the Islamic Middle Period 1200–1550* (London: Oneworld Publications, 2006), 39–46.

13 Al-Maqrīzī, *Kitāb al-Mawāʿiẓ*, 2:126; al-Badrī, *Rāḥa*, Ms D, f56a and Ms P, f3a–b. The English translation of al-Maqrīzī's version of this story is taken from Rosenthal, *The Herb*, 51–2.

14 Al-Maqrīzī, *Kitāb al-Mawāʿiẓ*, 2:126; al-Badrī, *Rāḥa*, Ms D, f57a and Ms P, f4a.

15 Ibid., Ms D, f58b and Ms P, f9a.

16 Taqī al-Dīn Aḥmad ibn Taymiyya, *Majmūʿ Fatāwā*, 37 vols (Cairo: Maktabat Ibn Taymiyya, 1985), 34:223.

17 Al-Badrī, *Rāḥa*, Ms D, f58a and Ms P, f8b.

18 ʿAbd al-Raḥmān ibn ʿUmar al-Jawbarī, *Kitāb al-Mukhtār fī Kashf al-Asrār*, ed. Manuela Höglmeier (Berlin: Klaus-Schwarz Verlag, 2006), 115. See also Karamustafa, *God's Unruly Friends*, 54.

19 Although hashish seems to have been the non-fermented substance used for recreational purposes, by the eighth/fifteenth century and especially from the ninth/sixteenth century other substances started to be in widespread use in Arab-Islamic societies. Among them coffee, tobacco and opium were particularly popular. See respectively Ralph S. Hattox, *Coffee and Coffeehouses: The Origins of a Social Beverage in the Medieval Near East* (Seattle, WA: University of Washington Press, 1985); Aḥmad al-Rūmī al-Aqḥiṣarī, *Against Smoking: An Ottoman Manifesto*, ed. and trans. Yahya Michot (Markfield: Kube Publishing; Oxford: Interface Publications, 2010); and Rudi Matthee, *The Pursuit of Pleasure: Drugs and Stimulants in Iranian History, 1500–1900* (Princeton, NJ: Princeton University Press, 2005).

20 See, for instance, Abū Manṣūr al-Thaʿalabī, *Mirʾāt al-Murūʾāt*, ed. Muḥammad Khayr Ramaḍān Yūsuf (Beirut: Dār Ibn Ḥazm, 2004), 57, according to whom: 'who has no

woman has no *murūʾa*, who has no son has no happiness but who has none of them has no sorrow'. Similarly, in an earlier source, Ibn al-Marzubān (d.309/921) says that '*murūʾa* is having a lot of goods and children', Ibn al-Marzubān, *al-Murūʾa*, ed. Muḥammad Khayr Ramaḍān Yūssif (Beirut: Dār Ibn Ḥazm, 1999), 115.

21 Karamustafa, *God's Unruly Friends*, 40–1.

22 Ibid., 19.

23 Khaled al-Rouayheb, *Before Homosexuality in the Arab-Islamic World, 1500–1800* (Chicago, IL: University of Chicago Press, 2005), 26. Facial hair plays a central role in the definition of masculinity in classical as well as modern Arab-Islamic societies; see, for instance, Faegheh Shirazi, 'Men's Facial Hair in Islam. A Matter of Interpretation', in Geraldine Biddle-Perry and Sarah Cheang (eds), *Hair: Styling, Culture and Fashion*, 111–22 (Oxford: Berg, 2008); and Cem Doğan, 'Modern Man in the Making: Facial Hair, Fashion and Medico-Social Construction of Masculinity in the Late Ottoman Society (1900–1920)', *Artuklu Human and Social Science Journal*, 1 (1) (2016): 46–54.

24 The beard was also a means of division between Muslims and non-Muslims according to a hadith: 'Be distinguished from disbelievers, grow your beards, and shave your moustaches'; Muḥammad ibn Ismāʿīl al-Bukhārī, *Ṣaḥīḥ al-Bukhārī*, ed. Muḥammad Zuhayr ibn Nāṣir al-Nāṣir, 9 vols (Damascus: Dār Ṭawq al-Najāh, 2000), 7:160n5892. The non-Muslims referred to here are the Zoroastrians, who used to shave their beards. Growing beards here represents an act of imitating the enemies of the religion.

25 Heghnar Z. Watenpaugh, 'Deviant Dervishes: Space, Gender, and the Construction of Antinomian Piety in Ottoman Aleppo', *International Journal of Middle East Studies*, 37 (4) (November 2005): 547–49; and Ahmet Karamustafa, 'Antinomian Sufi', in Lloyd Ridgeon (ed.), *The Cambridge Companion to Sufism* (Cambridge: Cambridge University Press, 2014), 121–22. This issue has also been analysed in Amanullah De Sondy, *The Crisis of Islamic Masculinities* (London: Bloomsbury, 2013), 153–78.

26 Watenpaugh, 'Deviant Dervishes', 549.

27 Durre S. Ahmed, 'Gender and Islamic Spirituality: A Psychological View of "Low" Fundamentalism', in Lahoucine Ouzgane (ed.), *Islamic Masculinities*, 11–34 (London: Zed Books, 2013), 18.

28 Éric Geoffroy, *Le soufisme: voie intérieure de l'islam* (Paris: Fayard, 2009), 185–86.

29 Karamustafa, *God's Unruly Friends*, 52–3.

30 Bichr Farès, 'Murūʾa', in C. E. Bosworth, E. van Donzel, W. P. Heinrichs and Ch. Pellat (eds), *Encyclopaedia of Islam*, 2nd edn., 636–38 (*EI2)*, 10 vols (Leiden: Brill, 1986–2000), 7:636–38; Salah Natij, '*Murūʾa*. Soucis et interrogations éthiques dans la culture arabe classique', *Studia Islamica*, 112 (2017); 206–63 and *Studia Islamica*, 113 (2018): 1–55.

31 Julia Bray, 'Men, Women and Slaves in Abbasid Society', in Leslie Brubaker and Julia M. H. Smith (eds), *Gender in the Early Medieval World: East and West 300–900*, 121–46 (Cambridge: Cambridge University Press, 2004), 138–41.

32 Farès, 'Murūʾa', 7:636–38.

33 Joseph Sadan, 'Vin – fait de civilisation', in Myriam Rosen-Ayalon (ed.), *Studies in Memory of Gaston Wiet*, 129–60 (Jerusalem: Hebrew University, 1977), 146–53.

34 Abū al-ʿAbbās ʿAbd Allāh ibn al-Muʿtazz, *Fuṣūl al-Tamāthīl fī Tabāshīr al-Surūr* (Beirut: Manshūrāt al-Jamal, 2011), 14.

35 Abū ʿUthmān al-Jāḥiẓ, *Min Risālatihi fī al-Shārib wa-l-Mashrūb*, in Ḥasan al-Sandūbī (ed.), *Rasāʾil al-Jāḥiẓ* (Cairo: al-Maktaba al-Tijāriyya al-Kubrā, 1933), 278.

36 Abū Muḥammad ʿAbd Allāh ibn Muslim ibn Qutayba, *Kitāb al-Ashriba*, ed. Muḥammad Kurd ʿAlī (Beirut: Dār al-Muqtabas, 2015), 73. See also Abū al-Faḍl ibn Manẓūr, *Lisān al-ʿArab*, 18 vols (Beirut: Dār Ṣādir, 1955–1956), 4:218 and Muḥammad Murtaḍā al-Husaynī al-Zabīdī, *Tāj al-ʿArūs min Jawāhir al-Qāmūs*, 10 vols (Beirut: Dār Ṣādir, 2011), 3:398. That men should not wear silk and gold is clearly stated in a well-known *ḥadīth* included in Sulaymān ibn al-Ashʿath ibn Isḥāq Abū Dāwūd, *Sunan Abī Dāwūd*, 7 vols (Damascus: Dār al-Risala al-ʿĀlamiyya, 2009), 6:165n4057.

37 Ibn Qutayba, *Kitāb al-Ashriba*, 79 and 89–90.

38 Abū Muḥammad ʿAbd Allāh ibn Muslim ibn Qutayba, *ʿUyūn al-Akhbār*, 2 vols (Cairo: Dār al-Kutub al-Miṣriyya, 1925), 1:295–96.

39 Abū Isḥāq Ibrāhīm ibn al-Qāsim al-Raqīq al-Qayrawānī, *Quṭb al-Surūr fī Awṣāf al-Anbidha wa-l-Khumūr*, ed. Sāra al-Barbūshī (Beirut: Manshūrāt al-Jamal, 2010), 783, 842, 909 and 911. Other similar instances are to be found also in the ninth/fifteenth-century Shams al-Dīn Muḥammad ibn al-Ḥasan al-Nawājī, *Ḥalbat al-Kumayt fī al-Adab wa-l-Nawādir al-Mutaʿallaqa bi-l-Khamriyyāt* (Cairo: Dār al-Ṭibāʿa al-Miṣriyya, 1859), 13.

40 The *hạdīth* commonly quoted was 'Everything that intoxicates is like a fermented substance and every fermented substance is illegal' (*kull muskir khamr wa-kull khamr ḥarām*); see Arent Jan Wensinck and Johan Peter Mari Mensing (eds), *Concordance et indices de la tradition musulmane. Les six livres, le Musnad d'al-Dārimī, le Muwattaʾ de Mālik, le Musnad de Ahmad Ibn Hanbal*, 8 vols (Leiden: Brill, 1936–1969), 2:491and Gautier H. A. Juynboll, *Encyclopedia of Canonical Ḥadīth* (Leiden: Brill, 2007), 171.

41 See also Edward William Lane, *Arabic-English Lexicon*, 8 vols (Beirut: Librairie du Liban, 1968), 1:1359: 'a state of intoxication produced by the *ḥashīsh* [or herb, or species of hemp] known by the name of *zīh*'. Another word used with a similar signification is *basṭ*, which is, according to Lane, 'a certain intoxicating thing [a preparation of hemp]', ibid., 2:204.

42 Shihāb al-Dīn Abī al-ʿAbbās Aḥmad al-Qarāfī, *Kitāb al-Furūq. Anwār al-Burūq fī Anwār al-Furūq*, ed. ʿAlī Jumʿa and Muḥammad Aḥmad Sirāj, 4 vols (Cairo: Dār al-Salām li-l-Ṭibāʿa wa-l-Nashr wa-l-Tawzīʿ wa-l-Tarjama, 2001), 1:363 and Rosenthal, *The Herb*, 109, for the English translation.

43 Al-Qarāfī, *Kitāb al-Furūq*, 1:363.

44 Abū al-ʿAbbās Aḥmad ibn Muḥammad ʿAlī ibn Ḥajar al-Haytamī, *Kitāb al-Zawājir ʿan Iqtirāf al-Kabāʾir*, 2 vols (Cairo: Maṭbaʿa al-Azhariyya, 1907), 1:173.

45 Abū al-ʿAbbās Aḥmad ibn Muḥammad ʿAlī ibn Ḥajar al-Haytamī, *al-Fatāwā al-Kubrā al-Fiqhiyya*, 4 vols (Beirut: Dār al-Fikr, 1983), vol. 4, 231.

46 Al-Haytamī, *al-Fatāwā*, 1:173. The hadith was already recorded in previous sources such as Abū Dāwūd, *Sunan Abī Dāwūd*, 5:529n3686.

47 Lozano, *Tres tratados*, 30–1. This is the standard list of negative physical and moral effects of hashish that was reported almost verbatim by later authors such as al-Zarkashī (d.794/1392), Ibn al-ʿImād al-Aqfahsī (d.808/1405), Ibn Ḥajar al-Haytamī (d.974/1567) and al-Ḥusayn al-Diyār Bakrī (d.966/1558–1559 or 982/1574), see ibid., 81; Indalecio Cámara Lozano, 'Un texto inédito para la historia del *ḥašīš* en el mundo islámico: *Ikrām man yaʿīš bi-taḥrīm al-jamr wa-l-ḥašīš*, de Ibn al-ʿImād al-Aqfahsī', in *Homenaje al Profesor Jacinto Bosch Vilá*, 2 vols (Granada: Universidad de Ganada, Departamento de Estudios Semíticos, 1991), 1:595; al-Haytamī, *Kitāb al-Zawājir*, 1:173; al-Diyār Bakrī, *Tārīkh al-Khamīs fī Aḥwāl Anfas al-Nafīs*, 2 vols (Cairo: Maṭbaʿa al-Faqīr ʿUthmān ʿAbd al-Rāziq, 1884), 2:31.

48 Ibn Taymiyya, *Majmūʿ al-Fatāwā*, 34:223.

49 Ibid., 34:205.

50 Ibid., 34:211 and Ibn Taymiyya, *al-Siyāsa al-Sharʿiyya*, ed. Ṣāliḥ al-Laḥḥām (ʿAmmān: Dār al-ʿUthmāniyya, 2004), 151–52. Ibn Taymiyya's position was adopted by one of his students, Shams al-Dīn Abū ʿAbd Allāh al-Dhahabī, *Kitāb al-Kabāʾir* (Beirut: Dār al-Nadwa al-Jadīda, 1988), 86.
51 For the difference between *liwāṭ* and *ubna*, see Al-Rouayheb, *Before Homosexuality*, 22 and 20–1.
52 As for *ghayra* being considered as a male virtue, see Pernilla Myrne, 'Discussing *Ghayra* in Abbasid Literature: Jealousy as a Manly Virtue or Sign of Mutual Affection', *Journal of Abbasid Studies*, 1 (1) (2014): 58–9.
53 Karamustafa, *God's Unruly Friends*, 20.
54 Biographical information about al-Badrī is very limited and is mostly reported in al-Sakhāwī's eighth/fourteenth-century biographical dictionary. See, for instance, Geert Jan van Gelder, 'al-Badrī, Abū al-Tuqā', in Kate Fleet, Gudrun Krämer, Denis Matringe, John Nawas, Everett Rowson (eds), *Encyclopaedia of Islam 3* (Leiden: Brill, 2012). http://dx.doi.org/10.1163/1573-3912_ei3_COM_22909.
55 Al-Badrī, *Rāḥa*, Ms D, f66a and Ms P, f30a.
56 Ibid., Ms D, ff58b–59b and Ms P, ff5b–7b.
57 Ibid., Ms D, f85a.
58 Michel Foucault, *Histoire de la sexualité I: La volonté de savoir* (Paris: Éditions Gallimard, 1976), 64.
59 Al-Badrī, *Rāḥa*, Ms P, f45a.
60 This is word play built around the grammatical terms *muḍāf ilayhi*, which indicates the attribution or genitive construction (*iḍāfa*) between two terms, the *muḍāf* and the *muḍāf ilayhi*. The latter here is used euphemistically to refer to the active role in a male–male intercourse: what is added, as opposed to the *muḍāf*/*ḍayf*.
61 Al-Badrī, *Rāḥa*, Ms P, f46a–b.
62 Ibid., Ms D, f42b and Ms P, f31a. In another case, a story reported in the *Rāḥa*, describing a hashish eater trying to gain the favour of a young boy, was already recorded in *The Pleasure of the Minds in What is not Found in the Book* (*Nuzhat al-Albāb fī mā lā Yūjad fī Kitāb*), written around three centuries before the *Rāḥa* by Shihāb al-Dīn al-Tīfāshī (d.651/1253). Although there are only slight differences between the two tales, in al-Tīfāshī's version there is no evidence whatsoever of hashish. See Shihāb al-Dīn Aḥmad al-Tīfāshī, *Nuzhat al-Albāb fī mā lā Yūjad fī Kitāb*, ed. Jamāl Jumaʿa (London: Riyāḍ al-Rayyās li-l-Kutub wa-l-Nashr, 1992), 155. This would explain why, in order to reproduce the widespread stereotype of the intoxicated pederast, al-Badrī embellishes his stories by replacing wine with another newly appeared intoxicant, hashish, which was also believed to function as an aphrodisiac.
63 Al-Badrī, *Rāḥa*, Ms P, f47a.
64 Foucault, *Histoire de la sexualité*, 55.
65 Al-Badrī, *Rāḥa*, Ms P, f33a.
66 Ibid., Ms P, ff38b–39a.
67 Badr al-Dīn Muḥammad al-Manhājī, *Basṭ al-Aʿdhār ʿan Ḥubb al-ʿIdhār*, ed. Muḥammad Yūsuf Ibrāhīm Banāt and Ḥasan Muḥammad ʿAbd al-Hādī (Beirut: Dār al-Kutub al-ʿIlmiyya, 2017), 36, mentions sixteen titles of books written between the fourteenth and sixteenth centuries dealing with the beauties of beardless boys.
68 For a detailed discussion of the motif of the sprouting beard compared to hashish, see Danilo Marino, 'Le plaisir de l'ivresse: Haschich et littérature homoérotique dans l'époque mamelouke', in Frédéric Lagrange (ed.), *Words of Desire: The Language of Arabic Erotica and its Translations* (Marseille: Diacritiques Editions, forthcoming).

69 Al-Badrī, *Rāḥa*, Ms D, f72b and Ms P, f50b.
70 Ibid., Ms P, f46a.
71 Ibid., Ms D, f72b and Ms P, f46a.
72 Zoltan Szombathy, *Mujūn: Libertinism in Medieval Muslim Society and Literature* (Exeter: E. J. W. Gibb Memorial Trust, 2013), 1–34.

References

Primary sources

Abū Dāwūd, Sulaymān ibn al-Ash ʿath ibn Isḥāq (2009), *Sunan Abī Dāwūd*, 7 vols, vol. 6, Damascus: Dār al-Risāla al- ʿĀlamiyya.

Al-Aqḥiṣarī, Aḥmad al-Rūmī (2010), *Against Smoking: An Ottoman Manifesto*, ed. and trans. Yahya Michot, Markfield: Kube Publishing; Oxford: Interface Publications.

Al-Bukhārī, Muḥammad ibn Ismā ʿīl (2000), *Ṣaḥīḥ al-Bukhārī*, 9 vols, vol. 7, ed. Muḥammad Zuhayr ibn Nāṣir al-Nāṣir, Damascus: Dār Ṭawq al-Najāh.

Al-Dhahabī, Shams al-Dīn Abū ʿAbd Allāh (1988), *Kitāb al-Kabā ʾir*, Beirut: Dār al-Nadwa al-Jadīda.

Al-Haytamī, Abū al- ʿAbbās Aḥmad ibn Muḥammad ʿAlī ibn Ḥajar (1907), *Kitāb al-Zawājir ʿan Iqtirāf al-Kabā ʾir*, 2 vols, vol. 1, Cairo: al-Maṭba ʿa al-Azhariyya.

Al-Haytamī, Abū al- ʿAbbās Aḥmad ibn Muḥammad ʿAlī ibn Ḥajar (1983), *al-Fatāwā al-Kubrā al-Fiqhiyya*, 4 vols, vol. 4, Beirut: Dār al-Fikr.

Al-Jāḥiẓ, Abū ʿUthmān (1933), *Min Risālatihi fī al-Shārib wa-l-Mashrūb*, in Ḥasan al-Sandūbī (ed.), *Rasā ʾil al-Jāḥiẓ*, 276–85, Cairo: al-Maktaba al-Tijāriyya al-Kubrā.

Al-Jawbarī, ʿAbd al-Raḥmān ibn ʿUmar (2006), *Kitāb al-Mukhtār fī Kashf al-Asrār*, ed. Manuela Höglmeier, Berlin: Klaus-Schwarz Verlag.

Al-Kutubī, Abū ʿAbd Allāh Muḥammad (1973), *Fawāt al-Wafiyāt*, 4 vols, vol. 3, ed. Iḥsān ʿAbbās, Beirut: Dār Ṣādir.

Al-Manhājī, Badr al-Dīn Muḥammad (2017), *Basṭ al-A ʿdhār ʿan Ḥubb al- ʿIdhār*, ed. Muḥammad Yūsuf Ibrāhīm Banāt and Ḥasan Muḥammad ʿAbd al-Hādī, Beirut: Dār al-Kutub al- ʿIlmiyya.

Al-Maqrizī, Taqī al-Dīn Abū al- ʿAbbās Aḥmad (1970s), *Kitāb al-Mawā ʿiẓ wa-l-I ʿtibār bi-Dhikr al-Khiṭaṭ wa-l-Āthār*, 2 vols, vol. 2, Beirut: Dār Ṣādir.

Al-Nawājī, Shams al-Dīn Muḥammad ibn al-Ḥasan (1859), *Ḥalbat al-Kumayt fī al-Adab wa-l-Nawādir al-Muta ʿallaqa bi-l-Khamriyyāt*, Cairo: Dār al-Ṭibā ʿa al-Miṣriyya.

Al-Qarāfī, Shihāb al-Dīn Abū al- ʿAbbās Aḥmad (2001), *Kitāb al-Furūq: Anwār al-Burūq fī Anwār al-Furūq*, ed. ʿAlī Jum ʿa and Muḥammad Aḥmad Sirāj, 4 vols, vol. 1, Cairo: Dār al-Salām li-l-Ṭibā ʿa wa-l-Nashr wa-l-Tawzī ʿ wa-l-Tarjama.

Al-Raqīq al-Qayrawānī, Abū Isḥāq Ibrāhīm ibn al-Qāsim (2010), *Quṭb al-Surūr fī Awṣāf al-Anbidha wa-l-Khumūr*, ed. Sāra al-Barbūshī, Beirut: Manshūrāt al-Jamal.

Al-Tha ʿalabī, Abū Manṣūr (2004), *Mir ʾāt al-Murū ʾāt*, ed. Muḥammad Khayr Ramaḍān Yūsuf, Beirut: Dār Ibn Ḥazm.

Al-Tīfāshī, Shihāb al-Dīn Aḥmad (1992), *Nuzhat al-Albāb fī mā lā Yūjad fī Kitāb*, ed. Jamāl Juma ʿa, London: Riyāḍ al-Rayyās li-l-Kutub wa-l-Nashr.

Al-Zabīdī, Muḥammad Murtaḍā al-Husaynī (2011), *Tāj al- ʿArūs min Jawāhir al-Qāmūs*, 10 vols, vol. 3, Beirut: Dār Ṣādir.

Bakrī, al-Ḥusayn al-Diyār (1884), *Tārīkh al-Khamīs fī Aḥwāl Anfas al-Nafīs*, 2 vols, vol. 2, Cairo: Maṭba ʿa al-Faqīr ʿUthmān ʿAbd al-Rāziq.

Ibn al-Bayṭār, Abū Muḥammad ʿAbd Allāh (1874), *Kitāb al-Jāmiʿ li-Mufradāt al-Adwiyya wa-l-Aghdiyya*, 4 vols, vol. 4, Būlāq: Maktabat al-Āmira.
Ibn al-Jawzī, Jamāl al-Dīn (2001), *Talbīs Iblīs*, Beirut: Dār al-Fikr li-l-Ṭibāʿa wa-l-Nashr.
Ibn Manẓūr, Abū al-Faḍl (1955–1956), *Lisān al-ʿArab*, 18 vols, vol. 4, Beirut: Dār Ṣādir.
Ibn al-Marzubān, Abū Bakr Muḥammad ibn Khalaf (1999), *al-Murūʾa*, ed. Muḥammad Khayr Ramaḍān Yūssif, Beirut: Dār Ibn Ḥazm.
Ibn al-Muʿtazz, Abū al-ʿAbbās ʿAbd Allāh (2011), *Fuṣūl al-Tamāthīl fī Tabāshīr al-Surūr*, Beirut: Manshūrāt al-Jamal.
Ibn Qutayba al-Dīnawarī, Abū Muḥammad ʿAbd Allāh ibn Muslim (1925), *Kitāb ʿUyūn al-Akhbār*, 4 vols, vol. 1, Cairo: Dār al-Kutub al-Miṣriyya.
Ibn Qutayba al-Dīnawarī, Abū Muḥammad ʿAbd Allāh ibn Muslim (2015), *Kitāb al-Ashriba*, ed. Muḥammad Kurd ʿAlī, Beirut: Dār al-Muqtabas.
Ibn Taymiyya, Taqī al-Dīn Aḥmad (1985), *Majmūʿ Fatāwā*, 37 vols, vol. 37, Cairo: Maktabat Ibn Taymiyya.
Ibn Taymiyya, Taqī ad-Dīn Ahmad (2004), *al-Siyāsa al-Sharʿiyya*, ed. Ṣālih al-Laḥḥām, ʿAmmān: Dār al-ʿUthmāniyya.

Secondary sources

Ahmed, Durre S. (2013), 'Gender and Islamic Spirituality: A Psychological View of "Low" Fundamentalism', in Lahoucine Ouzgane (ed.), *Islamic Masculinities*, 11–34, London: Zed Books.
Al-Rouayheb, Khaled (2005), *Before Homosexuality in the Arab-Islamic World, 1500–1800*, Chicago, IL: University of Chicago Press.
Al-Rouayheb, Khaled (2010), 'Heresy and Sufism in the Arab-Islamic World, 1550–1750: Some Preliminary Observations', *Bulletin of the School of Oriental and African Studies*, 73 (3): 359–80.
Bray, Julia (2004), 'Men, Women and Slaves in Abbasid Society', in Leslie Brubaker and Julia M. H. Smith (eds), *Gender in the Early Medieval World: East and West, 300–900*, 121–46, Cambridge: Cambridge University Press.
De Sondy, Amanullah (2013), *The Crisis of Islamic Masculinities*, London: Bloomsbury.
Doğan, Cem (2016), 'Modern Man in the Making: Facial Hair, Fashion and Medico-Social Construction of Masculinity in the Late Ottoman Society (1900–1920)', *Artuklu Human and Social Science Journal*, 1 (1): 46–54.
Farès, Bichr (1986–2000), 'Murūaʾ', in C. E. Bosworth, E. van Donzel, W. P. Heinrichs and Ch. Pellat (eds), *Encyclopaedia of Islam*, 2nd edn., 636–38 (*EI2)*, 13 vols, vol. 7, Leiden: Brill.
Foucault, Michel (1976), *Histoire de la sexualité I: La volonté de savoir*, Paris: Éditions Gallimard.
Geoffroy, Éric (2009), *Le soufisme: voie intérieure de l'islam*, Paris: Fayard.
Geries, Ibrahim (2015), 'Débat sur le Haschich dans les *maqāmas* d'Ibn al-Ḥaddād', in Mirella Cassarino and Antonella Ghersetti (eds), *Il dialogo nella cultura araba: strutture, funzioni, significati (VIII–XIII secolo)*, 107–21, Soveria Mannelli: Rubbettino.
Hattox, Ralph S. (1985), *Coffee and Coffeehouses: The Origins of a Social Beverage in the Medieval Near East*, Seattle, WA: University of Washington Press.
Juynboll, Gautier H. A. (2007), *Encyclopedia of Canonical Ḥadīth*, Leiden: Brill.
Karamustafa, Ahmet T. (2006), *God's Unruly Friends: Dervish Groups in the Islamic Middle Period 1200–1550*, London: Oneworld Publications.

Karamustafa, Ahmet T. (2014), 'Antinomian Sufi', in Lloyd Ridgeon (ed.), *The Cambridge Companion to Sufism*, 101–24, Cambridge: Cambridge University Press.
Kristeva, Julia (1982), *Powers of Horror: An Essay on Abjection*, trans. Leon S. Roudiez, New York: Columbia University Press.
Lane, Edward W. (1968), *Arabic-English Lexicon*, 2 vols, Beirut: Librairie du Liban.
Lozano Cámara, Indalecio (1991), 'Un texto inédito para la historia del *ḥašīš* en el mundo islámico: *Ikrām man ya 'īš bi-taḥrīm al-jamr wa-l-ḥašīš*, de Ibn al- 'Imād al-Aqfahsī', in *Homenaje al Profesor Jacinto Bosch Vilá*, 581–98, Granada: Universidad de Ganada, Departamento de Estudios Semíticos.
Marino, Danilo (forthcoming), 'Le plaisir de l'ivresse. Haschich et littérature homoérotique dans l'époque mamelouke', in Frédéric Lagrange (ed.), *Words of Desire: The Language of Arabic Erotica and its Translations*, Marseille: Diacritiques Editions.
Matthee, Rudi (2005), *The Pursuit of Pleasure: Drugs and Stimulants in Iranian History, 1500–1900*, Princeton, NJ: Princeton University Press.
Myrne, Pernilla (2014), 'Discussing *Ghayra* in Abbasid Literature: Jealousy as a Manly Virtue or Sign of Mutual Affection', *Journal of Abbasid Studies*, 1 (1): 46–65.
Natij, Salah (2017), '*Murū 'a*. Soucis et interrogations éthiques dans la culture arabe classique', *Studia Islamica*, 112: 206–63.
Natij, Salah (2018), '*Murū 'a*. Soucis et interrogations éthiques dans la culture arabe classique', *Studia Islamica*, 113: 1–55.
Rosenthal, Franz (1971), *The Herb: Hashish versus Medieval Muslim Society*, Leiden: Brill.
Sadan, Joseph (1977), 'Vin – fait de civilisation', in Myriam Rosen-Ayalon (ed.), *Studies in Memory of Gaston Wiet*, 129–60, Jerusalem: Hebrew University.
Shirazi, Faegheh (2008), 'Men's Facial Hair in Islam: A Matter of Interpretation', in Geraldine Biddle-Perry and Sarah Cheang (eds), *Hair: Styling, Culture and Fashion*, 111–22, Oxford: Berg.
Szombathy, Zoltan (2013), *Mujūn: Libertinism in Medieval Muslim Society and Literature*, Exeter: E. J. W. Gibb Memorial Trust.
van Gelder, Geert J. (2012), 'al-Badrī, Abū al-Tuqā', in Kate Fleet, Gudrun Krämer, Denis Matringe, John Nawas, Everett Rowson (eds), *Encyclopaedia of Islam 3*, Leiden: Brill. http://dx.doi.org/10.1163/1573-3912_ei3_COM_22909.
Watenpaugh, Heghnar Z. (2005), 'Deviant Dervishes: Space, Gender, and the Construction of Antinomian Piety in Ottoman Aleppo', *International Journal of Middle East Studies*, 37 (4): 535–65.
Wensinck, Arent Jan and Johan Peter Mari Mensing (eds) (1936–1969), *Concordance et indices de la tradition musulmane: Les six livres, le Musnad d'al-Dārimī, le Muwatta ' de Mālik, le Musnad de Ahmad Ibn Hanbal*, 8 vols, vol. 2, Leiden: Brill.

Chapter 4

THREE GENDERS, TWO SEXUALITIES: THE EVIDENCE OF OTTOMAN EROTIC TERMINOLOGY

İrvin Cemil Schick

During the second half of the twentieth century, the linguistic turn[1] made it possible (and meaningful) for historians to tackle subjects that, in past ages, they would have considered static simply by virtue of being 'natural'.[2] Thus, for example, when Marilyn Yalom published *A History of the Breast* in 1996,[3] it was immediately clear that her subject was not the site of the gland responsible in female primates for secreting milk to nourish infants, but rather the *meanings* ascribed to that organ over the course of human history. The fact that the various meanings with which the human female breast has been infused were socially constructed and have changed over time implies that the breast does indeed have a history – a cultural history. This is a notion that would have been nearly incomprehensible to historians a century ago.

A pioneer of this approach was, of course, Michel Foucault, who argued convincingly through his sizeable corpus that such notions as madness and sexuality were likewise socially constructed and therefore have histories of their own. His seminal *Histoire de la sexualité* (1976–1984),[4] which remained incomplete at the time of his death, investigated the development of sexuality as a discursive construct subject to society's intellectual vicissitudes. In particular, Foucault argued that 'homosexuality' is a modern construct – not, of course, in the sense that people did not engage in same-sex romantic or erotic relations in the past, but rather that what had been viewed merely as a practice came, during the nineteenth century, to be considered an innate nature, an identity:

> As defined by the ancient civil or canonical codes, sodomy was a category of forbidden acts; their perpetrator was nothing more than the juridical subject of them. The nineteenth-century homosexual became a personage, a past, a case history, and a childhood, in addition to being a type of life, a life form, and a morphology, with an indiscreet anatomy and possibly a mysterious physiology. Nothing that went into his total composition was unaffected by his sexuality. It was everywhere present in him. [...] Homosexuality appeared as one of the forms of sexuality when it was transposed from the practice of sodomy onto a kind of interior androgyny, a hermaphrodism of the soul. The sodomite had been a temporary aberration; the homosexual was now a species.[5]

Foucault has been criticized for being Eurocentric,[6] an accusation that, though factually correct, is not altogether fair since the main focus of his writing was always and avowedly Western Europe. Be that as it may, the absence of a global perspective in Foucault's work has left the door open for studies of lands and peoples outside Europe, and notably of the Muslim world. In this context, it is significant that Khaled el-Rouayheb chose to title his book *Before Homosexuality in the Arab-Islamic World, 1500–1800*.[7] Indeed, having been coined in or around 1868 by the Austro-Hungarian journalist and man of letters Károly Mária Kertbeny (formerly Karl-Maria Benkert, d.1882),[8] the German term *Homosexualität* is itself both modern and Western. This brings to mind the question of how people might have conceptualized what we now think of as homosexuality at a time when there was no word for it. Or perhaps this is the wrong question to ask. Should one then not speak instead of the 'invention' of homosexuality in late nineteenth-century Europe?[9]

That is in fact the idea underlying Rouayheb's analysis, at least for Arabic-speaking Muslims. Thus, he shows that the assessments of many Western Orientalists, from Sir Richard F. Burton to Bernard Lewis and beyond, concerning the ostensible prominence and acceptance of homosexuality in the Middle East and North Africa have been anachronistic, suffering as they did from the presentist presumption of the universal and transhistorical validity of a unitary notion of homosexuality.[10] Like several other scholars,[11] Rouayheb argues that pre- and early modern Arabic sources suggest the existence of a more nuanced, role- and age-differentiated view of same-sex relations. As Frédéric Lagrange puts it, 'the contemporary Western reader who has never perhaps questioned his holistic conception of homosexuality finds it "sliced up" into a multitude of role specializations, since medieval authors usually see no "community of desire" between, for instance, the active and the passive partners of homosexual intercourse'.[12] An examination of the sexual terminology used in Ottoman-era literature suggests that precisely the same held for Ottoman- and Turkish-speaking[13] Muslims, for whom 'homosexuality' as an all-embracing term covering partners male as well as female, young as well as old, active as well as passive, simply did not exist. Instead, the Ottoman language is extremely rich in highly specialized words that describe specific participants fulfilling specific roles.

Gender, sexuality and sexual orientation

Together with Helga Anetshofer and İpek Hüner-Cora of the University of Chicago, the present author has been working for some time on a dictionary of Ottoman erotic terminology.[14] While it has not been completed as of this writing, the vocabulary that has been compiled to date provides interesting evidence as to the historicity of sexual concepts and categories in the Ottoman- and Turkish-speaking Near East.

A sample of Ottoman and Early Anatolian Turkish texts ranging from the mid-fourteenth to the mid-nineteenth century have been surveyed in search of words of a sexual nature. The reason for limiting the chosen texts to pre-mid-nineteenth-century examples is that attitudes began to change fundamentally around that time, principally under European influence, so that new conceptions of gender and sexuality became normative in the course of cultural modernization, in Turkey as elsewhere.[15] The earliest texts surveyed include compilations of proverbs (e.g. *Oğuzname* [Book of Oğuz]), jokes (e.g. *Letâ'if-i Nasreddin Hoca* [Anecdotes of Nasreddin Hoca]) and tales (e.g. the anonymous *Ferec ba'de'ş-şidde* [Relief after Adversity] and *Dânişmend-nâme* [Book of Dânişmend]); later texts include medical-sexological treatises (e.g. various Ottoman translations/adaptations of *Rujū' al-Shaykh ilā Ṣibāh fī al-Quwwa 'alā al-Bāh* [Return of the Old Man to Youth Through the Power of Sex] commonly attributed to Kemâl Paşa-zâde, aka İbn Kemâl Paşa) and other works of prose (e.g. Deli Birâder's *Dâfi'ü'l-gumûm ve râfi'ü'l-humûm* [Repeller of Sorrows and Remover of Anxieties] and Cinânî's *Bedâyi'ü'l-âsâr* [Novelties]), as well as collections of poetry (e.g. Sünbül-zâde Vehbî's *Şevk-engîz* [Ardour-inducing] and Osman Sürûrî's *Hezliyyât* [Facetiae]).[16] Well over 650 words (nouns, verbs and metaphors) have been identified to date.

Although there is no doubt that this vocabulary is still not exhaustive, some very clear patterns have emerged, and they constitute the basis for the arguments put forward in the present essay.[17] In particular, the literature surveyed so far indicates that one can speak of three genders and two sexualities. First, rather than a male/female dichotomy, sources clearly view men, women and boys as three distinct genders.[18] Indeed, contrary to what some have assumed, boys are not deemed 'feminine', nor are they mere substitutes for women;[19] while they do share certain characteristics with them, such as the absence of facial hair, they are very clearly considered another gender.[20] Furthermore, since boys grow up to be men, gender can be fluid and in a sense every adult man is 'transgender', having once been a boy.

Second, sources suggest two distinct sexualities, but rather than a hetero/homosexual dichotomy, these sexualities are defined by penetrating or being penetrated.[21] For a man who penetrates, whom he penetrates was considered to be of little consequence and primarily a matter of personal taste. It is indeed significant that the words used for an active male's sexual orientation were quite devoid of value judgement: *matlab* (demands, wishes, desires), *meşreb* (temperament, character, disposition), *mezheb* (manner, mode of conduct, sect), *tarîk* (path, way, method, manner) and *tercîh* (choice, preference):

> Each travelled along a different path:
> One towards the public, the other, the private.
> They were two opposites in temperament;
> That is, each had a different mode of conduct.
> But sometimes those two obstinate opposites
> Would get together for a conversation.
> […]
> Clearly stating their desires,
> Recording their preferences and modes of conduct.[22]

The poem *Şevk-engîz* by Sünbül-zâde Vehbî (d.1224/1809), from which these lines are taken, is a debate between two men on the respective merits of sexual relations with women and with boys. It is quite symmetrical and non-judgemental, continuing a theme going back, through *Dâfi'ü'l-gumûm ve râfi'ü'l-humûm* by Deli Birâder (aka Mehmed Gazâlî, d. *c.* 942/1535) and *Kitāb Mufākharāt al-Jawārī wa-l-Ghilmān* (Book of praise for concubines and slave-boys) by al-Jāḥiẓ (d.255/869), to *Erōtes* (Lovers) by Lucian of Samosata (d. *c.* 180).[23]

In some cases, moreover, men were advised to switch between boys and women for reasons of health. Thus, a fifteenth-century Ottoman translation by Mercimek Aḥmed of the eleventh-century Persian book of counsel known as *Qābūs-nāma* (Book of Qābūs) advised its readers as follows:

> In the Summer, lean towards women, and in the Winter, towards boys, so as to be healthy. For a boy's body is warm, and two warms during the Summer will lead the body astray. And a woman's body is cold, and two colds during the Winter will dry up the body. And that is how it is.[24]

It is clear here that whether a man has sexual relations with boys or with women was not seen as determining of his essence or inner nature; he would be the penetrator in either case, and thus his sexuality did not depend on the gender of his partner.

Being penetrated, on the other hand, was a more complicated matter. While it was no dishonour for a boy to be penetrated, that was not true of a man. Indeed, qualifying a man as one who is penetrated was a common insult in satirical and polemical works: such a man was not viewed as akin to a juvenile; rather, he was considered feminized – also a common way of offending men. Thus, the poet Keşfî (d.945/1538–1539) belittled his colleague Vechî as follows:

> You're a black-faced hermaphrodite,[25] a crude rent-boy.
> Like a dog you become the enemy of whoever doesn't fuck you.
> Don't be hurt, O frequent fucker, if I don't fuck you.
> Is it your will to be the passive partner? I am not inclined toward that.
> [...]
> Moon-like, your black arse is a candlestick among the company.
> A thousand candles were stuck in [it], but your temperament didn't brighten.[26]

Here, the poet's references to his opponent as *hünsâ* (hermaphrodite, intersex), *kekez* (rent-boy, child prostitute)[27] and *mef'ûl* (object of an action, passive partner) all worked to cast aspersions on his manhood.

As this makes clear, a man who is penetrated was subject to opprobrium and ridicule. This confirms Rouayheb's contention that the so-called 'tolerance' of homosexuality often attributed to the Muslim world was in fact qualified. Relations between men and boys were not only tolerated, they were often praised, provided that they were experienced discreetly and with moderation;[28] relations between men and men, however, suffered severe social censure. But sexual relations between mature men and young boys are not considered homosexuality today, they are the domain of paedophilia (or at the very least of statutory rape). Thus, speaking of permissiveness towards 'homosexuality' in the context of Ottoman society is both anachronistic and misleading.

With the advent of Western-influenced heteronormativity during the nineteenth century, relations between men and boys also fell out of favour. In a much-quoted document entitled *Mârûzât* (Petitions) submitted to Sultan Abdülhamid II, the historian, statesman and jurist Ahmed Cevdet Pasha (d.1312/1895) wrote:

> Woman-lovers have increased in number, while boy-beloveds have decreased. It is as if the People of Lot have been swallowed by the earth. The love and affinity that were, in Istanbul, notoriously and customarily directed towards young men have now been redirected towards girls, in accordance with the state of nature. Among the notables, Kâmil Pasha and Âlî Pasha, so notorious as boy-lovers, and their followers are no more.[29]

The terms used here, such as *zen-dost* (woman-lover), *mahbûb* (boy-beloved) and *gulâm-pâre* (boy-lover), as well as several others, are discussed in greater detail in the sections that follow.

Boys

One might suppose that an indication of the significance of a concept for a given society may well be the wealth and internal consistency of the vocabulary corresponding to its various nuances. The suggestion that boys were considered a third gender in Ottoman society would seem to be borne out not only by the large number of words that signify boys as sexual objects but also by the ways in which they insistently differentiate boys from both men and women.

In the passage quoted above, Ahmed Cevdet Pasha mentioned the word *mahbûb* (from the Arabic *maḥbūb* = male beloved, from *ḥubb* = love), which was frequently used to denote a young boy who is the object of a man's romantic and/or erotic attention:

> There are those who love fresh flowerbuds of boy-beloveds, bashful and immature, with penises like ginger and testicles like walnuts …[30]

Taken from Deli Birâder's *Dâfi'ü'l-gumûm ve râfi'ü'l-humûm*, this passage is typical of its age, if rather more explicit than most. Indeed, it's not for nothing that Walter G. Andrews and Mehmet Kalpaklı titled their book on sixteenth-century Ottoman lyrical poetry *The Age of Beloveds*.[31]

The ideal age for boy-beloveds was described fairly precisely by Vehbî in his *Şevk-engîz*:

A new moon [shaped] like his eyebrows when a child,
He becomes a full moon when he reaches his fourteenth year.[32]
[...]
[First] a child, he becomes a beardless youth to play with;
Once his beard sprouts, playing with him goes bad.[33]

The word *emred* (from the Arabic *amrad*), which appears in the second couplet, signifies beardless youth and is a recurring theme in Ottoman – as well as Arabic and Persian – literature. Such boys were also called *sâde-rû* (from the Persian *sāda-rū* = clear-faced) or its Turkish equivalent, *yalın yüzlü*, as can be seen in the following lines from Sürûrî's (d.1229/1814) *Hezliyyât*:

Since the grief of the clear-faced ones has bent my back,
My beard sweeps the floor like a street broom.
[...]
Its glow was on the faces of the clear-faced ones.
My prick is the log that ignited the sphere of [their] buttocks.[34]

Between beardlessness and a mature beard is an intermediate stage, a boy with a freshly sprouting moustache (in Turkish, *bıyıkları yeni terlemiş*), which was considered quite erotic. This too was known by a term of Persian origin, *çâr-ebrû* (*chahār-abrū* = four eyebrows, i.e. two eyebrows and the two halves of a sparse moustache), and its Turkish equivalent, *dört kaşlu*. An example of the former is in a poem in Vehbî's *Dîvân* (Collected poetry):

In Isfahan, I watched a boy with four eyebrows
His lines resemble the hyacinths and gillyflowers of the Four Gardens.[35]

The first line of this couplet also features the word *püser* (from the Persian *pusar* = boy, son), which sometimes signifies catamite.

Other terms for a boy as sex-object included *civân* or *cüvân* (from the Persian *jawān* = young man), *gulâm* (from the Arabic *ghulām* = young man whose moustache is just sprouting),[36] *hîz* (from the Arabic *ḥīz* = catamite), *hûbân* (from the Persian *khūb* = beautiful, here pl.), *oğlan* (from the Old Turkic *oğul* = boy, son), *uşak* (from the Early Turkish *uşak* = little), *tâze* (from the Persian *tāza* = fresh, new, young), *puşt* (from the Persian *pusht* = back) and *vâsıla* (from the Arabic *wāṣala* = one who 'held communion, or commerce, of love').[37] A selection of couplets from Vehbî's *Şevk-engîz* illustrates some of these terms:

Know that the soul of the world is the young boy.
He turns the old lover into a young man.
[...]

When you get hold of such a young man,
Make sure you do not miss the opportunity of union [sex] with him.
[…]
Each was a leader in the kingdom of words;
From beginning to end, they sang the praises of boys.[38]

Sürûrî also used some of this vocabulary in his satires, including these two examples:

These days catamites are more favoured than poets who use language beautifully.
O Hevâyî, if only my arse were cleaner than your mouth![39]
[…]
Don't think that the number of catamites has decreased and that of pederasts increased.
Catamites have increased in number, and pederasts have decreased in relation to them.
Catamites and pederasts raced each other on the way to the house [domain] of fucking;
In the end, catamites got ahead and pederasts fell behind.[40]

Finally, another example from Deli Birâder, this time with the word *vâsıla*:

> 'Boyish masturbation' takes place during outings at the Hippodrome among bashful people. In such places, it sometimes happens that a glistening young boy comes next to a man, and the man loses control [lit. his faith softens] and grasps his [own] prick.[41]

These examples may be multiplied. The point is that boys were a well-defined category, and that they were distinguished not only from men but also from women. As Sürûrî wrote:

What is a woman-lover to do with a boy as pretty as a girl?
And what is a pederast to do with getting close to women?[42]

A boy may be as pretty as a girl, in other words, but he is no substitute for one when it comes to men who are partial to women. And the converse also holds true.

Men

Turning now to adult men who are sexually penetrated, the general tenor of poetic references to them can be inferred from the following couplet:

When pederasts become disabled they engage in [passive] homosexuality.
Every person gets punished, everyone gets his comeuppance.[43]

The word rendered here as '[passive] homosexuality', *ibnelik*, more often encountered as *ibne*, '(passive) homosexual', is derived from the Arabic *ubna* = 'fault, defect, or blemish', from *abana* = 'make an object of imputation, suspect of evil'.[44] Being a man who is penetrated is qualified here as a punishment for having once been a pederast. This is curious, since no negative judgement was generally attached to pederasty – at least in the domain of literature; nevertheless, these lines are significant for making explicit the contempt felt at the time towards a man who is penetrated. Deli Birâder described it as an 'ailment' for which intercourse was the only relief:

> For a pederast or a fornicator, fucking is another kind of wisdom;
> As for a (passive) homosexual (man), fucking cures his ailment.[45]

Indeed, another word for a passive male homosexual is *rencûr* (from the Persian *ranjūr* = sick, infirm, afflicted), whom Deli Birâder defined as follows:

> A *rencûr* is one who personally desires to be fucked, searches for men with large pricks and pays [them] aspers in order to get fucked by them.[46]

Other terms include *me'bûn* (from the Arabic *ma'būn* = one with whom wickedness is committed, also from *abana*) and *mukallib* (from the Arabic *muqallib* = that changes or turns, from *qalaba* = alter, change, turn around). For example:

> If young ones could not cure his afflication,
> Then he would need an old [passive] homosexual man.[47]

As the above examples make clear, men who are penetrated were generally scorned, unlike boys in the same role who were considered quite desirable. The role reserved for men was that of an omni-penetrator, in speaking of the two protagonists of *Şevk-engîz*, Vehbî mentioned:

> These two members of the blameworthy camp,
> That is, the woman-lover and the pederast …[48]

For placing their carnal desires above spiritual pursuits, both men were considered blameworthy, but equally so, for both were penetrators.

Pederasts – that is, men who have relations with boys – were variously known as *muğlim* (from the Arabic *mughlim* = 'excited by lust',[49] which shares a root with *ghulām*), *gulâm-pâre* (from the Arabo-Persian *ghulām-bāra* = friend of boys), *gulâmî* (from the Arabic *ghulāmī* = involved with boys), *mahbûb-perest* (from the Arabo-Persian *maḥbūb-parast* = male beloved-worshipper), *mahbûb-dost* (from the Arabo-Persian *maḥbūb-dost* = friend of male beloveds), *peçe-bâz* (from the Persian *bacha-bāz* = player with boys) and *püser-bâz* (from the

Persian *pusar-bāz* = player with boys). Some examples of the use of these terms follow. From Sürûrî:

> These days a kid would certainly offer his arse just for the spectacle,
> Were a pederast to show him a wren.[50]

From Vehbî:

> When hair becomes visible at his [the boy's] anus,
> Then a hair immediately grows in the pederast's eye.[51]

And from Deli Birader:

> O ascetic, do not blame me for loving catamites;
> For my master did not forbid me to play with boys.[52]

In short, men are of two kinds, those who penetrate and those who are penetrated. While the latter predilection was viewed as a defect, a blameworthy affliction, the former was considered the 'natural' state of affairs. The only exception was men who penetrate (adult) men, about whom reservations were sometimes voiced:

> Those who have this temperament [pederasts] blame and criticize those who like adolescents, saying that they love worthless fellows who have started to shave, so that their beloved boy turns into a porcupine if he lets the hairs on his arse grow, and into a rasp if he shaves them off.[53]

Note, however, that no moral judgement is implied in this criticism; the author is simply purporting to quote the opinion of men who prefer boys to young men. On the other hand, a negative value judgement was implied in a group of terms derived from the name of the Prophet Lūṭ, mentioned numerous times in the Qur'an. One of the sins for which the men of Sodom and Gomorrah were cursed and the cities destroyed was that they chose to 'approach men with lust rather than women'.[54] Thus, *lûtî* and *levvât* mean 'active' male homosexual, *livâta* means sodomy and the verb *televvut etmek* means to engage in sodomy. Deli Birader explains:

> If they should ask why sodomy is named *livâta*, say that this act first appeared among the people of the Prophet Lot. Satan taught it to Lot's people, because that accursed one wished for the people to go astray. For this reason, that ugly act [...] is named *livâta*.[55]

The part of his partner's anatomy a man penetrates could determine the term by which he would be known: *götçi* (arse-man, from the Turkish *göt* = arse), *künci* (likewise, from the Persian *kūn* = arse) and *kün-perest* (from the Persian *kūn-parast* = arse-worshipper), as opposed to *küs-bâz* (from the Persian *kus-bāz*

= cunt-player) and *küs-perest* (from the Persian *kus-parast* = cunt-worshipper). Other terms for men who are partial to women include *zen-pâre* (from the Persian *zan-bāra* = friend of women), *zen-dost* (from the Persian *zan-dūst* = one who cherishes women) and *zen-perest* (from the Persian *zan-parast* = woman-worshipper). For instance,

> O prisoners of the lustful carnal soul, and O owners of cunt-playing pricks that hold their heads high.[56]

Women

There is precious little in Ottoman art and literature by way of erotic and/or romantic relations *between* women. A rare example is Fâzıl Bey Enderûnî's (d.1225/1810) *Zenân-nâme* (Book of Women) – which has the distinction of being the first printed book to be banned by Ottoman authorities – where a same-sex scene at the women's public bath is briefly and only suggestively described.[57] Ottoman translations/adaptations of *Rujū' al-Shaykh ilā Ṣibāh fī al-Quwwa ʿalā al-Bāh*, attributed to Kemâl Paşa-zâde (d.940/1534), also contain some references, such as the story of how a woman who liked women was eventually convinced to abandon her ways and turn her attentions to men.[58]

Most terms used in Ottoman to denote women who engage in sexual relations with other women[59] are exact equivalents of the French *tribade*, that is, they refer to the act of rubbing or sometimes caressing. *Sahhâka* (from the Arabic *saḥḥāqa* = lesbian,[60] from *saḥaqa* = to pound, to pulverize)[61] *sevici* (Turkish for caresser, from *sevmek* = to caress), *sürtük* (Turkish for rubber, from *sürtmek* = to rub)[62] *tabak-zen* (from the Persian *ṭabaq-zan* = vulva striker, from *ṭabaq* = vulva)[63] and *mühre-zen* (from the Persian *muhra-zan* = burnisher). Some examples follow. From Sürûrî:

> A young beloved [a catamite] failed to perform on his wedding night.
> His wife said to that clear-faced one: 'You or me, what's the difference?'
> The whores gave his/her lover the following chronogram:
> 'The [passive] homosexual Ḥasan married his lesbian daughter to the catamite İsḥāḳ.'[64]

From Vehbî:

> Most are tribades, don't be fooled.
> A reasonable person does not like such tribades.
> [...]
> Those female burnishers rub themselves
> Up and down, just like hermaphrodites.
> Know that there are many lesbians,
> A dildo like a donkey's penis in their midsection [in their loins].[65]

One final example, from a slightly later date, is the following amusing couplet describing the poetess Leylâ Hanım (d.1264/1848), said to have been composed during her lifetime by a bookseller named Hâtif Efendi:

> The previous Leylâ was the tent-pitcher of her age;
> The present Leylâ Hanım is the burnisher of her age.[66]

In all these examples, lesbians are characterized by friction rather than penetration, and on those rare occasions where penetration is mentioned, it is by a dildo. It would not be a stretch to suggest that lesbianism was not viewed in Ottoman literature as a distinct sexuality, but rather as the absence of one: they were simply considered women who choose not to be penetrated.

On the other hand, 'straight' women – to use an anachronistic term – were characterized by being the object of penetration. Thus,

> Whenever you catch a woman, shove your prick into her.
> Don't scare her, flatter her with soft words, and thus shove it into her.
> [...]
> Is this a pine-tree? Is it an obelisk? What an ugly prick!
> A boy couldn't eat it, perhaps womenfolk [lit. virgins and mares] might be able to swallow it.[67]

Of course, those men who preferred the company of boys were quick to point out a likely result of penetrating women:

> Do not get yoked and become a seed-scatterer,
> A dizzy beast of burden for ploughing the fields of women.[68]

Furthermore, boys are preferable, they argued, being more faithful and truer:

> They do not know tricks and wiles like deceitful women, nor do they take multiple lovers and act inconstantly.[69]

There is, of course, a good deal of misogyny in Ottoman literature, and this offered the opportunity to condemn sexual relations with women just as often as with others. For example, the pederast in Vehbî's *Şehr-engîz* says:

> O wretched [lit. homeless] blatherer,
> Do not build a house on the path of a flood [i.e. penetrate a vagina].
> A man must be disposed towards a man.
> One who is not a man [i.e. one who is cowardly and contemptible] merits a woman.[70]

In other words, 'real' men do it with men rather than women; this is quite a change from the homophobic discourse generally prevailing today.

It is worth noting that although the women's role was defined as being penetrated, this does not mean that they were viewed as passive objects with no agency of their own. In fact, Ottoman literature is replete with stories of women who seek pleasure, often at the expense of men. To give but one example:

> But a woman whom her husband has divorced or has died, and who has gone on to another man; if his mace [penis] has a thicker base than the previous one and a larger and heavier head, or if his mace has strong semen, then the idea of her former husband will leave her.[71]

In many cases, women's sexual desire was even considered excessive and dangerous to men.

Indeed, women who assumed the role of pursuer rather than prey were often frowned upon.[72] The late fifteenth-century poetess Mihrî (d. *c.* 917/1512), for instance, was not shy about expressing her desires:

> Since I saw you, dear lord of beauties, in your neighbourhood
> I no longer desire Paradise and have given up on pretty boys
> [...]
> O Hatemî, you falsely passed as Mihrî's lover
> But by God, Mihrî loves you better than any boy.[73]

With what would appear to be grudging admiration, the biographer Âşık Çelebi noted in 1568 that:

> Though a woman, that non-man could kick many a brave man [...]. Her penmanship was a girl's needlework [but] her literary composition was whorish. Saying 'A male lion is a lion, is a female lion not a lion too?' she was not above playing with boys.[74]

That this was considered 'unfeminine' and therefore less than appropriate, however, is evident from the following comment about Mihrî in Latîfî's biographical dictionary (1546):

> Though the coquettishness of her poetry is woman-like and the style of her speech feminine, from the viewpoint of burning and being consumed [with passion] it is [male] lover-like and in the expression of passion and courting it is masculine, not feminine.[75]

In other words, 'active' women, like 'passive' men, could be subject to a certain degree of social censure.

Conclusion

In a notorious section of the 'Terminal Essay' that appeared in the first edition of his translation of the *Thousand and One Nights* (1886), Sir Richard F. Burton described what he called 'The Sotadic Zone' as encompassing both shores of the Mediterranean Sea, the Middle East, Central and South Asia, as well as the entire New World. There, he claimed, 'the Vice is popular and endemic, held at the worst to be a mere peccadillo'.[76]

While Burton did go on to speak specifically of pederasty, that is, of sexual relations between adult men and boys, his reference to 'the Vice' was widely taken to apply to homosexuality as the term is understood today. Whether credulous or critical, many readers and commentators have thus interpreted Burton as saying that homosexuality is widespread and socially accepted in broad regions of the world, notably the Middle East. As a number of scholars have recently pointed out, particularly in relation to the Arab world, this is a fundamental misunderstanding caused by presentism.

This chapter reviewed the vocabulary used in a limited but representative set of Ottoman literary sources to describe gendered and sexual concepts.[77] While it is very difficult, if not impossible, to determine what real people were actually doing behind closed doors, language goes a long way towards showing how they *thought* about what they did. The vocabulary surveyed here suggests that men and boys were considered distinct genders, and that sexuality was defined not by the gender of one's partner but by whether one penetrates or is penetrated.

A man who penetrates was not shamed or disgraced, regardless of his partner, provided that he exercised discretion and moderation; a man who is penetrated, on the other hand, was viewed with the deepest contempt. Being objects of penetration, boys and women were not considered quite as noble as men, but as sexual partners one was not more estimable than the other. Rather, which category a man favoured was viewed merely as a matter of personal taste.

On the one hand, the idea that having sexual intercourse with another man does not necessarily make one a 'homosexual' so long as he is the one who does the penetrating persists in Turkey today, notably among many of those who patronize transgender sex workers.[78] On the other, Ottoman literature has been used by Kemalists to belittle and delegitimize both the *Ancien Régime* and those seen today as their contemporary followers by painting Ottomans as degenerate and sexually 'deviant'.[79] The cultural context revealed here may prove beneficial both in interpreting studies of contemporary sexual mores and in re-evaluating the claims of republican ideologues.

Notes

Abridged versions of this chapter were presented at Pembroke College, University of Cambridge, and CETOBaC, École des Hautes Études en Sciences Sociales. I am grateful to Fabio Giomi, Sertaç Şehlikoğlu and Ece Zerman for making that possible, and to Serkan Delice and the participants in these seminars for their generous and incisive comments. I also thank Edith Gülçin Ambros, Helga Anetshofer, Esra Egüz, Didem Z. Havlioğlu, İpek Hüner-Cora, Ali Emre Özyıldırım, Pelin Tünaydın and Aslı Zengin, as well as the editors, for giving me the benefit of their thoughts and opinions.

1 The term 'linguistic turn' refers to a philosophical current that has centred language. Although it is traceable to the late nineteenth and early twentieth centuries (notably, the works of Ludwig Wittgenstein, Bertrand Russell and Ferdinand de Saussure), its influence in the humanities and social sciences dates primarily from the second half of the twentieth century and is associated with the movement known as post-structuralism.

2 The adoption of the concept of 'gender' to signify the sociocultural constructs that supplement the purely biological factor of sex (Joan W. Scott, 'Gender: A Useful Category of Historical Analysis', *American Historical Review*, 91 [5] [1986]: 1053–75), and the placement of the word 'race' between quotation marks to emphasize the arbitrariness of the sociocultural constructs that supplement the purely biological factor of skin colour (Henry Louis Gates Jr, 'Editor's Introduction: Writing "Race" and the Difference It Makes', *Critical Inquiry*, 12 [1] [1985]: 1–20) are two notable examples of this trend. But there are numerous other instances that, though perhaps less theoretically developed, have shed new light upon aspects of human existence once thought to be 'natural' and hence previously unproblematized.

3 Marilyn Yalom, *A History of the Breast* (New York: Alfred A. Knopf, 1996).

4 Michel Foucault, *Histoire de la sexualité*, 3 vols (Paris: Éditions Gallimard, 1976–1984).

5 Michel Foucault, *The History of Sexuality*, vol. 1, *An Introduction*, trans. Robert Hurley (New York: Vintage Books, 1980), 43.

6 Edward W. Said, 'Michel Foucault, 1927–1984', *Raritan*, 4 (2) (1984): 1–11; Robert J. C. Young, 'Foucault on Race and Colonialism', *New Formations*, 25 (1995): 57–65; Stephen Legg, 'Beyond the European Province: Foucault and Postcolonialism', in Jeremy W. Crampton and Stuart Elden (eds), *Space, Knowledge and Power: Foucault and Geography*, 265–88 (Aldershot: Ashgate, 2007).

7 Khaled el-Rouayheb, *Before Homosexuality in the Arab-Islamic World, 1500–1800* (Chicago, IL: University of Chicago Press, 2005).

8 Manfred Herzer, 'Kertbeny and the Nameless Love', *Journal of Homosexuality*, 12 (1) (1986): 1–26; Judit Takács, 'The Double-Life of Kertbeny', in Gert Hekma (ed.), *Past and Present of Radical Sexual Politics*, Working Papers, Fifth Meeting of the Seminar 'Socialism and Sexuality', 26–40, Amsterdam, 3–4 October 2003 (Amsterdam: Mosse Foundation, 2004).

9 Robert Beachy, 'The German Invention of Homosexuality', *Journal of Modern History*, 82 (4) (2010): 801–38.

10 Serena Tolino, 'Homosexuality in the Middle East: An Analysis of Dominant and Competitive Discourses', *DEP: Deportate, Esuli e Profughe*, 25 (2014): 72–91, notes that this tendency continues to this day in Samar Habib, *Female Homosexuality in the Middle East: Histories and Representations* (New York: Routledge, 2007) and Scott Siraj al-Haqq Kugle, *Homosexuality in Islam: Critical Reflection on Gay, Lesbian, and Transgender Muslims* (Oxford: Oneworld Publications, 2010), to which we could add many of the contributions to Stephen O. Murray and Will Roscoe, *Islamic Homosexualities: Culture, History, and Literature* (New York: New York University Press, 1997) and Samar Habib (ed.), *Islam and Homosexuality*, 2 vols (Santa Barbara, CA: Praeger, 2010). Certain other authors, by contrast, are more cautious,

questioning the applicability of this terminology to the Middle East and stressing its historical and cultural specificity, notably el-Rouayheb, *Before Homosexuality*, as well as Bruce Dunne, 'Homosexuality in the Middle East: An Agenda for Historical Research', *Arab Studies Quarterly*, 12 (1990): 55–83; Arno Schmitt, 'Liwāṭ im fiqh: männliche Homosexualität?', *Journal of Arabic and Islamic Studies*, 4 (3) (2001–2002): 49–110; Joseph A. Massad, *Desiring Arabs* (Chicago, IL: University of Chicago Press, 2007); and Afsaneh Najmabadi, 'Types, Acts or What? Regulation of Sexuality in Nineteenth-Century Iran', in Kathryn Babayan and Afsaneh Najmabadi (eds), *Islamicate Sexualities: Translations across Temporal Geographies of Desire*, 275–96 (Cambridge, MA: Center for Middle Eastern Studies, 2008).

11 Everett K. Rowson, 'The Categorization of Gender and Sexual Irregularity in Medieval Arabic Vice Lists', in Julia Epstein and Kristina Straub (eds), *Body Guards: The Cultural Politics of Gender Ambiguity*, 50–79 (New York: Routledge, 1991); Thomas Bauer, *Liebe und Liebesdichtung in der arabischen Welt des 9. und 10. Jahrhunderts: eine literatur- und mentalitätsgeschichtliche Studie des arabischen Ġazal* (Wiesbaden: Otto Harrassowitz, 1998), 163–74.

12 Frédéric Lagrange, 'The Obscenity of the Vizier', in Kathryn Babayan and Afsaneh Najmabadi (eds), *Islamicate Sexualities: Translations across Temporal Geographies of Desire*, 161–203 (Cambridge, MA: Center for Middle Eastern Studies, 2008), 162. Lagrange goes on to argue that satirical works may be said to create a homosexual 'identity' for their targets, but I disagree. It seems to me that the men derided as 'passive homosexuals' in such polemical works are no more endowed with an identity than if they had instead been called idiots or liars or thieves. An identity signifies membership in a socially meaningful imagined community; these are not identities, they are merely invectives.

13 The Ottoman language combines elements of Turkish, Arabic and Persian but is considerably more than the sum of its parts. It was by and large the language of the elite in the Ottoman Empire (1299–1923) and is no longer a living language. Turkish was and remains the language spoken by many of the common people in the area that roughly corresponds to present-day Turkey, as well as parts of the Balkans and the Levant. Muslim Ottoman culture was deeply influenced by Arab culture, but it is also worth remembering that a significant portion of post-medieval Arab culture was itself produced within the geographical boundaries of the Ottoman Empire.

14 Although Anetshofer and Hüner-Cora declined to be co-authors of this chapter due to other commitments, the research underlying the arguments presented here was conducted jointly.

15 Afsaneh Najmabadi, *Women with Mustaches and Men Without Beards: Gender and Sexual Anxieties of Iranian Modernity* (Berkeley, CA: University of California Press, 2005); Joseph A. Massad, *Desiring Arabs* (Chicago, IL: University of Chicago Press, 2007); Serkan Delice, '"Zen-dostlar Çoğalıp Mahbûblar Azaldı": Osmanlı'da Toplumsal Cinsiyet, Cinsellik ve Tarihyazımı', in Cüneyt Çakırlar and Serkan Delice (eds), *Cinsellik Muamması: Türkiye'de Queer Kültür ve Muhalefet*, 329–63 (Istanbul: Metis Yayınları, 2012); İrem Özgören Kınlı, 'Reconfiguring Ottoman Gender Boundaries and Sexual Categories by the mid-19th Century', *Política y Sociedad*, 5 [2] (2013): 381–95.

16 Ottoman words are transcribed according to the conventions of modern Turkish; Arabic and Persian words are transcribed according to the rules established by the *International Journal of Middle East Studies*.

17 Note that we are speaking here of societal perceptions and not of religious precepts. On the specifically religious/legal background of same-sex relations in Islam, see, for example, Schmitt, 'Liwāṭ im fiqh: männliche Homosexualität?'; Frédéric Lagrange, *Islam d'interdits, islam de jouissance* (Paris: Téraèdre, 2008): 125–33; Sara Omar, 'From Semantics to Normative Law: Perceptions of *Liwāṭ* (Sodomy) and *Siḥāq* (Tribadism) in Islamic Jurisprudence (8–15th Century CE)', *Islamic Law and Society*, 19 (2012): 222–56; Serena Tolino, 'Homosexual Acts in Islamic Law: *Siḥāq* and *Liwāṭ* in the Legal Debate', in Hatem Elliesie, Peter Scholz and Beate Backe (eds), *Gesellschaft für Arabisches und Islamisches Recht: Mitteilungen 2014*, 187–205 (2014). Available online: http://www.qucosa.de/fileadmin/data/qucosa/documents/15352/GAIR-Mitteilungen_2014.pdf (accessed 2 March 2017); and Jonathan Brown, 'A Pre-Modern Defense of the Hadiths on Sodomy: an Annotated Translation and Analysis of al-Suyuti's *Attaining the Hoped-for in Service of the Messenger(s)*', *American Journal of Islamic Social Sciences*, 34 (3) (2017): 1–44.

18 For a different context, see, for example, the exhibition catalogue Joshua S. Mostow and Asato Ikeda, with the assistance of Ryoko Matsuba, *A Third Gender: Beautiful Youths in Japanese Edo-Period Prints and Paintings (1600–1868)* (Toronto: Royal Ontario Museum, 2016). In recent years, we have come to view gender increasingly as not dimorphous nor even polymorphous but a continuum; and it is no doubt true that both gender and sexuality *as actually experienced by individual human beings* constitute continua. But a continuum is of limited use as an analytical category. Any classificatory system is a discrete (and preferably finite) collection of representations. When one speaks of gender in the context of politics, economics or social policy, one cannot help thinking primarily in discrete categories rather than in terms of an infinity of gradations. By the same token, to speak of three genders in Ottoman (or Japanese) culture is not to deny that real life is much more complex; these are merely a representation, at an appropriate level of abstraction, of experienced reality.

19 Abdülhamit Arvas is right to criticize the claim that boys were merely a substitute for the unavailable Ottoman women (Abdulhamit Arvas, 'From the Pervert, Back to the Beloved: Homosexuality and Ottoman Literary History, 1453–1923', in E[llen] L. McCallum and Mikko Tuhkanen [eds], *The Cambridge History of Gay and Lesbian Literature* [New York: Cambridge University Press, 2014], 147–49). On the other hand, it makes no sense to suggest, as he does, that attributing the near-universality of pederasty in Ottoman literature to gender segregation would be tantamount to 'naturalizing heterosexuality'. It is one thing to claim that an individual poet, say, Nedim (d.1143/1730), wrote about boys only because he had no access to women; it is something else altogether to seek historical reasons that might explain the overwhelming predominance of the theme across elite Ottoman culture as a whole. The suggestion that the near totality of Ottoman lyrical poetry was homoerotic simply because that was the native sexual orientation of every single Ottoman poet would strain credibility. Surely there were societal and cultural factors at work here, as there would have been had all Ottoman poetry instead featured a heterosexual bent. The fact that homoeroticism was much less prevalent in popular rural literature than in its elite urban counterpart gives strong – even if not conclusive – support to the hypothesis that gender segregation (which was always much more stringent in urban, upper-class settings) may have provided the impetus for the pervasiveness of pederasty in Ottoman classical literature.

20 In this respect, my findings do not confirm Abdallah Cheikh-Moussa's hypothesis that medieval Islamic society could be viewed as composed of two genders, namely bearded men and everyone else (including women, boys and eunuchs). See

Abdallah Cheikh Moussa, 'Ǧāḥiẓ et les eunuques, ou La confusion du même et de l'autre', *Arabica*, 29 (2) (1982): 184–214. I should note, in passing, that the subject of eunuchs well deserves careful treatment but is beyond the scope of the present chapter.

21 Cf. Schmitt, 'Liwāṭ im fiqh: männliche Homosexualität?'.

22 'Her biri başka tarîka pûyân / biri ʿâma birisi hâssa revân / böyle zıddeyn idiler meşrebde / yaʿnî kim her biri bir mezhebde / gâh ammâ o iki zıdd-ı ʿanîd/ cemʿ olub eyler idi güft ü şinîd / [...] / fikr-i tevzîh ile matlablarını / kayd-ı tercîh ile mezheblerini' (Sünbül-zâde Vehbî, *Şevk-engîz*, ed. Ahmet Yenikale [Kahramanmaraş: Ukde Kitaplığı, 2011], 67). All translations are mine, unless indicated otherwise.

23 Franz Rosenthal, 'Male and Female: Described and Compared', in J[erry] W. Wright Jr and Everett K. Rowson (eds), *Homoeroticism in Classical Arabic Literature*, 24–54 (New York: Columbia University Press, 1997); Jan Schmidt, 'Sünbülzāde Vehbī's *Şevk-engīz*, an Ottoman Pornographic Poem', *Turcica. Revue d'études turques*, 25 (1993): 9–37. Schmidt's use of the adjective 'pornographic' is unfortunate as well as inapt.

24 'Ve yaz olıcak avretlere meylet ve kışın oğlanlara, tâ ki tendürüst olasın. Zira ki oğlan teni ıssıdır, yazın iki ıssı bir yere gelse teni azıdur ve avret teni sovuktur, kışın iki sovuk bir yere gelse teni kurudur, vesselâm' (Keykâvus [ʿUnşur al-Maʿālī Kaykāvūs ibn Iskandar ibn Qābūs], Orhan Şaik Gökyay (ed.), *Kabusname*, trans. Mercimek Ahmed, 2nd edn. [Istanbul: Milli Eğitim Basımevi, 1966], 113). It is noteworthy, and more than a little amusing, that this passage was completely excised from a privately produced edition of Qābūs-nāma published in the 1970s in a series entitled '1001 Canonical Works' (Attilâ Özkırımlı [ed.], [ʿUnşur al-Maʿālī Kaykāvūs ibn Iskandar ibn Qābūs], *Kâbusnâme*, [trans.] İlyasoğlu Mercimek Ahmed, 2 vols [(Istanbul): Tercüman 1001 Temel Eser, n.d.], 1:188), even though it was present in a state-sponsored edition that appeared some three decades earlier.

25 I realize that this term is considered offensive by some, but the poet's intention here and in the example given later is clearly just that.

26 'Bir kara yüzlü hünsâ hâm-sıfat kekezsin / it big[i] her ki sikmez olursın ana düşmen / incinme ey sikişgen ger sikmesem sen[i] ben / mefʿûl mı irâde meyl itmezem inen ben / [...] / bir şemʿdândur ay tek meclisde kara götün / bin mûm sokıld[ı] tabʿun olmad[ı] lîk rûşen' (Edith Gülçin Ambros, 'On a Conventional Dimension of 16th Century Scurrilous Ottoman Satire: Keşfī's [d. 945/1538–9] Hicviyyāt', in *Life, Love and Laughter: In Search of the Ottomans' Lost Poetic Language. A Collective Volume in Memory of Arne A. Ambros* [Istanbul: The Isis Press, 2015], 513). The translation follows Ambros's, with some alterations, in particular, Ambros has 'ey tek'; I am grateful to Esra Egüz for suggesting this alternative reading, in which the candlestick is likened to the moon for shedding light upon the assembly and the man's posterior likewise for its roundness.

27 [Franciscus à Mesgnien] Meninski, *Thesaurus linguarum orientalium Turcicae-Arabicae-Persicae = Lexicon Turcico-Arabico-Persicum*, 6 vols (İstanbul: Simurg, 2000), 3986.

28 Needless to say, one should be wary of overstating this point: many jurists railed against the corrupting influence of young boys. What is significant, however, is that similar warnings were often voiced about women, and both practices were commonly qualified as *zinā'* (fornication). In other words, the problem was generally a believer's straying from spiritual pursuits and engaging in unsanctioned sex, not his doing so specifically with boys. See, for example, Rowson, 'The Categorization of Gender and Sexual Irregularity'.

29 'Zen-dostlar çoğalıp mahbûblar azaldı. Kavm-i Lût sanki yere batdı. İstanbul'da öteden beri delikanlılar için maʿrûf ve muʿtad olan aşk u alâka, hâl-i tabiʿisi üzre

kızlara müntakil oldu. Küberâ içinde gulâm-pârelikle meşhûr Kâmil ve Âlî Paşalar ile anlara mensûb olanlar kalmadı' (Ahmet Cevdet Paşa, *Ma'rûzât*, ed. Yusuf Halaçoğlu [Istanbul: Çağrı Yayınları, 1980], 9).

30 'Bir tâ'ife vardur ki mahbûbun tazesin ve gonçesin utancağın ve böncesin zencebîl çükcesin ve ceviz daşaklucasın sevüb ...' ([Deli Birader aka Mehmed Gazâlî] Selim S. Kuru, 'A Sixteenth-Century Scholar, Deli Birader, and His *Dāfi'ü'l-ġumūm ve rāfi'ü'l-humūm*', PhD dissertation [Department of Near Eastern Languages and Civilizations, Harvard University, 2000], 77).

31 Walter G. Andrews and Mehmet Kalpaklı, *The Age of Beloveds: Love and the Beloved in Early-Modern Ottoman and European Culture and Society* (Durham, NC: Duke University Press, 2005). On this subject, see also İsmet Zeki Eyuboğlu, *Divan Şiirinde Sapık Sevgi* (Istanbul: Okat Yayınevi, 1968); Halit Erdem Oksaçan, *Sultanlar Devrinde Oğlanlar* (Istanbul: Agora Kitaplığı, 2014); Arvas, 'From the Pervert, Back to the Beloved'; Rıza Zelyut, *Osmanlı'da Oğlancılık* (Istanbul: Kaynak Yayınları, 2016). On Ottoman sexual discourses more generally, see Dror Ze'evi, *Producing Desire: Changing Sexual Discourse in the Ottoman Middle East, 1500–1900* (Berkeley, CA: University of California Press, 2006).

32 By the lunar calendar, the moon is full on the fourteenth day of the month.

33 'Tıfl iken kaşı gibi ol hilâl / bedr olur varıcak on dördine sâl / [...] / tıfl iken oynayıcaķ emred olur / sakalı bitse oyunu bed olur' (Vehbî, *Şevk-engîz*, 83, 95).

34 'Sâde-rûlar gamı ham eyleyeli kametimi / süpürür yirleri çârûb-ı sokakdur sakalım / [...] / âteşi urdı yalın yüzlilerin rûyına kim / küre-i kûni tutuşdurmuş odundır yarağım' ([Osman Sürûrî], 'Afâllahu 'an seyyi'âtihi Hezliyyât-ı Sürûrî merhûm', no publication information, 15, 52).

35 'İsfahân'da çâr-ebrû bir püser seyr eyledim / hattı benzer çâr-bâğın sünbül ü şeb-bûsına' (Sünbül-zâde Vehbî, *Dîvân*, ed. Ahmet Yenikale [Kahramanmaraş: Ukde Kitaplığı, 2011], 505). In Ottoman poetry, the word *hat* (from the Arabic *khaṭṭ* = line; also script) often meant the silky down or 'peach fuzz' on a boy's face. The Four Gardens, *Chahār-Bāgh*, is a famous royal park near Isfahan.

36 Edward William Lane, *Arabic-English Lexicon* (London: Willams & Norgate, 1863), 2286.

37 Ibid., 3055.

38 'Nev-cüvândır bilesin cân-ı cihân / 'âşık-ı pîri ider tâze-cüvân / [...] / ele girdikde hemân öyle cüvân / fırsat-ı vuslatı fevt itme amân / [...] / her biri milk-i sühande server / ser-be-ser eylediler medh-i püser' (Vehbî, *Şevk-engîz*, 81, 87, 89, 95).

39 'Şimdi oğlan mu'teberdür şâ'ir-i hoş-lehceden / ey Hevâyî kâşki pâk olsa ağzından götüm' ([Sürûrî], *'Afâllahu 'an seyyi'âtihi Hezliyyât-ı Sürûrî merhûm*, 54). Hevâyî was the pen name used by Sürûrî in his satirical poetry.

40 'Sanma kim puşt azalub şimdi çoğaldı muğlim / çoğalub puşt ana nisbetle azaldı muğlim / itdi muğlimle yarış 'azm-ı sikiş-hânede puşt / 'âkıbet puşt oni geçdi giri kaldı muğlim' (ibid., 50).

41 'Calk-ı gulâmî At Meydânı seyrânında ve utancak âdamla yanında olur bunun gibi mahallerde gâh olur gişinün yanına bir garrâ vâsıla gelür imânı gevrer hemân sikin kavrar ...' (Deli Birâder, 'A Sixteenth-Century Scholar, Deli Birader', 131).

42 'Zen-pâre kız gibi güzel oğlanı neylesün / muğlim dahı takarrüb-i nisvânı neylesün' ([Sürûrî], *'Afâllahu 'an seyyi'âtihi Hezliyyât-ı Sürûrî merhûm*, 30).

43 'İbnelik eyler 'amel-mânde olınca muğlimân / her kişi görür mücâzât itdigin elbet bulur' (ibid., 37).

44 Lane, *Arabic-English Lexicon*, 9–10.

45 'Muğlim ü zânî yanında başka ʿirfândur sikiş / ibnenün ise hele derdine dermândur sikiş' (Deli Birâder, 'A Sixteenth-Century Scholar, Deli Birader', 46).

46 'Rencûr ana dirler ki sikilmegi bi'z-zât murâd ide büyük siklüler araya akçeler virüb gendüyi sikdire' (Deli Birâder, 'A Sixteenth-Century Scholar, Deli Birader', 138). On passive male homosexuality as a 'disease', see also Franz Rosenthal, 'ar-Râzî on the Hidden Illness', *Bulletin of the History of Medicine*, 52 (1) (1978): 45–60.

47 'Tâzeler derdine itmezse ʿilâc / köhne me'bûne olurdı muhtâc' (Vehbî, *Şevk-engîz*, 62).

48 'Bu iki şahs-ı melâmî-mezheb / yaʿnî zen-dost u gulâmî-meşreb' (Vehbî, *Şevk-engîz*, 109).

49 Lane, *Arabic-English Lexicon*, 2286.

50 'Seyrine zemâne çocuğı göt virir elbet / gösterse gulâm-pâre ana bokluca bülbül' ([Sürûrî], ʿAfâllahu ʿan seyyi'âtihi Hezliyyât-ı Sürûrî merhûm', 56). Wrens are small, brown songbirds. The Turkish word for wren, *bokluca bülbül*, literally means 'shitty nightingale', that is – metaphorically – a soiled penis.

51 'Halkasında dahı mûy olsa ʿayân / kıl biter çeşm-i gulâmîde hemân' (Vehbî, *Şevk-engîz*, 96). There is a subtle play on words here. *Gözünde kıl bitmek*, 'for a hair to grow in one's eye', is a Turkish expression of Persian origin that signifies great suffering. Thus, when the boy becomes hairy, it causes the pederast much grief. I am grateful to Ali Emre Özyıldırım for this interpretation.

52 'Zâhidâ oğlan seversin diyü taʿn itme bana / kim püser-bâz olmadan menʿ itmedi pîrüm benüm' (Deli Birâder, 'A Sixteenth-Century Scholar, Deli Birader', 88).

53 'Bu meşrebe tâbiʿ olan tâ'ife güzeşte sevenlere tırâşı gelmiş kürrezler sever sevdügi oğlan göti kılın korsa kirpiye kazır ise törpüye döner diyü taʿn u taʿrîz iderler' (Deli Birâder, 'A Sixteenth-Century Scholar, Deli Birader', 77).

54 Q 26.165–66, 27.54–5.

55 'Eger dirler ise livâtaya livâta didikleri niçündür eyit-ki evvel bu fiʿl Lût peygamber kavminden zâhir oldı Şeytân kavm-i Lûta gösterdi ol melʿûn halkun azduğın isterdi anunçün ol fiʿl-i kabîḥ [...] nâmına livâta dirler' (Deli Birâder, 'A Sixteenth-Century Scholar, Deli Birader', 103).

56 'Ey esîr-i nefs-i şehvet-sâz ve'y sâhibân-ı kîrân-ı küs-bâz ü ser-ferâz ...' (Deli Birâder, 'A Sixteenth-Century Scholar, Deli Birader', 46).

57 [Enderûnî Fâzıl Bey], *Defter-i Aşk, Hûbân-nâme, Zenân-nâme, Çengî-nâme*; Vehbî Bey, *Şevk-engîz* (Istanbul: Dârü't-Tıbaʿâti'l-ʿÂmire, 1253), 94–6.

58 'Efendim bu câriyeniz evâ'il hâlimde sahhâkalığa yeltenür idim baʿzı zarîfe hâtûnlar ile beraber görüşüb ...' (Sir, in the past your humble servant tried her hand at lesbianism; I frequented some gracious ladies ...) (*Bâh-nâme*, lithographed, no publication information [Istanbul, 1836–1878], 30). It is noteworthy that this detail is not present in the Arabic original. Both the French and the English translations interpret the word *sahhâka* (see below) literally: *polisseuse* (Abdul-Haqq Effendi, trans., *Le Livre de volupté [Bah Nameh]*, [Erzeroum: Qizmich-Aga, n.d.] [actually Brussels: Jules Gay, 1878–1879], 30); *polisher* ([İbn Kemâl Paşa], *The Secrets of Women; being the Second Part of 'The Old Man Young Again'* [Paris: Charles Carrington, 1899], 124).

59 In the text that follows I use the term 'lesbian' for brevity and not because I do not think that it needs to be problematized.

60 It is noteworthy that the more common Arabic term is *musāḥiqa* rather than *saḥḥāqa*. Both terms are derived from the same root.

61 Edward William Lane, *Arabic-English Lexicon* (London: Willams & Norgate, 1863), 1319.

62 In modern Turkish, *sürtük* has acquired the meaning 'street-walker'. It no longer appears to be used for lesbians.
63 Francis Joseph Steingass, *A Comprehensive Persian-English Dictionary, including the Arabic Words and Phrases to be met with in Persian Literature* (London: Routledge & Kegan Paul, 1892), 809.
64 'Bağlu çıkdı gerdeğe girdükde bir mahbûb uşak / kim dimiş ol sâde-rûya zevcesi ha ben ha sen / rûsbılar oynaşına muʿcemle târîhin didi / virdi puşt İshâka sahhâka kızın ibne Hasan' ([Sürûrî], ʿAfâllahu ʿan seyyi'âtihi Hezliyyât-ı Sürûrî merhûm', 82). The chronogram is said to be *muʿjam*, that is, it is calculated from the dotted letters only.
65 'Çoğı sahhâkadır olma gafil/ öyle sürtükleri sevmez ʿâkıyl / [...] / sürter ol mühre-zenân-ı ünsâ / zîr ü bâlâda misâl-i hünsâ / bil ki var nice tabak-zen nisvân/ kîr-i har gibi zıbık da be-miyân' (Vehbî, *Şevk-engîz*, 106–07).
66 'Leylâ-i pîşîn idi hayme-zen-i rûzigâr / şimdiki Leylâ Hanım mühre-zen-i rûzigâr' (Mehmed Zihnî, *Meşahîrü'n-nisâ*, 2 vols [Istanbul: Dârü't-tıbâʿati'l-ʿâmire, 1294–1295], 2:195). The play on words here is centred on the Persian suffix *-zan*, which means 'one who strikes'. Thus, *khayma-zan* is Persian for one who strikes (pitches) a tent, a reference to the fact that Leylâ of *Laylī u Majnūn* fame was an Arabian tribeswoman. At the same time, however, the word 'tent' signifies penile erection; thus, the first line of the poem stresses the fact that Leylâ had sexual relations with men. On the other hand, *muhra-zan* is Persian for 'burnisher', emphasizing the fact that the contemporary Leylâ Hanım was a lesbian.
67 'Gancuk elüne her ne zaman geçse yarak bas / ürkütme mülayim söz ile oğşayarak bas / [...] / çam-mudur bu dikilü taş-mu ne çirkün bi yarak / bunu oğlan yeyemez belkü yudar gız gısurak' ([ʿAbdülhalîm] Galib Paşa, *Mutâyyebât-ı Türkiyye*, lithographed, no publication information, 27, 33).
68 'Olma çifte koşulub tohm-efşân / gav-ı ser-geşte-i hars-ı nisvân' (Vehbî, *Şevk-engîz*, 91). This interestingly echoes the pejorative term used these days by some gays and lesbians for straight people: 'breeders'.
69 'Kahbe ʿavratlar gibi hîle ve hudʿa bilmezler bir nice oynaş dutuban hercâ'îlik kılmazlar' (Deli Birâder, 'A Sixteenth-Century Scholar, Deli Birader', 105).
70 Didi ey hâne-harâb-ı gep-zen / reh-i sîl-âbda yapma mesken / merd olan eyleye merde rağbet / şahs-ı nâ-merde sezâdır ʿavret' (Vehbî, *Şevk-engîz*, 80).
71 'Ammâ şol ʿavrat ki eri boşamış ya ölmiş ola andan bir gişiye dahı gelmiş ola eger evvelkisinden altı dibi yoğun başı sallı ağır gürze ya beli pek gürze râst gelürse eski erinün fikri içinden çıkar' (Deli Birâder, 'A Sixteenth-Century Scholar, Deli Birader', 52).
72 I am grateful to Didem Z. Havlioğlu for drawing my attention to the case of the 'active' woman and for the examples that follow, from her *Mihri Hatun: Performance, Gender-Bending, and Subversion in Early Modern Ottoman Intellectual History* (Syracuse, NY: Syracuse University Press, 2017).
73 'Göreli kûyında cânum sen güzeller şâhını / kalmadı rıdvâna meylüm geçmişem gılmândan / [...] / sen yalandan Hâtemî âşık geçersün Mihrîye / sümme vallâhi seni Mihrî [yeğ] sever oğlandan' ([Mihrî] Mikhri-Khatun, *Divan: Kriticheskij tekst i vstupitel'naja stat'ja*, ed. E[lena] I[nnokent'evna] Mashtakova [Moscow: Izdatel'stvo 'Nauka', 1967], 184–85. The translation follows Havlioğlu's, with some alterations.)
74 'Egerçi zendür ammâ ol nâ-merd niçe merd-i meydâna cüfte-zendür [...] ve yazısı kız nakşı ve inşâsı rûspiyânedür erkek arslan arslan dişi arslan arslan degül mi diyü şâhid-bâzlıkdan hâlî degül imiş' (Âşık Çelebi, *Meşâʿirü'ş-Şuʿarâ: İnceleme-Metin*, ed. Filiz Kılıç, 3 vols [Istanbul: İstanbul Araştırmaları Enstitüsü, 2010], 2:832–33). The term translated here as 'playing with boys' is the Persian *shāhid-bāzī*. This concept (also

known as *naẓar-bāzī*) is based upon the mystical practice of meditating by focusing on the beauty of God's creation (Leonard Lewisohn, 'Prolegomenon to the Study of Ḥāfiẓ 2: The Mystical Milieu: Ḥāfiẓ's Erotic Spirituality', in Leonard Lewisohn (ed.), *Hafiz and the Religion of Love in Classical Persian Poetry*, 3–73 [London: I.B.Tauris and the Iran Heritage Foundation, 2010], 42–51; Cyrus Ali Zargar, *Sufi Aesthetics: Beauty, Love, and the Human Form in the Writings of Ibn ʿArabi and ʿIraqi* [Columbia, SC: University of South Carolina Press, 2011], 85–119). For some Sufis, however, the object of contemplation soon became a beautiful boy and the term took the meaning of pederasty. As Mihrî is reputed to have died a virgin, here the 'playing' may have been fairly innocent.

75 'Egerçi işve-i eşʿârı zenâne ve şîve-i güftârı müʾennesânedür ammâ cihet-i sûz u güdâzda ʿâşıkane ve beyân-ı şevk u niyâzda merdânedür ne müʾennesânedür' (Latîfî, *Tezkiretüʾş-Şuʿarâ ve Tabsıratüʾn-Nuzamâ [İnceleme-Metin]*, ed. Rıdvan Canım [Ankara: Atatürk Kültür Merkezi Başkanlığı, 2000], 510).

76 Richard F. Burton (trans.), *A Plain and Literal Translation of The Arabian Nights' Entertainments, Now Entituled The Book of the Thousand Nights and a Night* (London: Burton Club, 1886), 10:207.

77 To date the Ottoman language has not been given the recognition it deserves for providing a direct, indeed intimate, channel into people's thoughts and perceptions. For a noteworthy exception, see Marinos Sariyannis, '"Mobs", "Scamps" and Rebels in Seventeenth-Century Istanbul: Some Remarks on Ottoman Social Vocabulary', *International Journal of Turkish Studies*, 11 (1–2) (2005): 1–15.

78 Hüseyin Tapınç, 'Masculinity, Femininity, and Turkish Male Homosexuality', in Kenneth Plummer (ed.), *Modern Homosexualities: Fragments of Lesbian and Gay Experiences*, 39–49 (London: Routledge, 1992); Tarık Bereket and Barry D. Adam, 'The Emergence of Gay Identities in Contemporary Turkey', *Sexualities*, 9 (2) (2006): 131–51.

79 İdris Muhtefi [pseud.], 'Mahbuplar Saltanatı', serialized in *İnkılâp*, 1 (5–14 January 1931): 126–35; Eyuboğlu, *Divan Şiirinde Sapık Sevgi*; Zelyut, *Osmanlıʾda Oğlancılık*.

References

Abdul-Haqq Effendi (trans.) (n.d.), *Le Livre de volupté (Bah Nameh)*, Erzeroum: Qizmich-Aga [Brussels: Jules Gay, 1878–1879].

Ahmet Cevdet Paşa (1980), *Maʿrûzât*, ed. Yusuf Halaçoğlu, Istanbul: Çağrı Yayınları.

Ambros, Edith Gülçin (2015), 'On a Conventional Dimension of 16th Century Scurrilous Ottoman Satire: Keşfî's (d. 945/1538–9) Hicviyyāt', in *Life, Love and Laughter: In Search of the Ottomans' Lost Poetic Language; A Collective Volume in Memory of Arne A. Ambros*, 503–26, Istanbul: The Isis Press.

Andrews, Walter G. and Mehmet Kalpaklı (2005), *The Age of Beloveds: Love and the Beloved in Early-Modern Ottoman and European Culture and Society*, Durham, NC: Duke University Press.

Arvas, Abdulhamit (2014), 'From the Pervert, Back to the Beloved: Homosexuality and Ottoman Literary History, 1453–1923', in E[llen] L. McCallum and Mikko Tuhkanen (eds), *The Cambridge History of Gay and Lesbian Literature*, 145–63, New York: Cambridge University Press.

Âşık Çelebi (2010), *Meşâ'irü'ş-Şu'arâ: İnceleme-Metin*, ed. Filiz Kılıç, 3 vols, Istanbul: İstanbul Araştırmaları Enstitüsü.
Bâh-nâme (*c*. 1836–1878), lithographed, no publication information, [Istanbul].
Bauer, Thomas (1998), *Liebe und Liebesdichtung in der arabischen Welt des 9. und 10. Jahrhunderts: eine literatur- und mentalitätsgeschichtliche Studie des arabischen Ġazal*, Wiesbaden: Otto Harrassowitz.
Beachy, Robert (2010), 'The German Invention of Homosexuality', *Journal of Modern History*, 82 (4): 801–38.
Bereket, Tarık and Barry D. Adam (2006), 'The Emergence of Gay Identities in Contemporary Turkey', *Sexualities*, 9 (2): 131–51.
Brown, Jonathan (2017), 'A Pre-Modern Defense of the Hadiths on Sodomy: an Annotated Translation and Analysis of al-Suyuti's *Attaining the Hoped-for in Service of the Messenger(s)*', *American Journal of Islamic Social Sciences*, 34 (3): 1–44.
Burton, Richard F. (trans.) (1886), *A Plain and Literal Translation of The Arabian Nights' Entertainments, Now Entituled The Book of the Thousand Nights and a Night*, London: Burton Club.
Cheikh Moussa, A[bdallah] (1982), 'Ǧāḥiẓ et les eunuques, ou La confusion du même et de l'autre', *Arabica*, 29 (2): 184–214.
[Deli Birâder aka Mehmed Gazâlî] Selim S. Kuru (2000), 'A Sixteenth-Century Scholar, Deli Birader, and His *Dāfi'ü'l-ġumūm ve rāfi'ü'l-humūm*', PhD dissertation, Department of Near Eastern Languages and Civilizations, Harvard University.
Delice, Serkan (2012), '"Zen-dostlar Çoğalıp Mahbûblar Azaldı": Osmanlı'da Toplumsal Cinsiyet, Cinsellik ve Tarihyazımı', in Cüneyt Çakırlar and Serkan Delice (eds), *Cinsellik Muamması: Türkiye'de Queer Kültür ve Muhalefet*, 329–63, Istanbul: Metis Yayınları.
Dunne, Bruce, (1990), 'Homosexuality in the Middle East: An Agenda for Historical Research', *Arab Studies Quarterly*, 12: 55–83.
Eyuboğlu, İsmet Zeki (1968), *Divan Şiirinde Sapık Sevgi*, Istanbul: Okat Yayınevi.
[Fâzıl Bey, Enderûnî] (1253), *Defter-i Aşk, Hûbân-nâme, Zenân-nâme, Çengî-nâme*; Vehbî Bey, *Şevk-engîz*, Istanbul: Dârü't-Tıba'âti'l-'Âmire.
Foucault, Michel (1976–1984), *Histoire de la sexualité*, 3 vols, Paris: Éditions Gallimard.
Foucault, Michel (1980), *The History of Sexuality*, vol. 1, *An Introduction*, trans. Robert Hurley, New York: Vintage Books.
Galib Paşa, ['Abdülhalîm] (n.d.), *Mutâyyebât-ı Türkiyye*, lithographed, no publication information.
Gates, Henry Louis Jr (1985), 'Editor's Introduction: Writing "Race" and the Difference It Makes', *Critical Inquiry*, 12, 1: 1–20.
Habib, Samar (2007), *Female Homosexuality in the Middle East: Histories and Representations*, New York: Routledge.
Habib, Samar (ed.) (2010), *Islam and Homosexuality*, 2 vols, Santa Barbara, CA: Praeger.
Havlioğlu, Didem Z. (2017), *Mihri Hatun: Performance, Gender-Bending, and Subversion in Early Modern Ottoman Intellectual History*, Syracuse, NY: Syracuse University Press.
Herzer, Manfred (1986), 'Kertbeny and the Nameless Love', *Journal of Homosexuality*, 12 (1): 1–26.
[İbn Kemâl Paşa] (1899), *The Secrets of Women; being the Second Part of 'The Old Man Young Again'*, Paris: Charles Carrington.
İdris Muhtefi [Pseud.] (1931), 'Mahbuplar Saltanatı', serialized in *İnkılâp*, 1 (5–14 January): 126–35.

Keykâvus [ʿUnṣur al-Maʿālī Kaykāvūs ibn Iskandar ibn Qābūs] (1966), Orhan Şaik Gökyay (ed.), *Kabusname*, trans. Mercimek Ahmed, 2nd edn., Istanbul: Milli Eğitim Basımevi.
Kugle, Scott Siraj al-Haqq (2010), *Homosexuality in Islam: Critical Reflection on Gay, Lesbian, and Transgender Muslims*, Oxford: Oneworld Publications.
Lagrange, Frédéric (2008), *Islam d'interdits, Islam de jouissance*, Paris: Téraèdre.
Lagrange, Frédéric (2008), 'The Obscenity of the Vizier', in Kathryn Babayan and Afsaneh Najmabadi (eds), *Islamicate Sexualities: Translations across Temporal Geographies of Desire*, 161–203, Cambridge, MA: Center for Middle Eastern Studies.
Lane, Edward William (1863), *Arabic-English Lexicon*, London: Willams & Norgate.
Latîfî (2000), *Tezkiretü'ş-Şuʿarâ ve Tabsıratü'n-Nuzamâ (İnceleme-Metin)*, ed. Rıdvan Canım, Ankara: Atatürk Kültür Merkezi Başkanlığı.
Legg, Stephen (2007), 'Beyond the European Province: Foucault and Postcolonialism', in Jeremy W. Crampton and Stuart Elden (eds), *Space, Knowledge and Power: Foucault and Geography*, 265–88, Aldershot: Ashgate.
Lewisohn, Leonard (2010), 'Prolegomenon to the Study of Ḥāfiẓ 2: The Mystical Milieu: Ḥāfiẓ's Erotic Spirituality', in Leonard Lewisohn (ed.), *Hafiz and the Religion of Love in Classical Persian Poetry*, 3–73, London: I.B.Tauris and the Iran Heritage Foundation.
Massad, Joseph A. (2007), *Desiring Arabs*, Chicago, IL: University of Chicago Press.
Mehmed Zihnî (1294–95), *Meşahîrü'n-nisâ*, 2 vols, Istanbul: Dârü't-tıbâʿati'l-ʿâmire.
Meninski, [Franciscus à Mesgnien] (2000), *Thesaurus linguarum orientalium Turcicae-Arabicae-Persicae = Lexicon Turcico-Arabico-Persicum*, 6 vols, İstanbul: Simurg.
[Mihrî] Mikhri-Khatun (1967), *Divan: Kriticheskij tekst i vstupitel'naja stat'ja*, ed. E[lena] I[nnokent'evna] Mashtakova, Moscow: Izdatel'stvo 'Nauka'.
Mostow, Joshua S. and Asato Ikeda, with the assistance of Ryoko Matsuba (2016), [exhibition catalogue] *A Third Gender: Beautiful Youths in Japanese Edo-Period Prints and Paintings (1600–1868)*, Toronto: Royal Ontario Museum.
Murray, Stephen O. and Will Roscoe (1997), *Islamic Homosexualities: Culture, History, and Literature*, New York: New York University Press.
Najmabadi, Afsaneh (2005), *Women with Mustaches and Men Without Beards: Gender and Sexual Anxieties of Iranian Modernity*, Berkeley, CA: University of California Press.
Najmabadi, Afsaneh (2008), 'Types, Acts or What? Regulation of Sexuality in Nineteenth-Century Iran', in Kathryn Babayan and Afsaneh Najmabadi (eds), *Islamicate Sexualities: Translations across Temporal Geographies of Desire*, 275–96, Cambridge, MA: Center for Middle Eastern Studies.
Oksaçan, Halit Erdem (2014), *Sultanlar Devrinde Oğlanlar*, Istanbul: Agora Kitaplığı.
Omar, Sara (2012), 'From Semantics to Normative Law: Perceptions of *Liwāṭ* (Sodomy) and *Siḥāq* (Tribadism) in Islamic Jurisprudence (8–15th Century CE)', *Islamic Law and Society*, 19: 222–56.
Özgören Kınlı, İrem (2013), 'Reconfiguring Ottoman Gender Boundaries and Sexual Categories by the mid-19th Century', *Política y Sociedad*, 5 (2): 381–95.
Özkırımlı, Attilâ (ed.) (n.d.), [ʿUnṣur al-Maʿālī Kaykāvūs ibn Iskandar ibn Qābūs], İlyasoğlu Mercimek Ahmed, [trans.]. *Kâbusnâme*, 2 vols, [Istanbul]: Tercüman 1001 Temel Eser.
Rosenthal, Franz (1978), 'ar-Râzî on the Hidden Illness', *Bulletin of the History of Medicine*, 52 (1): 45–60.
Rosenthal, Franz (1997), 'Male and Female: Described and Compared', in J[erry] W. Wright, Jr and Everett K. Rowson (eds), *Homoeroticism in Classical Arabic Literature*, 24–54, New York: Columbia University Press.

el-Rouayheb, Khaled (2005), *Before Homosexuality in the Arab-Islamic World, 1500–1800*, Chicago, IL: University of Chicago Press.

Rowson, Everett K. (1991), 'The Categorization of Gender and Sexual Irregularity in Medieval Arabic Vice Lists', in Julia Epstein and Kristina Straub (eds), *Body Guards: The Cultural Politics of Gender Ambiguity*, 50–79, New York: Routledge.

Said, Edward W. (1984), 'Michel Foucault, 1927–1984', *Raritan*, 4 (2): 1–11.

Sariyannis, Marinos (2005), '"Mobs", "Scamps" and Rebels in Seventeenth-Century Istanbul: Some Remarks on Ottoman Social Vocabulary', *International Journal of Turkish Studies*, 11 (1–2): 1–15.

Schmidt, Jan (1993), 'Sünbülzāde Vehbī's *Şevk-engīz*, an Ottoman Pornographic Poem', *Turcica. Revue d'études turques*, 25: 9–37.

Schmitt, Arno (2001–02), 'Liwāṭ im fiqh: männliche Homosexualität?', *Journal of Arabic and Islamic Studies*, 4 (3): 49–110.

Scott, Joan W. (1986), 'Gender: A Useful Category of Historical Analysis', *American Historical Review*, 91 (5): 1053–75.

Steingass, Francis Joseph (1892), *A Comprehensive Persian-English Dictionary, including the Arabic Words and Phrases to be met with in Persian Literature*, London: Routledge & K. Paul.

[Sürûrî, Osman], *ʿAfâllahu ʿan seyyiʾâtihi Hezliyyât-ı Sürûrî merhûm*, no publication information.

Takács, Judit (2004), 'The Double-Life of Kertbeny', in Gert Hekma (ed.), *Past and Present of Radical Sexual Politics*, Working Papers, Fifth Meeting of the Seminar 'Socialism and Sexuality', 26–40, Amsterdam, 3–4 October 2003, Amsterdam: Mosse Foundation.

Tapınç, Hüseyin (1992), 'Masculinity, Femininity, and Turkish Male Homosexuality', in Kenneth Plummer (ed.), *Modern Homosexualities: Fragments of Lesbian and Gay Experiences*, 39–49, London: Routledge.

Tolino, Serena (2014), 'Homosexual Acts in Islamic Law: *Siḥāq* and *Liwāṭ* in the Legal Debate', in Hatem Elliesie, Peter Scholz and Beate Backe (eds), *Gesellschaft für Arabisches und Islamisches Recht: Mitteilungen 2014*, 187–205. Available online: http://www.qucosa.de/fileadmin/data/qucosa/documents/15352/GAIR-Mitteilungen_2014.pdf (accessed 2 March 2017).

Tolino, Serena (2014), 'Homosexuality in the Middle East: An Analysis of Dominant and Competitive Discourses', *DEP: Deportate, Esuli e Profughe*, 25: 72–91.

Vehbî, Sünbül-zâde (2011), *Dîvân*, ed. Ahmet Yenikale, Kahramanmaraş: Ukde Kitaplığı.

Vehbî, Sünbül-zâde (2011), *Şevk-engîz*, ed. Ahmet Yenikale, Kahramanmaraş: Ukde Kitaplığı.

Yalom, Marilyn (1996), *A History of the Breast*, New York: Alfred A. Knopf.

Young, Robert J.C. (1995), 'Foucault on Race and Colonialism', *New Formations*, 25: 57–65.

Zargar, Cyrus Ali (2011), *Sufi Aesthetics: Beauty, Love, and the Human Form in the Writings of Ibn ʿArabi and ʿIraqi*, Columbia, SC: University of South Carolina Press.

Ze'evi, Dror (2006), *Producing Desire: Changing Sexual Discourse in the Ottoman Middle East, 1500–1900*, Berkeley, CA: University of California Press.

Zelyut, Rıza (2016), *Osmanlı'da Oğlancılık*, Istanbul: Kaynak Yayınları.

Part II

SUBVERTING THE SEXUAL NORM IN MODERN ARAB CULTURAL PRODUCTIONS

Chapter 5

EROS AND ETIQUETTE: REFLECTIONS ON THE BAN OF A CENTRAL THEME IN NINETEENTH-CENTURY ARAB WRITINGS

Nadia Al-Bagdadi

On the disappearance of Arabic erotic writings in the nineteenth century

As in other areas too, the Arab nineteenth century, characterized by colonial modernity, marks a turning point for Arabic *ars erotica* and its final repression. The profound transformative processes of modernization were reflected in the disappearance of those sites of discourse, both literary and other types, which traditionally dealt with *eros*, sexuality and social etiquette (*adab*). In addition to libertine and obscene poetry (*mujūn*), this also included love poetry (*ghazal*)[1] as well as the whole spectrum of erotic handbooks and philosophical treatises on the various forms of love – physical and spiritual.[2] Whether the banning of this central theme of Arabic writing was due to the presence of a critical 'view from outside' alone, or whether this disappearance reflected the continuation and final triumph of a current in Arabic literature and practice can at this point of my research only be proposed as a question and needs further interdisciplinary research.

This chapter will discuss the assertion of new forms of representation as well as new moral standards and sexual taboos that emerged during the Arab nineteenth century in tandem with a radically changing discourse about *ars erotica*. I shall attempt to clarify, firstly, the question of why a traditionally central theme, not only of the relevant erotic handbooks and literature but also of ethical and juridical writings, was superseded by a type of (non-)representation and prudery in written literature.[3] This will be achieved by a short reference to the historic dimension and genealogy of the Arab-Islamic literary genre and discourse on this theme as well as to the reactions to exogenous influences and the colonial, European view. Secondly, the chapter will engage with some of the classical keywords and metaphors used in this field of literary, moral and ethical literature. Finally, with reference to selected literary writings, the chapter highlights how, through this very theme and topos, we are able to illustrate elements of an entangled history between the European and Arab gaze, between observer and observed. This entanglement develops as a conscious, deliberately mutual reaction to each other: the changing attitudes towards eros and etiquette are deeply, but not exclusively, impacted upon by the

European experience and by colonial practices. Eros and etiquette, though studied here in literary testimonies, define a social space in which the representation of sex and sexual relationships – both homo- and heterosexual – relate to forms of social practices. That this examination of the profound change in *ars erotica* and the treatment of the theme of eros in the Arabic nineteenth century is to some degree based on a small body of textual evidence must be ascribed to the still fragmentary nature of the research in available sources.[4]

Ideas of eros and etiquette and representation of physicality, visibility and invisibility diverged sharply in the European and Arab worlds in the nineteenth century. Hence it is a historical irony that the pictures and projection screens of oriental painters, which in their naturalistic style suggest a mimetic representation, arise precisely in that historical moment in which in the thus 'portrayed world' itself forms of representation are changing in the opposite direction. While the great oriental painters and travellers conjure a world of oriental sensuality and permissiveness, both intoxicating and lasciviously cryptic, Arabic representations of sex and sexuality and the relationship of the sexes are moving away from this. Presented as a medium of seduction in the famous oriental female portraits of such European painters as Delacroix, Gérôme or Ingres, the *material veil* is instead of marginal importance as a theme of Arabic observations in the nineteenth century, even in the writings of important female Arabic authors such as ʿĀʾisha Taymūr (1840–1902) or Zaynab Fawwāz (1860–1914). Only towards the end of the century, particularly with the publication of Qāsim Amīn's famous writing *Taḥrīr al-marʾa* (*The Liberation of Woman and the New Woman,* 1899), in which the removal of the veil is posited as a condition of modernity, do the veil or veiling become themes relevant to political and literary discourse. Authors such as the Egyptian women's rights advocate Malak Ḥifnī Nāṣif (1886–1918) begin to deal also with the veil as a social practice, as an expression of cultural identity, and, with regard to the possibility of forbidding the veil, as a political question.

Eros and etiquette: The centrality of a philosophy of desire

The history of sexuality in the Arab world in general, and in particular the fracture with the Arabic *ars erotica*, still requires fundamental study. Although the question of whether the disappearance of Arabic *ars erotica* is due to those processes that were described for the European context of modernization and rationalization as subjective internalization in terms of Foucault is evident,[5] the following remarks must in this regard remain to some extent hypothetical. In order to make an attempt in this direction nonetheless, this chapter links two questions from critical dialectic and from a perspective of *entangled history*. On the one hand, it concerns the question of change or continuity and reconfiguration in the representation of eros, which finally led to the disappearance of the entire literary and semi-literary genres of erotological or similar nature. On the other hand, it concerns forms of social comparison and thereby the rise of dichotomous opposites ('we' vs 'them', 'own' vs 'foreign', etc.) that increasingly lead to hyperbolic confrontations in the field of moral and sexual behaviour expressed in such stereotypical categories as oriental–occidental, Islamic–Christian or masculine–feminine. This leads to the associated question of to what degree colonial relations in the nineteenth century influenced this process of reinterpretation of eros and the displacement of the value assigned to sexuality. This directly concerns the interaction of colonial circumstances and the continuance of Arabic theories of vision and scrutiny. This article is concerned primarily with the observers (not the observed) and the relation between observing subject and the observed object.

To illustrate the change in *ars erotica*[6] in the Arab nineteenth century and the subsequent break with tradition, a review of traditional Arabic forms of eros and the associated etiquette is necessary. These correlate with neither the image of the veiled woman and an Arab-Islamic society abstinent from any physical contact, if not positively hostile to contact, nor at the other extreme, the stereotype of the steamy atmosphere of the harem. Instead, social practices as well as various forms of representation display a very liberal discussion of sexual needs and eroticism, even if nevertheless conflictual when compared with later behaviour. Thus, it is precisely the centrality of this discourse that characterizes the Arab tradition of *ars erotica*. This observation is based on both the social function of *ars erotica* and the extensive treatment of this theme in non-erotological texts and genres.

The presentation of love and passion, seduction and rejection deals with the most elementary human needs and experiences such as fertility and reproduction or loss and death.[7] The spectrum of literature, both elite and popular, and the discourse about them stretch over a broad variety of genres, from pertinent erotological handbooks with their mixture of medical advice and sexual education through philosophical treatises to obscene anecdotic literature inclined to graphic detail. In the presentation of sexuality and relationships between the sexes, Arabic *ars erotica* is restricted to language and the word, written and spoken. Visual representations are virtually unknown in the Arab-Islamic world,[8] in contrast to Indian erotology, for example, which influenced Arabic erotology in other ways, not only through *The Book of the Thousand Nights and a Night* (*1001 Nights*).[9] In response, it would appear, Arabic erotology developed a unique linguistic repertoire and its own meta-language, as well as an extremely complex and multilayered intertextuality. Although still treated as marginalia of Arabic literature and literary studies,[10] erotic texts (*mujūn* and to some extent *ghazal*) occupy a central place in Arabic writings; including the thematically related and mutually referencing erotological handbooks and genres which, measured by the number of books printed, appear to be extremely popular.[11]

The naked and often intentionally provocative treatment of sex and sexual fantasies in this literature, which recognized few taboos, was frequently greeted not only with approbation but also with rejection or defensive reactions. This aspect of Arabic writing appeared particularly to Europeans as its greatest defect. Notoriously, Richard Burton (d.1890), the British Orientalist and translator of *1001 Nights*, banished the 'objectionable parts' to the footnotes – despite his obvious enthusiasm for the oriental works of *ars erotica*.[12]

As in Arabic love poetry the ideal of an ascetic love and ungratified desire was contrasted with physical union. From the twelfth century onwards, classical Arabic writings are characterized by radical anti-erotological criticism. It is to some degree a natural part of erotological discourse that tendencies opposed to the inherent dangers of free sexual and sensual intercourse soon developed and strengthened. The sociologist Abdelwahab Bouhdiba, whose study *La Sexualité en Islam*[13] remains the main general reference work in this field,[14] describes in summary this development as a regressive development from a previously relatively free and open society to a society increasingly subject to religious-conservative pressure.

But this view appears to reflect only one aspect and only one part of the literature in question. Certainly, in the twelfth century, currents that were opposed directly to *ars erotica* predominated. That these currents and works themselves serve as a platform for erotic discussion against uncontrolled desire and exaggeration of not merely physical love, belongs to one of the paradoxes of anti-erotic strategies, not only in the Arab world.

In view of the lack of systematic analysis and historiographic study of divergent strands in the field of Islamic law, certain tendencies, at times more stringent, at others more complying, can be ascertained but require further substantiation. However, strong directions can be discerned among Ḥanbalī jurists who tried to protect the individual and society from the assumed dangers arising from such unrestrained works. Scholars such as Ibn al-Jawzī (d.597/1200) and Ibn Qayyim al-Jawziyya (d.751/1350) should be mentioned here, while later on, the Egyptian theologian and adherent of the Shafiʿī school of law al-Suyūṭi (d.911/1505), for example, also advanced similar views. Here, a tendency appears based on a different concept of love, sexuality and desire, which seem to criticize and condemn directly and indirectly the theories of love and sexuality found in *ars erotica*. Whether discourses in legal and ethical and literary writings emerged in an interwoven fashion or in parallel remains to be shown. This led to a development in which that legal strand of anti-erotic discourse became an integral part of the erotic discourse itself and defines one of its specificities. The recognition of the ambivalent character or dual nature of eros, famously coined as 'bittersweet' by the Greek poetess Sappho, resurfaces ambivalently in Ibn al-Jawzī's Ḥanbalī view of non-divine love, *Dhamm al-Hawā* (Contra Passionem), and in his collection of prayers. To warn against erotic and love experiences described plainly and graphically in the great erotological anthologies, he reproduces, i.e. quotes, those at length and in detail.[15] For Ibn al-Jawzī, passion itself is to be condemned, as is its propagation. It's the Devil's work. Passion always ends tragically and painfully for the lovers, with unforeseeable consequences. Therefore, the argument continues, passion enslaves mankind and blinds its will. While Ibn al-Jawzī's *Contra Passionem* represents a strand of Ḥanbalī tendencies, Ibn Qayyim al-Jawziyya attempts a synthesis of al-Kharāʾiṭī's (d.327/939) erotological handbook *Iʿtilāl al-Qulūb* (Concerns of Hearts) and Ibn al-Jawzī's *Contra Passionem*. The theologian and muftī Ibn Qayyim al-Jawziyya offers in his book *Rawḍat al-Muḥibbīn wa-Nuzhat al-Mushtāqīn* (Garden of Lovers) a coherent theory of love and eros. Their goal is to find fulfilment on earth, but the ultimate goal, however, lies in the love of God. The *Garden of Lovers* strives to unite a good measure of earthly love and sexual joy with the advantages of the highest love, which lies in the worship of God (*'ibāda*). This differentiates this form of synthesis both from mystical ideas of love, whose highest fulfilment lies in union with God, and from those tendencies of *ars erotica* which concern solely physical and sexual fulfilment.

The grammar of unveiling

Secret and revelation are among the fundamental ideas of monotheistic religions. The victory march of Neoplatonic veil metaphors, advanced by the late antique philosophers, from Pseudo-Dionysius to Origen, did not halt before Muslim thinkers. The rigorous distinction between truth found at the surface and truth to be sought in the depth, or higher, echelons defines one of the most powerful figures of thought, describing as it does a practice of delimitation or discrimination, discrimination between the great mass of those in need of religion and those, usually the few, who arrive at truth by virtue of reason. Andalusian twelfth-century scholars such as Ibn Rushd (Averroes, d.595/1198) vividly describes this fundamental distinction in his treatise *Faṣl al-Maqāl*[16] (On the Harmony of Religion and Philosophy), as well as Ibn Ṭufayl (d.581/1185) in his allegorical parable on the life of *Ḥayy Ibn Yaqẓān* (Alive, Son of Awakening). This insight also plays a role in erotic poetry and the philosophy of desire, and developed into an idiosyncratic symbolic language and semiotic that seeks to discriminate between appearance and real-being and reality.

Thus, in dual fashion the transmission of 'truth' acquired specific relevance in different types of writing. Physical sexual dimensions expressed or depicted in realistic fashion in erotological texts appear to be in contradiction to assumptions about the nature of the relationship between the sexes in Arab societies. Does erotological literature then permit an alternate access to a societal sphere that, although depicted as private, is thus exposed to the public eye? Already the authors of *ars erotica* exploit the interplay between eros and etiquette and thus unambiguously indicate the subversive character of their writings. A particular attraction of erotic poetry consists precisely in its apparent naturalism and, on the other hand, in an indication that everything is but metaphor and play. For one example among many of this play between reality, appearance and (dis-)guise, one need look no further than the cryptic and subtle strategies of the Abbasid poet Abū Nuwās (d. *c.* 198–200/813–815), the greatest and most explicit of all poets of love and eros. In his poetry, eros and etiquette enter into a game of deception between that which one sees and that which is real, as well as between that which social norms allow and the violation of these norms. This is as true of his famous wine poems as it is of his homoerotic poetry.

Against this context, we are presented with the question about *fictionality* and the fictive nature of erotic and erotological works and the *factuality* of the accounts presented in these works. To what degree Arabic *ars erotica* should be read as a reflection of social reality or rather as a utopian alternative requires further social-historical and discourse analytical investigation.

In this regard, practices and rules of and for the gaze, looking and observation open up a central field of presentation, staging and representation.[17] The doctrine of the *ghaḍḍ al-baṣar*, the 'turning away of the gaze', in erotic, erotological and anti-erotological discourse was newly charged under colonial conditions and in debates about Europe. The regard and the taboo, the interdiction of the gaze, are now applied in a new situation, in which the object of temptation and the threatening glance of the observer are associated with Europe and the Europeans, as will be discussed further below.

Sight and insight

Traditionally, both currents, anti-erotological and erotological handbooks, as in the rest of the literature, recognize the eye as the most effective organ and at times as such condemn it for its very powers. The first glance, however, is generally regarded as impartial and therefore innocent. It is only the second glance that ignites carnal craving. 'But when', warns the jurist Ibn Qayyim al-Jawziyya, in accordance with tradition, 'someone intentionally casts a second glance, then he sins.'[18] And therefore, says Ibn Qayyim al-Jawziyya, with reference to the well-known verse in the Qur'an (24.30–1), the Prophet recommended turning away and not looking further. For the theologian al-Ghazālī (d.505/1111), there is no doubt that lascivious regard of a woman is nothing less than adultery (*fāḥisha*); as such a glance is equivalent to sexual penetration.

Eyes and the gaze are at the beginning of all temptation. They thus define an extensively reflected upon poetic motif and an object of moral-ethical observation. Glance, gaze and regard are the source of all suffering and all joy. They can even end in death, for glances can kill and thus belongs to the context of (feminine) *fitna* (lit. chaos, temptation) and the *ʿawra* (lit. shameful area) of the body. Thus all erogenous zones, the eye as well as the body, are subject to strict control and a social protocol that, it appears, becomes increasingly strict.[19] These regulations of the body in the public sphere and space are time bound, both in their application and interpretation and with regard to whom they apply to and when.

These ideas stemming from the ethico-religious domain reappear as themes and motifs in erotic literature, but with the aim of rebutting them – and thus they are subversive. Where anti-erotic and moralistic texts deal with the interdiction and the danger of the glance, literature is frequently concerned with an even more dangerous glance: the deadly look. In metaphoric exaggeration, the semantic field is expanded to include the hunt. Between hunter and prey, glances turn to spears that strike the eye.

Based on the same insight that determines the eye as the most potent erogenous zone of the body, literature regularly invokes the moment in which the eye first *creates* an object of desire.[20] The glance repeatedly wakens mistrust. Did an exchange of regards (*naẓar*) actually occur? What consequences did it have?

Many authors exploit these ambivalent situations with ironic gestures and thus reinforce the sign language. In this way, the eye and the glance play a central role not only in love poetry. The eye is the erogenous zone par excellence. The terrain of its presentation,[21] ostensible and ulterior, can be poignantly illustrated by the example of two intellectual currents and the radical change of conceptions of eros and etiquette, which will be dealt with in the following section.

The colonial view and taboos

This brief review of pre-modern conceptions does not serve the purpose of a quasi-apologetic fallback to some kind of 'more liberal' tradition in the relationship of eros and etiquette. In fact, the historic review emphasizes the degree to which the new paradigms of the nineteenth century presented a clear break with the past. Or, more precisely, the recourse to the pre-modern reveals the triumph of the predominantly Ḥanbalite, anti-erotic current over other more polyvalent attitudes rather than suggesting a radically new form of etiquette. This reduction to only one of the currents applies not only to *ars erotica* but correlates simultaneously with a development towards a monoculture and repression of variety, including in the field of religious textual exegesis.[22] This development was overlaid by the presence of external factors such as the 'foreign regard' of Europeans and their view of the Arab self. This exterior regard triggered reactions in turn. The concrete colonial presence and the intellectual confrontation with the West constitute not only a topos but also a central experience that, as numerous studies have shown, is reflected first of all in emerging comparisons between 'orient' and 'occident', or Europe, and between Islam and Christianity. The relationship of the sexes and gender issues become a central *tertium comparationis* not only in the metaphorical usage of 'raising the veil of the other' but as a measure of progressiveness or backwardness, or simply of the alien nature of the other society.[23]

In paradigmatic manner, two symptomatic situations illustrate the interplay between the genealogical change of *ars erotica* and the effect of the European presence. These are depicted in literary writing by two leading Arab writers of the time. In one instance, it is the demonstration of the power of the gaze of the other, as shown by the Egyptian writer, historian and reformer ʿAlī Mubārak in his novel-length *ʿAlam al-Dīn* (ʿAlam al-Dīn, 1882). In another, it is the multifaceted engagement with the Arab canon and the breach with Arabic *ars erotica* – investigated in Aḥmad Fāris al-Shidyāq's *al-Sāq ʿalā al-Sāq* (*Leg over Leg*, 1855). Both works represent not merely important milestones for the new genre of travel-novel and the changing experience of Europe by presenting these experiences and the resulting self-reflection in novelistic form. More significantly, they mark in general a turning point in Arabic concerns with 'own' and 'other'.

The gaze and observation had already been examined by one of the first authors of the new intellectual and literary movement, the *Nahḍa* (Renaissance). The Egyptian Rifāʿa al-Ṭahṭāwī (1801–1873), for instance, was challenged to explain in his travelogue the encounter with an unfamiliar and indeed strange medium, the 'stage-play' and theatre in Paris, which he described in terms of an interplay of appearance and reality.[24] Similarly, he compares the body language and exchange of regards of men and women as exercised in French public to etiquettes found back home. The theatre and its specific ways of creating authentic presentation and representation and the public as a space structured and conducted by diverting regimes of gaze and looking, also occupied ʿAlī Mubārak.

Overall, during the nineteenth century, the glance and the shame of looking acquire new significance. A sense of sharpened experience based on the perceived danger of denudation arises for the first time in the literary description of a situation, in which the glance itself as potent agent is examined.[25] Shame and the bounds that grow out of it are subject to reflection in ʿAlī Mubārak's autobiographical novel *ʿAlam al-Dīn*. This voluminous novel-like travelogue employs narrative strategies and techniques that were to become common stock in modern Arabic literature. Transfiguring Europe and Egypt through an inventory of typical representatives of those societies, the relationship between 'us' and 'them', modernization and modern lifestyle, tradition and religion, and, last but not least, gender and the role of woman in society are viewed through the eyes and experience of ʿAlam al-Dīn, an Azhar shaykh, and his family. The situation in question takes place, significantly, during a ride from Cairo to Alexandria on the latest of modern innovations, the train, which inspires awe and fear at the same time.[26] While in the first place the train ride allows the author to reflect on time and change, it provides another occasion to set in relation sight and insight. A conversation previously depicted as lively between the Egyptians and the British fell silent, both in narrative structure and in blocking of conversation and exchange, and hence the possibility of understanding. This point, when gazes are turned away and conversation ends, marks the emergence of new taboos whose effects *ʿAlam al-Dīn* envisions so clearly. The limits of understanding appear in two different but structurally similar ways; the lapse of conversation and closing of the eyes. Not allowing to see and perceive and keeping silent thus become constitutional parts of the experience with the European West. From such restrained experience arise not only problems of literary representation that, as suggested in *ʿAlam al-Dīn*, lead to new literary forms. Rather it defines a fundamental positioning of Arab society, for which the relationship between man and woman became an important indicator.

The shame of looking, for the seer and the seen, is examined in the context of the otherness of the French and the fear of seduction (*fitna*) by the woman. Here two spheres are abruptly conjoined and consolidated into a new taboo. This new taboo is illustrated in the literary text in a conversation between father and son, in which the youth's curiosity to look upon foreign girls is reproved with a reference to the traditional doctrine of the *ghaḍḍ al-baṣar* (turning away of the glance). The young man must stop looking at French girls. But the narrator has already violated this precept by allowing his son, fascinated by the girls' beauty, to describe at least a few of their superficial characteristics. This point reveals an ambivalence that the author is unable to resolve with either narrative technique or content, but upon the existence of which he focuses, as a problem of inhibited examination. At this point the proscription of looking is newly charged. The shaykh as incarnation of an aspect of Egyptian tradition and culture, namely Islam, represents those restrictions that the narrator wishes to escape. That the shaykh enounces a Qurʾanic taboo is intended to indicate the origin of this prohibition, but the current situation evidences a residue that can be recognized as a new puritanical attitude. The puritan gaze functions as an expression of defensiveness. That this new regulation of looking arises from the colonial situation is not merely implicitly mentioned in the novel but scenically illustrated. This new puritanism wants not only to protectively shield women's bodies from the glances of strange men but also to posit a new model in the relation between Arab men and women. The disembodied woman becomes a wife. Thus the moral codex of ʿAlī Mubārak's world bans the presence of corporality even in literary description. The unequal relationship between Europe and Egypt blocks the possibility of critical self-examination. The implicit narcissism arising from the confrontation with Europe is already broken on the cognitive and formal level when it is presented as such. Thus, analogically to the shame of looking, an insuperable taboo exists on the level of speech. The author presents this as a termination of communication where questions of personal belief are concerned. The conflict, or better the unexpressed conflict, is ignited by the relation of religion to the woman and the resulting role of the woman in the respective societies. Despite the curiosity of each about the other, the fear of rejection of one's own concepts by the other dominates. The limits of speech are established as blocked curiosity, which arises from inherent religious taboos. While everything else can be cognitively and argumentatively dealt with, here a conscious limit of vulnerable convictions and personal shame is drawn. But while the shame of looking can be localized as a culturally conditioned fixation, the termination of conversation arises from the inviolability of religion. Not least due to doubt of the other's tolerance, a taboo arises here, felt and respected equally by both sides, English and Egyptian. The taboo concerns the role of the woman in Egyptian society. Both sides are aware and fear that the current situation invokes prejudices. Therefore, they strive to rebut the image of the suppressed woman in Islam. The central issue is not the veil, that the shaykh's wife naturally wears, but polygamy. In accordance with the idea that every nation has the laws appropriate to it, the sheikh believes that monogamy is more appropriate for Europe than for the Orient, where polygamy is to be preferred due to the excess of women and the religious laws. This apologetic formulation, offered in the presence of a European, is nevertheless elsewhere opposed by statements of the modern reformer ʿAlī Mubārak, in which he explicitly attacks the institution of polygamy in Islam. The attraction and informative nature of his precursor semi-autobiographical fictional novel *ʿAlam al-Dīn* can also be found here; the title with its suggestive double meaning, namely of the personal name of the protagonist and the honorous *The Flag of Religion* stands programmatically for more than the name of the protagonist, in particular regarding the presentation of taboos. Literature demonstrates here poignantly the potential and limitations of reflection oriented towards individual feelings.

While this Egyptian literary work, with its newly achieved puritanical attitude, long determined the framework for the relationship between the sexes, doubly broken by the European perspective, another literary effort that offered a modern alternative was much less influential stylistically – and has only in recent decades been recognized for its vanguard nature.

Aḥmad Fāris al-Shidyāq's equally lengthy and, with an artfully developed fictional character, clearly semi-autobiographical novel *al-Sāq ʿalā al-Sāq*, published thirty years previously, took an altogether different approach to questions of Europe and us and in the development of a hitherto unfamiliar style that boastfully exploited what modern and classical literature, of Arabic and European provenance, have to offer. In this sense, *al-Sāq ʿalā al-Sāq* remained an exception to the emerging style, intellectual and literary, along the lines of *ʿAlam al-Dīn*. *Al-Sāq ʿalā al-Sāq* is centred on women in Arab and modern life, and thus on issues of sexuality and love, tradition and partnership, while another major lens through which individual experience in turbulent times and confrontations of changing regimes of knowledge, power and politics is offered in its reflection on language and linguistic criticism and fascinating plays with words, etymologies and neologisms. Not least because of the book's continuation of the tradition of *mujūn* and *ars erotica*, perceived, as we have seen, as untimely and inadequate, and because of the radicalism of the oeuvre's criticism of gender and the relations of the sexes in the author's own, Arab society, this attempt to ground an Arab and Arabic modernity was rejected not only by contemporaries.[27] Literary critics and historians long held these aspects of al-Shidyāq's work as irreconcilable with the dominant attitude towards modernity as expressed in ʿAlī Mubārak's work. Only today is the modernity of al-Shidyāq's work recognized – also and especially with regard to his attitude to women and to *ars erotica*.

To put it briefly, al-Shidyāq, the nineteenth-century Lebanese universal scholar and one of the first Arab intellectuals to focus on the relationship between the sexes, offers a completely different view of the repression of *ars erotica*. Already, the title of his novel, *al-Sāq ʿalā al-Sāq*, plays with the ambiguity of the formulation, which can certainly be read as sexual. But this was ignored in the book's reception.[28] Contemporaries condemned this work, which today – not least on account of his use of *mujūn*, the licentious poetry, bawdy language, pornographic descriptions and obscenities as well as his attitudes to women, sex and marriage, homoerotic shaykhs, etc. – is regarded as a milestone of Arabic modernity.[29] In contrast to the criticism of the *nahḍāwī*-s (reformist modernists), in pre-modern times homoerotic relationships or (porno-)graphic descriptions were criticized but not repressed. Or were they? In the absence of social-historic and literary accounts of their reception, we can only speculate.[30] In the nineteenth century, however, the rejection of *al-Sāq ʿalā al-Sāq* by the intellectual elite resulted not merely in stigmatization of the work in public discourse. Rather, the tradition of *mujūn* now disappeared by being excluded from the new canon of Arabic literature. Thus stories from the *1001 Nights* were still being published but only as adventure and fantasy tales – i.e. only the non-salacious stories.[31] Texts perceived as pornographic or in bad taste, the decisive criterion for in- or exclusion in the canon of the modern, were thus eliminated from the new 'institution literature'.[32]

The novel *al-Sāq ʿalā al-Sāq* is the unconventional report of a trip in the Arab West and Europe. The story tells of two protagonists, Faryāq and Faryāqiyya, a modern married couple, who, in their always distanced, frequently self-ironic reflections on love and marriage, function as a sort of model. The narrative contrast between a feminine and a masculine point of view, or feminine and masculine principle based on the names assigned to the protagonists, can also be read as the tension between two facets of a single person, the author Aḥmad Fāris al-Shidyāq.[33] While contemporary literature largely avoided physical descriptions of men or women, al-Shidyāq mobilized a complete repertoire of sensual to shameless descriptions of bodies. Thus women are compared not only with the full moon (*badr*) or have bodies like a banyan branch (*ghuṣn bān*), as was already familiar from love poetry, but are also described (using all the elements of old Arabic as well as classical aesthetic) with all their 'mountains of wrinkles' and fleshly 'hills'.

In *al-Sāq ʿalā al-Sāq*, al-Shidyāq offers a more complex comparison of Europe and the Arab world than his predecessor al-Ṭahṭāwī did thirty years before, instead resembling the challenging attitude of the Indian Mirzā Abū Ṭālib towards Europe. This is displayed in the structure and form of the novel, which enables a differentiated presentation of the observing subject and the observed object. This multidimensionality also informs the treatment of the sexes and sexuality. Four chapters entitled as *maqāma*-s (traditional literary genre, literally: assemblies) and concerned with love, sexuality and marriage, are embedded in the travel account. This elevated designation contrasts with the rest of the novel's structure and consciously associates a classical genre of Arabic literature with another genealogy and literary tradition. This leads to two experiential relations in the novel: a facility grounded in Arabic *ars erotica* of the treatment of sexual and moral questions, whose 'guards' are always women, and the modern cooperative relationship between Faryāq (the pseudonym combines the author's first and last names) and Faryāqiyya (the feminine form of the pseudonym), the first modern lovers and married couple in Arabic literature.

The part of the story occurring in Europe critically examines the social and cultural differences regarding the role and behaviour of women. This is not restricted to a merely external description, and thus a listing of aspects of the differences, but searches for the historical and cultural origins of these differences, both in Europe – namely, between England and France – and in the comparison with Arab countries. An alternative perspective is developed in the *maqāma*-s. The four *maqāma*-s, each of which forms the thirteenth chapter of its respective book, and which thus stand in the middle of the four books of which the novel is composed, are arranged like four columns in the novel. It is not only the placement of these *maqāma*-s in a new narrative structure that differentiates them from others of their time. Their thematic motives also have little in common with the *maqāma*-s of Nāṣīf al-Yāzijī (d.1871), published around the same time in Beirut. As he explains in his preface, al-Yāzijī also tried to introduce something new into Arabic literature by resurrecting a classical genre. Al-Yāzijī consciously adopted as a model the classical but rather edifying narrative structure as well as motifs of his prototype, the *maqāma*-s of the classical poet al-Ḥarīrī (d.516/1122), regarded by his contemporaries as outmoded.[34] As the title *Majmaʿ al-baḥrayn* (The Confluence of the Two Seas) augurs, he deals thematically with the most varied fields of Arabic knowledge (from astronomy to eating), but also with questions of education, as in the disputes with his daughter. The response was mixed, and even contemporary critics rejected this neoclassical attempt as anachronistic. In contrast, the *maqāma*-s embedded in al-Shidyāq's novel invoke other associations by their special placement, and other ways of reading through their use of language. They too are composed as rhymed prose, interrupted by poems, but their language is more fluid than al-Yāzijī's classical style. Thematically, the epic structure is concerned with only a single subject. Al-Shidyāq's *maqāma*-s are concerned with the advantages and disadvantages of marriage and celibacy, the advantages of monogamy and the joys of physical desire. Al-Shidyāq adopted the narrative structure of one of his *maqāma*-s from a tale of Jalāl al-Dīn al-Suyūṭī (d.911/1505),[35] an Egyptian legal scholar and author of relevant erotological works, in conscious allusion to it. In al-Suyūṭī's tale *Rashf al-zulāl min al-siḥr al-ḥalāl*, twelve young men who married on the advice of their *imām* report on the first night with their new wives. The charm and salacious humour of the accounts arise from the use in the twelve accounts, from first approach to sexual congress, of technical terms associated with the respective professions of the young men. The *imām* had recommended marriage because of its advantages. Al-Shidyāq's chapter entitled 'Maqāma Muqīma' (An Edifying Maqāma) clearly alludes to al-Suyūṭī's tale and modifies its motifs.[36] However, Faryāq encounters not twelve young men but twelve attractive women, who report in lively fashion one after the other on their sexual experiences with their husbands. After the hero of the story has plaintively expatiated on the moods of women in general, and those of his wife in particular, each of the women offers a short poem about her husband and her view of their relation. Al-Shidyāq makes one of these women an Indian, thus taking up again a common motif of Arabic erotology. Erotically informed Indian women are frequently to be found in classical texts of this type and in anecdotal literature, and this reference indicates the influence of Indian works on all Arabic writings – including other genres.[37] Here the author mobilizes Arabic *ars erotica*'s rich repertoire, including its long lists of words equivalent to a sexual dictionary. In view of the text's narrative structure and al-Shidyāq's incomprehension of the rejection with which European readers and Orientalists meet Arabic *ars erotica*, there can be no doubt that the author was not merely concerned with preserving erotological inventory. Rather al-Shidyāq marshals here historical and aesthetic characteristics of the Arab critique of civilization, one of his main themes and a further motif in his search for a specific articulation of modernity itself.

Thus al-Shidyāq's text reveals not only thematically, but also structurally and linguistically, a positively sensual relationship with the Arabic language – and with women. Completely in the sense of *ars erotica*, fulfilment arises from the act of describing love and passion. In both cases the author exploits the possibilities of representation and the conceivable to their limits. This is personified in the first modern couple in Arabic literature, Faryāq and Faryāqiyya,[38] a literary creation of whose innovative and critical strength the author is fully aware and which is indicated in the text. If this couple is original and unusual, it is thanks to a symbiosis of a resurrection of *ars erotica* with new experiences arising from contact with Europe. Al-Shidyāq's central examination of this theme and his intentional provocation by reanimating the genre of *ars erotica* in the medium of the new, breaks intra-social taboos. The interplay of European and Arabic taboos and criticism found here elevates the novel above its rivals. Thus he deals critically with a cliché common among Europeans: Arabs' sexual and moral intemperance, to which Arabs' civilizational backwardness is frequently ascribed.[39] Al-Shidyāq was familiar with European literature and culture, and attacked both polygamy and concubinage as irreconcilable with a relationship between the sexes based on mutual respect, and also as a cause of the general moral decay evidenced by the low level of Arabic educational institutions and the absence of sites dedicated to the conservation of Arabic traditions, such as modern libraries, but also in politico-religious matters, such as his intense personal occupation with the Maronite sect in Lebanon. Nevertheless, al-Shidyāq also criticized the European inability to appreciate the graphic qualities of Arabic *ars erotica*, but without formulating a theory of the different aesthetic reception or a philosophy of desire. He identified linguistic problems as the chief cause of this incomprehension and thus reduced the problem to an apparently linguistic level. On the one hand, he complained of European scholars' meagre knowledge of Arabic. On the other, he recognized peculiarities of different languages, and to some degree the untranslatable forms of thought thus expressed. Thus he mentions European incomprehension of the Arabic linguistic convention of using the same words to describe the physical attraction, seductiveness and Dionysian aspect of male adolescents as for females.[40] Against this background, al-Shidyāq's denigration of homosexual shaykhs in his novel is more comprehensible. This illustrates, on the one hand, the theme of anticlerical enlightenment which al-Shidyāq practised in his critique of the clergy. On the other hand, the denigration of Arabic priests as abandoned to masculine eroticism expresses less the author's homophobic reaction to a sexual abnormality as it does the recourse to a common motif of Arabic poetry: the sexual desire of religious scholars and clergy, treated ironically or as obscene, as for example, by Abū Nuwās. Al-Shidyāq completely ignored the fact that, besides the academic-Orientalist rejection of this aspect of the Arabic legacy, a great European enthusiasm and fascination existed for precisely these works. This fascination and the presumed associated degradation of Arabic culture was an offence in the eyes of those Arab contemporaries and critics who sought to protect the Arabic literary canon from its own traditions by keeping it 'pure'.

In lieu of a conclusion

Today, *al-Sāq ʿalā al-Sāq* is understood as a modern work, not least because of its associations with *ars erotica*. This has to do with developments of the last two decades, during which the relevant classics of Arabic *ars erotica* have been newly published in numerous editions in the Arab metropolises of Tunis, Beirut and Damascus, and systematic occupation with Arabic erotological literature has boomed – evidenced among other things by the appearance of a new Arabic sexual dictionary.[41] Add to that contemporary Arabic literature, in which transgression of sexual and moral taboos is the rage, not least in women's literature, as in the works of various female authors such as the Algerian Aḥlām al-Mustaghānamī or Rajā' al-Ṣāni' (Rajaa Alsanea: *Girls of Riyadh*) from Saudi Arabia. After the *Nahḍa* and its lingering effects, offensively libertine poetry and literature reappear first in the mid-twentieth century, after the representation of love, sexuality and the relationship of the sexes had been so long restricted to only non-physical aspects. But these no longer connect with the tradition and spectrum of Arabic *ars erotica*. This illustrates how profound the break with the pre-modern is. The novel *Burhān al-'Asal* (*The Proof of the Honey*, 2007)[42] by Salwā al-Nu'aymī excited so much attention not least for this reason, because it strikingly announced a new interest in classical erotic writing and connected a sexual revolution in the Arab world with its own tradition. That such a book touched a nerve not only in the Arab world is attested by the numerous translations. The prevailing stereotype about Arab sexuality is still determined by the veil and veil metaphors, which explains in reverse the European book market's fascination with libertine Arabic literature. We can also observe this parallelism in the nineteenth-century European reception to *ars erotica*. In contrast to today, the Arabic nineteenth century marked the beginning of a period of upheaval and transfiguration. And as the beginning of repression of *ars erotica* as etiquette, an upheaval that, as this chapter has hopefully demonstrated, was much too complicated to be subsumed under the heading of Victorian prudery.

Notes

Revised version and translation from the German: Nadia Al-Bagdadi, 'Eros und Etiquette', in Bettina Dennerlein, Elke Frietsch and Therese Steffen (eds), *Verschleierter Orient – Entschleierter Okzident?: (Un-)Sichtbarkeit in Politik, Recht, Kunst und Kultur seit dem 19. Jahrhundert*, 117–34 (Munich: Wilhelm Fink Verlag, 2012).

1 Regarding the disappearance of *ghazal* in the nineteenth century, cf. Thomas Bauer and Angelika Neuwirth (eds), *Ghazal as World Literature*, vol. 1, *Transformations of a Literary Genre*, Beiruter Texten und Studien 89 (Beirut: Orient Institut, 2005).

2 For this chapter, the concept *ars erotica* includes all currents and genres. Naturally the significant distinctions between love poetry and *ars erotica*, or between the pornographic and obscene should not be obliterated. But for the purposes of this chapter these distinctions are of subordinate importance. In recent years a large number of new studies on sex and sexuality in Muslim countries have appeared. Everett K. Rowson and J.W. Wright (eds), *Homoeroticism in Classical Arabic Literature* (New York: Columbia University Press, 1997) remains a good introduction to the subject. For the later Ottoman period, see Khaled El-Rouayheb, *Before Homosexuality in the Arab Islamic World, 1500–1800* (Chicago, IL: Chicago University Press, 2005).

3 One must however mention that the theme survived in farces!

4 As far as I know, there are no thorough studies of the practice and survival of the frequently very sexual burlesques of the so-called 'people's theatres' or popular street

theatre in the nineteenth century. But adaptation to the new taste also appears likely here. For the theatre in the nineteenth century, see Philip C. Sadgrove, *The Egyptian Theatre in the Nineteenth Century: 1799–1822* (Reading: Ithaca Press, 1996), as well as Muḥammad Yūsuf Najm, *al-Masraḥiyya fī al-Adab al-ʿArabī al-Ḥadīth* (Beirut: Dār al-Thaqāfa, 1956).

5 Michel Foucault, *The History of Sexuality*, 3 vols (New York: Pantheon Books, 1978–1986).

6 *Ars erotica* is not an Arabic concept. In modern Arabic, concepts such as *ʿilm al-jins* or *al-jinsiyya* are used; in classical Arabic, higher-level terms refer to the various genres, for example, *kutub al-bāh* (books about sexual congress) or *mujūn* (in poetry).

7 Herbert Marcuse, *Eros and Civilization: A Philosophical Inquiry into Freud* (Boston, MA: Beacon Press, 1955).

8 With known exceptions such as the early Islamic frescoes in Qusayr ʿAmra or other private visual presentations. Cf. Gabriele Mandel, *Islamische Erotik*, trans. Karsten Diettrich (Fribourg: Liber SA, 1983).

9 Richard F. Burton (trans. and ed.), *The Book of the Thousand Nights and a Night* (London: Burton Club, 1886).

10 See, for example, Julie Scott Meisami, 'Arabic Mujūn Poetry: The Literary Dimension', in Frederick de Jong (ed.), *Verse and the Fair Sex: Studies in Arabic Poetry*, 8–30 (Utrecht: Stiching, 1993).

11 So far science has had little to say about the history of the reception and use of these works.

12 Richard Burton translated the Indian Kamasutra from Sanskrit and the sixteenth-century text *Rawḍ al-ʿĀṭir fī Nuzhat al-Khāṭir*, ed. Jamāl Jumʿa (London: Riad El-Rayyes Books, 1990), by the Tunisian ʿUmar ibn Muḥammad al-Nafzāwī, from the French (translated by a French officer from Arabic) into English. Judging by the numerous references and translations, the work was much more popular in Europe than in the Arabic world, where it was only one among many.

13 Abdelwahab Bouhdiba, *La sexualité en Islam* (Paris: Presses Universitaires de France, 1986).

14 See also currently the studies of Rajāʾ b. Slāma influenced by French psychoanalysis.

15 Cf. Stefan Leder: *Ibn al-Ǧauzi und seine Kompilation wider die Leidenschaft: Der Traditionalist in gelehrter Überlieferung und originärer Lehre* (Beirut: Orient Institut der DMG; Wiesbaden: Steiner Verlag, 1984).

16 Frank Griffel (trans.), *Ibn Rushd: Maßgebliche Abhandlung Faṣl al-Maqāl* (Berlin: Suhrkamp, 2010).

17 For a survey of the role of observation see also Nadia Al-Bagdadi (ed.), 'Mapping the Gaze: Vision and Visuality in Classical Arab Civilization', special issue of *Medieval History Journal*, 9 (1) (2006). For an attempt at a systematic comparison of Western and Eastern regimes of observation, see Hans Belting's thesis of the dominance of the theory of seeing in Arabic society contrasted with the European theory of the picture. Cf. Hans Belting, *Florenz und Bagdad: Eine westöstliche Geschichte des Blickes* (Munich: Beck Verlag, 2008).

18 Ibn Qayyim al-Jawziyya, *Rawḍat al-Muḥibbīn wa-Nuzhat al-Mushtāqīn*, ed. Aḥmad ʿUbayd (Damascus: al-Taraqqī, 1956), 94.

19 In view of the absence of social and other studies, not much can presently be said in this regard.

20 Thus the moment in which the sight of a beautiful naked body triggers uncontrolled desire and passion is already to be found in Mesopotamian myths.

21 In the sense of Goffman's use of the metaphor of presentation as social strategy, see Erving Goffman, *The Presentation of Self in Everyday Life* (Edinburgh: Edinburgh University Press, 1959).
22 Cf. Muḥammad Ḥaddād, *Muḥammad ʿAbduh. Qirāʾa Jadīda fī al-Khiṭāb al-dīnī* (Beirut: Dār al-Ṭālīʿa., 2003).
23 Here see also the first studies on this theme by Jūrj Ṭarābīshī, *al-Rujūla wa-Idiyūlūjiyya al-Rujūla fī al-Riwāya al-ʿArabiyya* (Beirut: Dār al-Ṭālīʿa, 1983) and *Ramziyat al-Marʾa fī al-Riwāya al-ʿArabiyya* (Beirut: Dār al-Ṭālīʿa, 1985).
24 Rifāʿa al-Ṭahṭāwī, *Takhlīṣ al-Ibrīz fī Talkhīs Bārīz* (Cairo: Būlaq, 1849). See also Reinhard Schulze, 'Schauspiel oder Nachahmung: Zum Theaterbegriff arabischer Reiseschriftsteller des 19. Jahrhundert', *Die Welt des Islam*, 34 (1994): 67–84. Mubārak also dealt with this problem. How much the problem of realistic or true representation and depiction occupied Mubārak is illustrated by his irritation after visiting a theatre in Marseille: 'From where do they have a picture [*ṣūra*] of paradise and hell, of deserts and punishment, although they have never seen them? How can they represent [*yuṣawwirūna*] what no one has seen?'
25 For more on this subject, see Nadia al-Bagdadi, *Vorgestellte Öffentlichkeit: Zur Genese moderner Prosa in Ägypten 1860–1908; Dargestellt am Beispiel von vier Autoren* (Wiesbaden: Reichen Verlag, 2010), esp. 115–20.
26 This is the first depiction of a train ride on the new connection between the cities, inaugurated in 1854.
27 Raḍwā ʿĀshūr, *al-Ḥadātha al-Mumkina* (Cairo: Dar al-Shurūq, 2010), offers a summary of the work's reception.
28 There are not yet any studies of al-Shidyāq's perspective on and treatment of *ars erotica*, however, see Tarek el-Ariss, *Trials of Arab Modernity: Literary Affects and the new Political* (New York: Fordham University Press, 2013). Critics such as Jurjī Zaydān or later ʿImād al-Ṣulḥ have criticized but not studied these aspects of his work. Cf. in contrast ʿAzīz al-ʿAẓma and Fawwāz Trābulsī, *al-Aʿmāl al-Majhūla li-Aḥmad Fāris al-Shidyāq* (Beirut: Riad El-Rayyes Books, 1994), which was the first to remark upon the ambiguity of the title.
29 See also Joseph Massad, *Desiring Arabs* (Chicago, IL: Chicago University Press, 2007).
30 Nonetheless, see Samah Selim, *The Novel and the Rural Imaginary in Egypt* (London: Routledge, 2007).
31 Cf. Al-Bagdadi, *Vorgestellte Öffentlichkeit.*
32 Peter Bürger, *Theory of the Avant-Garde*, trans. Michael Shaw (Minneapolis, MN: University of Minnesota Press, 1984).
33 Cf. Kamran Rastegar, *Literary Modernity Between the Middle East and Europe: Textual Transactions in the Nineteenth Century in Arabic and Persian Literature* (London; Routledge, 2007), as well as in Al-Bagdadi, *Vorgestellte Öffentlichkeit.*
34 Nāṣīf al-Yāzijī, *Majmaʿ al-Baḥrayn* (Beirut, 1855). See also Thomas Bauer, 'Die Badiʿyya des Nasif al-Yazigi und das Problem der spätosmanischen Arabischen Literatur', in Andreas Christian Islebe and Angelika Neuwirth (eds), *Reflections on Reflections: Near Eastern Writers Reading Literature*, 49–118 (Wiesbaden: Reichert Verlag, 2006), which offers a successful treatment of the difficulty of reading *maqāma*-s, regarded as obsolete, as modern texts at the beginning of the Arabic modern period.
35 A French translation exists: 'Abd al-Rahmane al-Soyoûti, *Nuits de Noces : Ou Comment Humer le Doux Breuvage de la Magie Licite*, trans. René Khawam (Paris: Albin Michel, 1972).
36 Aḥmad Fāris al-Shidyāq, *al-Sāq ʿalā al-Sāq* (Beirut: Dār al-Ḥayāh, 1996), 475–84.

37 The theme of Indian influence on Arabic storytelling has been thoroughly handled for the *1001 Nights*. But to my knowledge there has been no comparable research in the field of *ars erotica*.
38 See also Boutrous Hallaq, 'Love and the Birth of Modern Arabic Literature', in Roger Allen and Hilary Kilpatrick (eds), *Love and Sexuality in Modern Arabic Literature*, 16–23 (London: Al-Saqi, 1995), 19.
39 Here however Massad's reference to al-Shidyāq is inaccurate as he recognizes only this aspect of the work. Cf. Massad, *Desiring Arabs*, 35–6.
40 Hāshim Yāghī, *al-Naqd al-Adabī al-Ḥadīth fī-Lubnān*, vol. 1 (Cairo: Dār al-Maʿārif 1965), 102, 117.
41 ʿAbd al-Ḥalīm Ḥamza, *al-Qāmūs al-Jinsī ʿinda al-ʿArab* (Beirut: Riad El-Rayyes Books, 2002).
42 Salwā al-Nuʿaymī, *Burhān al-ʿAsal* (Beirut: Riad El-Rayyes Books. 2007), published in English as *The Proof of the Honey*.

References

ʿAbd al-Ḥalīm Ḥamza (2002), *al-Qāmūs al-Jinsī ʿinda al-ʿArab*, Beirut: Riad El-Rayyes Books.

Al-ʿAẓma, ʿAzīz and Fawwāz Trābulsī (1994), *al-Aʿmāl al-Majhūla li-Aḥmad Fāris al-Shidyāq*, Beirut: Riad El-Rayyis Books.

Al-Bagdadi, Nadia (2010), *Vorgestellte Öffentlichkeit: Zur Genese moderner Prosa in Ägypten 1860-1908; Dargestellt am Beispiel von vier Autoren*, Wiesbaden: Reichert Verlag.

Al-Bagdadi, Nadia (2012), 'Eros und Etiquette', in Bettina Dennerlein, Elke Frietsch and Therese Steffen (eds), *Verschleierter Orient – Entschleierter Okzident?: (Un-)Sichtbarkeit in Politik, Recht, Kunst und Kultur seit dem 19. Jahrhundert*, 117–34, Munich: Wilhelm Fink Verlag.

Al-Bagdadi, Nadia (ed.) (2006), 'Mapping the Gaze: Vision and Visuality in Classical Arab Civilization', special issue of *Medieval History Journal*, 9 (1).

Al-Nafzāwī, ʿUmar b. Muḥammad (1990), *Rawḍ al- ʿĀṭir fi-Nuzhat al-Khāṭir*, ed. Jamāl Jumʿa, London: Riad El-Rayyes Books.

Al-Nuʿaymī, Salwā (2007), *Burhān al-ʿAsal*, Beirut: Riad El-Rayyes Books.

Al-Shidyāq, Aḥmad Fāris (1996), *al-Sāq ʿalā al-Sāq*, Beirut: Dār al-Ḥayāh.

al-Soyoûti, 'Abd al-Rahmane (1972), *Nuits de Noces: Ou Comment Humer le Doux Breuvage de la Magie Licite*, trans. René Khawam, Paris: Albin Michel.

Al-Ṭahṭāwī, Rifāʿa (1849), *Takhlīṣ al-Ibrīz fī Talkhīs Bārīz*, Cairo: Būlaq.

ʿĀshūr, Raḍwā (2010), *al-Ḥadātha al-Mumkina*, Cairo: Dar al-Shurūq.

Bauer, Thomas (2006), 'Die Badiʿyya des Nasif al-Yazigi und das Problem der spätosmanischen Arabischen Literatur', in Andreas Christian Islebe and Angelika Neuwirth (eds), *Reflections on Reflections: Near Eastern Writers Reading Literature*, 49–118, Wiesbaden: Reichert Verlag.

Bauer, Thomas and Angelika Neuwirth (eds) (2005), *Ghazal as World Literature*, vol. 1, *Transformations of a Literary Genre*, Beiruter Texten und Studien 89, Beirut: Orient Institut.

Belting, Hans (2008), *Florenz und Bagdad: Eine westöstliche Geschichte des Blickes*, Munich: Beck Verlag.

Bouhdiba, Abdelwahab (1986), *La Sexualité en Islam*, Paris: Presses Universitaires de France.

Bürger, Peter (1984), *Theory of the Avant-Garde*, trans. Michael Shaw, Minneapolis, MN: University of Minnesota Press.
Burton, Richard F. (trans. and ed.) (1886), *The Book of the Thousand Nights and a Night*, London: Burton Club.
El-Ariss, Tarek (2013), *Trials of Arab Modernity: Literary Affects and the New Political*, New York: Fordham University Press.
El-Rouayheb, Khaled (2005), *Before Homosexuality in the Arab Islamic World, 1500–1800*, Chicago, IL: Chicago University Press.
Goffman, Erving (1959), *The Presentation of Self in Everyday Life*, Edinburgh: Edinburgh University Press.
Griffel, Frank (trans.) (2010), *Ibn Rushd: Maßgebliche Abhandlung Faṣl al-Maqāl*, Berlin: Suhrkamp.
Ḥaddād, Muḥammad (2003), *Muḥammad ʿAbduh: Qirāʾa jadīda fī al-Khiṭāb al-Dīnī*, Beirut: Dār al-Ṭālīʿa.
Hallaq, Boutrous (1995), 'Love and the Birth of Modern Arabic Literature', in Roger Allen and Hilary Kilpatrick (eds), *Love and Sexuality in Modern Arabic Literature*, 16–23, London: Al-Saqi.
Ibn Qayyim al-Jawziyya (1956), *Rawḍat al-muḥibbīn wa-nuzhat al-mushtāqīn*, ed. Aḥmad ʿUbayd, Damascus: al-Taraqqī. Reprint Cairo.
Leder, Stefan (1984), *Ibn al-Ǧauzi und seine Kompilation wider die Leidenschaft: Der Traditionalist in gelehrter Überlieferung und originärer Lehre*, Beirut: Orient Institut der DMG; Wiesbaden: Steiner Verlag.
Mandel, Gabriele (1983), *Islamische Erotik*, trans. Karsten Diettrich, Fribourg: Liber SA.
Marcuse, Herbert (1955), *Eros and Civilization: A Philosophical Inquiry into Freud*, Boston, MA: Beacon Press.
Massad, Joseph (2007), *Desiring Arabs*, Chicago, IL: Chicago University Press.
Meisami, Julie Scott (1993), 'Arabic Mujūn Poetry: The Literary Dimension', in Frederick de Jong (ed.), *Verse and the Fair Sex: Studies in Arabic Poetry and in the Representation of Women in Arabic Literature*, 8–30, Utrecht: Stiching.
Mubārak, ʿAlī (1882), *ʿAlam al-Dīn*. Alexandria: Mt. Jarīdat al-Maḥrūsa.
Najm, Muḥammad Yūsuf (1956), *al-Masraḥiyya fī al-Adab al-ʿArabī al-Ḥadīth*, Beirut: Dār al-Thaqāfa.
Najm, Muḥammad Yūsuf (1961), *al-Masraḥ al-ʿArabī: Dirāsāt wa-Nuṣūṣ*, Beirut: Dār al-Thaqāfa.
Rastegar, Kamran (2007), *Literary Modernity Between the Middle East and Europe: Textual Transactions in the Nineteenth Century in Arabic and Persian Literature*, London: Routledge.
Rowson, Everett K. and J. W. Wright (eds) (1997), *Homoeroticism in Classical Arabic Literature*, New York: Columbia University Press.
Sadgrove, Philip C. (1996), *The Egyptian Theatre in the Nineteenth Century: 1799–1822*, Reading: Ithaca Press.
Schulze, Reinhard (1994), 'Schauspiel oder Nachahmung: Zum Theaterbegriff arabischer Reiseschriftsteller des 19. Jahrhundert', *Die Welt des Islam*, 34: 67–84.
Selim, Samah (2007), *The Novel and the Rural Imaginary in Egypt*, London: Routledge.
Ṭarābīshī, Jūrj (1983), *al-Rujūla wa-Idiyūlūjiyya al-Rujūla fī al-Riwāya al-ʿArabiyya*, Beirut: Dār al-Ṭālīʿa.
Ṭarābīshī, Jūrj (1985), *Ramziyat al-Marʾa fī al-Riwāya al-ʿArabiyya*, Beirut: Dār al-Ṭālīʿa.
Yāghī, Hāshim (1965), *al-Naqd al-Adabī al-Ḥadīth fī Lubnān*, vol. 1, Cairo: Dār al-Maʿārif.
al-Yāzijī, Nāṣīf (1855), *Majmaʿ al-Baḥrayn*, Beirut.

Chapter 6

WOMEN'S LITERATURE AS COUNTER-NARRATIVE IN BAʿTHIST IRAQ?

Achim Rohde

Introduction

Cultural and artistic production in authoritarian systems has long caught the attention of scholars, in works that have addressed the dissemination of official ideology, the degree of political control over a society attained by a given regime or the perseverance of autonomous spaces and dissident voices within authoritarian polities.[1] Building on a growing body of scholarship on modern and contemporary Iraqi fiction, particularly on literature written by women, this chapter focuses on the work of the renowned Iraqi feminist novelist and journalist, Luṭfiyya al-Dulaymī (b.1942).[2] In the context of this volume, the chapter singles out sexual and gender norms as negotiated through one of al-Dulaymī's wartime novels and its reception by Baʿthist literary critics. It points to spaces of contestation within Baʿthist Iraq, specifically in the sphere of cultural and artistic production, that are often unaccounted for in conventional political history narratives.

The chapter contributes to the historiography of Baʿthist Iraq by offering a fresh reading of literature published by Iraqi writers who continued to live and work in the country under Saddam Hussein's (Ṣaddām Ḥusayn) rule.[3] It builds on the work of Miriam Cooke, who discussed al-Dulaymī's work as evidence for the existence of critical voices among novelists in Saddam's Iraq.[4] This chapter extends the discussion begun by Cooke by locating al-Dulaymī's novel in the broader social and political context of the time. Cooke was mainly interested in detecting possible resistances and hidden criticism of the regime in state-sponsored literary works, and in establishing the subversive potential of literary works even under repressive circumstances. This chapter discusses literary production in Baʿthist Iraq as a discursive space defined by the regime, which served its purpose precisely through its ambiguity and multivalence, including even dissident works such as al-Dulaymī's novel. Needless to say, no genuine public sphere existed in Baʿthist Iraq, where the public domain was heavily censored and mostly reflected official discourse.[5] The regime tightly controlled the realm of cultural production just as it did any other aspect of life in Baʿthist Iraq, and it recruited writers and novelists to serve its agenda. Yet, in order to be effective, propaganda does not invent entirely new discourses. Its success depends on its ability to confirm and manipulate opinions and attitudes rather than radically alter them.[6] Moreover, Baʿthist ideology itself is not homogenous but a contradictory fusion of conservative and nativist, as well as modernist, aspects. This created room for changes of emphasis within this discourse over time and for the voicing of competing agendas.[7] Expressions of discontent and more or less hidden critiques of the regime's policies therefore functioned both as a technology of government aimed at stabilizing existing power structures and simultaneously illustrate the agency of writers.

The 1980s saw a sustained rise in the share of women in the wage labour force, and birth rates declined. As a consequence, women's visibility in public life increased to a degree that triggered resentments among the more conservative strata in Iraqi society, until in 1986/7, the regime officially distanced itself from its former cautiously modernist agenda of gender reforms and called upon women to give highest priority to marriage and procreation. However, such calls had no measurable effects on the employment rate of women or the birth rate.[8] These developments formed the backdrop for al-Dulaymī's work and affected its reception inside Iraq. Al-Dulaymī's novel reflects a tension arising during the war years between ideals of companionate marriage, which had been at the core of the modernist agenda in the Middle East since the end of the nineteenth century and which the Iraqi Baʿth regime embraced in no uncertain terms throughout the first decade of its rule in Iraq, and more conservative authoritarian models of patriarchy.[9] The novel mourns the decay of the companionate model in favour of the authoritarian one in the context of war.

The following section locates this novel in the broader context of the Baʿth regime's cultural and gender policies, by portraying a debate between two Baʿthist literary critics regarding the significance of Western feminist thought and literature written by women authors, which was published in the party-owned leading daily *al-Thawra* at the time al-Dulaymī's novel was released. The chapter subsequently zooms in on the novel *Budhūr al-Nār* (Seeds of Fire, 1988), published by al-Dulaymī during the final year of the Iran–Iraq War (1980–1988), through a review article published in *al-Thawra*, and it concludes by discussing the significance of these findings regarding the question of dissident voices acting within Baʿthist Iraq.

Literature between mobilization and resistance

The Baʿth regime consciously turned culture and the sciences, particularly historiography, into an instrument for moulding Iraqi society in its own image.[10] These efforts became most accentuated in the 1980s, after Saddam Hussein's ascension to the presidency and the beginning of the war against Iran. The state sponsored cultural activities in the fields of painting/sculpture, theatre/cinema, literature/poetry, monumental architecture, etc. Right from the beginning of the war against Iran, it sponsored the evolution of a whole new genre of nationalist war poetry and literature, which, like its counterparts in the figurative arts, was rife with references to Iraq's ancient Mesopotamian and Islamic past.[11] Just as the Mesopotamian discourse in the regime-sponsored war propaganda alluded to established trends in the Iraqi art scene, so did the discourse of heroism and sacrifice nurtured during the war years refer to established patterns in Iraqi poetry and prose.[12] Miriam Cooke observes that within the first year of the war, 'the Qadisiyyat Saddam series had already published two anthologies of short stories, which must have been written immediately after the start of the war',[13] and a total of 452 short stories were published in Iraq during the first two years of the war, most of them eulogizing the war effort. Propaganda efforts by the former regime centring on war-related issues disseminated a crude kind of heroic heterosexual masculinity as an embodiment of Iraqi national virtue, depicting manly soldiers sacrificing themselves in defence of a feminized homeland. Regime-sponsored visual art and literature were equally recruited for disseminating this kind of propaganda, which often included notably eroticized imagery of romantic relationships between soldiers and women on 'the home front', warfare as an act of love and death, battle as an orgasmic experience, etc.[14] In her analysis of novels and short stories written by women authors during the war, Cooke has suggested reading the eroticization visible in Iraqi war literature in a Freudian sense, as interplay between Eros and the death instinct.[15] According to her, in eroticized accounts of the war 'death is enmeshed with fantasies that provide a libidinal sublimation'. In this sense, the use of such imagery was a mobilizing tool and a way of distracting the public from the real horrors of war.

However, feminist literary scholars have noted that literature generally narrates and presents wars in particularly gendered ways, often against the grain of the kind of 'engaged' war literature.[16] Indeed, in her sizable though random sample of regime-sponsored Iraqi 'war literature', Cooke identified hidden motifs signalling non-compliance with the regime's propaganda efforts that were subtly woven into the plots:

> Not all men's and women's war stories are as ideologically driven [...]. Sometimes the preface and the contents of a book may be at odds with each other so that the critical commentary, the most transparent genre, is patriotic and the plot is not [...]. The triumphalist introduction does not spill over into all the stories. Their message may not be explicit, but it colors the deliberate ambiguity or irony of the language.[17]

Similarly, Nadia Al-Bagdadi contends that Iraqi writers had developed techniques to circumvent the censors, for instance by composing abstract and metaphorical short stories and novels whose hidden criticism of the regime was, however, easily understood by a conscious reader.[18] Indeed, despite unprecedented levels of repression of real or imagined dissent during the years of the Iran–Iraq War, the regime left certain spaces for nonconforming social behaviour and contestation, and to some degree it tolerated non-Baʿthist voices, particularly in the arts but also in the media.[19] For example, it tolerated the existence of a queer subculture in Baghdad and elsewhere in Iraq, even as its gender discourse grew more socially conservative during the late 1980s, and more so during the 1990s.[20]

Salām ʿAbbūd has voiced diametrically opposing views in this regard, and strongly criticizes Iraqi intellectuals and artists who remained in the country for political complicity with the regime. He analysed short stories and poetry published by Iraqi authors during the 1980s and paints a bleak picture of Iraqi cultural decline, which really set in after Hussein's ascension to the presidency in 1979 and the start of the war against Iran. This decline was part and parcel of the militarization of the society under Saddam Hussein, which the author regards as the essence of the regime's rule.[21] ʿAbbūd's discussion of the Iraqi 'culture of violence' mirrors the argument first coined by Kanan Makiya in his *Republic of Fear*, according to which civil society had been thoroughly destroyed and absorbed into a totalitarian system.[22] Later works further developed Makiya's approach and elaborated on his findings.[23]

The tension between these two positions mirrors a long-running controversy among Iraqi intellectuals in exile and those who had remained in Iraq during Saddam Hussein's rule regarding restrictions and possibilities for cultural production under dictatorship.[24] According to accounts by exiled Iraqi literary critics such as ʿAbd Jāsim al-Sāʿadī, there was a fundamental difference between the state-sponsored 'official' war literature, on the one hand, which 'the military authority seeks to have published, in order to strengthen feelings of masculinity, toughness, and power among the soldiers', and, on the other hand, 'oppositional' literature written by exiled Iraqis who, rather, focus on the destruction and the individual and human costs of war.[25] In defence of those who remained inside Iraq, Muhsin al-Musawi presents Iraqi culture and arts as an authentic expression of popular patriotism, which the various rulers in the course of the twentieth century never completely succeeded in co-opting and manipulating.[26] Leaving aside the dubious dichotomy visible in al-Musawi's work between a regime-sponsored and an 'authentic' Iraqi culture, this chapter traces evidence from the field of literary production and its public perception that suggests the perseverance of a 'grey zone' in Baʿthist Iraq, where differing and partly contradictory points of view concerning a variety of issues would be voiced, not necessarily in keeping with official ideology.[27] Given the gendered and sexualized imagery notable in regime-sponsored 'war literature', this chapter zooms in on a literary work of a female Iraqi novelist that addresses issues of gender and sexuality in different ways.

The majority of Iraqi women writers did not focus on the war experience in the sense propagated by the regime. Nor were they published under the category of 'war literature'. Their work therefore enjoyed far less support by the state and was far less acknowledged in Iraqi reviews. These female authors thus operated from a position of marginality, depriving them of the visibility and prestige that went along with being promoted by the regime. But a relative lack of attention on the part of the regime towards female writers may also have afforded them a larger degree of autonomy and the ability to express dissident views.[28] Many women writers left the country or were able to publish their works abroad rather than in Iraq itself. At the same time, Iraqi critics occasionally acknowledged literature written by women throughout the 1980s and 1990s. Thus, an anthology of poetry written by Iraqi women was published by Salmān Hādī Āl Ṭaʿma, who cites other such compilations and poetry collections published by individual women writers during these years.[29] His work was first published in 1955 and consequently features a majority of women writers who published mainly before the rise of the Baʿth regime. The updated and expanded edition of 1995 also includes writers from later generations and poems that were written as late as the 1980s. Few of the thirty-nine writers introduced in this volume were active members of the party-affiliated civilian mass organizations such as the General Federation of Iraqi Women (GFIW).[30] During the 1970s, the GFIW had served as a symbol of the Baʿthist regime's Modernism, culminating in a reform of the Personal Status Law and further legal reforms to support women's access to education and the labour market. For the most part, the poems assembled in this volume did not fit into the category of 'war literature', not even as home front stories, but rather relate to a more general Iraqi patriotism and/or to specific locations, personal feelings in the context of daily life, work and the family.[31] Indeed, that Iraqi public discourse increasingly took notice of literature written by women at this point is illustrated by a controversy in the party-owned daily newspaper *al-Thawra* between the literary critics ʿAbd al-Wāḥid Muḥammad and Fāḍil Thāmir concerning linguistic problems in the translation into Arabic of the term 'feminism', and the reception by an Iraqi audience of an edited volume of Elaine Showalter, an internationally acknowledged work on feminist literary theory.[32]

In his essay opening the debate in late 1987, Thāmir noted an increased interest during this period in Iraq in literature written by women. To develop the analytical tools necessary to interpret these works, and understand the significance of literature written by women as compared with that written by male authors, he called for the examination of relevant developments in Western countries and, in this context, he discussed Showalter's book and other Western works on literary theory. Thāmir used the Arabic term 'al-naqd al-nisāʾī al-jadīd' to translate the title of Showalter's book. Yet, by the late 1980s, Arab feminists started to replace the older term *al-nisāʾiyya* (which can mean 'feminism' but also simply 'women's') with the more unambiguously feminist neologism *al-niswiyya*.[33] Thāmir's use of terminology suggests that he remained out of sync with contemporary developments in Arab feminist thought. His colleague Muḥammad translated an extract of Showalter's book into Arabic and presented it in *al-Thawra*. He was more visibly distanced from feminist ideas and argued that the book's title should rather be translated as 'naqd al-musāwā al-jadīd'. For Muḥammad, the feminist movement was striving for equality between women and men, and therefore he presented the term *musāwā* (equality) as the most appropriate translation. He rejected the idea that literature written by women differed in any qualitative way from literature written by men.[34] This all but explicit rejection of any consciously feminist agenda reflected the Baʿthist regime's turn towards a more socially conservative political line during the late war years, when it emphasized family values and personal sacrifice for the sake of the nation and distanced itself from the cautiously reformist agenda of the party-affiliated civilian mass organization GFIW.

During the war years of the 1980s, this kind of reformism was increasingly rejected as promoting the interests of women at the expense of men, thus endangering national unity.[35] In his response to Muḥammad, Thāmir seemed to offer a cautious defence of the regime's original 'state feminism', arguing that contemporary Arabic literature written by women differed from its counterpart written by men as well as from the 'international feminist movement'. In distancing himself from the latter, he argued that Western feminists at times seemed to argue for women's superiority over men. Precisely at this point, when he negatively refers to a consciously feminist agenda, Thāmir introduces the term *niswī* and links it with timeworn anti-feminist and implicitly homophobic platitudes: lesbian-feminist literary criticism ('al-naqd al-niswī al-līsbūnī'), which he presents as striving to establish a society made up exclusively of women, which in the realm of literature translated into a separate literary realm. Still, he insisted that contemporary Arabic literature written by female authors displayed unique features, and argued that any serious assessment of such works had to be aware of feminist theory produced in Western academia as well.[36] But he did not name any such unique features, suggesting that this phrase is mainly a rhetorical figure paying lip service to the regime's own modernist ideological package, which Thāmir half-heartedly defended in his article against Muḥammad's more openly conservative views.

Luṭfiyya al-Dulaymī and writers of the 'inside'

This debate signals a certain polarity in Iraq of the 1980s between conservatives and modernists regarding gender norms in general and the relation between Arab and Western feminists in particular. At first glance, this discursive context seems to obscure the degree of repression and fear that was a hallmark of Baʿthist Iraq, in particular during the 1980s. Yet this atmosphere transpired occasionally in literature published during this period. For example, after her return to Iraq in 1986, Dayzī al-Amīr, a distinguished and internationally known author who had previously headed the Iraqi Cultural Center in Beirut and published two volumes of short stories on the Lebanese Civil War, published a volume of short stories that did not address the ongoing Iraqi war experience at all. An atmosphere of loneliness and anxiety prevails in this volume, a degree of bitterness and dread permeates the narrative.[37] Similar works from this period have been published by Muḥammad Khuḍayr, an outstanding author of short stories who lived and worked in Basra during the years of Baʿthist rule.[38]

Writers who did not participate in writing propagandistic war literature and who continued to depict scenes from everyday civilian life insisted on an artist's autonomy to reflect upon society in a way they considered appropriate. Some writers who had initially joined the patriotic fervour of the early war years and whose short stories were published under the category of 'war literature' had, by the late 1980s, apparently developed more critical thoughts about the war. Among these authors, according to ʿAbbūd,[39] was Luṭfiyya al-Dulaymī, a former teacher and journalist, who had become famous for her 'impeccably patriotic' works. Al-Dulaymī is a prolific author of short stories, novels and theatre plays. During the 1980s, she took residence in Amman without, however, leaving Iraq for good. She went into exile only in 2006, at the height of the civil war, and eventually settled in Amman.[40] Her works were not banned in Iraq.

In 1988 she published a remarkable novel entitled *Seeds of Fire*, which is only superficially a 'conventional home front novel about two couples on the margins of the war whom circumstances have separated'.[41] The main characters are Laylā, a graphic designer working in an advertising company, and her husband Yāsir, who leaves home to work in an unnamed place in the desert. At work Laylā grows increasingly critical of the subtle ways in which her art is instrumentalized to sell products, and she starts to produce different designs, much to the dismay of her employer, who is said to have lost 'an important contract with an insecticide company' because of Laylā's controversial new designs.[42] Meanwhile, Yāsir leads a monotonous life working in the middle of nowhere, imagining his wife while visiting prostitutes and only rarely visiting home. He starts to become envious and jealous of Laylā and is no longer able to relate to her on an emotional level. The two become completely estranged from each other. In a notable departure from the rest of the story, the closing scene depicts Yāsir finally returning home to find Laylā in the kitchen with their new-born baby son, preparing dinner. While the development of the plot up to the closing scene would rather have implied the couple's break-up, the author probably chose this 'happy' ending to divert the attention of the censors. It is evident that *Seeds of Fire* was written as an allegory of wartime Iraq, devoid of any heroism and patriotic eulogies, but rather reflecting upon the very process of producing 'war literature' from a notably critical perspective, with an implicit but unmistakable reference to the massacres of the Kurds committed by the Baʿth regime in 1987/8 – as part of its so called Anfāl campaign,[43] the regime used chemical weapons against Kurdish villages and towns in what was officially presented as a counter-insurgency measure but in practice constituted an atrocious mass murder of a civilian population that many observers considered as genocidal in its proportions – as well as to the use of poison gas against Iranian troops during the war:

> In fact, this is a novel that traces through the transformation of Layla, a woman working within the system, into a dissident as she uses art to forge an oppositional discourse [...]. Layla's art makes explicit what was meant to remain hidden, but in the very same process it hides another message that is the story of its purpose. Her art demystifies the information the company is disseminating and changes consumers from unconscious participants into observers [...]. Literature becomes the site of a struggle over the interpretation and definition of the war.[44]

At the same time, the novel addresses the divisive effects of the war on a personal level. It describes how lovers become strangers to each other, instead of praising the cohesive national family, as did many other works published under the rubric 'war literature'. In this novel, the struggle over the meaning of the war is also expressed in the changing gender roles represented in the plot. Thus, as the two spouses become estranged from each other over the years, Laylā is left alone with her unborn child and with memories of Yāsir from the time of their engagement, when he had possessed so much 'beauty, femininity, and gentleness'.[45] The novel thereby implicitly criticizes the model of a heroic military masculinity that was endlessly promoted in Iraqi 'war literature'. Notably, Yāsir's change of attitude towards Laylā is presented as part of a process of his loss of the compassionate 'female' aspects of his character.[46] Moving beyond Cooke's discussion of the dissident political subtext of the novel, the remainder of this chapter focuses on the personal dimension of the war experience that is addressed in the novel and was also raised in the Iraqi media. It is here that an explicit 'struggle over the interpretation and definition of the war' can be observed. Al-Dulaymī's novel offered a clear challenge of the regime's wartime gender policies, which was refuted by loyalist literary critics, without, however, banning the publication and dissemination of the novel inside Iraq.

Ba'thist literary criticism and sexual norms

Al-Dulaymī's novel was reviewed in *al-Thawra* without any reference to its dissident character in the stricter political sense, which formed the focus of Cooke's interpretation of the novel.[47] The critic Dāwūd Salmān al-Shuwaylī was himself a writer of 'proper' war literature and had previously published a study entitled 'The Issue of Sexuality in the Iraqi Novel'.[48] His review mainly discusses the representation of sexuality in al-Dulaymī's novel, namely, he focuses on the dynamics of Yāsir and Laylā's relationship from the perspective of gender roles. He characterizes the relationship between Laylā and Yāsir in a way that is equally critical of both.

According to al-Shuwaylī, prior to Yāsir's departure their relationship is very close, and Laylā's personality is said to have almost melted into her husband's. To some degree, this description of their early relationship seems to delineate Yāsir and Laylā as two figures whose gendered identities were not clearly distinguishable from one another, who put the highest emphasis on their common humanity rather than stressing their physical differences. Thus, Laylā is quoted saying: 'I do not desire worldly lust from you, like other women do.' Rather, she misses the spiritual fulfilment her husband and their relationship offered her. Her loneliness is intensified by the fact that her brother, too, has left home to fight in the war. Rather dismissively, in his review article al-Shuwaylī contends that Laylā misses her brother even more than her husband. The heroine of this novel, Laylā, evidently represents educated middle-class women. Laylā's husband Yāsir starts his new life as a worker among many other men working in the desert. This is a metaphor referring to men who were drafted into the military and sent to the frontline, a strictly male environment where women rarely figured and then only in medical professions. Yāsir misses Laylā but, unlike her, he dreams of her regularly at night in a clearly eroticized way. This leads al-Shuwaylī to maintain that Yāsir remembers her not as his wife and a human being, that he misses not her 'body and soul' but rather her 'things': her sex. He describes Yāsir's refusal when Laylā begs him to let her join him at his workplace in the desert, pointing to the male surroundings in his workplace and arguing that she would never be happy with him there, that out there men viewed women 'only as a body, as an object of desire and a nightly dream'.

These remarks can be read as a subtle critique of the eroticized imagery used in Iraqi war propaganda for mobilization purposes, in which the Iraqi homeland was habitually depicted as a sleeping beauty in need of protection by heroic male soldiers, and the relation between the frontline and the rear was often depicted as a love relationship between a male soldier and his beloved woman, at times with rather overt sexual overtones and from a thoroughly masculinized perspective.[49]

Laylā's request to join her husband 'at the front' recalls demands raised by the GFIW during the 1970s and early 1980s to include women in the armed forces, which were rejected by the regime, and which pointed to a lack of acceptance in Iraqi society for such moves and to the 'natural' gender order of things.[50] Against this background, the novel was easily understood as a critical comment on the regime's sexualized war propaganda and its gender policies more generally, as well as the way the war impacted on gender relations in Iraqi society.

The dissident nature of al-Dulaymī's novel was not lost on al-Shuwaylī, who criticizes it for being 'filled with a lot of empty talk'. Yet, he refrains from tackling the broader issues related to the regime's wartime policies that were implicitly raised in the novel. By the late 1980s, the regime was aware of a growing war fatigue among the Iraqi population, and al-Dulaymī's novel was an expression of this trend. In this case, a literary critic loyal to the regime chose simply to ignore this dimension of the novel's plot. Instead, the review focuses exclusively on the two main protagonists and their relation as a married couple. Al-Shuwaylī identifies the issue of sexuality and the ways Yāsir and Laylā experience it as the leitmotif of al-Dulaymī's novel. According to him, both Yāsir and Laylā are incapable of facing their own sexuality and prefer to run away from it. Sexuality, he explains, is a fundamental dimension of relationships between men and women. However, he warns, it should never be an end in itself, 'even if some people think of it that way', but always merely a means to an end, namely procreation. He clearly disapproves of the fact that Laylā still 'awaits her first child after ten years of unfertile marriage' and of the ways both Laylā and Yāsir view their relationship, either as purely spiritual or as purely sexual. In a healthy relationship, he implies, husband and wife should live together and reconcile 'body and soul' by acting out their sexuality for procreative purposes. His intervention mirrors the explicitly anti-feminist line taken by ʿAbd al-Wāḥid Muḥammad regarding Showalter's book discussed in the previous section, according to which women would be denied agency of their own, independent of men.

Between the lines he appears to offer a critique of Laylā's and Yāsir's way of life, which the Baʿthist regime had promoted as a positive ideal in the 1970s, the model of a nuclear family with few children and two educated spouses who both work in their respective professions, sometimes at the expense of conjugal and family life. Al-Shuwaylī attacks this model: he approves of sexuality only for procreative purposes, and thus views women exclusively as mothers. Luṭfiyya al-Dulaymī offers her readers a sceptical outlook on the possibility of meaningful relationships between women and men in Iraq under the circumstances of the time, which in fact reinforced the gender segregation that the regime's earlier reform policies had helped to blur to some degree. In contrast, al-Shuwaylī's agenda echoes the regime's renewed emphasis on family values and procreation since the late 1980s,[51] a prelude to its religious turn in the 1990s. Al-Shuwaylī insists on a binary gender regime as a natural given, where women are defined through motherhood while men provide for the family in dangerous and faraway places. He thereby implicitly criticizes al-Dulaymī's novel for portraying both women and men as leading their own professional lives and for blurring the binary gender order through its description of Laylā and Yāsir's early relationship.

It is significant that despite the criticism levelled against al-Dulaymī's novel, which reflected official regime discourse during the late 1980s, her work was published and publicly acknowledged in Iraq. The regime would not completely silence such voices. Al-Shuwaylī's review of al-Dulaymī's work echoes reports of an emerging domestic 'cultural opposition' challenging official discourse during the 1990s. ʿAbbūd dismisses such developments as mere fig leaves or even fabrications aimed at diverting attention from the tyrannical character of Saddam Hussein's rule.[52] Arguably, though, tolerating the emergence of such voices might also be a tactic by the regime to neutralize political discontent by acknowledging it, however ambivalently.[53] Underlying are questions regarding the functioning on the ground of authoritarian or dictatorial systems in general, and Saddam Hussein's Iraq in particular.[54]

Conclusion

Luṭfiyya al-Dulaymī has been highlighted here as an Iraqi novelist operating from within the system, whose works indicate her increasingly critical stance towards the regime's war policies over the years. Instead of reinforcing a masculinist and heroic narrative as favoured by the regime, in *Seeds of Fire* she critically reflects on the price Iraqi society paid for the regime's war policies. Her novel reflects the experiences of many educated Iraqi middle-class women whose husbands were called up for military service during the Iran–Iraq War. Al-Dulaymī's novel and its reception by literary critics thus seem to mirror an ongoing power struggle within Iraq between modernists and a more conservative social strata. Educated middle-class women formed an important part of the modernist camp, and they found ways to publicly articulate their views. Although by the late 1980s the regime had abandoned its former Modernism, symbolized by its official commitment to gender reforms, it didn't prevent such debates from being staged in public. The oppositional political subtext of this novel becomes visible when looking at the gendered characters it presents as well as when scrutinizing the public reception of al-Dulaymī's work inside Iraq. But allowing a degree of debate and certain spaces of contestation to emerge in the public realm reflected a communication strategy on the part of the regime meant to reproduce the existing order by showing a degree of flexibility towards expressions of discontent, provided the dictator himself was not mentioned.[55] In this sense, one should not consider al-Dulaymī's work a straightforward expression of political dissidence. Rather, her novel reflects the modernist wing of the Baʿthist constituency and a central tenet of the party's original ideological costume, which the regime pushed to the margins in the late war years, albeit without completely delegitimizing it. The ambiguities of literary production in Iraq and its reception in public discourse, which I have tried to outline in this chapter by focusing on a work by one prominent author published during the most repressive period of the 1980s, should be understood as reflections of a continuous struggle for cultural hegemony in Baʿthist Iraq within the parameters set by the regime, in which artists were not simply irresponsible and thoroughly indoctrinated puppets in the service of Saddam Hussein but rather proved their agency through the way they bargained their position vis-à-vis the apparatus and decided on their actions throughout the years.

Notes

1 Eric Davis, *Memories of State: Politics, History and Memory in Modern Iraq* (Berkeley, CA: University of California Press, 2005); Miriam Cooke, *Dissident Syria: Making Oppositional Arts Official* (Durham, NC: Duke University Press, 2007).

2 For women in Iraq generally, see, for example, Nadje Al-Ali, *Iraqi Women: Untold Stories from 1948 to the Present* (London: Zed Books, 2007); Nadje Al-Ali, 'Iraqi Women and Gender Relations: Redefining Difference', *British Journal of Middle Eastern Studies*, 35 (3) (2008): 405–19; Noga Efrati, 'The Other "Awakening" in Iraq: The Women's Movement in the First Half of the Twentieth Century', *British Journal of Middle Eastern Studies*, 31 (2) (2004): 153–73; Noga Efrati, 'Competing Narratives: Histories of the Women's Movement in Iraq, 1910–1958', *International Journal of Middle East Studies*, 40 (2008): 445–66; and Noga Efrati, *Women in Iraq: Past Meets Present* (New York: Columbia University Press, 2012). For useful overviews of the evolution of modern Iraqi literature, see Fabio Caiani and Catherine Cobham, *The Iraqi Novel: Key Writers, Key Texts* (Edinburgh: Edinburgh University Press, 2013) and Ronen Zeidel, 'On Dictatorship, Literature and the Coming Revolution: Regime and Novels in Iraq 1995–2003', *Nidaba: An Interdisciplinary Journal of Middle East Studies*, 2 (1) (2017): 62–74, although neither work specifically addresses literature written by women authors.

3 Lisa Wedeen, 'Conceptualizing Culture: Possibilities for Political Science', *American Political Science Review*, 96 (4) (2002): 713–28.

4 Miriam Cooke, *Women and the War Story* (Berkeley, CA: University of California Press, 1996).

5 Eric Davis, 'The Historical Genesis of the Public Sphere in Iraq, 1900–1963: Implications for Building Democracy in Post-Baʿthist Iraq', in Seteney Shami (ed.), *Publics, Politics and Participation: Locating the Public Sphere in the Middle East and North Africa*, 385–427 (New York: Social Science Research Council, 2009).

6 In this vein, see Davis, *Memories of State*, 275; Pierre Darle, *Saddam Hussein, maître des mots: du langage de la tyrannie à la tyrannie du langage* (Paris: L'Harmattan, 2003), 34–5. For comparable processes in Nazi Germany, see David Welch, 'Nazi Propaganda and the Volksgemeinschaft: Constructing a People's Community', *Journal of Contemporary History*, 39 (2) (2004): 213–38. Regarding Syria, see Aurora Sottimano, 'Ideology and Discourse in the Era of Baʿthist Reforms: Towards an Analysis of Authoritarian Governmentality', in Aurora Sottimano and Kjetil Selvik (eds), *Changing Regime Discourse and Reform in Syria*, 3–40 (Boulder, CO: Lynne Rienner, 2009).
7 Achim Rohde, 'Echoes from Below? Democracy Talk in Baʿthist Iraq', *Middle Eastern Studies*, 53 (4) (2017): 551–70.
8 Noga Efrati, 'Productive or Reproductive? The Roles of Iraqi Women during the Iraq-Iran War', *Middle Eastern Studies*, 35 (2) (1999): 27–44; Amatzia Baram, 'The Effects of Iraqi Sanctions: Statistical Pitfalls and Responsibility', *Middle East Journal*, 54 (2) (2000): 194–223; Achim Rohde, 'War and Gender in Baʿthist Iraq', in Moha Ennaji and Fatima Sadiqi (eds), *Gender and Violence in the Middle East*, 97–114 (London: Routledge, 2011).
9 Achim Rohde, *State-Society Relations in Baʿthist Iraq: Facing Dictatorship* (London: Routledge, 2010), 75–85.
10 Amatzia Baram, *Culture, History and Ideology in the Formation of Baʿthist Iraq* (London: Macmillan, 1991); Samir al-Khalil, *The Monument: Art, Vulgarity and Responsibility in Iraq* (London: André Deutsch, 1991); Davis, *Memories of State*.
11 Baram, *Culture, History and Ideology in the Formation of Baʿthist Iraq*.
12 Muḥammad al-Jazāʾirī, *al-Qātil wa-l-Ḍaḥiyya: Mīthūlūjiyā wa-Shiʿr* (London: Dār al-Warrāq, 1998); Terri DeYoung, *Placing the Poet: Badr Shakir al-Sayyab and Postcolonial Iraq* (Albany, NY: State University of New York Press, 1998).
13 Cooke, *Women and the War Story*, 232–34.
14 Andrew Parker, Mary Russo, Doris Sommer and Patricia Yaeger (eds), *Nationalisms and Sexualities* (London: Routledge, 1992); Achim Rohde, 'Opportunities for Masculinity and Love: Cultural Production in Iraq during the 1980s', in Lahoucine Ouzgane (ed.), *Islamic Masculinities*, 184–210 (London: Zed Books, 2006); Rohde, *State-Society Relations in Baʿthist Iraq*; Rohde, 'War and Gender in Baʿthist Iraq'; Wiebke Walther, 'From Women's Problems to Women as Images in Modern Iraqi Poetry', Die *Welt des Islams*, 36 (2) (1996): 219–41.
15 Cooke, *Women and the War Story*, 249.
16 Evelyne Accad (ed.), *Sexuality and War: Literary Masks of the Middle East* (New York: New York University Press, 1990); Miriam Cooke and Angela Woollacott (eds), *Gendering War Talk* (Princeton, NJ: Princeton University Press, 1993).
17 Cooke, *Women and the War Story*, 240.
18 Nadia Al-Bagdadi, 'Nachwort', in Ikbal Hasson (ed.), *Die schwarze Abaya: Irakische Erzählungen*, 113–15 (Berlin: EXpress Edition, 1986).
19 Rohde, *State-Society Relations in Baʿthist Iraq* and 'Echoes from Below?'.
20 Achim Rohde, 'Gays, Cross-Dressers, and Emos: Non-Normative Masculinities in Militarized Iraq', *Journal of Middle East Women's Studies*, 12 (3) (2016): 433–49.
21 Salām ʿAbbūd, *Thaqāfa al-ʿUnf fī al-ʿIrāq* (Cologne: al-Kamel Verlag, 2002).
22 Samir al-Khalil, *Republic of Fear: The Politics of Modern Iraq* (London: Hutchinson Radius, 1989).
23 Joseph Sassoon, *Saddam Hussein's Baʿth Party: Inside an Authoritarian Regime* (Cambridge: Cambridge University Press, 2012); Aaron M. Faust, *The Baʿthification of Iraq. Saddam Hussein's Totalitarianism* (Austin, TX: University of Texas Press, 2015).

24 Fatima Mohsen, 'Debating Iraqi Culture: Intellectuals between the Inside and the Outside', in Stefan Millich, Friederike Pannewick and Leslie Tramontini (eds), *Conflicting Narratives: War, Trauma and Memory in Iraqi Culture*, 5–24 (Wiesbaden: Reichert, 2012); Leslie Tramontini, 'The Struggle for Representation: The Internal Iraqi Dispute over Cultural Production in Baathist Iraq', in Stefan Millich, Friederike Pannewick and Leslie Tramontini (eds), *Conflicting Narratives: War, Trauma and Memory in Iraqi Culture*, 25–48 (Wiesbaden: Reichert, 2012).

25 ʿAbd Jāsim al-Sāʿadī, *al-Dhākira wa-l-Ḥanīn fī al-Qiṣṣa al-ʿIrāqiyya al-Qaṣīra fī al-Manfā* (London: al-Rāfid, 1996), 103–24.

26 Muhsin Jassim al-Musawi, *Reading Iraq: Culture and Power in Conflict* (London: I.B.Tauris, 2006).

27 Mark LeVine, 'Chaos, Globalization, and the Public Sphere: Political Struggle in Iraq and Palestine', *Middle East Journal*, 60 (3) (2006): 489, considers 'a "gray zone" between authoritarianism and democracy as the space in which politics can be contested' in most countries in the contemporary Middle East.

28 bell hooks, 'Choosing the Margin as a Space of Radical Openness', *Framework: The Journal of Cinema and Media*, 36 (1989): 15–23.

29 Salmān Hādī Āl-Ṭaʿma (ed.), *Shāʿirāt ʿIrāqiyyāt Muʿāṣirāt*, 2nd edn. (Damascus: Dār al-Barāq li-l-Ṭibāʿa wa-l-Nashr, 1995); see also Nathalie Handal (ed.), *The Poetry of Arab Women: A Contemporary Anthology* (New York: Interlink Books, 2001).

30 After seizing power through a coup d'état in 1968, the Iraqi Baʿthist regime sought to stabilize its rule through repression and co-optation. The party-affiliated civilian mass and corporatist organizations, among them the GFIW, served to streamline all sectors of Iraqi civil society and to draw them into the governing apparatus. The GFIW's agenda amounted to a moderate reformism of gender relations in Iraqi society, focusing on education and the integration of women into the wage labour force. Its biggest achievement was a modest reform of the Personal Status Law in 1978, although it fell short of its original demands, which were rejected by the regime's leadership. See Rohde, *State-Society Relations in Baʿthist Iraq*, 76–85.

31 For an English language survey of literature written by Iraqi women, see Ferial J. Ghazoul, 'Iraq', in Radwa Ashour, Ferial J. Ghazoul and Hasna Reda-Mekdashi (eds), *Arab Women Writers: A Critical Reference Guide, 1873–1999*, 178–203 (Cairo: American University of Cairo Press, 2007).

32 Elaine Showalter (ed.), *The New Feminist Criticism: Essays on Women, Literature and Theory* (London: Virago, 1986). It is interesting that this debate between the two literary critics refers only to Showalter, a landmark of white feminist critical literary theory, and they do not refer to black or postcolonial feminist literary criticism, as formulated by Alice Walker and bell hooks, among others, who greatly influenced Arab feminist thought.

33 Margot Badran, 'Between Secular and Islamic Feminism/s: Reflections on the Middle East and Beyond', *Journal of Middle East Women's Studies*, 1 (1) (2005): 6–28: 13; Samia Mehrez, 'Translating Gender', *Journal of Middle East Women's Studies*, 3 (1) (2007): 106–27. See *al-Thawra*, 19 December 1987.

34 *Al-Thawra*, 9 January 1988.

35 Rohde, 'War and Gender in Baʿthist Iraq'.

36 *Al-Thawra*, 15 and 16 January 1988.

37 Cooke, *Women and the War Story*, 223; Amal Boumaaza, 'War in Iraqi Feminist Writings', MA thesis (Duke University, 2016). Available online: http://dukespace.lib.

duke.edu/dspace/handle/10161/11975 (accessed 8 February 2017), 20–1, see also Al-Bagdadi, 'Nachwort', 114.

38 ʿAbbūd, *Thaqāfa al-ʿUnf fī al-ʿIrāq*, 268, explicitly mentions Khuḍayr and other writers from Basra as exceptions to the rule. For translations into English of some of his works, see also Denis Johnson-Davies (ed.), *Under the Naked Sky: Short Stories from the Arab World* (Cairo: American University of Cairo Press, 2000), 153–65, and Shakir Mustafa (ed.), *Contemporary Iraqi Fiction: An Anthology* (Syracuse, NY: Syracuse University Press, 2008).

39 ʿAbbūd, *Thaqāfa al-ʿUnf fī al-ʿIrāq*, 43–4.

40 For biographical information, see Radwa Ashour, Ferial J. Ghazoul and Hasna Reda-Mekdashi (eds), *Arab Women Writers: A Critical Reference Guide, 1873–1999* (Cairo: American University of Cairo Press, 2007), 385–86, and Boumaaza, 'War in Iraqi Feminist Writings', 23–33. For some of al-Dulaymī's short stories in English translation, see Mustafa, *Contemporary Iraqi Fiction*, as well as several issues of the literary journal *Banipal* (http://www.banipal.co.uk/). See also Rana F. Sweis, 'Iraqi Artists, Actors and Designers Try to Build New Lives in Jordan', *The New York Times*, 23 March 2011.

41 Cooke, *Women and the War Story*, 245–6; Luṭfiyya al-Dulaymī, *Budhūr al-Nār* (Baghdad: Dār al-Shuʾūn al-Thaqāfiyya al-ʿĀmma, 1988).

42 Cooke, *Women and the War Story*, 246.

43 The name Anfāl is taken from the eighth sūra of the Qurʾan and literally means 'the spoils'. The sūra al-Anfāl recalls the battle of Badr between the Prophet's men from Medina and the Meccans (year 2/624). It is important in Islamic jurisprudence as a source of regulations concerning the conduct of war, specifically war against infidels and rules concerning the distribution of booty. *Kuffār* (i.e. polytheists) or, even worse, apostates (*ahl al-ridda*), are considered in Islamic jurisprudence as having forfeited all their rights. If defeated in battle, they are to expect particularly harsh treatment, their property is distributed among the victors, their communities are destroyed, sometimes even the right to a decent burial according to Islamic rites is denied. Such utter destruction was exactly what the inhabitants of the rebellious areas of northern Iraq experienced in 1987/8. Alluding to the Prophet's wars against the Meccans, the units employed in the Anfāl campaign were heralded as Badr forces (Quwwāt Badr). Using Qurʾanic discourse to designate atrocities of the worst kind is not simply a matter of cynicism and concealing the facts, but also an indication of the Baʿthist understanding of such acts of extreme violence as being legitimized by some form of higher justice, one that sees the idea of national unity, embodied in the acceptance of Baʿthist (or, for that matter, Saddam Hussein's) rule, as the absolute source of political legitimacy. The metaphorical use of Qurʾanic discourse in this context underlines the pseudo-religious trait inherent in Baʿthism, one that places loyalty to the regime in the same category as adherence to the Islamic faith (an apostasy in its own right, as it implicitly deifies Saddam Hussein as leader of the Baʿthist state). Kurds refer to the Anfāl campaign as genocide and put the number of victims at 180,000. According to the Baʿth regime's own account, the Anfāl campaign cost about 100,000 human lives. See Rohde, *State-Society Relations in Baʿthist Iraq*, 35–41.

44 Cooke, *Women and the War Story*, 246, 261.

45 Al-Dulaymī, *Budhūr al-Nār*, 38.

46 The estrangement between lovers resulting from long periods of separation during the war was also addressed in a poem by Yūsuf al-Ṣāʾigh. It was about a soldier who had already spent some two years at the front. When one day he phoned his girlfriend

back home, she did not even recognize his voice; he hung up the phone without identifying himself. See *al-Thawra*, 6 July 1986.

47 *Al-Thawra*, 3 May 1990. The following quotations will all be taken from this article.

48 Unfortunately, no bibliographical details are given either for Shuwaylī's study or for another study mentioned in the article by Ghālī Shukrī, entitled 'The Problem of Sexuality in the Arabic Narrative'. For an article on sexuality in literature in general, see *al-Thawra*, 14 July 1990. See also Shujāʿ Musallam al-ʿĀnī, *al-Marʾa fī al-Qiṣṣa al-ʿIrāqiyya*, 2nd edn. (Baghdad: Dār al-Shuʾūn al-Thaqāfiyya al-ʿĀmma, 1986), who, among other topics, discusses female and male sexuality and the ways society dealt with them in Iraqi novels dating back to the 1940s. His work is free of moralistic judgements and presents sexuality as given, while discussing in depth the problems evolving around it in contemporary Iraqi society.

49 Rohde, 'Opportunities for Masculinity and Love', and *State-Society Relations in Baʿthist Iraq*.

50 Ibid., and Rohde, 'War and Gender in Baʿthist Iraq'.

51 For more details, see Efrati, 'Productive or Reproductive?'; Rohde, 'War and Gender in Baʿthist Iraq'.

52 ʿAbbūd, *Thaqāfa al-ʿUnf fī al-ʿIrāq*, 242.

53 Rohde, 'Echoes from Below?'.

54 Ronen Zeidel, 'On Dictatorship, Literature and the Coming Revolution: Regime and Novels in Iraq 1995–2003', *Nidaba: An Interdisciplinary Journal of Middle East Studies*, 2 (1) (2017): 62–74.

55 Rohde, 'Echoes from Below?'.

References

ʿAbbūd, Salām (2002), *Thaqāfa al-ʿUnf fī al-ʿIrāq*, Cologne: al-Kamel Verlag.

Accad, Evelyne (ed.) (1990), *Sexuality and War: Literary Masks of the Middle East*, New York: New York University Press.

Al-Ali, Nadje (2007), *Iraqi Women: Untold Stories from 1948 to the Present*, London: Zed Books.

Al-Ali, Nadje (2008), 'Iraqi Women and Gender Relations: Redefining Difference', *British Journal of Middle Eastern Studies*, 35 (3): 405–19.

Al-ʿĀnī, Shujāʿ Musallam (1986), *al-Marʾa fī al-Qiṣṣa al-ʿIrāqiyya*, 2nd edn., Baghdad: Dār al-Shuʾūn al-Thaqāfiyya al-ʿĀmma.

Al-Bagdadi, Nadia (1985), 'Nachwort', in Ikbal Hasson (ed.), *Die schwarze Abaya: Irakische Erzählungen*, 113–15, Berlin: EXpress Edition.

Al-Dulaymī, Luṭfiyya (1988), *Budhūr al-Nār*, Baghdad: Dār al-Shuʾūn al-Thaqāfiyya al-ʿĀmma.

Al-Jazāʾirī, Muḥammad (1998), *Al-Qātil wa-l-Ḍaḥiyya: Mīthūlūjiyā wa-Shiʿr*, London: Dār al-Warrāq.

Al-Khalil, Samir [Makiya, Kanan] (1989), *Republic of Fear: The Politics of Modern Iraq*, London: Hutchinson Radius.

Al-Khalil, Samir [Makiya, Kanan] (1991), *The Monument: Art, Vulgarity and Responsibility in Iraq*, London: André Deutsch.

Al-Musawi, Muhsin Jassim (2006), *Reading Iraq: Culture and Power in Conflict*, London: I.B.Tauris.

Āl-Ṭaʿma, Salmān Hādī (ed.) (1995), *Shāʿirāt ʿIrāqiyyāt Muʿāṣirāt*, 2nd edn., Damascus: Dār al-Barāq li-l-Ṭibāʿa wa-l-Nashr.
Ashour, Radwa, Ferial J. Ghazoul and Hasna Reda-Mekdashi (eds) (2007), *Arab Women Writers: A Critical Reference Guide, 1873–1999*, Cairo: American University of Cairo Press.
Badran, Margot (2005), 'Between Secular and Islamic Feminism/s: Reflections on the Middle East and Beyond', *Journal of Middle East Women's Studies*, 1 (1): 6–28.
Baram, Amatzia (1991), *Culture, History and Ideology in the Formation of Baʿthist Iraq*, London: Macmillan.
Baram, Amatzia (2000), 'The Effects of Iraqi Sanctions: Statistical Pitfalls and Responsibility', *Middle East Journal*, 54 (2): 194–223.
Boumaaza, Amal (2016), 'War in Iraqi Feminist Writings', MA thesis, Duke University. Available online: http://dukespace.lib.duke.edu/dspace/handle/10161/11975 (accessed 8 February 2017).
Caiani, Fabio and Catherine Cobham (2013), *The Iraqi Novel: Key Writers, Key Texts*, Edinburgh: Edinburgh University Press.
Cooke, Miriam (1996), *Women and the War Story*, Berkeley, CA: University of California Press.
Cooke, Miriam (2007), *Dissident Syria: Making Oppositional Arts Official*, Durham, NC: Duke University Press.
Cooke, Miriam and Angela Woollacott (eds) (1993), *Gendering War Talk*, Princeton, NJ: Princeton University Press.
Darle, Pierre (2003), *Saddam Hussein, maître des mots: du langage de la tyrannie à la tyrannie du langage*, Paris: L'Harmattan.
Davis, Eric (2005), *Memories of State: Politics, History and Memory in Modern Iraq*, Berkeley, CA: University of California Press.
Davis, Eric (2009), 'The Historical Genesis of the Public Sphere in Iraq, 1900–1963: Implications for Building Democracy in Post-Baʿthist Iraq', in Seteney Shami (ed.), *Publics, Politics and Participation: Locating the Public Sphere in the Middle East and North Africa*, 385–427, New York: Social Science Research Council.
DeYoung, Terri (1998), *Placing the Poet: Badr Shakir al-Sayyab and Postcolonial Iraq*, Albany, NY: State University of New York Press.
Efrati, Noga (1999), 'Productive or Reproductive? The Roles of Iraqi Women during the Iraq-Iran War', *Middle Eastern Studies*, 35 (2): 27–44.
Efrati, Noga (2004), 'The Other "Awakening" in Iraq: The Women's Movement in the First Half of the Twentieth Century', *British Journal of Middle Eastern Studies*, 31 (2): 153–73.
Efrati, Noga (2008), 'Competing Narratives: Histories of the Women's Movement in Iraq, 1910–1958', *International Journal of Middle East Studies*, 40: 445–66.
Efrati, Noga (2012), *Women in Iraq: Past Meets Present*, New York: Columbia University Press.
Faust, Aaron M. (2015), *The Baʿthification of Iraq. Saddam Hussein's Totalitarianism*, Austin, TX: University of Texas Press.
Ghazoul, Ferial J. (2007), 'Iraq', in Radwa Ashour, Ferial J. Ghazoul and Hasna Reda-Mekdashi (eds), *Arab Women Writers: A Critical Reference Guide, 1873–1999*, 178–203, Cairo: American University of Cairo Press.
Handal, Nathalie (ed.) (2001), *The Poetry of Arab Women: A Contemporary Anthology*, New York: Interlink Books.

hooks, bell (1989), 'Choosing the Margin as a Space of Radical Openness', *Framework: The Journal of Cinema and Media*, 36: 15–23.
Johnson-Davies, Denis (ed.) (2000), *Under the Naked Sky: Short Stories from the Arab World*, Cairo: American University of Cairo Press.
LeVine, Mark (2006), 'Chaos, Globalization, and the Public Sphere: Political Struggle in Iraq and Palestine', *Middle East Journal*, 60 3: 467–92.
Mehrez, Samia (2007), 'Translating Gender', *Journal of Middle East Women's Studies*, 3 (1): 106–27.
Millich, Stefan, Friederike Pannewick and Leslie Tramontini (eds) (2012), *Conflicting Narratives: War, Trauma and Memory in Iraqi Culture*, Wiesbaden: Reichert.
Mohsen, Fatima (2012), 'Debating Iraqi Culture: Intellectuals between the Inside and the Outside', in Stefan Millich, Friederike Pannewick and Leslie Tramontini (eds), *Conflicting Narratives: War, Trauma and Memory in Iraqi Culture*, 5–24, Wiesbaden: Reichert.
Mustafa, Shakir (ed.) (2008), *Contemporary Iraqi Fiction: An Anthology*, Syracuse, NY: Syracuse University Press.
Parker, Andrew, Mary Russo, Doris Sommer and Patricia Yaeger (eds) (1992), *Nationalisms and Sexualities*, London: Routledge.
Rohde, Achim (2006), 'Opportunities for Masculinity and Love. Cultural Production in Iraq during the 1980s', in Lahoucine Ouzgane (ed.), *Islamic Masculinities*, 184–210, London: Zed Books.
Rohde, Achim (2010), *State-Society Relations in Baʿthist Iraq: Facing Dictatorship*, London: Routledge.
Rohde, Achim (2011), 'War and Gender in Baʿthist Iraq', in Moha Ennaji and Fatima Sadiqi (eds), *Gender and Violence in the Middle East*, 97–114, London: Routledge.
Rohde, Achim (2016), 'Gays, Cross-Dressers, and Emos: Non-Normative Masculinities in Militarized Iraq', *Journal of Middle East Women's Studies*, 12 (3): 433–49.
Rohde, Achim (2017), 'Echoes from Below? Democracy Talk in Baʿthist Iraq', *Middle Eastern Studies*, 53 (4): 551–70.
al-Sāʿadī, ʿAbd Jāsim (1996), *al-Dhākira wa-l-Ḥanīn fī al-Qiṣṣa al-ʿIrāqiyya al-Qaṣīra fī al-Manfā*, London: al-Rāfid.
Sassoon, Joseph (2012), *Saddam Hussein's Baʿth Party: Inside an Authoritarian Regime*, Cambridge: Cambridge University Press.
Showalter, Elaine (ed.) (1986), *The New Feminist Criticism: Essays on Women, Literature and Theory*, London: Virago.
Sottimano, Aurora (2009), 'Ideology and Discourse in the Era of Baʿthist Reforms: Towards an Analysis of Authoritarian Governmentality', in Aurora Sottimano and Kjetil Selvik (eds), *Changing Regime Discourse and Reform in Syria*, 3–40, Boulder, CO: Lynne Rienner.
Sweis, Rana F. (2011), 'Iraqi Artists, Actors and Designers Try to Build New Lives in Jordan', *The New York Times*, 23 March. Available online: https://www.nytimes.com/2011/03/24/world/middleeast/24iht-m24-jordan.html (accessed 26 June 2020).
Tramontini, Leslie (2012), 'The Struggle for Representation: The Internal Iraqi Dispute over Cultural Production in Baathist Iraq', in Stefan Millich, Friederike Pannewick and Leslie Tramontini (eds), *Conflicting Narratives: War, Trauma and Memory in Iraqi Culture*, 25–48, Wiesbaden: Reichert.
Walther, Wiebke (1996), 'From Women's Problems to Women as Images in Modern Iraqi Poetry', *Die Welt des Islams*, 36 (2): 219–41.

Wedeen, Lisa (2002), 'Conceptualizing Culture: Possibilities for Political Science', *American Political Science Review*, 96 (4): 713–28.
Welch, David (2004), 'Nazi Propaganda and the Volksgemeinschaft: Constructing a People's Community', *Journal of Contemporary History*, 39 (2): 213–38.
Zeidel, Ronen (2017), 'On Dictatorship, Literature and the Coming Revolution: Regime and Novels in Iraq 1995–2003', *Nidaba: An Interdisciplinary Journal of Middle East Studies*, 2 (1): 62–74.

Chapter 7

FRAMING THE CLOSET: GAY MEN IN EGYPTIAN CINEMA IN THE 1970S

Koen M. Van Eynde

Egyptian cinema has a long – albeit sparse – history of showing gay and queer characters on the screen.[1] An early example of a gay man on the screen is in the adaptation of the eponymous novel by Naguib Mahfouz (Najīb Maḥfūẓ), *Zuqāq al-Midaqq* (*Midaq Alley*). In it, the gay character Kirsha, a masculine moustache-wearing *muʿallim*,[2] sees most of his sexuality erased compared to the original novel, only occasionally alluding to his homosexuality in the film. Another famous type is the '*ṣabī al-ʿālima*', the servant 'boy' of a dancer who is portrayed as a stereotypical effeminate gay. Actor Fārūq Falawkas played the servant 'boy' type in a couple of films, most notably in *al-Rāqiṣa wa-l-Siyāsī* ('The Dancer and the Politician', Samīr Sayf, 1990) and in *Darb al-Hawā* (*Darb El Hawa*, Ḥussām al-Dīn Muṣṭafā, 1983). Lesbian characters have been portrayed too, as in the 1975 film *Junūn al-Shabāb* ('Crazy Youth', Khalīl Shawqī) and the 1978 film *al-Ṣuʿūd ilā al-Hāwiya* ('Rise to the Abyss', Kamāl al-Shaykh). A commonality of most of the films is their tendency to represent homosexuality negatively, as an affliction or as part of a generally libertine lifestyle. This changed in the 1990s, particularly with the unique film *Mercedes* (Yusrī Naṣrallāh, 1993). Gay men appeared for the first time as men with other interests in life, as ordinary men enjoying football and time out with their friends, although associated with anarchy and living on the streets.[3]

Not only homosexual characters but also other queer representations have found a welcome refuge in Egyptian cinema. A very popular trope in Egyptian comedies is cross-dressing, which falls under the broader category of queer representations on the screen. Like homosexuality, cross-dressing characters allow the films to address, question and possibly subvert traditional concepts of what is deemed to be masculine and feminine behaviour. Through the medium of comedy, it allows the film to address these issues more directly, safe in the knowledge that the elaborate ruse will come to light eventually. Cross-dressing as such exposes the social construct of gender roles, as tongue-in-cheek representations of masculinity and femininity. However, cross-dressing should not be conflated with homosexuality. Cross-dressing is not necessarily queer or gay; instead it could reinforce male and female stereotypes. This chapter will focus on the portrayal of male homosexuality, and in doing so will try to answer the question of how the films assert, challenge and reframe gender norms.

I have chosen two films with a prominent gay character produced in the 1970s, during Anwar Sadat's presidency (1970–1981), boasting famous and popular star actors of their time.[4] The first of the two main films is *Ḥammām al-Malāṭīlī* ('Malatili Bath', Ṣalāḥ Abū Sayf, 1973), with star actor Yūsuf Shaʿbān (b.1936), famous for his roles as an oppressive, Westernized 'liberal',[5] together with the then little-known actor Muḥammad al-ʿArabī (b.1946). The second film I will look at in more detail is *Qiṭṭa ʿalā Nār* ('Cat on Fire', Samīr Sayf, 1977), an adaptation of Tennessee Williams's 1955 play *Cat on a Hot Tin Roof*, with popular actors Nūr al-Sharīf (1946–2015), known for his underdog roles, and Būsī (b.1953).[6] The reason for choosing these two films in this specific time frame is that they appear to digress from the more common practice of simply depicting the existence of same-sex sexual acts. Instead, both films appear to make a case for the possibility of gay identities.

Homosexuality and heteronormativity

Joseph Massad[7] argues that a Western discourse on homosexuality was imposed on the Arab world, forcing the subject onto the table and inevitably sparking a backlash from conservative Islamist and nationalist forces. Massad's claims were met with fierce criticism from local gay rights groups, who insisted that they should not be portrayed solely in terms of a Western neocolonial framework.[8] Massad's point of view has some merits, in the sense that it is difficult and possibly dangerous to transpose a 'gay identity' as fostered in Western discourse across the globe without regard to cultural sensitivities and individual preferences. Human Rights Watch's (2009) report *Together, Apart* notes that 'sexual orientation and gender identity issues have begun to enter the agendas of some mainstream human rights movements' but warns that 'these vital developments were not won through identity politics'. Instead, it continues, 'the urge of some western LGBT activists to unearth and foster "gay" politics in the region is potentially deeply counterproductive'.[9] However, not recognizing the existence and rights of gay people, and indeed the right to fight for them and give them a voice, is a valid criticism against Massad's strong opposition to presumed 'Western' lesbian, gay, bisexual, transgender and intersex (LGBTI) rights groups. It is therefore important to recognize the presence of gay men and women in Egypt, while treating with caution Western discursive practices and identity politics when talking about Egyptian gay subjects.

The dialectic between the international and the local debate should be articulated taking into consideration multiple factors, including political contingencies. In the case of Egypt, the theme of 'indigeneity' and 'cultural authenticity' has been used by conservative political actors – both religious and secular – and the current backlash against gay people confirms the inherent link between gender representations, the governing of sexuality and authoritarianism.[10] The very notion of a gay identity along with other discussions on identity politics[11] could be construed by authorities and conservative forces alike as a Western construct and import, and used by authoritarian regimes to justify a crackdown on minority or disadvantaged groups. As a case in point, some critics of *Cat on Fire* describe the film's story as 'foreign to Egyptian society'.[12] This does not mean that people are unaware of the existence of Egyptian homosexuals, or that they believe Egyptian homosexuals do not exist. Instead, what these statements indicate is that the concept of a gay identity, of someone identifying publicly as gay, is something most people would rather not have to confront. What, then, is a gay identity, and how could we approach the subject in an Egyptian context?

In that respect, gender is understood as a performance, as defined by Judith Butler in *Gender Trouble* ([1990] 2007). Gender is neither stable nor coherent, but rather a 'stylized repetition of acts' that the actors (in a broad sense, namely those performing gender) come to believe through continuous repetition.[13] However, gender performances can only meaningfully exist within a 'highly rigid regulatory frame'.[14] Informed by Butler, Samira Aghacy, in her account of masculine performance in Arabic novels since 1967, asserts that gender is also always 'in accordance with socially constituted norms and patterns of masculinity and femininity'.[15] This approach allows us to deconstruct hegemonic power structures and lay bare those individual performances of gender and identity, which are in turn informed by hegemonic gender performances or what is commonly held as masculine (or feminine) behaviour in Egypt at any given time.

The question that springs to mind is whether Egyptian cinema offers the possibility, tacitly or explicitly, for alternative gender performances, and what role they could play. The argument that runs through this chapter is that the Egyptian film industry has always been inclined to question dominant gender roles, offering a space for discussing taboo subjects, without necessarily offering alternatives to these dominant roles and instead asserting a new hegemonic ideal for masculine or feminine identity. For example, even in the earliest Egyptian films, traditional concepts of marriage – as an agreement between families – and love were reconstituted as a private understanding between individuals and the concept of romantic love respectively. Although it is easy to draw parallels with Egyptian cinema's Western counterpart, it is important to bear in mind that the films often promote a message of 'evolutionary change' without questioning patriarchal authority.[16] In other words, the modern relationships, whilst remaining safely within the boundaries of heterosexual love and reaffirming heteronormativity, show a potential for change, challenging the presumed static Arab (gender) identities in Egyptian cinema. Egyptian cinema could thus be a space where new gender roles and identities are discussed, including the supposed West-originating categories of gay identities, placing them within a localized, Egyptian, cultural context. The specific roles of homosexual characters in the discussed films are to be read in this context of Egyptian popular culture and in particular Egyptian cinema. Egyptian cinematic practices accept the existence of what they deem to be old-fashioned gender norms and roles, and try to address these, albeit by asserting reconstituted heteronormative identities in the films' resolution.

Melodrama and the nation

Themes of family, heritage and nation-building held and continue to hold centre stage in Egyptian cultural products.[17] Ella Shohat asserts that Egyptian cinema conveyed a 'nationalist ideology [that] aimed to provide the people with an interpretation of reality that claimed to transform them from traditional subjects to active citizens'.[18] This ideology, aimed at transforming subjects into citizens, is not unique to Egyptian cinema. Writing about Arab New Realist films, Malek Khouri argues that themes of nation, identity and self-determination 'in many ways echo [...] the early stages of [the] *al-Nahḍa* movement in the 19th century'.[19] A modernist narrative was given shape, manifesting itself in Egyptian films. Armbrust writes that the country's industry had created a filmic language recognizable to Egyptian viewers, suffused with images synthesizing local and foreign elements[20] such as the 'ibn al-balad'[21] and the educated class. A new nation was envisioned on the screen, with themes such as family life and gender relations, women's rights, education, a modern notion of self and the role of Arab and Egyptian heritage in the construction of the modern self, which could eventually contribute to social and national progress. Lila Abu-Lughod described these narratives as 'development realism', a model for cultural products that purports to 'educate' citizens into becoming national subjects. These state narratives, however, were at times also subverted in Egyptian films, more so after the 1967 defeat in the Six Day War and the collapse of pan-Arabism as a viable political ideology.

From the late 1960s onwards, the country's film industry started to portray an identity crisis engulfing the country (and the Arab world). They started to approach the modern ideals of social progress critically, some more explicitly so than others, without changing their paradigm of film-making practices. Elsewhere I have argued that one of the crises portrayed in films of this era was the crisis of man.[22] As protectors and providers of the nation (and family), hegemonic ideals that films continued to represent, men fell short of their tasks in order to perform their masculinity successfully on-screen. It was, as such, a crisis of masculinity that manifested itself primarily in two ways: (1) through portrayals of 'defeated men', men unable to cope with the new political situation and the shattering of the ideal of Arab unity promised by the Nasserist regime; and (2) through men reinventing themselves and asserting a new-found dominant position. Actor Nūr al-Sharīf (*Cat on Fire*) is famous for his roles as a 'defeated man', while Yūsuf Shaʿbān (*Malatili Bath*) is an advocate of the second type.

The 1970s could be described as a relatively liberal period in terms of depicting sexuality on the silver screen in Egypt.[23] In this decade, the Egyptian film industry underwent a number of changes, including being partly reprivatized and experiencing a lack of investment from the state as compared to previous decades.[24] In the early 1970s, Egypt's economy was weakened by the aftermath of the expensive Six Day War in 1967, which resulted in Israel occupying the Sinai and the closure of the Suez Canal, a major source of revenue for the country. Early in Sadat's presidency, however, the country made some political gains in the aftermath of the October War of 1973, which is portrayed as a victory by the

Egyptian official narrative. Afterwards, the country started to look towards the United States as a major ally, which became more and more visible in films from this period too. Egyptian cinema in the 1970s portrayed a modern lifestyle, encompassing Western commodities and embracing a consumer society. The films under discussion here were made before social conservatism became more prevalent in the country in the late 1970s and early 1980s, around the time of Sadat's economic policy changes, known as *Infitāḥ*.[25]

Malatili Bath *(1973)*

The director of the film, Ṣalāḥ Abū Sayf (1915–1996), was well known and often lauded for his films' realism, and described as the Director of Realism by Egyptian critics.[26] Many of his films top the list of Egyptian classics.[27] According to critic Ḥassan Ḥaddād, the realist style of Ṣalāḥ Abū Sayf meant more than depicting a truthful portrait of reality; it meant looking for reasons behind the present state.[28] He is particularly known for his films portraying misery and injustice, sometimes inferred to be in monarchical Egypt (prior to the 1952 Free Officers' coup d'état).[29] According to Joel Gordon, Abū Sayf's films, together with other films of the Nasser era, have contributed to the 'construction of a new civic identity for an independent Egypt'.[30] *Malatili Bath* is one example of a film exploring the sociopolitical crisis in the country behind the defeat against Israel in 1967, according to the director's own artistic views.

The film opens with long shots of Cairo's busy streets, zooming in on stop signs, police regulating traffic and the statues of Cairo's major squares, with close-ups of their hands, held up straight as if to say 'stop'. The film's introduction sets the mood: chaos, limitations, restrictions and difficulties await the protagonists. The camera zooms in on a young man, Aḥmad (Muḥammad al-ʿArabī), who has recently moved to the city in search of education and a job, a better life for himself and his family, who stayed behind in Ismailia.[31] He is soon confronted with the economic realities in Cairo – a city suffering from increasing unemployment, high living costs and insufficient housing – and finds himself living on the streets. This is where he meets his future girlfriend, the prostitute Naʿīma (Shams al-Barūdī, b. 1945), with whom he is immediately infatuated – although remembering, through a flashback, his mother's warning of 'the immoral women of Cairo'. Eventually he finds a place to sleep indoors, in a public bath owned by a virile and moustachioed *muʿallim*. The *muʿallim* immediately takes Aḥmad under his protection, possibly due to the latter's youthful good looks, though the *muʿallim* is also visibly pleased to help out a boy from the distraught city of Ismailia.

The sweating bodies of the men frequenting the bathhouse make Aḥmad noticeably uncomfortable, yet he has no other choice but to stay at night. Soon after settling down, Raʾūf (Yūsuf Shaʿbān) enters the bathhouse. Several signifiers make it clear he is from a different socio-economic background to the other patrons of the bath: he is addressed respectfully, drives a large American car, wears expensive Western clothes and is an artist. Before long, it is inferred from the sound of commotion off-screen that Raʾūf is being physically attacked by the other patrons of the bathhouse, though the reason for this is unknown to the viewers. We then learn that he frequents the bath to draw the men, under the pretence of being an artist, but in reality uses it as a venue to pick up men. Raʾūf is an uncomfortable character, out of place in the bathhouse. He does not fit in, not only in terms of class but also in terms of sexuality. He proudly wears a moustache as a symbol of manliness,[32] but it becomes clear that this manly looking character has other interests than just his artistic expression, and perhaps his moustache is only a cover to hide his closeted feelings for other men. The other patrons as well as the bathhouse's employees know what is going on and why he is there, with one of the employees constantly repeating the phrase 'may God have mercy on us' in his presence, which will eventually become a running gag throughout the movie.

The film is not a comedy, yet it does have regular comedic relief like this. The employee's sarcastic comments show he is well aware of what is going on inside, but he will never say anything explicitly. Ṣalāḥ Abū Sayf's films often tackle serious topics with a hint of humour,[33] perhaps in an attempt to make the plot more enjoyable, but in this case, it may well serve to explore some Egyptian attitudes towards non-hegemonic practices of sexuality. By repeating this phrase, the employee, who is in a class-sense inferior to Raʾūf, shows a sense of moral superiority with comedic effect. Jeroen Vandaele has argued that a combination of the theories of incongruity and superiority are essential to study the role of humour in film.[34] Incongruity exposes the unexpected and superiority is 'understood as the social aspect of humor',[35] where viewers can show they have understood the situation and the seemingly incongruous statements made by the bathhouse employee. In this case, the employee steps out of his expected subservient role and makes an innocent comment. By doing so, a situation is created for the audience to laugh at the situational humour and to show their peers that they understand what is going on (by laughing) but not explicitly by having to talk about it. The film, however, forces us to confront Raʾūf's homosexuality, Naʿīma's sexual liberty and Aḥmad's sexual awakening.

Aḥmad is still a virgin, who will experience sex for the first time with Naʿīma. Once he is no longer a virgin and it is inferred his moral decline is complete, he gives in to Raʾūf's repeated invitations to come to his place, described by the *muʿallim* as a beautiful house overlooking the Nile – raising the question of whether he himself has visited Raʾūf at his home. Aḥmad is asked to take off his shirt, showing his youthful body for Raʾūf to draw. At one point, Aḥmad changes the radio channel and an awkward moment ensues when Raʾūf hears the tunes of James Brown's *Sex Machine* and starts dancing, shirtless. Exhausted, he sits down next to Aḥmad and asks him if he has 'tried love', before thrashing the large portrait of his mother hanging in the living room. He then tells Aḥmad and the viewers about his painful journey as a homosexual man in Egypt, being treated with hormones and pills to curb his 'unnatural inclinations': his father left the country when he found out about his son's sexuality; his mother initially stayed but eventually left him to fend for himself after she realized he could not be cured.

Besides exploring themes of sexuality, the film is also a critique of the corrupted mindset of people in the country, specifically the capital. The older Raʾūf claims the country used to be open-minded, allowing for more personal freedoms, suggesting that nowadays people are preoccupied with regulating each other's whereabouts, looks and who they fall in love with. Raʾūf, whose assimilation into a Western lifestyle is repeatedly emphasized, and Aḥmad, whose interest in the country's and Cairo's Islamic and Arab history is frequently mentioned, have contrasting visions for the future and contrasting explanations for what has caused the current crisis. Aḥmad's youthfulness extends beyond his body and good looks. Raʾūf believes he is naïve for having hopes for a better future. Aḥmad believes in the promises of the regime and that through education and hard work, rather than sitting idly by, he can contribute to building a stronger nation. Raʾūf on the other hand is fatalistic – for which Aḥmad blames the artist – and argues that the people's self-regulating behaviour inevitably results in a narrow-minded focus away from the things that matter in life. Aḥmad's and Raʾūf's private discussions are part of the director's attempt to lay bare and explore the reasons behind the country's socio-economic demise. Aḥmad, however, slowly allows Cairo's fatalism to take hold and forgets about his idealism, until his girlfriend Naʿīma's brutal murder by her rural family serves as a violent wake-up call; the film ends with a moralizing message telling the audience, and Egypt, to 'wake up'.[36]

The film appears to expose constructed social roles that restrain diversity using a cinematic language, a 'myth of modernity', that is commonly understood by its audience. Instead of positively depicting these new gender roles, the film denounces the failure of the modernist project that had resulted in complacency. In order to get its point across, the film explores the nadir of Egyptian society, in doing so associating homosexuality with criminality and disease, prostitution and possibly a non-Egyptian, unpatriotic lifestyle. However, although Raʾūf is clearly a sick man, suffering from the effects of mind-numbing medication, his homosexuality is not portrayed as repulsive. Indeed, it is clearly depicted as something natural, something he was born with, albeit well hidden beneath the filth of everyday life in the corrupted city. The film allows for a certain amount of sympathy for the character, who has been a victim of his surroundings, forcing him to stay in the closet. The same is true for Naʿīma, the prostitute, who is the victim of a harsh economic environment and an unwelcoming society for single working women. The film acknowledges her and Raʾūf 's agency, but they are forced to live a life of limitations and restrictions, treading and transgressing the line of propriety and living the ideal masculine and feminine roles society has carved out for them, from which they have tried to escape.

Cat on Fire *(1977)*

Cat on Fire was directed by Samīr Sayf (b.1947), a mainstream director whose films are often big commercial successes, such as *al-Mashbūh* ('The Suspect', 1981), *al-Nimr wa-l-Unthā* ('The Tiger and the Female', 1987) and *al-Mutawaḥḥisha*

('The Savage Girl', 1979), with popular actress Su'ād Ḥusnī (1943–2001).[37] *Cat On Fire* also boasts a number of stars of its time, with actor Nūr al-Sharīf (who received numerous prizes for his role in the film)[38] and his wife Būsī[39] in the roles of estranged husband and wife Amīn and Jījī, as well as Farīd Shawqī[40] (1920–1998) and Maryam Fakhr al-Dīn (1933–2014) in the roles of 'Big Daddy' Maḥmūd and 'Big Mama' Amīna. Nūr al-Sharīf was a rising star in the 1970s, playing controversial characters and addressing sensitive topics such as religion and homosexuality,[41] or portraying the downtrodden in society as well as playing roles of political opponents and prisoners throughout his long career – which spanned over forty years and includes more than 230 films and TV series, many of them much less controversial and more commercial in nature. He also played the controversial role of the assassinated Palestinian cartoonist Nājī al-ʿAlī (murdered in London in 1987) in the eponymous film by acclaimed director ʿĀṭif al-Ṭayyib (a protégé of Ṣalāḥ Abū Sayf), for which Egyptian newspapers lambasted him at the time.[42] In *Cat on Fire* he plays the role of Amīn, a former football star whose relationship with his best friend ʿIzzat – who committed suicide – is under intense scrutiny from his family and friends. His wife and family have heard rumours of their close and possibly sexual relationship, which Amīn strongly denies. The majority of the film consists of flashbacks exploring how husband and wife felt, hinting at the possibility of the homosexual relationship between Amīn and ʿIzzat, before ending in husband and wife reconciling and reaffirming heterosexual bonds.

The Egyptian adaptation of Williams's play was adapted for a 1970s Egyptian audience. One noticeable difference is the presence of the homosexual character ʿIzzat (in the same role as Skipper in the original), played by Lebanese actor Shawqī Matā (b.1948),[43] a character physically absent in the American play (and its Hollywood adaptation of 1958).[44] Unhindered by the Hays Code,[45] Egyptian cinema could address a topic such as homosexuality more explicitly than its Hollywood counterpart could, and could therefore include a character like ʿIzzat in the plot. The Egyptian adaptation portrays ʿIzzat's and Amīn's friendship through flashbacks from both Amīn's and Jījī's points of view, to give the viewer an impression of the heavy weight they carry on their shoulders as a result of ʿIzzat's suicide. Most of the memories are Jījī's, showing how she always felt second to ʿIzzat, while the only flashback exclusive to Amīn is to when he is asked to identify ʿIzzat's body. Amīn blames Jījī and is unable to face his own responsibility for the death of his best friend; instead he turns to heavy drinking, leaving behind professional football and losing one job after another.

The themes of avarice, malfunctioning families, gender and sexuality were very present in Egyptian cinema at the time.[46] For example, all the characters except Amīn and his mother Amīna already knew that Amīn's father Maḥmūd was dying, but preferred to keep it quiet and throw him a birthday party, angling for a larger share of his wealth, a storyline taken from the original play. It is a dysfunctional family with everyone talking behind each other's backs; Niṣriyya, Maḥmūd's second daughter-in-law, eavesdrops on others and has been resentful of Jījī's and Maḥmūd's proximity from the very beginning; and Amīn's brother Mukhtār, embodying virility with his moustache, keeps asking his father for more money to cover the costs of raising his many children. Amīn's assumed heroic masculinity as an idolized football player from a wealthy background is questioned on several accounts too: he drinks and is unwilling to sleep with his wife, adding to the rumours of his presumed relationship with his friend ʿIzzat. Amīn, however, remains unable to deal with his possible romantic feelings for ʿIzzat, a constant burden resting on his shoulders.

At the end of the film, the big confrontation happens between father and son, two men struggling to uphold their respective male performances. Maḥmūd wrestles with his sense of manliness as the sick and ageing family patriarch, unwilling to confront his own weakness as well as his son's possible homosexuality. Maḥmūd is forced to talk man to man, something to which he is visibly unaccustomed. He raises the topic carefully, ordering his son Amīn to stop drinking and asking him why he shuns his wife. Maḥmūd then takes the whole family to a new factory that his business is constructing and tells everyone he will leave it in Amīn's hands, in a bid to convince his son to take responsibility as a man. In the ensuing private conversation, Maḥmūd asks the ultimate question about 'what happened between him and the dead boy'. Only at that point does it occur to Amīn that his love for ʿIzzat was obvious to everyone, but denied by himself. Patriarchy, embodied by Maḥmūd, compels Amīn to confront his ambivalent sexual identity, while simultaneously stifling it and denying him the opportunity to explore his feelings for ʿIzzat. The film does not make explicit the nature of the relationship Amīn and ʿIzzat had, although there are several occasions that subvert Amīn's narrative that he 'did not know' about his friend's homosexuality. For instance, ʿIzzat is always present in the flashbacks, seen hugging Amīn tightly when he scored a goal, or looking intently at Amīn and Jījī at a party; or when Amīn argues he did not want his wife to come with them on an 'all-male trip' to Luxor during which he was to share his train cabin with ʿIzzat; or the shock on Amīn's face when he found out ʿIzzat had a night-time visitor in his hotel room that ultimately led to ʿIzzat killing himself.

Cat on Fire is a film developing modernist state narratives of family and gender subversively, seemingly avoiding an idealization of family life and portraying a more univocal human experience. The film's narratives are reminiscent of the cinematic language heralding the development of the nation-state.[47] Carla Marcantonio noted that melodrama has also 'retained an elastic ability to adapt to varying incarnations of modernity',[48] allowing it to explore and express new narratives that run counter to the hegemonic state narratives of social progress. However, through the characters of Amīn on the one hand, and his brother Mukhtār on the other, the film strikes an intricate balance between the former's difficulties in adhering to the ideal expected of him, and the latter's almost caricaturesque portrayal of idealized heterosexual masculinity, while afflicted with money problems, raising the question whether the ideal is desirable or indeed sustainable.

Conclusion

In her study of British comedy actor John Mills's nonconformist roles, Gill Plain argues that the actor's roles 'articulate the failure of heroic masculinity', which, according to Plain, 'suggests an uncomfortable dialogue between the dominant and subordinate masculinities the actor was capable of embodying'.[49] A similar dialogue is at work between and within the different characters in the films discussed here. In *Malatili Bath*, there is a generational clash between the older fatalistic Ra'ūf and the young idealistic Aḥmad. The actor playing Ra'ūf, Yūsuf Sha'bān, is known for portraying domineering and corrupt masculinity, contradicting his presumed enlightened westernized character. His role as an upper-class artist with a moustache and all the symbols of a dominant masculinity is paradoxical because of his subversive sexual identity. In *Cat on Fire*, the dialogue occurs between the old-world masculinity of the family patriarch Maḥmūd and the young idol Amīn, both uncomfortable with the roles in which they have been placed. Simultaneously, actor Nūr al-Sharīf's role as a possibly homosexual football player in this film embodies subordinate and dominant masculinity simultaneously, suggesting the failure of heroic masculinity, possibly reminding viewers of the general mood in a country experiencing socio-economic and political changes many felt they could not keep up with.

The erosion of state narratives and the exposure of the failure of idealized gender roles in films from the late 1960s onwards could be read as an attempt to propose an alternative way of thinking and talking about gender and sexuality. The films do not seem to suggest that homosexual relations are unnatural or repulsive, although the gay characters are associated with mental illness (*Malatili Bath*) and alcohol abuse (*Cat on Fire*), and homosexual relations remain within the realm of the *other*, ending in murder or suicide respectively in order to restore a certain normalcy. Nevertheless, family life is a source of conflict in the films, particularly in *Cat on Fire*, but family is also the solution proposed at the end, reaffirming heteronormativity. At the end of the film, normalcy appears to be restored when Amīn accepts his responsibility for the death of his best friend and agrees to take up his role as husband and provider. *Malatili Bath* refuses to redeem Na'īma or Ra'ūf, although it has gone to great lengths to invoke sympathy for both characters. As such, one could say that both films explore the possibility that heteronormativity is not naturally inscribed onto all of us, while the resolution the films propose requires accepting restrictive norms affecting how we live our lives and experience our bodies.

Both films further highlight difficulties with approaching homosexuality, as an act and an identity. Even though the act is rejected, for a mix of religious, social and cultural preconceptions, its existence is acknowledged and often, as the films show, dealt with as a private matter. Within this context, the films contribute to creating a discourse on homosexuality in Egypt. If heteronormativity is a constructed gender identity and not naturally inscribed onto male and female bodies, the films also seem to suggest that same-sex desire could forge a possible gender identity that certain people associate with. Perhaps queer viewers would have liked the films to take a more explicit position on queer identities, without resorting to a heteronormative resolution. But on the other hand, this could be a better reflection of everyday experiences of homosexual men and women in 1970s Egypt. And could it not be argued that the redemption of the characters and the solutions proposed at the very end of the films – postponed as much as was possible time-wise – seem to have come too late? The films' resolution remains ambiguous and inconclusive, leaving the door to the closet open and the possibility of its contents bursting out onto the screen one day.

Notes

1 Even though gay characters are occasionally depicted in Egyptian cinema, their portrayal is subject to censorship just like any other topic dealing with sex. Film censorship in Egypt has taken on many forms over the course of more than a century of Egyptian film production. Taboo topics such as class and religion were problematic in the 1930s and 1940s; after the 1952 revolution politics became a thornier issue (unless it was anti-colonial). Sex was slightly more tolerated, although explicit sex scenes were out of the question. Nevertheless, censorship was and still is used in a bid to uphold 'what is deemed to be culturally, morally or religiously appropriate' (Dina Mansour, 'Egyptian Film Censorship: Safeguarding Society, Upholding Taboos', *Alphaville*, 4 [2012]. Available online: http://www.alphavillejournal.com/Issue%204/HTML/ArticleMansour.html [accessed 20 October 2017]). This means that there is no explicit rule on what is allowed or not as regards homosexuality on the screen, but film-makers have had to take into account the censorship committee when considering portraying normative and non-normative sexual acts and identities.

2 A *mu ʿallim* is a common character in popular and lower-class areas in Egypt. The term literally translates to 'teacher' or 'educated person'. In the cultural imagination of the type, a *mu ʿallim* is often represented as an abusive, masculine and violent man. He receives some respect from those around him mainly out of fear, but also because of his financial standing and sometimes thanks to his ability to keep the peace in the local neighbourhood.

3 Egyptian directors did not continue portraying gay characters in this unique way after Naṣrallāh's *Mercedes*, instead returning to more stereotypical portrayals of homosexuality, including in the critically acclaimed film *ʿImārat Ya ʿqūbiyān* (*The Yaqoubian Building*, Marwān Ḥāmid, 2006). The film features a sexually active gay character, which was uncommon in Egyptian cinema, but the character was still portrayed as 'becoming' gay after having been abused as a child by older men. At the end of the film, normality was restored when he was murdered by one of his lovers. The most recent portrayal of a gay character in Egyptian cinema, in *Asrār ʿĀ ʾiliyya* ('Family Secrets', Hānī Fawzī, 2013), also repeats the common misbelief that homosexuality is an affliction and the result of childhood abuse or absent father figures.

4 Films exemplary of Yūsuf Sha ʿbān's star persona are, for example, *Midaq Alley* (Ḥassan al-Imām, 1963), in which he plays a pimp, or *Imra ʾa Sayyi ʾat al-Sum ʿa* (*A Woman With a Bad Reputation*, Henry Barakāt, 1973), in which he plays an abusive

husband. Films exemplary of Nūr al-Sharīf's underdog persona include *al-Karnak* (*Karnak Cafe*, ʿAlī Badrakhān, 1975), in which he plays a university student arrested and tortured by Nasser's security services, or *Sawwāq al-Utūbīs* ('The Bus Driver', ʿĀṭif al-Ṭayyeb, 1982) in which he portrays a middle-aged bus driver trying to make ends meet, taking care of his family and sick father.

5 Liberal in this context does not mean politically or socially liberal. Instead, his famous characters often portray abusive men professing to be or looking like modern Western liberals but behaving in the exact opposite way. However, in *Malatili Bath* he does portray a character with liberal thought, valuing personal freedom.

6 The film is based on the play, but it is not the first cinematic adaptation. In 1958, Richard Brooks directed *Cat on a Hot Tin Roof* with Elizabeth Taylor and Paul Newman. The Egyptian adaptation is most likely based on the play, as Būsī herself stated in a 2017 interview that she was inspired by the story written by Tennessee Williams (Ṣāḥibat al-Saʿāda, 'Isʿād Yūnis, Interview with Būsī', YouTube, 21 February 2017. Available online: https://www.youtube.com/watch?v=YAg20nLRLnU [accessed 30 October 2017]).

7 Joseph Massad, 'Re-orienting Desire: The Gay International and the Arab World', *Public Culture*, 14 (2) (2002): 361–85, and Joseph Massad, *Desiring Arabs* (Chicago, IL: University of Chicago Press, 2007).

8 Ghassan Makarem, 'We Are Not Agents of the West', 14 December 2009. Available online: http://www.resetdoc.org/story/we-are-not-agents-of-the-west/ (accessed 15 October 2017).

9 Human Rights Watch, 'Together, Apart: Organizing Around Sexual Orientation and Gender Identity Worldwide', 11 June 2009, 18. Available online: https://www.hrw.org/report/2009/06/11/together-apart/organizing-around-sexual-orientation-and-gender-identity-worldwide (accessed 25 October 2017).

10 At the moment, Egypt applies laws for 'debauchery' when trying people arrested for supposedly engaging in 'homosexual acts'. However, at the time of writing, Egypt's parliament is set to debate a new bill criminalizing homosexuality more explicitly (Scott Long, 'Egypt's Wipe-out-the-Queers Bill', [Blog] *A Paper Bird*, 30 October 2017. Available online: https://paper-bird.net/2017/10/30/egypts-wipe-out-the-queers-bill/ [accessed on 31 October 2017]).

11 For discussions on masculine identity, see Farha Ghannam, *Live and Die Like a Man: Gender Dynamics in Urban Egypt* (Stanford, CA: Stanford University Press, 2013); Paul Amar, 'Discourses of "Men in Crisis", Industries of Gender in Revolution', *Journal of Middle East Women's Studies*, 7 (3) (2011): 36–70; for studies on Islam and identity, see Meir Hatina, *Identity Politics in the Middle East: Liberal Thought and Islamic Challenge in Egypt* (London: Tauris Academic Studies, 2007); Lahoucine Ouzgane (ed.), *Islamic Masculinities* (London: Zed Books, 2006).

12 Al-Zahrāʾ ʿAbd al-Wahhāb, 'Fī Dhikra Raḥīlihi al-Ūlā: Nūr al-Sharīf ʿAlāmāt Mumayyiza wa-Tajārub Sayyiʾa' (One Year After Nūr al-Sharīf's Death: Distinction and Bad Experiences), *El-Tareeq*, 11 August 2016. Available online: http://www.el-tareeq.net/Article.aspx?Article_ID=6536 (accessed 27 October 2017); Duʿā Abū al-Ḍiyāʾ, 'Alāqāt Khafiyya fī al-Mujtamaʿ al-Miṣrī bi-l-Ṭarīqa al-Amrīkiyya' (Hidden Relations in Egyptian Society, the American Way), *El-Cinema*, 31 December 2015. Available online: https://www.elcinema.com/review/1237331/ (accessed 26 May 2018).

13 Judith Butler, *Gender Trouble: Feminism and the Subversion of Identity* (New York: Routledge, [1990] 2007), 140.

14 Ibid., 25.

15 Samira Aghacy, *Masculine Identity in the Fiction of the Arab East since 1967* (Syracuse, NY: Syracuse University Press, 2009), 4.
16 Walter Armbrust, 'Long Live Patriarchy: Love in the Time of ʿAbd al-Wahhab', *History Compass*, 7 (1) (2009): 259.
17 Egyptian films were influenced by other cultural products, such as theatre and literature, which espoused themes of nation-building and Arab identity, and discussed notions of family and romantic love (Viola Shafik, *Arab Cinema: History and Cultural Identity* [Cairo: American University in Cairo Press, 1998]; Walter Armbrust, 'New Cinema, Commercial Cinema, and the Modernist Tradition in Egypt', *Alif*, 15 [1995]: 81–129; Walter Armbrust, 'Transgressing Patriarchy: Sex and Marriage in Egyptian Film', *Middle East Research and Information Project*, 206 [1998]: 29–31; and Walter Armbrust, 'Long Live Patriarchy').
18 Ella Shohat, 'Egypt: Cinema and Revolution', *Critical Arts*, 2 (4) (1983): 22–32, 27.
19 Malek Khouri, 'Origins and Patterns in the Discourse of New Arab Cinema', *Arab Studies Quarterly*, 27 (1/2) (2005): 4.
20 Armbrust, 'New Cinema, Commercial Cinema'.
21 Sawsan El-Messiri, *Ibn al-Balad: A Concept of Egyptian Identity* (Leiden: Brill, 1978).
22 Van Eynde, 'Men in the Picture: Representations of Men and Masculinities in Egyptian Cinema Since 1952', PhD thesis, Katholieke Universiteit Leuven, Belguim (2015): 123–5.
23 Other examples of 1970s films portraying taboo topics include *Urīdu Ḥallan* (*I Want a Solution*, Saʿīd Marzūq, 1975), portraying a middle-aged woman trying to get a divorce while entering a romantic relationship with a younger man – the film is said to have influenced the divorce law of 1979 (see Mona Abdel-Fadil and Koen Van Eynde, 'Golden Age Divas on the Silver Screen: Challenging or Conforming to Dominant Gender Norms?', *Journal of African Cinemas*, 8 [1] [2016]: 20). The film *Biʾr al-Ḥirmān* ('Well of Deprivation', Kamāl al-Shaykh, 1969) is about a woman who has nightly bouts of sexual promiscuity, a double personality as a sexual predator of which she remembers nothing the day after. A taboo film of the era is *al-Dhiʾāb lā Taʾkul al-Laḥm* (*Kuwait Connection*, Samīr Khūrī, 1975), a film featuring nudity, produced in Lebanon but including several famous Egyptian actors such as ʿIzzat al-ʿAlaylī (b.1934) and Nāhid Sharīf (1942–1981).
24 Shafik, *Arab Cinema*, 32.
25 Sadat's presidency is mostly remembered for the so-called *Infitāḥ* or Open-door policy, a change in economic policy away from Nasser's socialist-inspired economy towards a capitalist economy attracting foreign investment. But Sadat was also a social conservative and very religious, something that is sometimes overlooked in favour of his presumed liberal economic policies. Although Sadat adopted a more liberal constitution in 1971, he subsequently amended it in 1980, near the end of his presidency. In 1980, he included the amendment that read that *Sharīʿa* was to be the primary source of legislation, in a possible attempt to appease Islamists in the country, who were angered by the signing of the Camp David Accords with Israel in 1978.
26 Ibrahim Al-Aris, 'The Legacy of Salah Abu Seif, Master of Realism in Egyptian Cinema', *Al Jadid*, February 1997, trans. Elie Chalala. Available online: http://www.aljadid.com/content/legacy-salah-abu-seif-master-realism-egyptian-cinema (accessed 29 November 2016).
27 Some of his most famous and lauded films are *Shabāb Imraʾa* (*The Leech*, 1956), *Lā Anām* (*Sleepless*, 1957) – with angelic star actress Fātin Ḥamāma in a rare 'evil' role – *al-Qaḍiyya 68* ('Case 68', 1968) and *al-Saqqā Māt* (*The Water Bearer Is Dead*, 1977).

28 Ḥassan Ḥaddād, 'Al-Futuwwa: Ruʾya Naqdiyya' (The Tough Guy: A Critical View), *Huna*, 2 September 1993. Available online: http://www.cinematechhaddad.com/Rowad/SAbuSaef_1.HTM (accessed 31 July 2013).
29 See, for example, *Al-Futuwwa* ('The Tough Guy', 1957).
30 Joel Gordon, *Revolutionary Melodrama: Popular Film and Civic Identity in Nasser's Egypt* (Chicago, IL: University of Chicago Press, 2002).
31 The city of Ismailia on the Suez Canal is branded in Egyptian collective memory as being on the forefront of the war against Israel, which had occupied the Sinai desert since 1967. In the October War of 1973, the city was witness to the Battle of Ismailia, during which Egyptian forces were able to defend the surrounded city prior to a UN-brokered ceasefire.
32 David Gilmore, *Manhood in the Making: Cultural Concepts of Masculinity* (New Haven, CT: Yale University Press, 1990), ch. 2; Christopher Oldstone-Moore, 'Social Science, Gender Theory and the History of Hair', in Jennifer Evans and Alun Withey (eds), *New Perspectives on the History of Facial Hair: Framing the Face*, 15–31 (New York: Palgrave Macmillan, 2018).
33 See also, for example, *Al-Zawja al-Thāniya* (*The Second Wife*, 1967) with Suʿād Ḥusnī and Ṣalāḥ Manṣūr, about the mayor of a village taking a second wife. The film talks about religiously sanctioned polygamy but parodies it, portraying it as awash with misunderstandings, leading to abuse.
34 Jeroen Vandaele, 'Humor Mechanisms in Film Comedy: Incongruity and Superiority', *Poetics Today*, 23 (2) (2002): 221–49.
35 Ibid., 246.
36 The end scenes are a fast sequence of events: from the moment Naʿīma's uncle tracks her down, to her murder and Aḥmad's realization the time has come to return to Ismailia does not take more than a few minutes. It is a common trope in Egyptian films for the nation to be depicted by a female character, often abused by outdated traditions and ignorance. Abū Sayf's films tend to broach political topics through metaphors, and it is likely that Naʿīma is a reference to a battered motherland, abused and unable to live up to its full potential through backwardness and corruption, and that Aḥmad's decision to return to his family living in a city on the frontline of the 1967 war could be interpreted as a direct call for action against complacency.
37 *The Savage Girl* is an adaptation of a French play called *La Sauvage* (*Restless Heart*, 1938) by Jean Anouilh. For more on this film, the on-screen and off-screen persona of actress Suʿād Ḥusnī and how various state narratives and counter-narratives inform the film, see Abdel-Fadil and Van Eynde, 'Golden Age Divas on the Silver Screen'.
38 Nūr al-Sharīf received three prizes for his role in the film, from the Writers and Cinema Critics Association and the Film Association ('Nūr al-Sharīf' [Nūr al-Sharīf], *Al-Jazeera*, 11 August 2015. Available online: http://www.aljazeera.net/encyclopedia/icons/2015/5/11/%D9%86%D9%88%D8%B1-%D8%A7%D9%84%D8%B4%D8%B1%D9%8A%D9%81 [accessed 27 October 2017]).
39 Other films in which husband and wife are playing together are *Ḥabībī … Dāʾiman* ('My Love … Forever', Ḥusayn Kamāl, 1980), *Futuwwāt Bulāq* ('Tough Men From Bulaq', Yaḥya al-ʿIlmī, 1981) and *Ākhir al-Rijāl al-Muḥtaramīn* ('Last of the Respectable Men', Samīr Sayf, 1984). They often produced their films themselves under the production company N. B. Film, as they did with *Cat on Fire*.
40 Farīd Shawqī is also known as *malik al-tirso*, or 'king of the third-class cinemas', referring to the cheap cinemas offering multiple film screenings for the price of one ticket. He was a popular actor and his name alone on the billboard could attract huge numbers.

41 Nūr al-Sharīf's 'forbidden roles' included atheists (*al-Ikhwa al-A'dā'* ['Enemy Brothers', Ḥusām al-Dīn Muṣṭafā, 1974]) and playing the role of a young Muslim man falling in love with a Christian girl (*Liqā' Hunāk* ['A Meeting There', Aḥmad Ḍiyā' al-Dīn, 1973]). His role in *Cat on Fire* is the only time he has played a homosexual character.

42 After the making of the film, which was only screened for two weeks, artists boycotted working with Nūr al-Sharīf and newspapers attacked him because the film was said to be critical of Arab regimes' handling of the Palestinian cause, according to the online Egyptian news site *al-Masry al-Youm Lite* (Ghāda Ghālib, 'Aswa' Sitt Ashhur 'Āshahā Nūr al-Sharīf fī Ḥayātihi' [The Worst Six Months of Nūr al-Sharīf's Life], *Al-Masry al-Youm Lite*, 15 August 2015. Available online: http://lite.almasryalyoum.com/extra/66227/ [accessed 2 December 2016]).

43 Shawqī Matā and Nūr al-Sharīf have worked together in several films, such as *al-Kull Yuḥibb* ('Everybody's in Love', Maḥmūd Farīd, 1976) and *al-Shayāṭīn* ('The Devils', Ḥusām al-Dīn Muṣṭafā, 1977).

44 The homosexual character Skipper was physically absent in the original play and the 1958 Hollywood adaptation. His existence was only made known through Brick, the protagonist, and the other characters mentioning Skipper. Another difference is that in the original, Skipper attempted to sleep with Brick's wife in an effort by Brick to prove to her that his friend is not homosexual, something that would be out of the question in an Egyptian context. *Cat on Fire* possibly alludes to this scene, when 'Izzat dances in a close embrace with Jījī, under Amīn's watchful eye who is nevertheless visibly uncomfortable with the situation. It remains unclear whether he is uncomfortable with his wife dancing with another man or because his best friend is dancing with his wife, giving her the chance to ask him private questions about his relationship with Amīn.

45 The Hays Censorship Code was first published in 1930 and was named after its creator, Will Hays. The code presented guidelines to film-makers, and influenced most films made in the United States between 1930 and 1966, when a ratings system was introduced (Michael Brooke, 'The Hays Code', BFI Screen Online, 2014–2014. Available online: http://www.screenonline.org.uk/film/id/592022/ [accessed 25 April 2017]).

46 See, for example, the films *al-Khayṭ al-Rafī'* ('The Thin Line', Henry Barakat 1971), *Dammī wa-Dumū'ī wa-Ibtisāmātī* (*My Blood, Tears and Smile*, Ḥusayn Kamāl, 1973) and *al-Ṣa'ālīk* (*The Vagabonds*, Dāwūd 'Abd al-Sayyid, 1985).

47 Armbrust 'New Cinema, Commercial Cinema'; Lila Abu-Lughod, *Dramas of Nationhood: The Politics of Television in Egypt* (Chicago, IL: University of Chicago Press, 2005).

48 Carla Marcantonio, *Global Melodrama: Nation, Body, and History in Contemporary Film* (New York: Palgrave Macmillan, 2015), 2.

49 Gill Plain, *John Mills and British Cinema: Masculinity, Identity and Nation* (Edinburgh: Edinburgh University Press, 2006), 216.

References

'Abd al-Wahhāb, al-Zahrā' (2016), 'Fī Dhikra Raḥīlihi al-Ūlā: Nūr al-Sharīf 'Alāmāt Mumayyiza wa-Tajārub Sayyi'a' (One Year After Nūr al-Sharīf's Death: Distinction and Bad Experiences), *El-Tareeq*, 11 August. Available online: http://www.el-tareeq.net/Article.aspx?Article_ID=6536 (accessed 27 October 2017).

Abdel-Fadil, Mona and Koen Van Eynde (2016), 'Golden Age Divas on the Silver Screen: Challenging or Conforming to Dominant Gender Norms?', *Journal of African Cinemas*, 8 (1): 11–27.
Abū al-Ḍiyā', Du'ā (2015), ''Alāqāt Khafiyya fī al-Mujtama' al-Miṣrī bi-l-Ṭarīqa al-Amrīkiyya' (Hidden Relations in Egyptian Society, the American Way), *El-Cinema*, 31 December. Available online: https://www.elcinema.com/review/1237331/ (accessed 26 May 2018).
Abu-Lughod, Lila (2005), *Dramas of Nationhood: The Politics of Television in Egypt*, Chicago, IL: University of Chicago Press.
Aghacy, Samira (2009), *Masculine Identity in the Fiction of the Arab East since 1967*, Syracuse, NY: Syracuse University Press.
al-Aris, Ibrahim (1997), 'The Legacy of Salah Abu Seif, Master of Realism in Egyptian Cinema', *Al Jadid*, February, trans. Elie Chalala. Available online: http://www.aljadid.com/content/legacy-salah-abu-seif-master-realism-egyptian-cinema (accessed 29 November 2016).
Amar, Paul (2011), 'Discourses of "Men in Crisis", Industries of Gender in Revolution', *Journal of Middle East Women's Studies*, 7 (3): 36–70.
Armbrust, Walter (1995), 'New Cinema, Commercial Cinema, and the Modernist Tradition in Egypt', *Alif*, 15: 81–129.
Armbrust, Walter (1998), 'Transgressing Patriarchy: Sex and Marriage in Egyptian Film', *Middle East Research and Information Project*, 206: 29–31.
Armbrust, Walter (2009), 'Long Live Patriarchy: Love in the Time of 'Abd al-Wahhab', *History Compass*, 7 (1): 251–81.
Brooke, Michael (2014–2014), 'The Hays Code', BFI Screen Online. Available online: http://www.screenonline.org.uk/film/id/592022/ (accessed 25 April 2017).
Butler, Judith [1990] (2007), *Gender Trouble: Feminism and the Subversion of Identity*, New York: Routledge.
El-Messiri, Sawsan (1978), *Ibn al-Balad: A Concept of Egyptian Identity*, Leiden: Brill.
Ghālib, Ghāda (2015), 'Aswa' Sitt Ashhur 'Āshahā Nūr al-Sharīf fī Ḥayātihi' (The Worst Six Months of Nūr al-Sharīf's Life), *Al-Masry al-Youm Lite*, 15 August. Available online: http://lite.almasryalyoum.com/extra/66227/ (accessed 2 December 2016).
Ghannam, Farha (2013), *Live and Die Like a Man: Gender Dynamics in Urban Egypt*, Stanford, CA: Stanford University Press.
Gilmore, David (1990), *Manhood in the Making: Cultural Concepts of Masculinity*, New Haven, CT: Yale University Press.
Gordon, Joel (2002), *Revolutionary Melodrama: Popular Film and Civic Identity in Nasser's Egypt*, Chicago, IL: University of Chicago, Press.
Ḥaddād, Ḥassan (1993), 'Al-Futuwwa: Ru'ya Naqdiyya' (The Tough Guy: A Critical View), *Huna*, 2 September. Available online: http://www.cinematechhaddad.com/Rowad/SAbuSaef_1.HTM (accessed 31 July 2013).
Hatina, Meir (2007), *Identity Politics in the Middle East: Liberal Thought and Islamic Challenge in Egypt*, London: Tauris Academic Studies.
Human Rights Watch (2009), 'Together, Apart: Organizing Around Sexual Orientation and Gender Identity Worldwide', 11 June. Available online: https://www.hrw.org/report/2009/06/11/together-apart/organizing-around-sexual-orientation-and-gender-identity-worldwide (accessed 25 October 2017).
Khouri, Malek (2005), 'Origins and Patterns in the Discourse of New Arab Cinema', *Arab Studies Quarterly*, 27 (1/2): 1–20.

Long, Scott (2017), 'Egypt's Wipe-out-the-Queers Bill', [Blog] *A Paper Bird*, 30 October. Available online: https://paper-bird.net/2017/10/30/egypts-wipe-out-the-queers-bill/ (accessed 31 October 2017).
Makarem, Ghassan (2009), 'We Are Not Agents of the West', 14 December. Available online: http://www.resetdoc.org/story/we-are-not-agents-of-the-west/ (accessed 15 October 2017).
Mansour, Dina (2012), 'Egyptian Film Censorship: Safeguarding Society, Upholding Taboos', *Alphaville*, 4. Available online: http://www.alphavillejournal.com/Issue%204/HTML/ArticleMansour.html (accessed 20 October 2017).
Marcantonio, Carla (2015), *Global Melodrama: Nation, Body, and History in Contemporary Film*, New York: Palgrave Macmillan.
Massad, Joseph (2002), 'Re-orienting Desire: The Gay International and the Arab World', *Public Culture*, 14 (2): 361–85.
Massad, Joseph (2007), *Desiring Arabs*, Chicago, IL: University of Chicago Press.
'Nūr al-Sharīf' (Nūr al-Sharīf) (2015), *al-Jazeera*, 11 August. Available online: http://www.aljazeera.net/encyclopedia/icons/2015/5/11/%D9%86%D9%88%D8%B1-%D8%A7%D9%84%D8%B4%D8%B1%D9%8A%D9%81 (accessed 27 October 2017).
Oldstone-Moore, Christopher (2018), 'Social Science, Gender Theory and the History of Hair', in Jennifer Evans and Alun Withey (eds), *New Perspectives on the History of Facial Hair: Framing the Face*, 15–31, New York: Palgrave Macmillan.
Ouzgane, Lahoucine (ed.) (2006), *Islamic Masculinities*, London: Zed Books.
Ṣāhibat al-Saʿāda (2017), 'Ṣāḥiba al-Saʿāda – Būsī: Nūr al-Sharīf "Istaʿbaṭnī" fī Dhālika al-Fīlm Taʿarraf ʿalā al-Qissa' (Ṣāhiba al-Saʿāda – Būsī: Nūr al-Sharīf "Fooled Me" in That Film, Get To Know the Story), YouTube, 21 February. Available online: https://www.youtube.com/watch?v=YAg20nLRLnU (accessed 30 October 2017).
Plain, Gill (2006), *John Mills and British Cinema: Masculinity, Identity and Nation*, Edinburgh: Edinburgh University Press.
Shafik, Viola (1998), *Arab Cinema: History and Cultural Identity*, Cairo: American University in Cairo Press.
Shohat, Ella (1983), 'Egypt: Cinema and Revolution', *Critical Arts*, 2 (4): 22–32.
Vandaele, Jeroen (2002), 'Humor Mechanisms in Film Comedy: Incongruity and Superiority', *Poetics Today*, 23 (2): 221–49.
Van Eynde, Koen (2015), 'Men in the Picture: Representations of Men and Masculinities in Egyptian Cinema Since 1952', PhD thesis, Katholieke Universiteit Leuven, Belgium.

Primary filmography

Ḥammām al-Malāṭīlī (Malatili Bath) (1973), Dir. Ṣalāḥ Abū Sayf, Wrs Ismāʿīl Walī al-Dīn and Muḥsin Zayyid, Egypt: Ṣalāḥ Abū Sayf, 93 minutes.
Qiṭṭa ʿalā Nār (Cat on Fire) (1977), Dir. Samīr Sayf, Wrs Hānī Muṭāwiʿ and Rafīq al-Ṣabbān, Egypt: N. B. Films, 108 minutes.

Secondary filmography

Ākhir al-Rijāl al-Muḥtaramīn (Last of the Respectable Men) (1984), Dir. Samīr Sayf, Wr. Waḥīd Ḥāmid, Egypt: N. B. Films, 94 minutes.
Biʾr al-Ḥirmān (Well of Deprivation) (1969), Dir. Kamāl al-Shaykh, Wr. Iḥsān ʿAbd al-Quddūs, Yūsif Fransīs, Egypt: Ramsīs Najīb, 120 minutes.

al-Dhiʾāb lā Taʾkul al-Laḥm (Kuwait Connection) (1975), Dir. Samīr Khūrī, Wr. Samīr Khūrī, Lebanon: Arab Film Distribution, 91 minutes.

Futuwwāt Bulāq (Tough Men from Bulaq) (1981), Dir. Yaḥya al-ʿIlmī, Wrs. Najīb Maḥfūẓ, Waḥīd Ḥāmid, Egypt: Gamāl al-Tābiʿ Films, 120 minutes.

Ḥabībī … Dāʾiman (My Love … Forever) (1980), Dir. Ḥusayn Kamāl, Wrs. Kawthar Haykal, Rafīq al-Shaʿbān, Egypt: N. B. Films, 120 minutes.

ʿImārat Yaʿqūbiyān (*The Yaqoubian Building*) (2006), Dir. Marwān Ḥāmid, Wrs. ʿAlāʾ al-Aswānī and Waḥīd Ḥāmid, Egypt: Good News For Film, 130 minutes.

Imraʾa Sayyiʾat al-Sumʿa (*A Woman with a Bad Reputation*)(1973), Dir. Henry Barakāt, Wr. Mamdūḥ al-Liṯī, Egypt: Studio Miṣr, Films Īhāb al-Liṯī, 110 minutes.

Junūn al-Shabāb (Crazy Youth) (1975), Dir. Khalīl Shawqī, Wrs. Wafiyya Khairī and ʿAlī al-Zarqānī, Egypt: Cinema, Theatre and Music Authority, 201 minutes.

al-Karnak (*Karnak Café*) (1975), Dir. ʿAlī Badrakhān, Wrs. Najīb Maḥfūẓ and Mamdūḥ al-Līthī, Egypt: Mamdūḥ al-Līthī, 140 minutes.

Mercedes (1993), Dir. Yusrī Naṣrallāh, Wr. Yusrī Naṣrallāh, Egypt: Miṣr International Films, 110 minutes.

Sawwāq al-Utūbīs (The Bus Driver) (1982), Dir. ʿĀṭif al-Ṭayyeb, Wrs. Bashīr al-Dīk and Muḥammad Khān, Egypt: Hādīrāmā, 108 minutes.

al-Ṣuʿūd ilā al-Hāwiyya (Rise to the Abyss) (1978), Dir. Kamāl al-Shaykh, Wr. Ṣāliḥ Mursī, Egypt: Amūn Films, Muḥsin ʿAlam al-Dīn, 128 minutes.

Urīdu Ḥallan (I Want a Solution) (1975), Dir. Saʿīd Marzūq, Wr. Fātin Ḥamāma, Saʿīd Marzūq, Egypt: Ṣalāḥ Dhū al-Fiqār, 115 minutes.

al-Zawja al-Thāniya (*The Second Wife*) (1967), Dir. Ṣalāḥ Abū Sayf, Wr. Aḥmad Rushdī Ṣāliḥ, Ṣalāh Abū Sayf, Egypt: Ramsīs Najīb, 112 minutes.

Zuqāq al-Midaqq (*Midaq Alley*) (1963), Dir. Ḥassan al-Imām, Wrs. Najīb Maḥfūẓ and Saʿd al-Dīn Wahba, Egypt: Ramsīs Najīb, 125 minutes.

Part III

SEXUALITY, POWER AND RESILIENCE IN THE MIDDLE EAST AND NORTH AFRICA TODAY

Chapter 8

LIVING ARCHIVES OF THE EGYPTIAN HUMAN RIGHTS MOVEMENT: THE POLITICAL BIOGRAPHY OF AIDA SEIF AL-DAWLA

Lucia Sorbera

Introduction: 'Women's Rights are Human Rights'. The hidden history of an idea

The notion that women's rights are human rights has been part of the feminist lexicon since the early 1980s, when Cecilia Medina, the Chilean jurist, eloquently articulated it in relation to freedom, equal rights and equality of all human beings before the law, arguing that human rights cannot be fulfilled unless women enjoy their full rights. In a groundbreaking article for feminist theory, Medina stated: 'As a logical consequence of the fact that women's rights are human rights, feminism, in theory, is a movement to achieve a democratic society, without which human rights may not be fully enjoyed.'[1] Ten years later, Charlotte Bunch questioned why human rights and women rights were still seen as distinct and, analysing the experience of the GABRIELA women's coalition in the Philippines, she invited scholars to explore the transformative effect of including a feminist perspective in the human rights concept.[2] In the early 1990s this idea was no longer limited to academic circles but permeated the spaces of social activism. In fact, in 1993, when the World Conference on Human Rights was held in Vienna, women activists mobilized to ensure that women's human rights were on the agenda of the international community.[3]

The idea that women's rights are human rights became mainstream after the fourth International Conference on Women in Beijing (1995), when the then US First Lady Hillary Rodham Clinton stated it during her inaugural speech. It was then adopted in the Beijing Declaration and Platform for Action, which was focused on twelve areas concerning the implementation of women's human rights and set out an agenda for women's empowerment.[4] The paradox is that as soon as the idea was attributed to Clinton and adopted by the UN, its long history was lost and, with it, some of its subversive power vanished. In this chapter I argue that the revolutionary potential of feminist human rights activism can be recuperated by shifting the focus of the narrative from the institutional history to the political biographies of women human rights defenders. I do so by exploring the trajectory of women in the human rights movement in Egypt from the early 1980s until today, through a detailed analysis of the political biography of a veteran in the field, Aida Seif al-Dawla (ʿĀyda Sayf al-Dawla), from whom I collected a long oral history in January 2018.

A psychiatrist and a founding member of the New Woman Foundation (NWF), one of the leading feminist organizations in Egypt, which started as a feminist reading group in 1984, and of El-Nadeem (*al-Nadīm*) Center for Rehabilitation of Victims of Violence (1995), Aida Seif al-Dawla's political experience goes back to the late 1970s, when she was part of the student movement, and the Communist Egyptian Labour Party. Politics has shaped Aida's life since she was born, as it was an integral part of her family history, which she remembered with pride and fondness when she gave me her oral history. Aida Seif al-Dawla is considered a mentor and a point of reference by young psychiatrists, feminist activists and public intellectuals. The transgenerational positive impact of Aida's work is apparent in the words used by the journalist Lina Attalah (Līnā ʿAṭā Allāh) and the human rights defender Yara Sallam (Yārā Sallām), who have featured her work in their writings on human rights and feminism.[5] As the focus of my research is the genealogies of feminism and the transgenerational transmission of feminist thought, my encounter with Aida Seif al-Dawla is a small yet one of the most significative samples of some seventy oral histories of feminist intellectuals and human rights activists I have collected in Cairo since the early 2000s, when I first started researching Egyptian feminist history.

Before I get into the analysis of Aida Seif al-Dawla's political biography and how its understanding is crucial to the possibility of writing a gendered history of the Egyptian human rights movement, I need to provide some theoretical and methodological insights, which will allow me to situate my research at the crossroad between feminist and human rights history.

From the feminist postcolonial critique to a decolonial feminist epistemology of human rights

The four UN Conferences on Women (Mexico City, 1975; Copenhagen, 1980; Nairobi, 1985; and Beijing, 1995), alongside the parallel non-governmental organization (NGO) forums, the preparatory regional meetings and the follow-up conferences have been a significant marker of what in the 1990s became known as global and transnational feminism, around which a copious amount of scholarly literature developed in the late 1990s and early 2000s.[6]

Egyptian feminist activists and academics enthusiastically participated in the Beijing conference and in the parallel NGO meetings. Shereen Abouelnaga (Shirīn Abū al-Najā), Professor of English and Comparative Literature at Cairo University, wrote, twenty years later: 'In 1995, I enjoyed the privilege of attending the fourth UN World Conference on Women, held in Beijing, China. Stamped on my mind are two things: the group of stunning women I met and the World Public Hearing on Crimes against Women.'[7]

The enthusiasm was not unanimous. Critics of the process, most notably Gayatri Chakravorty Spivak, have labelled the four UN women's conferences as 'global theatre', where women represent the unity of the world, a necessary mise en scène that serves the needs of globalization, and have criticized these conferences' lack of connections with grassroots activism.[8]

Indeed, a neoliberal human development framework shines through the documents produced during these conferences and their preparatory meetings, as it does through the Convention on the Elimination of all Discrimination against Women (CEDAW) and the 2005 United Nations Development Program's (UNDP) Human Development Report on the Arab World (*Towards the Rise of Women in the Arab World*).[9] The ideological and political underpinnings of the UN – and through it, the international underpinnings also – agenda for women's rights and equality were reproached by postcolonial feminist scholars based on a sharp critique of the universalism of the women's rights discourse that frames CEDAW,[10] arguing that the development logic reinforced rather than challenged Arab state power, Western state interests and transnational governance,[11] and that overall what remained unchallenged was the paradigm of Western urban and middle-class modernity as inherently emancipatory for women, while fieldwork research in rural areas shows that the reality is far more complex.[12] Inderpal Grewal has been critical of this hegemonic trend of practice and discourse, naming it 'transnational feminist governmentality'.[13]

Arab feminist scholars criticized the processes generated by the international organizations' global agenda for development in the Arab world, where, since the mid-1990s, the social movement's organizations have turned into professional NGOs and lost their subversive potential (the 'NGOisazion' of the social movements).[14] In addition, the culturalist approach of the international organizations – which overemphasized the weight of 'local traditions', 'religion' and 'patriarchy' in shaping the discourse about women in Muslim-majority countries – allowed the secular authoritarian and corrupted Egyptian regime to manipulate women and gender discourses to legitimize itself during the years in which both its domestic and international policies led to a crisis of legitimacy. So, on the one hand, the Egyptian state presented itself as 'gender friendly' by hosting the UNDP conference in 1994 and facilitating the preparatory works towards it, by approving the *khul*ʿ law in 2000, establishing the National Council for Women (2000) and by appointing the first women to the Supreme Constitutional Court in Egyptian history. On the other hand, these were the years when the Egyptian state also reverted to conservative discourses about women and gender to contain the growing popularity of the Salafi and other Islamist forces (especially the Muslim Brotherhood). As has happened frequently in modern history, women's bodies were the ideal terrain to fight ideological battles, and political leaders used them to portray themselves as 'the guardians of morality'. All the women political activists I spoke to remember the 1990s as a very difficult decade, when the state was trying to either co-opt or repress women who were politically active in secular independent organizations that were trying to promote progressive views on gender. The case of the Arab Women's Solidarity Association, led by Nawal al-

Saadawi (Nawāl al-Saʿdāwī), which was shut down after the outspoken writer took a stand against Egypt's participation in the 1991 US-led military campaign against Iraq, is a notorious case, albeit not the only one. The link between human rights and women's rights has always been controversial terrain, because, on one side, it was easy to neutralize it by reducing it to a neoliberal global feminist slogan (as Clinton did), while on the other, the study of the biographies of women human rights defenders shows a far more complex picture, where the role that individuals can have in their societies is not predetermined but changes significantly according to what they do with the circumstances in which they live. This applies to both the global and the local levels.

In this chapter I aim to contribute to the effort of both decolonizing and gendering the history of the human rights movement by illustrating the historical link between human rights and the feminist activism in Egypt. I believe that the first (decolonizing through positioning at the centre the historical narratives produced by non-Western subjects) can't be done without the latter (gendering), because gender is a key category to understanding power relationships, especially in colonial and postcolonial settings. Human rights are a crucial field in decolonizing feminism (and in feminist studies), not only because, as is well known, the human rights paradigm has contributed a central framework to feminist activism and shaped feminist language at least since the early 1990s, if not before, but also because, as is less known, women human rights defenders from the Arab world (and other non-white women) have been crucial actors in the international human rights movement. Showing that women have been key actors in the human rights movement in the Arab world since its inception in the mid 1980s, and that today they are playing a central role in keeping it alive under serious constraints and in transmitting its memory, the stories I collected challenge culturalist myths, contributing to a decolonial understanding of both human rights and feminism.

Oral history and memory

My work draws on some of the Italian feminist oral historian Luisa Passerini's critical insights, especially her emphasis on memory as a type of subjectivity and the mutual constitutional relationship between memory and the present.

Passerini pioneered criticism of populist and positivist approaches to oral history, which were dominant in the 1970s, criticizing the idea that oral history was 'giving voice to the voiceless' and reconceptualizing the interview as a process that draws out forms of cultural identity and shared tradition rather than social history facts.[15] In her recent work, Passerini further extends her relational conceptualization of the interview process as intersubjectivity: 'The interview is the product of a relation – at least dual – between embodied subjects, a construction which requires, in order to be understood, that there is more than one interlocutor and that memory is a highly mobile process, according to which interlocutors and circumstances are involved.'[16] The interview does not simply record history but, through the process of memory, understood as the interplay between what is remembered and what is forgotten, it creates historical subjects and their personal 'archive' or repositories of memory. The stories collected through the interviews are not made up only of words. Narratives are seldom linear and coherent but are inhabited by omissions, silences, pauses, the change in the tone of the voice, sobs, glances and smiles. Interviews are embodied and gendered, like the historical subjects they contribute to creating. Temporality is also important. The interviews are situated in a specific time, and the spirit of the time influences the flows of memory. What follows is also my own memory of the encounter with Aida Seif al-Dawla at a moment that was perceived as extremely challenging for the Egyptian and the global community of human rights defenders.

The eloquent silences of memory: Meeting a veteran of Egyptian human rights activism in times of repression

> The seventies, oh … I don't want to go through any of this again, neither to the seventies, although I challenged the seventies a lot, I tried, although I was not in the leadership of anything […]. Hānī[17] will tell you about the student movement. He was in the leadership.

Differently from other women of her generation, who were born in the early 1950s, with a similar educational background, all of whom graduated in the 1970s and participated in the student movements, Aida Seif al-Dawla does not appear eager to talk about the years when the students' contestation emerged from the Egyptian university campuses and took to the streets.

When we first met, at the end of 2017, the atmosphere was gloomy. The activities of the El-Nadeem Center for Rehabilitation of Victims of Violence, which she has founded in 1993 with her colleagues Sūzān Fayyāḍ and ʿAbd Allāh Manṣūr, had been severely reduced. The clinic had been closed since February 2016, on the order of the Ministry of Health, an order that El-Nadeem's doctors have questioned both on substantial and procedural grounds,[18] up to the time of writing, with no success. At the time of our second meeting, in January 2018, Aida, like her colleague Sūzān Fayyāḍ and the human rights defenders Azza Soliman (ʿAzza Sulaymān) and Mozn Hassan (Muzn Ḥasan), respectively the founder of Center for Egyptian Women's Legal Assistance (CEWLA, 1995) and Nazra for Feminist Studies (2007), were under a travel ban. At the time of writing, the travel ban on the four women continues.

Aida appeared troubled, especially for the future of the young people. There was no joy in her narrative of the student movement in the 1970s. As I was listening to her, I was wondering if the melancholy atmosphere surrounding the community of human rights defenders was the subtext of Aida's account. She tended to underplay her role, and when I tried to encourage more detailed stories, she referred me to other of her comrades, such as the journalist and her ex-husband Hani Shukrallah

(Hānī Shukr Allāh), his sister Hāla, her friends Laila Soueif (Laylā Suwayf), Mājda ʿAdlī, Āmāl ʿAbd al-Hādī and Nawla Darwīsh. I had already spoken to most of them, and thanks to Aida I met the others over the next few days, but I insisted on knowing more about the beginnings of her political activism. This was the moment when her memory went back to her grandparents.

Becoming a feminist human rights defender in twentieth-century Egypt

> I was brought up in a political family. From my grandfather down to today. My paternal grandfather was from Upper Egypt, and he was a sort of community leader. His name was ʿAbbās.

Aida Seif al-Dawla's political biography is framed within her family history. In her voice one can hear the echoes of the salient moments in the national history, from the 1919 anti-British uprisings, to the 1967 defeat against Israel, to the repression of the Marxist dissidents by Gamal Abdel Nasser's regime. Her narrative is reminiscent of the autobiographies of the Egyptian feminists who came before her, stories where family's memories shape a sense of history and in Aida's case her approach to human rights activism.

> ʿAbbās left his village, al-Badārī, in Asyūṭ, as a child, on his own. He came to Cairo and studied in al-Azhar, where he became a shaykh. Then he returned to his village. He was not the official major, but he was the de facto major and led several peasants' mutinies over land …
>
> My mother comes from the other end of the (*laughs*) … from the other end of the country. I mean, my fathers' families are basically peasants. My mother's family is aristocracy from the Delta. Her father, Yusūf al-Jindī, is the one upon whom the street in downtown Cairo, close to the American University, is named. They lived in an area called Ziftā, in the Gharbiyya governorate. It is a town through which the railways carrying cotton to be transported to Europe go through. So, this Yusūf al-Jindī in 1919 declared Ziftā independent for eighteen days. They cut the railways (*laughs*). They cut the railways, they set-up a town orchestra, they ruled the town for eighteen days. Of course, after that he was arrested for a short time, but later he became member of the Wafd, and was nominated to be a member of the Cabinet […].[19]
>
> My father was also a political activist. He was a lawyer: ʿIṣmat Sayf al-Dawla. He was a famous lawyer, an excellent one, and he was an activist who developed his own theory, which was neither Marxist nor Trotskyist, nor Islamist, nor Nasserite. Something different, which he called the theory of the Arab revolution. And he has many, many, many, many followers but not in Cairo, not in Egypt. He has followers in Syria in Iraq, Libya, in Tunis … who call themselves actually the ʿIṣmatī-s. So, this man brought us up with stories from his family and stories of resistance, and, he brought us up, basically this way. His main two principles were: not to lie and not to tolerate injustice … And that, within injustice, under

> injustice, political resistance is a must. And that there is not political resistance without a political organization; and that in a dictatorship you can't have a political organization unless this political organization is underground. So, he was telling this to me, these stories when I was fifteen, seventeen, a daughter who was not allowed out on her own from the house. For me, this was totally abstract. I remember, the first time I left the house on my own was to go to university.

Somehow, the family that Aida describes appears like many middle-class conservative families in the late 1960s, certainly in Cairo, but also in other cities in the Mediterranean region. Once women's political rights had been granted (in 1956), the idea that women had to achieve a high level of education and then work was quite common. Middle-class young women at that time considered higher education to be a passport for financial independence. Many of the women I interviewed remember the experience of being at university as 'absolutely natural'. This was what both the republican state and the family were expecting from them. Notwithstanding the challenges faced by women in achieving leadership positions (something that was still exceptional at that time), equality in the public space was formally acknowledged. Yet, families still exercised a strict control on women's personal lives, as Aida's comment about not going out before enrolling in university suggests. Sexuality was conceived as legitimate only within the context of the marriage, leading many to get married at a relatively young age (seventeen or eighteen), and the limitations to personal freedom had nothing to do with being Muslim or Christian. As a matter of fact, the narratives of the Coptic and Muslim women I met over the years do not vary much one from the other, and intermarriage is not an exceptional fact. Moreover, most of the time religious affiliation is not a theme that comes up during the interviews, and social behaviour does not differ, to the point that sometimes I can't tell whether my interviewee is a Coptic or a Muslim. The control over women's bodies as a site of the family's honour was a practice that transcended social class, but it was exercised in different ways by different classes. Class is not the only factor shaping women's experience, but it intersects generations alongside other variables, such as the specific family life. In the narrative produced by Aida about her life, the fact that her father was a political activist plays a central role in shaping her identity:

> What happened was that in the last year of my school he got arrested. The patriarch. The kind hardly democratic slash patriarch of the house got arrested … He was sentenced to ten years, but he spent two years in prison. And so … while he was absent, I entered the university and … the university was … ON FIRE … there were demonstrations, for the '67 defeat, and … lack of democracy, and hiking price […]. But even before my father was arrested – because my father got arrested twice, once in early '71 – or '72 … I don't remember – and then again in this widespread arrest that Sadat did in 1981, before that, I had an uncle who was a communist, and who had escaped prison. He was one of the communists who was sentenced in '59 by Nasser's regime. They were sent to the al-Wāḥāt [the Oasis] detention centre. And, I had another, the cousin of

> my mother, basically was killed by prison, because he died immediately after the release. So, the idea of people going to prison and out of prison and struggling an unjust regime for me was the way good people live. And, for a long time, without … without ideology. It is not like I developed my ideology. Until now I can't describe myself as a real learned person. Ever since then, that was the drive and that's how it has been.

Up to this point Aida had defined her political identity along the line of continuity with a genealogy of male activists. There is a shift in her narrative when she joined the feminist reading group that became the New Woman Foundation, in 1984, a space where she familiarized herself with the Egyptian and international feminist thought, as transmitted through the archives of *L'Égyptienne*, the Egyptian Feminist Union's magazine launched in 1925, copies of which were conserved by one of the NWF members. The New Woman Foundation developed a critique of the different forms of domination and discrimination that oppress women: the family, state institutions and the way the job market is organized. These were the same years when Kimberlé Crenshaw theorized intersectionality,[20] the analytical category that today recurs in all the public interventions of young feminist Egyptian women.

Aida studied in a German school and, notwithstanding her personal inclination for English literature and for political sciences, her mother plotted to dissuade her from her plans:

> I completed the high school with very high grades, and I applied to enrol in the Faculty of Political Science. My mother was devastated … how could I have such high grades and not enter medicine? And then she … she told me … She lied to me … and told me … because we used to rotate my father's visits, as I had a brother who was only two years old. So, once my mother would go with my older brother, and I stayed with the baby, and once I would go with her and Muhammad would stay with the baby. So, she came back, and she told me: 'Baba was very upset that you registered to political sciences and he would like you to become a doctor.' And of course, that was the end, I mean, that was a big burden, and …. (*smiles*) I changed … of course, and it turned out to be a lie. Actually, my father would have been very happy if I'd register in political sciences … Ah ah … my mother was … she had a way, and not even God could stop her!

Aida was a good student, she completed medical school with high grades, but she knew from the first day that she would not become a doctor: 'It took six years (*laughs*). Six years during which I never made an injection, I never made a stitch, I never attended an operation, I never entered the morgue. But I got excellent marks in surgery and anatomy, because I knew how to learn things well (*laughs*).'

She decided to specialize in psychiatry because she seemed to find it easier to talk to people than to operate on their bodies. But over time she realized that psychiatry was transforming her into a different person: 'I have changed a lot. Through psychiatry … I was a terrible person … a terrible …' Then, maybe reading a shade of scepticism on my face, she insisted:

> No really ... I mean, I entered this profession when I was still training, and I was ... I was indoctrinated by my family, by my father especially, what is right, and what is wrong, there is only black and white, no grey zones, no excuses to make mistakes. Of course, for my father what he considered mistakes were mostly things related to moral issues. My father was ... as progressive as he was politically, he was otherwise extremely, extremely conservative. And he was mistrustful of women.

In a recent study about psychology and Islam in Egypt, and based on a one year ethnographic observation of a centre for psychological counselling in Cairo in 2009 and 2010, the anthropologist Aymon Kreil questions the idea – mostly developed in the circles of Foucauldian critique – that the use of psychology to address individual problems results in a negation of politics, especially in an authoritarian regime such as Hosni Mubarak's, where the arbitrariness of the state was obvious. This is not always true. On the contrary, Kreil writes: 'The psychologizing of political and social issues entails a politicization of psychological matters.'[21] I argue that this observation can be very productively applied to the analysis of the nexus between second-wave feminism and psychiatry (but more in general, the medical professions) in Egypt. Feminist Egyptian psychiatry was certainly inspired by the pioneering work of Nawal al-Saadawi, whose first book, *al-Marʾa wa-l-jins* (*Women and Sex*), first published in Arabic in 1972,[22] was a landmark for second-wave feminism, and deeply influenced all future generations. The biographies of feminists from the medical and especially psychiatric professions have shed light on a complex interweaving between opportunities created by institutional policies (such as the generalization of free higher education and the opening-up of opportunities for work in hospitals) and an activist's career anchored over a longer time frame, which goes against certain simplistic readings of biopolitics as a sole tool of domination. In the experience and the life-narrative of Aida Seif al-Dawla, psychiatry was not the science that pathologizes non-normative subjects but the practice of care and compassion, which can't be but politicized, and whose main aim is care for the subjects who are treated. In her own words:

> Working with people through psychiatry showed me that there was not only a grey zone, there are all colours, and all human beings are all very, very very ... complicated. And so ... I became more tolerant, and more self-critical, and .... and learned to listen a lot before I open my mouth. No, it was educational and therapeutic.

From its early days, Aida's work was a combination of feminism, psychiatry and democratic activism, as witnessed by her experience in the dispensary of Qaṣr al-ʿAynī:

> In '86 I joined a small group of friends and colleagues who decided to set up a primary health-care unit in al-Wāylī. This neighbourhood had a strong leftist

> presence and, of course, the community was largely conservative. It was two years before the parliamentary elections, and we wanted to set foot in the area. I joined the clinic and I was working in the child monitoring, length, weight, development, and of course children come with their moms, and … and then at some point, the issue of FGM [female genital mutilation] was brought up, and we decided to hold meetings with the mothers. I would have a closed meeting, where we are going to talk about FGM and its impact on women's health: physical, psychological and sexual … So, we had this meeting and they were listening to me. I was talking about the bleeding and the infections, talking about the implications, and the difficulties in giving birth and so on, and then (*laughs*) I started talking about the sexual implications of women genital mutilations, and, of course, they are very polite, I am a doctor and they have to listen (*laughs*), but … I noticed there were smiles and winks between the women, then I stopped and said: 'OK, obviously I am saying something you are not in agreement with … so … what is it? What have I said wrong?' It ended up that for an hour I was sitting there and women talking about (*laughs*) their sexual adventures and creativity with their husbands, and what they do if their husbands don't please them. And I remember one of them saying: '*khitān* [FGM] has nothing to do with sexual pleasure. What has to do with sexual pleasure is how he comes to you, how he approaches you in bed. That's what either leads to pleasure or does not lead to pleasure.'

This experience prompted Aida to challenge the idea that the main argument that feminists can use against FGM is the control of women's pleasure. She rather suggests that the real point is the violence inflicted on young girls. Actually, she argues that, as long as the campaigns against FGM focus on the theme of sexual pleasure, they remain on the same epistemic level as those who support it.

Aida's feminism was cultivated through a combination of grassroots work and extensive readings, especially the biographies of the modern women writers such as Malak Ḥifnī Nāṣif (better known under the pen name of Bāḥithat al-Bādiya), the nationalist feminists who created the Egyptian Feminist Union, such as Hudā Shaʿrāwī, Nabawiyya Mūsā and Sayzā Nabarāwī, and Nawal al-Saadawi. Without dismissing the intellectual roots of feminism, she pointed out many times during the interview that the fieldwork experience and the clinical work were what opened her eyes:

> I read about what Nawal al-Saadawi had written about circumcision and it was very abstract for me. I never saw an actual circumcised woman except when I graduated from the medical school. And I didn't think that this was still been done until I started working in 1993, with a wonderful, wonderful elderly woman called Mārī Asʿad. Mārī Asʿad is an elderly woman who together with ʿAzīza Ḥusayn, a little bit older, has been working with marginalized communities ever since the '20s. They had been working mainly in Manshiyyat Nāṣir, close to al-Muqaṭṭam, and they addressed whatever it was that was an issue for the poor women there. And then in 1993, there was the preparation of the international

> population conference in Egypt. So, all the reproductive issues were on the agenda. And to produce papers for that conference we had to do research. At the time, we were not a task force, we were just a group meeting at Mārī Asʿad's house. To do this research we did fieldwork. And the field revealed a lot that we did not know.

After the conference, in 1994, Mārī Asʿad set up the Task Force against Female Genital Mutilation. The task force produced papers and organized training and several workshops for both men and women, across the country. They worked with young girls, physicians and the clergy.

The next step in Aida's trajectory as a feminist human rights defender was the creation of El-Nadeem Center for Rehabilitation of the Victims of Violence, which, in her own words, took her to 'a completely different level of understanding psychiatry and therapist–client relationship'. In 1989, the Egyptian Organization for Human Rights (EOHR), of which Aida was part, supported the iron workers who had been arrested for taking part in a strike. They published a statement demanding the release of the workers. The government retaliated by arresting many EOHR members and reopening their old files on their political activities in the leftist groups. Muḥammad al-Sayyid Saʿīd, Hishām Mubārak and Kamāl Khalīl were among those who were arrested and were brutally tortured in jail:[23]

> Some of our friends were arrested and were tortured. And when they came out some of them were injured. At that time, I was working at ʿAyn Shams hospital, Sūzān was the head of psychiatry at the Palestine Hospital in Heliopolis, and ʿAbd Allāh was at the Airport hospital. Doctors in Egypt are very important. I mean, when they give orders, orders are executed. And yet, we could not have those friends of ours examined, and the one time they were examined we could not get a report of their conditions. Because, the hospitals would not give a report, when they found out that they had been in prison and that they were injured in prison. So that was one reason: to set something that would provide people the reports of what happened to them.
>
> The second thing is that because they were friends, were our friends, and when they came out, we had gatherings and we talked, we came to see an aspect of torture that we have not seen before. I had three people in my family, who were detained for long period of time, and were very brutally tortured, during Abdel Nasser and during Sadat. But when they came out, they came out as heroes. I never heard them talk, and nobody talked about what they did to them. These tortures. With those friends, they talked. So, we saw the other side of being a hero. We saw people who are very angry, who are humiliated, who … some of them were angry with themselves because they didn't try to fight back, and … so, we saw these traumas, this effect of the trauma, and we felt that these needed intervention.

At that time, Aida and her colleagues were all volunteers at the EOHR, one of the oldest civil society organizations in Egypt (it was created in 1985 and registered as an NGO in 2003). They first considered opening a centre to treat the victims of torture inside the organization, but eventually they could not agree on how to deal with the privacy of the clients, and they decided to create a new organization, specializing in this treatment. In an interview given to *Mada Masr*'s Lina Attalah, Aida explained that there were also multiple visions about how to work on human rights within the EOHR. Some of them believed that human rights work should be led by professionals, others – and Aida being one of them – that human rights should be developed at the level of street activism, as happened later, during the 2011 revolution.[24] El-Nadeem focused on the clinical work, even if it was soon evident that this kind of clinical work could not but have political implications. When they started El-Nadeem, Aida and her colleagues were expecting to receive political activists who had been subject to torture. This was not the case, and it pushed her to think critically of how the human rights movement was positioned within the society:

> After a year we realized that we, the people who come from political movements, and some of us were in the political parties, and worked in human rights, we had absolutely *no idea* of what was actually happening in the country. Because from 1993 until 2000, until the breakout of the demonstrations in solidarity with the al-Aqṣā Intifada, we did not receive a single political activist as a client. Everybody we received, everybody we reached out, were people from the very low social classes, who are poor, who are marginalized who did not have the right phone number to call when they got in trouble, and … and we realized that … people do not get tortured only to 'confess'.

She continued:

> People can get tortured just to be intimidated or to give up a piece of land, or to leave a flat that is designed for somebody up, or to teach somebody a lesson on behalf of the third party. That the torture can take place for the weirdest reasons you can think of, and … and that is happening everywhere. Wherever there are police, there is torture, or possible torture. It is in police stations, in state security headquarters, in the security offices in the universities, in the metro station, in public hospitals. Wherever there is police, maltreatment and torture can take place. When we reached that conclusion, we realized that torture is an issue that cannot be addressed only through a clinic, that people must know what is happening in the country. We also realized that the people who come to us for help because they had been tortured, or women who came to us because they were subjected to domestic violence, they are not patients in the classic sense. They are normal people who were subjected to extreme traumas, and so, the treatment is not just to listen, and give advice or a prescription, the treatment has to include rehabilitation, it has to be a reformulation of this person's life, to make sense of this terrible trauma they have been subjected to. The rehabilitation needs to happen according to what this person actually needs. If it was legal aid,

we refer to legal aid, if it was campaign, we would campaign with the person, if it was publishing their real story, we did that.

El-Nadeem decided to go public with the stories they collected, using multiple channels. In 1994, Dr Sūzān Fayyāḍ published an article in an opposition party newspaper, but they also used TV talk shows. Aida told me that at the time there was a perception of more freedom on television, information that was confirmed, in a separate interview, by the TV presenter and politician Gameela Ismail (Jamīla Ismāʿīl).[25] Aida emphasized that one of the main challenges was to gain people's trust: 'At the time nobody really believed us … People who are unlikely to be subjected to torture, or who do not know people who have been tortured, they still don't believe. They either don't believe, or they think that this happens to people who deserves it. And with the climate created after 2013 it is even worse.'

In 1998 the then Minister of Social Affairs Mervat Tallawy (Mīrvat Talāwī) presented a proposal to reform Law 32/1964, the law of associations, to the government. The cabinet altered it and passed a reform that was never enacted because it was declared unconstitutional.[26] The new associations' law (Law 84/2002) mandated that all NGOs were to register at the Ministry of Social Affairs. Aida was then part of the Egyptian Association to Combat Torture. They applied and were refused registration.[27] In early 2000 the human rights community was mature, but some incoherence remained, which made it difficult to qualify it as a movement. For instance, during the Queen Boat case in 2001, when over fifty men faced charges of debauchery, obscene behaviour and contempt of religion (which allowed the case to be judged by the security court), the human rights community was divided: 'There were human rights organizations whose directors announced that they were against homosexuality.'[28] People who were charged were never recognized for being homosexual, not even by their own lawyer. Even the human rights lawyers at that time framed the debate in a different way. While thinking retrospectively about the early 2000s, Aida Seif al-Dawla acknowledged that there had been a generational gap in the human rights community, and that 2001 was a landmark, a moment of real change, when a new generation of human rights defenders, less ideological and more aware of the interconnection between human rights, personal and sexual rights and political freedom, emerged. This generation began to be active in the early 2000s in informal spaces, especially the street demonstrations in support of the Palestinian al-Aqṣā Intifada. At that time, the kind of clientele that El-Nadeem received began to change. The psychiatrists at El-Nadeem were also participating in the demonstrations; it was therefore natural to reach out to young people. Young protesters who were abused started to hear about El-Nadeem, and El-Nadeem became the place to go to seek help.

The protests continued in 2003 against the participation of Egypt in the US-led coalition that attacked Iraq, the movement in solidarity with the judiciary against the corruption of the political system in 2004, then through the Egyptian Movement for Change Kifāya[29] and, since 2008, the April 6 Youth Movement, in which the students joined the workers claiming the right to strike and better working conditions.[30]

Political dissent intersected the fight for social and economic rights in the 2000s, and it involved not only politicized urban middle-class intellectuals and activists, but also young and working-class women and men who had not previously been part of any political movement. Aida Seif al-Dawla narrates the campaign 'We are all Khaled Said' (which started as a Facebook page in 2010 upon the outrage created by the death in police custody in Alexandria of a young computer programmer, Khaled Said [Khālid Saʿīd], and the dissemination of the photographs of his tortured body after his death)[31] and the 2011 uprisings along a line of continuity with this long movement, producing a story that is grounded in historical contextualization and avoids idealizations.[32] She remembers that during the eighteen days of the 2011 uprising, which not only toppled the regime of Hosni Mubarak, but also inspired a human revolution in Egypt and beyond it,[33] there was an 'emotional unity' but regrets that this never translated into political unity. The revolution forced El-Nadeem to deal with the violence happening in the square:

> People who were arrested, people who were taken to be informants and infiltrators in the square, during the eighteen days, were frequently taken by revolutionaries in the square, tied to trees, and beaten. Something that we did the day after the Battle of the Camels[34] was searching tents for torture, there were torture tents. [...] Some friends brought us once two people, who were taken to be informants, and they were badly beaten, they were smashed for suspicion of being informers, so even within the mess of the eighteen days it was not completely ... It was not utopia. It was not utopia. But of course, the good overshadowed the bad. There was a lot of good in the square. *In the squares*. And I am sure that a lot of things that happened in Tahrir [Taḥrīr], did not happen in Suez, did not happen in Alexandria. You know, the thing is the eighteen days have been reduced to Tahrir Square. Ok. Just like the horrible crimes committed by al-Sisi on 14 August 2013, have been reduced to what happened in Rābiʿa, plus minus al-Nahḍa.[35] What happened on that day, happened in all governorates. And the number of the killed far exceeds the number of those reported in Rābiʿa.

The dispersal of the two pro-Muslim Brotherhood sit-ins in Rābiʿa al-ʿAdawiyya in the district of Naṣr City and al-Nahḍa Square in Giza recurs in the narrative of the feminist revolutionary activists as a traumatic experience. Many of them regret the lack of empathy that the society, including many activists, showed for the victims. The number of deaths is disputed between government sources, which tried to minimize it, and human rights organizations. Nazra for Feminist Studies (Naẓra li-l-dirāsāt al-nisawīyya) published a report based on women's testimonies (both paramedics who were operating there and those who were sitting-in), and they found that at least nineteen women died during the attack.[36] Three of them remained unknown. Paramedics and doctors described the situation they witnessed as a 'complete disaster'.[37] Nazra also documented fifty-two arrests of women in the aftermath of the dispersal operation and reported open violations of human rights, including sexual assault and vaginal inspection of the women arrested.[38]

Rābiʿa al-ʿAdawiyya was a landmark in recent Egyptian history, the beginning of the age of terror when, in the name of security, the state violates human rights and persecutes human rights defenders and their families.

Conclusion

I collected Aida Seif al-Dawla's and other women's human rights testimonies at a time when a battle over the memory of the uprising was happening in Egypt. The new regime was trying to appropriate the memory of the uprising and wipe out experiences of resistance to the military rule, reducing the battle to the polarization between terrorism and the army. In this environment, the narrative of the history related by Aida and other human rights defenders represents a challenge to this hegemonic account. The intertwining between old and recent memories, the 1970s and 2011, can be better understood in the light of Passerini's concept of memory's 'double character' and her assertion that 'memory has a history'.

The women I interviewed knew modern Egyptian history and experienced other phases of repression, but they all agreed that repression had never been so brutal, and the sense of fear was pervasive. Whoever did not identify with the state was perceived as a terrorist or a traitor. President al-Sisi and his European supporters did not hesitate to resort to culturalist arguments to dismiss the work of human rights defenders in Egypt. For instance, during a joint press conference, the President of France Emmanuel Macron stated that France cannot give lessons on human rights to Egypt, and President Abd al-Fattah al-Sisi reinforced the idea, affirming that Egypt cannot afford 'the luxury of human rights [*sic*]'.[39] However, the stories I am collecting document a vital and well rooted human rights community, whose history has yet to be written. The conclusion to be drawn from an analysis of my interviews is that writing a global history of human rights implies a pluralistic approach, going beyond the archives of international organizations and documenting the experiences developed by human rights defenders in non-Western contexts. This will contribute to a decolonization of human rights history.

Women have been part of human rights organizations since the beginning. Many of the Egyptian second-wave secular feminists came to the realm of political activism through student movements and the underground Marxist organizations of the 1970s. Human rights activism paralleled other forms of political activism, especially leftist and feminist, and today some of the most prominent figures in the human rights community, such as Aida Seif al-Dawla, Mājda ʿAdlī, Sūzān Fayyaḍ, Āmāl ʿAbd al-Hādī, Nawla Darwīsh, Ragia Omran (Rājya ʿUmrān), Heba Morayyef (Hiba Murayyaf), Mahienour al-Massry (Māhī al-Nūr al-Maṣrī), Mozn Hassan, Azza Soliman, Yara Sallam, Sallī Tūma and Dāliā ʿAbd al-Ḥamīd, to name only some of the many I met, are women. In this chapter, I have begun drafting a genealogy of feminist human rights activism through the biography of one of the veterans in the field. A more comprehensive, even if not exhaustive, collective biography of women human rights defenders in Egypt should also feature the biographies of at least some artists and writers, who work more explicitly on human rights in their literary and artistic work: Lina Attalah, Laila Soliman (Laylā Sulaymān), Basma Abdel Aziz (Basma ʿAbd al-ʿAzīz) and Bahia Shehab (Bahiya Shihāb) are some of the most thought-provoking voices from the new generation.

Human rights are today at the centre of the agenda of the main feminist organizations, the historical ones, such as the New Woman Foundation, and the more recent, such as Nazra for Feminist Studies (created in 2007 and forced to close its headquarters in 2018, following the freezing of its assets), Ikhtiyār for a Feminist Choice (created in 2012), CEWLA (since 1995) and many others beyond Cairo, such as Janūbiyya Ḥurra in Aswan (since 2012) and Daughters of the Nile in the Buḥayra Governatorate (since 2011). On the other side, feminism informs the work of human rights organizations that recognize gender as an intersectional category for understanding inequalities, discriminations and human rights violations, such as the Egyptian Initiative for Personal Rights. There are also groups created around campaigns, such as No to Military Trials for Civilians (created by Mona Seif and her mother Laila Soueif in 2011), a Nation Without Torture and Freedom for the Brave.

I encountered a number of challenges while I was working on these interviews. They contain a number of phrases such as 'I don't know', 'I don't remember … ', 'This does not matter anymore' or even 'Why do you keep asking about that?' How to make sense of the silences, the incoherencies, the untold stories? The ambiguous relationship between the interviewer and the interviewee, alternating between trust and suspicion, bears its own history. Part of it has to do with the traumatic experience of the past eight years, which is a matter of investigation for other studies. Part of it is the history of the hegemonic perception of Arab and Muslim women, and the essentialist depiction of the Middle East, where women are portrayed only as victims of patriarchy. What I have tried to do here is to transform the suspicion into intersubjectivity, and to produce a narrative that sheds light on the agency. I consider my interviewees not as victims of history but as agents of history in the making. When I collect their testimonies about violence, I focus on their acts of resistance to violence; when they share with me their experience as daughters or wives, I am interested in understanding how they contribute, through an in-depth self-reflection on their personal experience, to transforming family relationships.

There is not much about Islam and Muslims in my interviews. This is partly due to the positioning of my interviewees in the field of secular feminism, which is made up of women who, whatever their personal attitude towards religion, do not use Islamic arguments to uphold their political discourse. Overall, they tend to distinguish between social conservatism and Islam, and they attribute women and gender discriminations to the former more than the latter.

There is also an element of intertextuality in the interviews. The interviewees often refer to documents (articles they have written, papers they have presented or even public statements) they clearly remember but that can't be located: 'I will check in my computer/at home/in my bookshelves, and if I find it I will send it to you.' Every time I hear these words, I remember what Passerini, drawing on Agostino's *Confessions*, describes as the paradox of memory or the intertwine between memory and oblivion: 'it is impossible to search for something that has been lost, unless we remember at least part of it'.[40]

Most of the documents produced by women in the Egyptian human rights community are not archived. This is partly due to the fact that human rights were first articulated within spontaneous and underground groups. Plus, in the process of so doing, its main actors did not perceive themselves as historical subjects and they did not create archives until very recently. Their memories today are usually the only available archive. They are a living archive in the meaning that oral historians gave to the word in the 1970s and 1980s, namely, historical sources that allow us to rewrite history from the perspective of non-institutional and non-hegemonic, sometimes even marginal, subjects.[41]

The testimonies I used in this chapter are part of a broader corpus that I am using to write about the history of Egyptian feminism. Here, I have extrapolated some fragments that specifically refer to the human rights movement in Egypt, as it has been experienced by some of the women activists I met. Interestingly enough, my interviewees began to talk explicitly about 'human rights' and to position themselves as members of the 'human rights community' – also retrospectively – since 2015, when the crackdown against human rights activists became extremely violent. As I noticed this shift in the narrative, I considered it important to record and narrate the emergence of women human rights activists' historical subjectivity as an integral part of both feminism and the human rights movement.

My oral histories reveal an understudied aspect of feminism in Egypt and, more broadly, in Arab and Muslim majority societies: similar to the experiences in the United States and in Europe during this period, here also there was a deep sense that feminism, in order to continue to be relevant, needed to care about other inequalities and to engage in policies of both local and global governance. These narratives challenge one of the many accusations that has been made against Egyptian feminist, of being elitist and 'not close enough to people'. Interestingly enough, other – male dominated – social and political movements, whose roots were in the same social environments of the feminists (middle-class and highly educated people), never faced the same accusations.

Looking at these particular figures, who have been active both at the grassroots and the international level and who are all connected through transnational networks and platforms of civil society activism, allows me to prove that the scholarship on women in the Arab and Muslim majority societies that draws on revised modernization theory – which asserts that modernization results in greater gender equality and less rigid sexual norms,[42] that Islam is the main obstacle for gender egalitarianism,[43] and that continues to influence the work of contemporary political scientists[44] – is not just wrong but also contributes to silencing women's voices in Arab and Muslim societies. While the public discussion on women and development, reproductive health and sexual rights flourished in governmental and international spaces, in good measure by stressing the burden imposed by 'traditional cultures' in order to enhance their agenda of 'modern development', independent feminist activists and emerging women's collectives and associations emphasized that, more than 'traditions' and 'culture', it was the economic factor – in particular, the severe economic crisis that followed the years of *infitāḥ* policy and the adoption of a structural adjustment programme – that most reinforced cultural and social conservatism. My research, narrating history through the collection of personal stories, shifts the focus from the institutional accounts produced by the government to activists' lived experiences and contributes to the epistemological debate about decolonizing feminism and to a larger discussion on corporeality through feminist history lenses. By asking how feminism addressed neoliberal governments' attempts to police and discipline women's bodies, this research leads to a deeper understanding of Egyptian political history in that period.

A feminist scholarship that relies on living archives can contribute to a more nuanced understanding of the intertwining between gender, sexuality and politics in the Arab world and beyond.

Notes

This chapter is researched using a feminist oral history methodology, as outlined in the second paragraph. This implies that how people refer to themselves is a core epistemic element of the historical narrative. To reflect this, the Arabic names of the public feminist figures are given as they appear in their own publications or social media profiles. In some cases, they also reflect the Egyptian not the Arabic standard pronunciation. To ensure consistency throughout the volume, the *International Journal of Middle East Studies* (*IJMES*) transliteration is provided between parentheses the first time they are quoted.

1 Cecilia Medina, 'Women's Rights are Human Rights: Latin American Countries and the Organization of American States (OAS)', in Myriam Díaz-Diocaretz and Iris M. Zavala (eds), *Women, Feminist Identity, and Society in the 1980s: Selected Papers*, 63–79 (Amsterdam: Benjamins, 1985), 63.

2 Charlotte Bunch, 'Women's Rights as Human Rights: Toward a Re-Vision of Human Rights', *Human Right Quarterly*, 12 (4) (1990): 486–98.

3 United Nations Human Rights Office of the High Commissioner, *Women's Rights are Human Rights* (New York, 2014), 13. Available online: https://www.ohchr.org/Documents/Events/WHRD/WomenRightsAreHR.pdf (accessed 8 January 2019).

4 Ibid.

5 Lina Attalah, 'Human Rights in Focus, Aida Seif al-Dawla' (*Mada Masr*, 10 October 2015). Available online: https://madamasr.com/en/2015/10/10/feature/politics/human-rights-in-focus-aida-seif-al-dawla/ (accessed 21 March 2019); Yara Sallam, 'Aida Seif el-Dawla' (*Even the Finest Warriors*, 26 January 2019). Available online: https://eventhefinestofwarriors.org/en/profile/aida-seif-el-dawla/ (accessed 21 March 2019).

6 The literature on this topic is broad. For the Muslim world, see at least: Mahnaz Afkhami, *Faith and Freedom: Women's Human Rights in the Muslim World* (Bethesda, MD: Women's Learning Partnership, 1995); and Valentine M. Moghhadam, *Globalizing Women: Transnational Feminist Networks* (Baltimore, MD: Johns Hopkins University Press, 2005).

7 Shereen Abouelnaga, *Women in Revolutionary Egypt. Gender and the New Geographics of Identity* (Cairo: American University in Cairo Press, 2016), 107.

See also Niamh Reilly, *Without Reservation: The Beijing Tribunal on Accountability for Women's Human Rights* (Brunswick, NJ: Center for Women's Global Leadership, 1996).

8 Gayatri Chakravorty Spivak, '"Woman" as Theatre: United Nation Conference on Women, Beijing 1995', *Radical Philosophy*, 75 (1996).

9 United Nations Development Programme (UNDP), 'The Arab Human Development Report 2005: Towards the Rise of Women in the Arab World', 2006. Available online at http://hdr.undp.org/sites/default/files/rbas_ahdr2005_en.pdf (accessed 8 January 2019).

10 Sardar Shaheen Ali, 'Women's Rights, CEDAW and International Human Rights Debates', in Jane L. Parpart, Shirin M. Rai and Kathleen Staudt (eds), *Rethinking Empowerment: Gender and Development in a Global/Local World*, 61–78 (London: Routledge, 2002).

11 Lila Abu-Lughod, Fida J. Adely and Frances Hasso, 'Overview: Engaging the Arab Human Development Report 2005 on Women', *International Journal of Middle East Studies*, 41 (1) (2009): 59–60.

12 Ibid.

13 Inderpal Grewal, *Transnational America: Feminisms, Diasporas, Neoliberalisms* (Durham, NC: Duke University Press, 2005).

14 Islah Jad, 'The "NGOization" of the Arab Women's Movements', *Al-Raida Journal*, 38–47, July 2016. Available online: http://www.alraidajournal.com/index.php/ALRJ/article/view/442 (accessed 31 March 2019); Maha Abdelrahman, *Civil Society Exposed: The Politics of Civil Society in Egypt* (London: I.B.Tauris, 2004).

15 Luisa Passerini, *Fascism in Popular Memory: The Cultural Experience of the Turin Working Class* (Cambridge: Cambridge University Press, 1987).

16 Luisa Passerini, 'Living Archives: Continuity and Innovation in the Art of Memory, Working Paper', 1. Available online: https://babe.eui.eu/wp-content/uploads/sites/21/2014/06/Paper_Passerini_1_15_2014.pdf (accessed 20 January 2019).

17 Hani Shukrallah (Hānī Shukr Allāh), a prominent journalist and political analyst, who served as the Chief Editor of *al-Ahrām Weekly* from 1998 to 2005. He came back from his studies in Canada in 1970 and in 1971 he was already in an underground political organization that, at the time, was called the Egyptian Communist Organisation and later changed its name to the Egyptian Workers Communist Party. He was also one of the co-founders of the Egyptian Organization for Human Rights (1985). Interview, Hani Shukrallah, Cairo, 4 January 2018. Some of his writings have been collected in the volume *Egypt, the Arabs and the World: Reflections at the Turn of the Twenty-First Century* (Cairo: American University in Cairo Press, 2011).

18 'Our Reply to the MOH Allegations Regarding Closure of El Nadim', [Press release] 25 February 2016. Available online: https://www.alnadeem.org/en/content/our-reply-moh-allegations-regarding-closure-el-nadim (accessed 3 January 2019).

19 Interview, Aida Seif El-Dawla, Cairo, 4 January 2018.

20 Kimberlé Crenshaw, 'Demarginalizing the Intersection of Race and Sex: A Black Feminist Critique of Antidiscrimination Doctrine, Feminist Theory, and Antiracist Politics', in Katharine Bartlett (ed.), *Feminist Legal Theory*, 139–68 (London: Taylor & Francis, 1989).

21 Aymon Kreil, 'Science de la psyché et authorité de l'Islam: quelle conciliation? Le cas d'une association de conseil psychologique au Caire', *Archives de Sciences Sociales des Religions*, 170 (2015): 279.

22 Nawāl al-Saʿdāwī, *al-Marʾa wa-l-jins* (*Women and Sex*) (Cairo: Maktabat Madbūlī, 1972).
23 Attalah, 'Human Rights in Focus'.
24 Ibid.
25 Interview, Jamīla Ismāʿīl, Cairo, 9 January 2018.
26 Human Rights Watch, 'Egypt: Margins of Repression State Limits on Nongovernmental Organization Activism', 17 (8). Available online: https://www.hrw.org/reports/2005/egypt0705/egypt0705.pdf (accessed 20 January 2019).
27 Attalah, 'Human Rights in Focus'.
28 Ibid.
29 The Egyptian Movement for Change Kifaya was the most well-known and active social movement between 2004 and 2006. Gathering Marxist, Nasserite, Islamist, and liberal veteran activists under a trans-ideological political platform calling for the end of the one-party rule and more broadly the liberalization of the political sphere, it is generally considered the most influential social movement in Egypt in the years before the 2011 revolution. See Michaelle Browers, 'The Egyptian Movement for Change: Intellectual Antecedents and Generational Conflicts', *Contemporary Islam*, 1(1) (2007): 69–88; Joel Beinin, 'Workers' Protest in Egypt: Neo-liberalism and Class Struggle in 21st Century', *Social Movements Studies*, 8(4) (2009): 449–54; Rabab El-Mahdi, 'Enough! Egypt's quest for democracy', *Comparative Political Studies*, 42(8) (2009): 1011–39.
30 The movement takes its name from the date (6 April 2008) when a strike was forbidden in the industrial district of Maḥalla al-Kubra. The union between young well-educated people and workers in this movement is considered one of the triggers of the Egyptian revolution. For a history of the Egyptian student movement, see Ahmed Abdallah, *The Student Movement and National Politics in Egypt, 1923–1973* (Cairo: Al Saqi Books, 1985; reprinted Cairo: American University Press, 2008). For the history of the workers movement in Egypt, see Joel Beinin and Zachary Lockman, *Workers on the Nile: Nationalism, Communism, Islam, and the Egyptian Working Class, 1882–1954* (Cairo: American University Press, 1998). For the workers' movement and the Egyptian revolution, see Joel Beinin, *Workers and Thieves: Labour Movements and Popular Uprisings in Tunisia and Egypt* (Stanford, CA: Stanford University Press, 2015), 75–81.
31 The anthropologist Walter Ambrust features the commemorations of Khaled Said among the political protests that, through the commemoration of the martyrs (those who died for the revolution), express grievances and demands. Walter Ambrust, *Martyrs and Tricksters: An Ethnography of the Egyptian Revolution* (Princeton, NJ: Princeton University Press, 2019), 99–123.
32 Recent scholarship confirms this thesis. See Joshua Stacher, *Watermelon Democracy: Egypt's Turbulent Transition* (Syracuse, NY: Syracuse University Press, 2020); Ambrust, *Martyrs and Tricksters*; Sherine Hafez, *Women of the Midan: The Untold Stories of Egypt's Revolutionaries* (Bloomington, IN: Indiana University Press, 2019); Nicola Pratt, *Embodying Geopolitics: Generations of Women's Activism in Egypt, Jordan, and Lebanon* (Berkeley, CA: University of California Press, 2020).
33 I discuss the international reverberations of the Egyptian 2011 Revolution in Lucia Sorbera, 'Writing Revolution: New Inspirations, New Questions', *Postcolonial Studies* 17(1) (2014): 104–08.
34 On 2 February 2011, pro-Mubārak thugs on horses and camels attacked protesters in Taḥrīr Square, causing popular outrage. One year later, the twenty-four officials who had been accused of sending the thugs were acquitted.

35 Rābiʿa Square and al-Nahḍa Square were the two places where the supporters of the Muslim Brotherhood gathered to protest the ousting of President Mohammed al-Mursī in July 2013. The Muslim Brotherhoood sit-in in Rābiʿa and al-Nahḍa squares were brutally cleared on 14 August 2013, in what Egyptian and international human rights organizations described as the most violent attack against civilians in Egyptian modern history.

36 Nazra for Feminist Studies, 'The Dispersion of the Rābiʿa Sit-in and its Aftermath'. Available online: https://nazra.org/sites/nazra/files/attachments/report_on_police_treatment-with_women_protesters_en.pdf (accessed 30 January 2019).

37 Ibid., 8.

38 Ibid., 13.

39 Joint Press Conference by Emmanuel Macron and Abd al-Fattah al-Sisi, 25 October 2017.

40 My translation from the original Italian: 'Non è possibile cercare qualcosa che si è perso a meno che non lo si ricordi almeno in parte'; Luisa Passerini, *Memoria e Utopia: Il Primato dell'Intersoggettività* (Torino: Bollati Boringhieri, 2003), 26.

41 Luisa Passerini (ed.), *Storia orale: Vita quitidiana e cultura materiale delle classi subalterne* (Torino: Rosenberg & Sellier, 1978); Paul Thompson, *The Edwardians: The Remaking of British Society* (London: Routledge, 1973); Philippe Joutard, *Le voci del passato* (Torino: Sei, 1987).

42 Ronald Inglehart and Wayne E. Baker, 'Modernization, Cultural Change, and the Persistence of Traditional Values', *American Sociological Review*, 65 (1) (2000): 19–51.

43 Pippa Norris and Ronald Inglehart, *Sacred and Secular: Religion and Politics Worldwide* (Cambridge: Cambridge University Press, 2011).

44 Veronica Kostenko, Eduard Ponarin, Musa Shteiwi and Olga Strebkova, 'Historical Legacies and Gender Attitudes in the Middle East', *Economic Research Forum*, Working Paper 1105 (Giza: Economic Research Forum, 2017).

References

Abdalla, Ahmed (1985), *The Student Movement and National Politics in Egypt, 1923–1973*, Cairo: Al Saqi Books.

Abdelrahman, Maha (2004), *Civil Society Exposed: The Politics of Civil Society in Egypt*, London: I.B.Tauris.

Abouelnaga, Shereen (2016), *Women in Revolutionary Egypt: Gender and the New Geographics of Identity*, Cairo: American University in Cairo Press.

Abu-Lughod, Lila, Fida J. Adely and Frances S. Hasso (2009), 'Overview: Engaging the Arab Human Development Report 2005 on Women', *International Journal of Middle East Studies*, 41 (1): 59–60.

Afkhami, Mahnaz (1995), *Faith and Freedom: Women's Human Rights in the Muslim World*, Bethesda, MD: Women's Learning Partnership.

Ali, Sardar Shaheen (2002), 'Women's Rights, CEDAW and International Human Rights Debates', in Jane L. Parpart, Shirin M. Rai and Kathleen Staudt (eds), *Rethinking Empowerment: Gender and Development in a Global/Local World*, 61–78, London: Routledge.

al-Saʿdāwī, Nawāl (1972), *al-Marʾa wa-l-jins* (*Women and Sex*), Cairo: Maktabat Madbūlī.

Ambrust, Walter (2019), *Martyrs and Tricksters: An Ethnography of the Egyptian Revolution*, Princeton, NJ: Princeton University Press.

Attalah, Lina (2015), 'Human Rights in Focus, Aida Seif al-Dawla', *Mada Masr*, 26 January. Available online: https://madamasr.com/en/2015/10/10/feature/politics/human-rights-in-focus-aida-seif-al-dawla/ (accessed 21 March 2019).
Beinin, Joel (2009), 'Workers' Protest in Egypt: Neo-liberalism and Class Struggle in 21st Century', *Social Movements Studies*, 8 (4): 449–54.
Beinin, Joel (2015), *Workers and Thieves: Labour Movements and Popular Uprisings in Tunisia and Egypt*, Stanford, CA: Stanford University Press.
Beinin, Joel and Zachary Lockman (1998), *Workers on the Nile: Nationalism, Communism, Islam, and the Egyptian Working Class, 1882–1954*, Cairo: American University in Cairo Press.
Browers Michaelle (2007), 'The Egyptian Movement for Change: Intellectual Antecedents and Generational Conflicts', *Contemporary Islam*, 11: 69–88.
Bunch, Charlotte (1990), 'Women's Rights as Human Rights: Toward a Re-Vision of Human Rights', *Human Right Quarterly*, 12 (4): 486–98.
Crenshaw, Kimberlé (1989), 'Demarginalizing the Intersection of Race and Sex: A Black Feminist Critique of Antidiscrimination Doctrine, Feminist Theory, and Antiracist Politics', in Katharine Bartlett (ed.), *Feminist Legal Theory*, 139–68, London: Taylor & Francis.
El Mahdi, Rabab (2009), 'Enough! Egypt's Quest for Democracy', *Comparative Political Studies*, 42(8): 1011–39.
El-Nadeem (2016), 'Our Reply to the MOH allegations regarding closure of El Nadim', [Press release] 25 February 2016. Available at https://www.alnadeem.org/en/content/our-reply-moh-allegations-regarding-closure-el-nadim (accessed 3 January 2019).
Grewal, Inderpal (2005), *Transnational America: Feminisms, Diasporas, Neoliberalisms*, Durham, NC: Duke University Press.
Hafez, Sherine (2019), *Women of the Midan: The Untold Stories of Egypt's Revolutionaries*, Bloomington, IN: Indiana University Press.
Human Rights Watch (2004), 'Egypt: Margins of Repression State Limits on Nongovernmental Organization Activism', 17 (8). Available online: https://www.hrw.org/reports/2005/egypt0705/egypt0705.pdf (accessed 20 January 2019).
Inglehart, Ronald and Wayne E. Baker (2000), 'Modernization, Cultural Change, and the Persistence of Traditional Values', *American Sociological Review*, 65 (1): 19–51.
Jad, Islah (2016), 'The "NGOization" of the Arab Women's Movements', *Al-Raida Journal*: 38–47. Available online: http://www.alraidajournal.com/index.php/ALRJ/article/view/442 (accessed 31 March 2019).
Joutard, Philippe (1987), *Le voci del passato*, Torino: Sei.
Kostenko, Veronica, Eduard Ponarin, Musa Shteiwi and Olga Strebkova (2017), 'Historical Legacies and Gender Attitudes in the Middle East', *Economic Research Forum*, Working Paper 1105, Giza: Economic Research Forum.
Kreil, Aymon (2015), 'Science de la psyché et authorité de l'islam: quelle conciliation? Le cas d'une association de conseil psychologique au Caire', *Archives de Sciences Sociales des Religions*, 170: 267–82.
Medina, Cecilia (1985), 'Women's Rights as Human Rights. Latin American Countries and the Organization of American States (OAS)', in Myriam Díaz-Diocaretz and Iris M. Zavala (eds), *Women, Feminist Identity, and Society in the 1980s: Selected Papers*, 63–79, Amsterdam: Benjamins.
Moghhadam, Valentine M. (2005), *Globalizing Women: Transnational Feminist Networks*, Baltimore, MD: Johns Hopkins University Press.

Nazra for Feminist Studies (2013), 'The Dispersion of the Rābi'a Sit-in and its Aftermath'. Available online: https://nazra.org/sites/nazra/files/attachments/report_on_police_treatment-with_women_protesters_en.pdf (accessed 30 January 2019).
Norris, Pippa and Ronald Inglehart (2011), *Sacred and Secular: Religion and Politics Worldwide*, Cambridge: Cambridge University Press.
Passerini, Luisa (1987), *Fascism in Popular Memory: The Cultural Experience of the Turin Working Class*, Cambridge: Cambridge University Press.
Passerini, Luisa (2003), *Memoria e Utopia: Il Primato dell'Intersoggettività*, Torino: Bollati Boringhieri.
Passerini, Luisa (2014), 'Living Archives. Continuity and Innovation in the Art of Memory, Working Paper'. Available online: https://babe.eui.eu/wp-content/uploads/sites/21/2014/06/Paper_Passerini_1_15_2014.pdf (accessed 20 January 2019).
Passerini, Luisa (ed.) (1978), *Storia orale: Vita quitidiana e cultura materiale delle classi subalterne*, Torino: Rosenberg & Sellier.
Pratt, Nicola (2020), *Embodying Geopolitics: Generations of Women's Activism in Egypt, Jordan, and Lebanon*, Berkeley, CA: University of California Press.
Reilly, Niamh (1996), *Without Reservation: The Beijing Tribunal on Accountability for Women's Human Rights*, New Brunswick, NJ: Center for Women's Global Leadership.
Sallam, Yara (2019), 'Aida Seif el-Dawla', *Even the Finest Warriors*, 26 January. Available online: https://eventhefinestofwarriors.org/en/profile/aida-seif-el-dawla/ (accessed 21 March 2019).
Shukrallah, Hani (2011), *Egypt, the Arabs and the World: Reflections at the Turn of the Twenty-First Century*, Cairo: American University in Cairo Press.
Sorbera, Lucia (2014), 'Writing Revolution: New Inspirations, New Questions', *Postcolonial Studies*, 17(1): 104–08.
Spivak, Gayatri Chakravorty (1996), '"Woman" as Theatre. United Nation Conference on Women, Beijing 1995', *Radical Philosophy*, 75: 2–4.
Stacher Joshua (2020), *Watermelon Democracy: Egypt's Turbulent Transition*, Syracuse, NY: Syracuse University Press.
Thompson, Paul (1973), *The Edwardians: The Remaking of British Society*, London: Routledge.
United Nations Development Programme (UNDP) (2006), 'The Arab Human Development Report 2005: Towards the Rise of Women in the Arab World'. Available online at http://hdr.undp.org/sites/default/files/rbas_ahdr2005_en.pdf (accessed 8 January 2019).
United Nations Human Rights Office of the High Commissioner (2014), *Women's Rights are Human Rights*, New York. Available online: https://www.ohchr.org/Documents/Events/WHRD/WomenRightsAreHR.pdf (accessed 8 January 2019).

Interviews

Aida Seif al-Dawla, interview with author, Cairo, 4 January 2018.
Gameela Ismail, interview with author, Cairo, 9 January 2018.
Hani Shukrallah, interview with author, Cairo, 4 January 2018.

Chapter 9

SEX WORK IN TANGIER AND THE EMERGENCE OF NEW YOUTHFUL SUBJECTIVITIES

Mériam Cheikh

Introduction

> I don't go out [*tan-khruj*] [to prostitute]. I go out mostly during the summer. And, in the winter, I would go out just when I need some money for my daily expenses [*bach nṣarraf*]: I have to eat. I have to pay the rent, I have expenses. [...] I don't go out every night: everyday disco, everyday disco, I have never done that. I don't go out very often. I don't like this way of going out [all the time]. I don't run after money. I don't have any responsibility, I don't have to send money to my family. I can live without going out every day. And then, when I go out the thing is not that I go with one and then another one and so on. I try to be with one only, to create a relationship with him, stay with him and go out to the disco with him. Before I met you, I was with a guy from the Rif [region], he was used to send me sometimes two million, three million [2,000–3,000 euros]. I was rolling in money. So, I was not going out. He took good care of me. You know dating someone [*l-mṣaḥba*] is better. You feel hope, you feel it's your man. Then I went out and met another one, I dated him. He was also used to send me money and we were used to party [*nqasru*] together. (Badīʿa, Tangier, 2008)

Badīʿa is a 'girl who goes out' (*tat-khruj* in Moroccan), that is to say, a girl who frequents nightclubs and bars at night to make a living. She belongs to what among social commentators (journalists, politicians, social workers, social scientists, experts) is called 'the world of prostitution'. However, her own words stress immediately to the reader that the trajectories and pathways of young women experiencing transactional sex have not had and do not have the universe of prostitution as their sole outlook. She was twenty-four years old when, in 2008, she explained to me her way of experiencing 'the going out', or *l-khrīj*. In her speech, different layers of experiences come to define what is 'going out'. We see it being alternately associated with the very idea of commercial sex ('expenses', 'money'), with the idea of dating (*l-mṣaḥba*) and finally with the idea of fun ('party', or *nqasru*). Badīʿa not only refers to the *khrīj* as a specific sexual practice (prostitution) but in relation to her entire intimate and sexual trajectory.

The young women I met during my research and who were in their late teens and in their twenties articulated the same ideas about going out. Although they admitted that they were going out to sell sex for money, they insisted on making clear that their going out was more complex to understand. The entanglement of sexuality, intimacy and amusement was irreducible to the category of 'prostitution'. This category is analytically insufficient in accounting for underclass young women's sexual practices involving money. From this perspective, the *khrīj* also refers to the idea of distancing oneself from norms, morality and respectability.

While referring to the positive idea of self-valorization through amusement and the flouting of moral rules and conventions, *khrīj*, in professional terms, refers also to an activity that fosters the constitution of careers in sex work, a path negatively seen by the young women in this research who try to navigate between the lines of a profitable and a disadvantageous *khrīj*.

This double aspect that has marked the trajectories of these young women is better grasped if we consider the *khrīj* as a social space, to use Bourdieu's terminology, assembling very different ways of practising commercial sex.[1] Hierarchical, this space differentiates between women according to the value they derive from the type of avenues they patronize, the type of men they associate with and the body capital they are able to constitute.[2]

Taking into account the triple dimension of 'the going out' (prostitution, date and fun) involves recognizing the way in which women want to voice their practices, frame their stories and tell their experiences. It fosters the understanding of the formation of their subjectivities. Accepting the need to follow them beyond the prostitution dimension of their going out highlights how some actresses in the sexual economies in Morocco position themselves within the field of prostitution,[3] how they relate to the entertainment dimension of the leisure avenues where they sell sex and how they struggle to position themselves positively within this dimension.

Moreover, their narratives allow us to connect their present experiences with their past in terms of intimacy and sexuality. Their accounts of the ways they became sexually active and physically learnt about intimate relationships highlight specific spaces of the formation of subjectivities. In this respect, school and friendships are fundamental in the elaboration of their sexuality that evolves around values of fun. Positively seen,[4] these youth values are a serious competitor to the hegemonic morality preventing young people from expressing their inner youthful self. They contribute to building a sense of self-worth and respectability.

Spatially speaking, the flats that the young women share are the main site of observation of the constitution of this emancipatory female collective. Within the limits of my social position, I participated in such a collective by joining two young women sharing the same flat with another three young women at the very beginning and, later, by joining a group of friends sharing another flat. Therefore, in Tangier, my knowledge of female friendship, shared flats and the reworking of family ties comes from two distinct women's networks to which I managed to belong and that I was able to follow in the city. By observing their use of the city because of moves or friendly visits that they made to other young women living in shared residency, I was able to trace a geography of this residential mode: type of apartments, neighbourhoods, relations with the neighbours, etc.

This chapter seeks to highlight one side of the multiple and variable ways in which sex work is practised in Morocco: one that sheds light on an important change that I will define as being the process of sexual morality loosening disembodiment. I argue that the youth culture of leisure, situated at the background of sex-work practices, invites us to look at what would be limited to the universe of deviance and the spheres of lack as a process of intimate transformation that is bringing a new sexual order. Sexual transactions by lower-class youths are participating in the subversion of and the shift in sexual and moral norms in Morocco. They reflect the broader changes in the sexual order in Morocco. To consider this, I will, after a brief discussion of the literature on the subject, present ethnographical evidence highlighting aspects of amusement as experienced while in school and after.

In terms of methodology, my discussion of the *khrīj* activity is based on data gathered through a seventeen-month ethnography (2008–2009) followed by five year-long ongoing observations and interviews with the young women I lived with in Tangier. I observed and analysed the trajectories of young single women aged eighteen to thirty, coming from the lower classes and born and/or raised in urban settings (mainly Tangier). All the information gathered during the immersion and afterwards allowed me to develop a longitudinal analysis of their trajectories that could assess not only the activity of 'the going out' at a specific time but also the construction of subjectivities at stake.

Framing the phenomenon of prostitution, silencing the multidimensional aspect of 'the going out'

In Morocco, prostitution has long been presented (and still is today, to a lesser extent) in the media discourses as a growing phenomenon, a 'plague' that has turned Morocco into a destination for sex tourism.[5] In the last three decades, the theme has informed the headlines of an emergent press increasingly interested in crime news.[6] It has also been at the centre of several scandals that generated polemics and divided society into two camps: a moralist camp and a compassionate camp, informed by a comprehensive approach towards sex work.[7] The (still difficult) destigmatization of prostitutes is being supported by the humanistic agenda set in a society where discourse about the 'poor' has become gradually codified and politicized by officials (the king, MPs, governmental agencies, non-governmental organizations, etc.). Social justice has been built up in principle and is seen as the translation of good governance[8] – in rhetoric at least – since the alternance era of 1998, and mainly through the creation of the National Initiative for Human Development Support Project (INDH).

Feminist social scientists in Morocco contributed to encouraging a compassionate vision towards different women's issues.[9] They helped to oppose moralistic views on social phenomena concerning stigmatized women and to include ideas of vulnerability and precariousness in the grid analysis. As far as prostitution is concerned, rare studies[10] were able to frame prostitution as a valuable sociological subject[11] by defining it as a social rather than a moral problem. Their descriptions and analysis consisted mainly in putting emphasis on the social and economic difficulties that pushed women to engage in this activity. They breached the hegemonic definition of prostitution concerned more with the illegitimacy and immorality of women. The breach is fragile, however, and while succeeding in framing women as victims of social conditions, they failed in giving voice to them by describing the complexity of the *khrīj* configuration. Part of the experience is passed over and the voices of the actresses are silenced. For instance, self-accomplishment, formation of subjectivities or the construction of positive values within 'the going out' have been constantly ignored by these studies.

This complexity has nevertheless been pointed out by a number of new studies over the last two decades. Approaching transactional sex through a multidimensional lens, these new studies give importance to the multiple meanings of the exchanges at play and the uses of money. The overlapping of amusement and self-desire within practices of prostitution has been observed widely, especially in the Global South, where sexual transactions are far from being clearly defined as mere sexual services.[12] For instance, in Mozambique, the word *curtidoras*,[13] in Cuba, the words *jinetaras* and *el hi-life*,[14] or in Senegal, the word *aventurières*[15] refer to women who derive personal benefits from making money with the men they meet at night, to support themselves and their families. Lately, the same can be seen in Western countries such as France: within minority groups, specific terms such as the stigmatizing *beurette à chicha*[16] are used to qualify that kind of heterosexual intimacy. These studies, while offering in-depth analyses that bring out the entertainment aspect of the sex transactional practices especially, do not shed light on the formation of the young women's sexuality or the formation of their desire as adolescents, which some of them still are, neither do they frame their practices as youthful practices.

Young, transgressive and at school

During my stay in the shared flats, my room-mates often talked about their experiences of 'fun' when they were at school. The regular visits of some of their friends, who were still pursuing a chaotic schooling, were a good reason to talk about the recent past when they experienced 'craziness', or *tkeḥkiḥ*,[17] to use their own expression, together. Experiences of 'craziness' took place while they were at school. Dating back only two or three years for some of my room-mates, these experiences allowed them to have a good time despite being poor. By a good time, they meant being able to afford some leisure with their male and female peers who belonged to the friendly collectives they were growing up with:

> You go out to have fun, you have good time. You don't have the feeling of being belittled. You're like anyone. I used to see all these girls going out and everything so me too I wanted to go out, see these nightclubs, date boys and go with them in fancy cars. (Salīma, 2013)

These collectives were constituted within and outside schools. The importance of schooling has to be understood not only from an institutional point of view, where school is seen only as an educational space, but from an interactional point of view, where school is seen as a space of social relations between peers. This difference can be grasped if we look not at the role of school but at the work of socialization that happens within the institution (classrooms, playgrounds) but also around it (peer-group meeting spaces outside of schools):

> I was not interested in school at all. For example, I used to have class from 2 to 4 pm but I would skip it. Girls and boys would come to you and start telling you: 'Skip class. Come on, we'll meet with this boy, I know him, he's got cigarettes.' We would go and have nice walks with boys around the city. I used to do that: have fun and enjoy myself. The teachers didn't give a shit if I was there or not. It was better for them if I was missing, they would not see me and bear me. I was used to doing nothing in class except laughing. (Salīma, 2013)

Truancy is an opportunity to date young men who, according to the gift ideology between the sexes they are embodying, will also give them presents and money. Recalling her time at school, one of my room-mates told me:

> At that time [adolescence], I thought that was the life. You go with boys and you start to get dizzy. You're having fun, and then the boy tries to kiss you, he wants to touch your breasts. He offers you 100 or 200 dirhams telling you 'hey this is for you' or he offers you restaurants. I thought that was the way of living. I liked it very much because everyone would tell me I was beautiful, and I appealed to everybody. (Salīma, 2013)

It is also an occasion to make different use of the city and time. The young women linger in cafes or in poolrooms (*golfazurs*), smoke, date boys and experience intimacy at an early stage. For them, the small tourist city of Aṣīlā, on this side of the Gibraltar Strait, constitutes a space assimilated into Europe that builds their imaginary more than their immediate desire for migration. In this space within easy reach, they can smoke freely without ever feeling the weight of a transgression that would, ordinarily, put them in the category of 'bad girls':[18]

> Amaya: We were in Aṣīlā and we thought we were at the end of the world. We were young. As soon as we arrived in Aṣīlā, we used to walk and smoke in the street like we were in Europe.
>
> Salīma: It was as if we had taken the boat and we had left this country. (Amaya [eighteen years old in 2009, still in high school] and Salīma, 2009)

This sentiment of worthiness is made possible because they associate themselves at that moment to school, an institutional sphere that gives social meaning. In other words, their feeling of being transgressive was attenuated because they felt they were having these experiences as pupils. The pupil category gave them the possibility of claiming the youthfulness of their experiences of 'craziness' and fun. Being a pupil, being at school, is being a young person. This explains the pride they felt about being associated with school when telling their stories. Through this pride and sense of dignity, I could read the specificity of being a pupil and the importance of belonging to the school institution *while* having these noncomformist ('crazy') experiences. Because they were pupils, they were able to have these 'transgressive' experiences *and* to frame them as experiences of fun rather than experiences of *ḥarām*. In other words, recalling the school experiences was a way to explain how they drifted from school but, most importantly, to valorize and legitimize practices otherwise easily reduced to the 'bad' (*ma mzyansh*) and the 'ugly' (*khayb*). Being pupils meant falling within a category acknowledging the fact that at a certain moment some persons could be seen as young or adolescent, and their practices – transgressive or not – could be considered as emanating from the specific habitus and dispositions that constitute young selves.[19] One of the young women told me how her father – who was a school director in a small village near Tangier – would not beat her for skipping school and the *khrīj* but would rather try to open a dialogue showing her that he understood that she was going through 'adolescence age' (*hadhā huwa sinn al-murāhaqa*).

Increased schooling for girls in working-class and urban settings, associated with a decline in marriage, lead to a reorganization of juvenile time: alongside the time slots devoted to school also came time for fun in the company of classmates not only of the same sex but also of the opposite sex. The young women I studied are what we call millennials. They were all born at the end of the 1980s, after the 1983–1984 reforms that precipitated the deterioration of the public school without resolving the problem of mass education. Unlike what has been said about the sociological background of women who go out in Morocco, the young women of my research are, with one exception, part of the almost 90 per cent of girls who went to secondary school in the administrative region of Tangier at that time.[20] They almost all went to school even when living in a rural area. The only kind of school they knew produced disaffected and 'useless' people.[21] Being a dropout or still putting a great deal of effort into trying to obtain the baccalaureat, the young women would often say that 'education is not profitable'.[22] But they spent most of their time and adolescence in school, which constituted the main context of their personal development.

The transgressions of dominant norms were fitting within the youthfulness socially constructed by schooling and socially accepted as far as young persons, going to school, are concerned. And they were not marginal or uncommon, since they were a product of the mass-schooling realm and were practised by a large proportion of the young population attending school. In discourses about their time at school, young women kept coming back to being part of a larger group. This affiliation made sense of the values and norms they identified with.

The pupil category appeared crucial in the formation of their youthful identity. This formation occurred through specific desires related to leisure consumption and the discovery of intimacy and sexuality. But it was also informed by the distance the pupil category allowed them to take from the universes of work and marriage. Being a pupil allowed them to blossom as a subject entirely determined by deprivation and the 'natural' path to adulthood through marriage that has, reductively, long described youth trajectories in Muslim countries.

Young women used to cherish school, although they all were in a position of failure. They cherished it because it permitted them to show that they were affiliated to something; that they were affiliated to an institution and not affiliated to nothing. It was better to pretend to be a student than to be identified as a 'single woman staying at home and doing nothing'. It is less the school's producing honourable positions that matters and more that it gives them affiliation to a universe that allows them to distance themselves from the ways illiterate young women become adults. The fun they could have while being students also distanced them from social and mental spheres of deprivation. Young women were in search of an idleness that did not remind them of their economic conditions – that is why they constantly resisted being confined in the home doing nothing.

Thus, in order not to break with the school universe, when they reached fourteen or fifteen years old some young women went to work in restaurants or in domestic jobs to enable them to pay for their education. Although their experiences at school were unfortunate, they consented to maintain their status of pupil, which was more comfortable than the indeterminacy of a social status that implies a definitive exit from school, early employment in a non-skilled sector of the labour market and long-term celibacy. The importance of an affiliation to school also appeared through the determination of some young women to stay at school although their results were poor. The desire to pursue an education, although chaotic, was also strong in young women who tried to better their skills when reaching their early and mid-twenties. The majority of those dreaming of resuming school did so through professional avenues available to them, while others dropped out.

The pursuit of youthfulness: Sharing flats

The exploration of the significance of schools and the everyday life at schools gives a better understanding of the subjectivities but also affectivities at work in the lives of these underclass young women. Although some of my room-mates were no longer at school, they were still attached to the positive narratives of fun and amusement and, while going out and dating to make ends meet, they struggled to pursue the cultural meaning they were giving to their empowering way of life. Living in shared flats contributed to this empowerment as well as to the continuity between emotions felt during the time of their 'craziness' experiences and those still felt while engaging more and more in the prostitution aspect of 'the going out'.

In addition to entertainment spaces (discotheques, bars, cafes, etc.) frequented by the young women I met, the flats that I shared with them constituted the main site of my observations. The flats were the context of their stories about schools; they were the receptacle of their aspirations to reconnect with a universe that allowed them to feel free. Through shared flats and the persistence of discourses on school as a 'lost heaven', we understand better that their personal investment in schooling explains their need to distance themselves from the urgency of social integration and to appear respectable, while cultivating an art of leisure at the heart of the *khrīj*.

But this residential mode was also what prolonged their experiences of 'the going out', of the professionalization of prostitution, of sexuality and heterosexuality, and of femininity. The private spheres of the young women appeared to be a good site of observation to make sense of an activity associated with the public space.

The young woman Badīʿa quoted above told me that she 'would go out just when [she] need[s] some money [...] [she] ha[s] to pay the rent'. She added: 'I don't have to send money to my family.' She clarified this point to make sure that I understand from which 'place' she was speaking. Insisting on having rent to pay and not having a family to sustain, she clarified to me that her main objective in 'the going out' is to sustain herself and her way of life. Part of this way of life consisted in living away from her family in shared flats.

The experience of sharing a flat with other young women, often friends, is a crucial step, which usually had happened early in the lives of the women in this study. Despite being a widespread youth residential phenomenon in urban Morocco, however, shared flats are little taken into account. They are ignored and even unimaginable in statistics and studies that think of housing only within the framework of the family institution. Yet, as a practice of living, shared flats reflect juvenile behaviour and values in today's urban society.[23] The shared flats' residential mode, which used to apply mainly to single men, is nowadays increasingly used by young women: single women who take charge of themselves away from the family home, where unmarried girls traditionally live. This residential mode is adopted by those whose family homes are far away as well as those with their family situated in the same city, sometimes just a few minutes walk in nearby neighbourhoods. Shared flats therefore contradict many stereotypes of Moroccan women, and also Arab and Muslim women in general. Moreover, they contradict a commonplace in Morocco that depicts prostitutes as foreigners in the city who came there to perform sexual transactions. This idea persists especially because, in a context of moralization of 'untied' women, it is supposed that one must be far from their family to have the opportunity to be immoral. Immorality and distance are no longer enough to explain transgressive practices.

Shared flats are the ideal place to measure the emergence of a female identity structured around a celibacy, deliberate or not. A celibacy hitherto the prerogative of men. Moreover, being a matter of a social network constituted outside of the families' circles, it highlights two points: the centrality of female friendships and the reworking of family ties that informs the formation of subjectivities. In other words, shared flats are an excellent site for observing changes in norms and transformations of the intimate order in Morocco.

Young women rarely rent apartments alone, instead, they rent a single room within a flat with several other persons or a 'mattress' in a room shared with other persons, which is cheaper. They share flats and rooms at the same time. The material situation contributes de facto to the formation of a female collective. Through this collective we are able not only to see how friendship is constituted and valued but also to approach it as a space where practices and discourses are scrutinized and legitimized or delegitimized. They thus create a deeply hierarchized social space, where the dominant gaze and moral values are both mobilized to judge the value of friends and room-mates or neutralized to disarm the power of the stigma. In this light, the formation of subjectivities is a relational process that is linked to the collective. I was part of it as well, and the dominant gaze I introduced helped me to shed light on this formation from a relational point of view.

While shared flats are the best way to observe the constitution of the subject of single woman and celibacy, they are also useful for understanding the relationship young women have with their families. The female residential circulation also concerns the comings and goings between living with the family and living with room-mates in shared flats. Some events, usually the lack of money to continue paying rent or the decision to stop 'the going out', mean that young women intermittently return to their family homes. This way of alternating strongly affects interpersonal relationships within the families and reconfigures the positions held by siblings. It also shows that leaving home is rarely a sudden break with the family: it is, rather, a progressive process of remoteness that allows the construction of an autonomous subject. Becoming a single person (*célibataire*) is the result of a construction developed both inside and outside the family.

Lack of money or dramatic biographical events regularly result in rental interruptions, changes or evictions by the owners for non-payment. These developments promote residential instability and increase the urban circulation of women as much as they affect their mental geography of the city, where we see how they describe and prioritize neighbourhoods according to whether or not enforcement of moral values by neighbours prevents them from or allows them to move freely without being harassed.

Performance of appearances

If the young women were living in shared flats because of their activities, these flats helped them build specific female subjectivities. This construction came at a price: the violent confrontation with hegemonic femininity that pushes them to seek to perform respectable identities through the way they look but also through their attempt to embody modern dominant ideals of middle-class femininity. Performance of respectability signified for them not only showing off their ability to consume but also their willingness to be reckoned as valuable subjects, as valuable 'citizens'. Fun and amusement participate in the valorization of individuals. This is at least what one of the young women suggested when she described how she was seen: 'Everyone is nice to you. I was like a girl in need of nothing, a *rich girl, free*. I felt I was someone' (Salīma, 2013; Salīma's emphasis).

Three of the young women I lived with told me a story, worthy of a situation comedy, in which we can observe this performance of appearances, which is not always successful, but also grasp the dramatic articulation between personal values and material condition:

> Once with Salīma, at the time of high school, we met some guys in the city centre of Tangier. We met them, they were friendly and they invited us. We did not have money and we did not want to appear as those who 'don't have nothing'. So, we stole a chicken from Salīma's parents and we went to the market to sell it. What a shame! We had the chicken in a bag. I remember well, we were going up the boulevard when we saw handsome men in a 4x4 car that were hitting on us. We started to show off. That day we believed that we were irresistible. Since we had to meet those guys, we got all dressed up. We straightened our hair, we wore the latest fashionable *jellabas*. So, we passed in front of these guys who were staring at us. We wiggled our hips, we pretended to snub them meaning: 'we are worth more than you'. In fact, we were dying to get into their car, we had forgotten the other guys that were waiting for us for the night. But what happened at that moment: the chicken tried to get out of the bag, it started to beat its wings in all directions. What a shame! The guys sped up their car and left quickly, they were ashamed for us. I bet that today they must still talk about 'the yokels [*jebliyyāt*][24] who pathetically showed off'. (Salīma and Amaya, 2009)

We see how they develop fictions of social and cultural mobility. They also learn that their sexuality has a value and that they could positively trade it since they correspond to modern dominant ideals of femininity (independence, autonomy, appropriately fashionable and appropriately desirable). They learn to generate value by transposing onto their sexual body the marks of middle-class respectability. Middle-class respectability's marks are learnt through the social meanings of having an education and, most importantly, of having a social status that postpones an uncertain future. Through these marks they mirror a legitimate existence. For the young women I worked with, looking like a middle-class young woman is to have beautiful clothes, appear to have a job and be mobile. One young woman used to tell me when she was back from the nightclubs in the early morning that again that morning she had appeared in the street as one of those white-collar women employees who go to work in banks or in public institutions. She could appear this way because she always changed her clothes before coming back home. Instead of walking around in her party clothes and offering the sad and dangerous spectacle of a 'walk of shame', she used to take in her bag clean and respectable clothes that resembled what an employee would wear, to change into them.

As for mobility, the possibility of renting cars and having fun going to the beach or to other cities was a sign of respectability, something that could mean you could meet the right one at a crossroad:

> I stopped at a pedestrian crossing and could not restart. The car stalled. I see one arriving, he was crossing. He looked at me and smiled. I thought he was

> laughing at me. He looked at me insistently and I said to myself: why is he looking this way? That day I was stunning, I had sunglasses, I was driving the car. He approached me and he asked me for my phone number. I did not want to give it to him. I left. But, the guy followed me with his car. Wherever I went, he followed me. I was with girlfriends in the car. We laughed. He did not let go. Until I stop. When he came out, he came to talk to me, I made him run but he insisted so much that I gave him the number. (Laṭīfa, 2008)

She did indeed end up dating him for several years after this encounter, until they were both found dead due to a domestic gas accident. However, the possibilities young women struggle to create for themselves, such as this kind of intimate encounter, are poorly understood by the local press in term of hustling because they involve recognizably working-class young women. For example, this is what a moral entrepreneur of a local newspaper wrote about women renting cars:

> Whores have found new techniques to solicit their clients. They rent cars on Fridays and Saturdays and then hang around high-standing hotels where prey is in excess.[25]

Through the means of 'the going out', they construct specific selves pursuing the formation of their subjectivities that started when they were at school. Schooling nurtured these imagined possibilities of becoming someone (a 'person') by letting the fun aspect related to youth and adolescence be part of the socialization process a large majority of young Moroccans go through at school. However, the diffusion of a dominant leisure culture where social, cultural and economic resources are displayed implies at the same time relegation, discrimination and classification,[26] rendered here through their feelings of humiliation.

Conclusion: A new intimate order?

Prostitution remains an issue of socio-economic conditions. It is related to labour and female labour in many ways. This link does not, however, prevent an approach from another dimension. The young women's narratives give insight into the way they engaged in it and invite us to adopt a biographical approach to the activity of prostitution. Sticking as close as possible to the different elements of their stories brings a more complex overview of it. For the majority of the women I interviewed and lived with, if 'the going out' meant gaining some money through intimate and sexual services, it was also seen as a means to pursue youthful desires. Beyond the mere commercial transaction, accounts on 'the going out' practices are first and foremost about youth, friendship and the discovery of intimacy and sexuality at adolescence. Being part of the nightlife enabled them to discover their self-worth. Young women felt they were constructing valuable and respectable subjectivities mirrored in the new leisure economies. Aimed at more privileged social groups, leisure avenues that have increasingly come to define the urban economies of major Moroccan cities (Tangier, Marrakech, Casablanca) over the two last decades are also shaping new ways of expressing youthfulness. Fun and entertainment have become criteria to assess and decide who is acceptable to be seen as a young person, as someone allowed to live their youthfulness.

Notes

This chapter has received funding from the European Union's Horizon 2020 research and innovation programme under the Marie Skłodowska-Curie grant agreement No. 753562.

1 Lilian Mathieu, *La condition prostituée* (Paris: Textuel, 2007).

2 Ibid.; Mériam Cheikh, *Les filles qui sortent : Jeunesse, sexualité et prostitution au Maroc* (Brussels: Éditions de l'Université de Bruxelles, 2020).

3 Ibid.

4 Although it is not the objective of this chapter, it is worth noting that the positive aspect of these youth values tends to change according to the trajectories within 'the going out' that can lead to social careers within sex work. Being professionally involved in sex work and experiencing dramatic economic conditions can produce a reformulation of the values in negative terms.

5 See, for example, Majdouline El Atouabi, 'Marrakech, Agadir, Tanger, Essaouira … Des destinations préférées pour le tourisme du vice et de la dépravation. Le Maroc est-il devenu un paradis sexuel?' (*Maroc Hebdo*, 23 March 2006). Available online: https://www.maghress.com/fr/marochebdo/69109 (accessed 20 October 2018); Mohamed Semlali, 'Le Maroc sur la voie thaïlandaise?' (*L'Observateur du Maroc*, 27 May 2009). Available online: https://www.maghress.com/fr/lobservateur/1842 (accessed 20 October 2018); H. M., 'Le Maroc, destination de tourisme sexuel? Ce qu'on en dit sur les "forums spécialisés"' (*Médias24*, 6 June 2014). Available online: https://www.medias24.com/SOCIETE/12179-Le-Maroc-destination-de-tourisme-sexuel-Ce-qu-on-en-dit-sur-les-forums-specialises.html (accessed 20 October 2018).

6 Jonathan Smolin, *Moroccan Noir: Police, Crime, and Politics in Popular Culture* (Bloomington, IN: Indiana University Press, 2013).

7 The last scandal was about the movie *Much Loved* by Nabil Ayouch, portraying the life of three young women engaged in sex work: Claire Diao, 'Nabil Ayouch dévoile ses prostituées sur la Croisette et fait scandale au Maroc' (*Le Monde*, 23 May 2015). Available online: http://www.lemonde.fr/afrique/article/2015/05/23/nabil-ayouch-devoile-ses-prostituees-sur-la-croisette-et-fait-scandale-au-maroc_4639386_3212.html (accessed 28 December 2017). See Mériam Cheikh and Lidia Peralta Garcia, 'Moralistic versus Compassionate Portrayal of Prostitution in Moroccan Cinema: Casablanca by Night *versus* Much Loved as a Case Study', *Mediterranean Journal of Communication*, 10 (2) (2019): 179–92.

8 Béatrice Hibou and Irène Bono, *Le Gouvernement du Social au Maroc* (Paris: Karthala, 2016).

9 This feminist approach informed the work of Moroccan sociologists and especially women who started gathering in research groups particularly around the figure of Fatima Mernissi and the collection of books concentrating on women's issues in Morocco she launched in the 1980s. On this dimension of Fatima Mernissi's work, see Raja Rhouni, *Secular and Islamic Feminist Critiques in the Work of Fatima Mernissi* (Leiden: Brill, 2010).

10 Fatima Rafik, 'La Prostitution féminine à Essaouira (Maroc)', Phd dissertation, Th. 3e cycle, Anthropologie sociale et culturelle, Paris 5, 1980; Touria Hadraoui, 'Dhāhirat al-Baghā' fī al-Dār al-Bayḍā'', in Mohamed Al Ahyane (ed.), *Portraits de femmes*, 51–71 (Casablanca: Le Fennec, 1987); Fatima Zryouil, *al-Baghā', aw, al-Jasad al-Mustabāḥ* (Casablanca: Ifrīqiyā al-Sharq, 2001); Sara Carmona Benito, *La prostitution dans les rues de Casablanca* (Casablanca: Les Editions Toubkal, 2008).

11 The legitimacy of such sociological study is still very fragile, as I experienced while doing my research. My research study was mocked, provoked disgust and anger, or contributed to oversexualizing my person.

12 For a bibliographical analysis of the huge amount of studies available, see Ronald Weitzer, 'Sociology of Sex Work', *Annual Review of Sociology*, 35 (2009): 213–34.

13 Christian Groes-Green, '"To Put Men in a Bottle": Eroticism, Kinship, Female Power, and Transactional Sex in Maputo, Mozambique', *American Ethnologist*, 40 (1) (2013): 102–17.

14 Coco Fusco, 'Hustling for Dollars. Jineterismo in Cuba', in Kamala Kempadoo and Jo Doezema (eds), *Global Sex Workers: Rights, Resistance, and Redefinition*, 151–66 (New York: Routledge, 1998).

15 Thomas Fouquet, 'Les aventurières de la nuit dakaroise : Esquisse d'un art de la citadinité subalterne', in Mamadou Diouf and Rosalind Fredericks (eds), *Les arts de la citoyenneté au Sénégal: Espaces contestés et civilités urbaines*, 131–57 (Paris: Karthala, 2013).

16 My own observation. *Beurette* is the feminine of *Beur*, both stigmatizing words used to refer to French with North African descent. And *Beurette à chicha* refers to women frequenting cafes where it is possible to smoke the hookah (*shisha*) and meet their boyfriends or other men who are taking care of them.

17 In Tangier's Moroccan language the word means 'very loud laughs', and the young women were using it as a noun to describe joyful experiences related to adolescence.

18 Nadia Yaqub and Rula Quawas, *Bad Girls of the Arab World* (Austin, TX: University of Texas Press, 2017).

19 Mounia Bennani-Chraïbi and Imane Farag (eds), *Jeunesses des sociétés arabes: Par-delà les promesses et les menaces* (Montreuil: Aux lieux d'être, 2007); Asef Bayat and Linda Herrera, *Being Young and Muslim: New Cultural Politics in the Global South and North* (New York: Oxford University Press, 2010).

20 Ministère de l'Éducation Nationale, *Recueil statistique de l'éducation 2009–2010*. Available online: https://www.men.gov.ma/Ar/Documents/02-Reuil2009-10Final.pdf (accessed 26 June 2020).

21 The sentiment of uselessness conveyed by the women echoes the two concepts ('disaffiliation' and 'supernumerary') developed by the critical sociologist Robert Castel on social exclusion: Robert Castel, *La montée des incertitudes: Travail, protections, statut de l'individu* (Paris: Seuil, 2009).

22 For a similar observation on the emergent defiance towards education in Morocco, see Sophie Cerbelle, 'Enfants hors l'école: Faible remédiation et faible demande. Le cas du Maroc', *Cahiers de la recherche sur l'éducation et les savoirs*, 11 (2012): 149–67; Etienne Gérard and Bernard Schlemmer, 'Le rapport à l'école dans les milieux populaires de Fès (Maroc)', in Marc Pilon, Jean-Yves Martin and Alain Carry (eds), *Le droit à l'éducation, quelle universalité?*, 183–206 (Paris: Archives contemporaines, 2010).

23 Françoise Navez-Bouchanine, *Habiter la ville marocaine* (Paris: l'Harmattan, 1997).

24 *Jebliyyāt* refers to *Jebala* people from the north-west mountains of Morocco. The term has a stigmatized sense when used by people considering themselves more 'civilized'.
25 *La Dépêche de Tanger*, 4 October 2003.
26 Mériam Cheikh, 'De l'ordre moral à l'ordre social: L'application des lois pénalisant la sexualité prémaritale selon des lignes de classe' (From the Moral to the Social Order: The Application of Laws Penalizing Premarital Sexuality Along Class Lines), *L'Année du Maghreb*, 17 (2017): 49–67.

References

Bayat, Asef and Linda Herrera (2010), *Being Young and Muslim: New Cultural Politics in the Global South and North*, New York: Oxford University Press.

Bennani-Chraïbi, Mounia and Imane Farag (2007), *Jeunesses des sociétés arabes: Par-delà les promesses et les menaces*, Montreuil: Aux lieux d'être.

Boris, Eileen and Rhacel Parrenas (2010), *Intimate Labors: Cultures, Technologies, and the Politics of Care*, Stanford, CA: Stanford University Press.

Carmona Benito, Sara (2008), *La prostitution dans les rues de Casablanca*, Casablanca: Les Editions Toubkal.

Castel, Robert (2009), *La montée des incertitudes: Travail, protections, statut de l'individu*, Paris: Seuil.

Cerbelle, Sophie (2012), 'Enfants hors l'école: Faible remédiation et faible demande; Le cas du Maroc', *Cahiers de la recherche sur l'éducation et les savoirs*, 11: 149–67.

Cheikh, Mériam (2017), 'De l'ordre moral à l'ordre social: L'application des lois pénalisant la sexualité prémaritale selon des lignes de classe' (From the Moral to the Social Order: The Application of Laws Penalizing Premarital Sexuality Along Class Lines), *L'Année du Maghreb*, 17: 49–67.

Cheikh, Mériam (2020), *Les filles qui sortent: Jeunesse, sexualité et prostitution au Maroc*, Brussels: Éditions de l'Université de Bruxelles.

Cheikh, Mériam and Lidia Peralta Garcia (2019), 'Moralistic versus Compassionate Portrayal of Prostitution in Moroccan Cinema: Casablanca by Night *versus* Much Loved as a Case Study', *Mediterranean Journal of Communication*, 10 (2): 179–92.

Diao, Claire (2015), 'Nabil Ayouch dévoile ses prostituées sur la Croisette et fait scandale au Maroc', *Le Monde*, 23 May. Available online: http://www.lemonde.fr/afrique/article/2015/05/23/nabil-ayouch-devoile-ses-prostituees-sur-la-croisette-et-fait-scandale-au-maroc_4639386_3212.html (accessed 28 December 2017).

El Atouabi, Majdouline (2006), 'Marrakech, Agadir, Tanger, Essaouira … Des destinations préférées pour le tourisme du vice et de la dépravation: Le Maroc est-il devenu un paradis sexuel?', *Maroc Hebdo*, 23 March. Available online: https://www.maghress.com/fr/marochebdo/69109 (accessed 20 October 2018).

Fouquet, Thomas (2013), 'Les aventurières de la nuit dakaroise: Esquisse d'un art de la citadinité subalterne', in Mamadou Diouf and Rosalind Fredericks (eds), *Les arts de la citoyenneté au Sénégal: Espaces contestés et civilités urbaines*, 131–57, Paris: Karthala.

Fusco, Coco (1998), 'Hustling for Dollars: Jineterismo in Cuba', in Kamala Kempadoo and Jo Doezema (eds), *Global Sex Workers: Rights, Resistance, and Redefinition*, 151–66, New York: Routledge.

Gérard, Etienne and Bernard Schlemmer (2010), 'Le rapport à l'école dans les milieux populaires de Fès (Maroc)', in Marc Pilon, Jean-Yves Martin and Alain Carry (eds), *Le droit à l'éducation, quelle universalité?*, 183–206, Paris: Archives contemporaines.

Groes-Green, Christian (2013), '"To Put Men in a Bottle": Eroticism, Kinship, Female Power, and Transactional Sex in Maputo, Mozambique', *American Ethnologist*, 40 (1): 102–17.
Hadraoui, Touria (1987), 'Dhāhirat al-Baghā' fī al-Dār al-Bayḍā'', in Mohamed Al Ahyane (ed.), *Portraits de femmes*, 51–71, Casablanca: Le Fennec.
Hibou, Beatrice and Irène Bono (2016), *Le Gouvernement du Social au Maroc*, Paris: Karthala.
H. M. (2014), 'Le Maroc, destination de tourisme sexuel? Ce qu'on en dit sur les "forums spécialisés"', *Médias24*, 6 June. Available online: https://www.medias24.com/SOCIETE/12179-Le-Maroc-destination-de-tourisme-sexuel-Ce-qu-on-en-dit-sur-les-forums-specialises.html (accessed 20 October 2018).
Kempadoo, Kamala (2004), *Sexing the Caribbean*, New York: Routledge.
Mathieu, Lilian (2007), *La condition prostituée*, Paris: Textuel.
Ministère de l'Éducation Nationale (n.d.), *Recueil statistique de l'éducation 2009–2010*. Available online: https://www.men.gov.ma/Ar/Documents/02-Reuil2009-10Final.pdf (accessed 26 June 2020).
Navez-Bouchanine, Françoise (1997), *Habiter la ville marocaine*, Paris: l'Harmattan.
Rafik, Fatima (1980), 'La Prostitution féminine à Essaouira (Maroc)', Phd dissertation, Th. 3e cycle, Anthropologie sociale et culturelle, Paris 5.
Rhouni, Raja (2010), *Secular and Islamic Feminist Critiques in the Work of Fatima Mernissi*, Leiden: Brill.
Semlali, Mohamed (2009), 'Le Maroc sur la voie thaïlandaise?', *L'Observateur du Maroc*, 27 May. Available online: https://www.maghress.com/fr/lobservateur/1842 (accessed 20 October 2018).
Smolin, Jonathan (2013), *Moroccan Noir: Police, Crime, and Politics in Popular Culture*, Bloomington, IN: Indiana University Press.
Weitzer, Ronald (2009), 'Sociology of Sex Work', *Annual Review of Sociology*, 35: 213–34.
Yaqub, Nadia and Rula Quawas (2017), *Bad Girls of the Arab World*, Austin, TX: University of Texas Press.
Zryouil, Fatima (2001), *al-Baghā', aw, al-Jasad al-Mustabāḥ*, Casablanca: Ifrīqiyā al-Sharq.

Chapter 10

THE STRAIGHT STORY: CHALLENGING HETERONORMATIVITY IN BEIRUT

Erica Li Lundqvist

As we passed by the streets of Ādam's hometown with the coffin, I heard a voice calling out for prayer from a distant speaker. We had come a long way from Beirut to attend this funeral. It was my first Muslim funeral, it was in the middle of my fieldwork period[1] and unfortunately it was one of my research subjects and close friends that we were about to bury.[2] We had all been given a small Qur'an with a portrait (similar to a bookmark) of the deceased inside, as of a martyr. I had just seen a glimpse of the corpse of Ādam before the ritual cleansing of his body.[3] I did not know what was going to happen at that point. However, I, along with many other relatives and friends, was pushed into a small room where we could see Ādam lying in his decay, just before members of the family wrapped him in a white cloth and put him on a bier and carried him to the graveyard.

Women were not allowed near the grave during the burial, so I stood among the other women watching the ceremony from a distance. After the funeral, family and friends gathered for dinner and I joined my friends again in a big tent the family had put up in the middle of the village. Following the dinner, my friends and I were separated again, and I was directed to a small room in a family member's house. The mother, sisters, cousins and other women sat on the floor in the small room and reminisced over the deceased. Among the women was a veiled young girl that I had seen at the burial earlier. She presented herself to me as Ādam's promised wife. This was the first time I heard about Ādam's fiancée and I was wondering – while sipping my tea on the floor in the small room – how much she knew about her dead fiancé's life in Beirut, his sexuality or the fact that many of his male friends from Beirut attending the funeral were gay. And if the family knew about his sexuality, did they use silence as an effective 'don't ask don't tell' strategy?

Silence, and in particular silencing, has throughout history been a successful strategy and controlling mechanism for societies to keep certain behaviours at bay and dissident people in the margin. There are many examples of this silent strategy. Regarding homosexuality, Kecia Ali refers to it as 'the open secret', where the unwillingness to condemn cases of same-sex activity in the past, 'the preference to let them pass by, if not unnoticed then unnamed and therefore unpunished', works as a strategy to avoid dealing with the problem in speech and therefore in public.[4]

If you do not talk about it, it does not exist. Stephen Murray named it 'the will not to know', as something that people are aware of but are unwilling to acknowledge in public.[5] For Michel Foucault, silence was imbedded in the concept of *scientia sexualis* as a way of controlling sexuality, and as part of the knowledge/power's dynamic. Silence is a tool to signify that power is constituted through accepted forms of knowledge, scientific understanding and 'truth'.[6]

The Foucauldian view on dissidence is also applicable to the Lebanese situation. Foucault writes about deviants as revolutionaries, as they are, simultaneously, socially marginal yet discursively central. Ideas of deviance and the deviant have always had a central place in society, paradoxical as it may sound, and there have been different strategies on how to deal with and control deviance.[7]

In this chapter, I will discuss the strategy of silence, not only as a mechanism for controlling what is seen as diverting from the norm but also as a useful tactic for some personal liberation. Instead of discussing silence as only oppressive or as a consequence of fear, shame and guilt, or as an approval of the heteronormative way of life, I will focus on silence as a navigating tool and a useful tactic among young men in Lebanon who self-identified as Muslim and gay.

Heteronormativity is related to a hegemonic heterosexuality that sets norms for actions and identification. The term is also used to highlight how different behaviours, sexualities and identifications are punished and marginalized in various ways. In the heterosexual matrix, the sexual desire derives from gender, which in turn derives from the biological sex.[8] As the introductory story suggests, secrecy and silence are part of everyday tactics, which, given the marginal position in society, gave agency to and empowered the men of this study.

I had eight main research subjects. They were connected in many ways, as friends, lovers, colleagues or acquaintances, and the study as a whole is therefore not only representative of the voices of a few young men, it also describes a network of relationships in Beirut's gay community. Six of the eight were Sunni Muslims, one was Shi'ite and one was Druze. I met the young men in their homes, with their families, at their places of work, at parties, funerals, birthdays and other festivities. They were all in their twenties or early thirties and were at the time living in Beirut, although some came from and had been raised in different parts of Lebanon. The socio-economic status of the young men varied. Some of them had left their home villages to move to Beirut, others lived with their parents in Beirut or had their parents close by. While most of them had a university degree and were working within their respective field, others were still studying and were about to get a bachelor's degree or were in the process of finding a job. One was a high school dropout with several jobs. Their different religious backgrounds did not necessarily indicate that they had a more or less difficult time dealing with the heteronormative societal demands than for some having been raised with a different religious background. However, religion had, and still has, a great impact on how they viewed themselves and the world around them.

The formation of queer identities in Lebanon is closely linked to global processes of circulation and translation of gender models and ideas.[9] This chapter positions the importance of gender and sexual identities at the centre of an often over-simplified political understanding of the very notion of identity. As Merabet has noted, also in Lebanon, that notion has traditionally been defined on the basis of sectarian and religious affiliation.[10] Marginalized sexual positions correlate not only with gender and sexual differences, but also with categories such as ethnicity, religion, class and age, and point towards identities in transition. These intersectionalities are not to be seen from a purely abstract structural level but rather as 'lived' phenomena, and are important to examine in order to highlight both the inequalities between and the privileges of different intersections.[11]

From the stories told and the narratives I gathered through interviews and observations in Beirut, it seems to me that gay liberation is far from a unified struggle in Lebanon. None of the individuals that are part of this study felt an immediate need to walk the streets of Beirut waving a rainbow flag or intended to openly reconcile a religious identity with being gay. The heteronormative society does not stigmatize the young men as deviant, as they do not formally and publicly violate social norms. In the heteronormative Lebanese society, however, there is much talk about the homosexual deviant, and everyone knows that being exposed as homosexual or living as a pure deviant homosexual is severely stigmatizing. There is a variety of ways in which gay men in Lebanon are responding to their deviant position. The most common is to act straight in public, while living a gay life 'in the closet'. Secrecy and silence enable them to create a life of some choice beyond the demands of the family and the heteronormative society. Silence about sexuality is connected to both the silence of the young men and the silence of the majority, the latter's silence cleverly summarized in the expression 'the will not to know'. Silence about personal homosexuality, at times by discursively imposing homophobia, exists everywhere and is produced at all levels of Lebanese society. In Lebanon, many regard same-sex acts as a sin, a conscious choice or something that can be changed voluntarily, and this is also reflected in the law. In fact, the legal system in Lebanon has tended to punish those who publicly display homosexual affection more than it has paid attention to the practice or existence of homosexuality in private spheres. Any relations that are 'contradicting the laws of nature' are criminalized under Article 534 of the Penal Code,[12] and until recently homosexuality was also regarded as a symptom of mental illness.[13]Explorations of the connection between sexual and religious identities are also important, particularly between religious beliefs and practices and ideas of homoeroticism and narratives of sexual identities.

Staying 'in line': Unconsciously performed queer tactics

To be able better to address the above, I will use Sara Ahmed's concepts of *orientation* and *the straight line*.[14] I will utilize these concepts to investigate how the young men in the study are being directed or 'oriented' towards 'home' or certain objects, and what happens when they deviate from the normative way of life. According to Ahmed, being 'in line' means finding our way. The lines we follow, the paths we walk on, function as forms of alignment and as ways of being and keeping in line with others: when we are in line, we are oriented. We are in line when we face the direction that is already faced by others. To follow a straight line regarding sexual orientation is to 'become straight'. In my understanding of Ahmed, heteronormativity, or 'the straight line' – as a way of situating heterosexuality as seemingly neutral, normative and dominant – is not only a well-trodden path but also it becomes a compass to navigate with when young men deviate. To follow 'the straight line' is to live by the norms, linear and over time, and while young men might deviate in one aspect, they might not in another.

A lot of questions arose after my experience at the funeral. I was thinking that even if Ādam had still been alive, I could never imagine the marriage between him and his fiancée ever happening. The grieving family and the closest kin did not share the same stories about Ādam and his life as the rest of his friends and I. Or maybe he someday would have conceded to his family's will and followed the straight path leading back to this home town. And what about his gay friends? Would they someday have to get married to a woman too? Possibly Ādam's background could explain why he was not already married. His family being poor and located far from the city of Beirut might have delayed the marriage plans and made it easier for him to hide from his family's eyes and live a life of his own choice. Or was it just his parents' hope that their son would someday return to his hometown, settle down and start a family? And if the family where aware of his homosexuality, might they presume that it was a phase, or that it did not matter as long as he could father children with a woman? What social and economic pressures exist that might encourage a young woman to ignore possible signs that their husband-to-be is having sex with men? Unfortunately, his final return was in a coffin, dressed in white as 'the groom of death', as this local Sunni custom requires when a man dies before he gets married.[15]

Marriage was something that was desirable in the quest to mimic the heteronormative among the young men. To explain how homonormativity is created, it is important to note that homonormativity is not the same as heteronormativity, as it does not assume that every person is gay; rather, it assumes that queer people want to be just like heteronormative people and rewards those who mimic heteronormative life schedule standards. The politics of homonormativity becomes a new way of controlling sexuality and deviance, by normalizing it and incorporating it into the heteronormative politics of life. Duggan, although she writes from a neoliberal American context, claims this 'new homonormativity' is:

> A politics that does not contest dominant heteronormative assumptions and institutions, but upholds and sustains them, while promising the possibility of a demobilized gay constituency and a privatized, depoliticized gay culture anchored in domesticity and consumption.[16]

In Lebanon, without marriage one is not considered a real man, not a full member of society, as marriage is the ultimate confirmation of a man's status. For sex to be good, it has to be reproductive, egalitarian, monogamous, between two people preferably of the same age, and from the same class and religion, as inter-sectarian marriage is a complex issue in Lebanon.[17] Marriage and the possibility of having children was something present in the stories of the young men in the study, not only as an obligation and a problem but also as something desirable and as a possible goal for most of them in the future. While waiting for the compulsory heterosexual marriage to happen, the relationships that many of the young men engaged in did, in many ways, resemble that of a mature heterosexual monogamous relationship. Still, gay marriage was not an option for the young men and their relationships were not accepted in the eyes of society. Marriage in Lebanon is intimately interconnected with religion. However, the young men found support in homonormativity by honouring monogamy and love as positive values, also in the eyes of God.

When it came to marriage (to a woman), ʿAlī believed it was in the hands of God: 'if God wants me to marry I will. It is the same with being gay, it is God's will.'[18] While marriage was seen as a necessity, the choice of partner did not ultimately depend on parental approval. In the minds of the young men, love was still a prerequisite when it came to premarital relationships but not so much when it came to heterosexual marriage. Bilāl was totally against open relationships. He believed that any sexual act outside of marriage was sinful. This applied to straight couples as well. Even though he thought of his actions as sinful and wrong, he could not neglect the feelings he had towards other men. Bilāl kept his sexuality a secret from his ex-girlfriend in the hope of getting back with her one day to start a family. He claimed that the only reason for lying to her was because he still loved her. Since it was impossible for him to adopt children, he saw this possible marriage with his ex-girlfriend as his only option if he wanted to procreate and not break the family line, he explained. Thus, in Sara Ahmed's vocabulary, marriage and children are the 'home' they are supposed to direct themselves towards, according to society and their families' expectations.[19]

Although love is not a prerequisite in arranged heterosexual marriages, it became one justification for the young men's relationships with other men, as it is still believed to be a 'good' form of sexual relation within the 'straight line', minimizing every 'perverse' trace of their still deviant sexual orientation. We can see that by maintaining heteronormative lifestyles, which included monogamy and love, the young men's sexual orientation may therefore have appeared less deviant than other sexual aberrations. Monogamy, as in the meaning of staying true to one partner, became important, as it applies to everyone. Casual promiscuity threatened their possibilities of navigating in alignment with the 'straight line'.

Rabīʿ had known since he was a child that he liked boys as he used to watch beautiful boys on TV and in magazines. His first sexual experience was with another boy, and although he also had some sexual experiences with girls he never had what he refers to as 'full sex' with a girl. (A distinction between 'soft sex' and 'full sex' is common among the interviewees, where 'full sex' refers to sex including penetration, because for them, what determines a sexual act is penile penetration.) He thought that it was more difficult for a man to find a girl to have sex with than another man, since girls, according to Rabīʿ, are more reluctant to have sex with penetration before marriage. His sexuality, however, was a secret he would never tell. He knew early on that his feelings were forbidden, and therefore it became a well-kept secret for many years to come. If Rabīʿ could have told those that thought what he was doing and feeling was wrong, he would have said:

> This is very personal and each person has the right to live the way he wants, as long as I'm not giving harm to anyone then it's not wrong, I'm the only one who knows what's right and what's wrong for me. I'm a respectful educated decent person and what I do does not change that.[20]

The will of the young men to be included played on the premises of a heteronormative society, to be absorbed and acknowledged as serious and normal, and was also built on normative views on sexuality and how life should be organized. Thus, inclusion in the heteronormative world would in this case mean a heteronormative structured gay world, namely, a well-organized homonormativity. Another story from the field might help to explain the complicated relationship to the 'straight line' and the expectations of marriage.

As a bisexual,[21] Ziyād occasionally met and dated women. At one time, he had started a relationship with a woman and they planned to get married. She had always been aware of his gay life since they had been close friends for a long time. But the day they started to talk about marriage, she asked him to stop having sex with men. He promised and tried to distance himself from his former life but it was too hard, not only because all his friends were gay but also because he worked in gay venues and he wanted to have sexual intercourse with men. Consequently, she became very jealous of all of his (and her) gay friends and eventually they broke the whole thing off. He told me that the main reason for their marriage had not been love but that they both wanted children, and an arranged marriage between the two would facilitate that and speed up the process. Still, since Lebanon does not legally or socially accept non-normative sexualities and homonormative gay couples (and probably will not in the foreseeable future), homonormativity only has a function on a personal level, in the intimacy of couples and with close friends, as a justification for continuation on 'the straight line'. By adjusting to monogamy and dreaming of marriage, however, gay couples can connect to a narrative about the normal even though they always risk being rejected.

Opacity and the idea of 'coming out'

Another aspect of a non-confrontational tactic, closely related to the discussion on silence, is the idea of 'coming out' as the hegemonic and quintessential gesture of publicly acknowledging who you really are. The idea of the closet and the coming out process is more an ideology than a real possibility for most in Lebanon. Coming out (confession) has become the required way for sexual minorities to free themselves and to assert their rights. As such, it is seen as a central tool in identity politics, while silence has been primarily understood as a weapon against sexual minorities, exercised in the form of censorship, bans and denial. Repressive silence, rather than the use of the prohibition of homosexual acts in the Penal Code, has been the most common strategy. Yet again, silence has also been useful for the young men to avoid classification and thus avoid being stigmatized at the expense of an undisturbed homophobic discourse.

Rabīʿ had, since the first day I met him, grown to become a confident, successful man who enjoyed his life, his friends, both gay and straight, and his job, which gave him the means to live an enjoyable and easy middle-class life in Beirut. At my last visit to Beirut in 2013 we reminisced over the past seven years, and when later, in an email interview, I asked him if anything had changed in Lebanon since we first met, he answered:

> Yes, indeed, and for the better. Years ago the gay subject was a taboo, we could never even make a joke about it specially in front of family. Now people have a clear idea of what gay men are, they used to think that the gay man is a transvestite, we talk about gay issues in public places even with family members. Famous people are known gay and yet accepted and have fans, you see people more comfortable with gay fashion, even when you see people who look gay on the roads you don't hear laughs. So in Beirut, life is much easier for gay people.[22]

Despite all this, or maybe because of it, he would never reveal his gay life to anyone but his close gay friends and 'gay friendly friends' as he called them, 'people who are educated enough and aware of gay people's presence and do not judge people on their sexuality', he said. He believed that the least judgemental people were people outside of Lebanon, mainly from Europe and America, or Lebanese who had travelled a lot and had gay friends. These were people he could tell about his sexuality, he stated. Maybe if he lived somewhere else he could consider 'coming out', partially at least, since telling his parents was something he would never do, he explained. Rabīʿ also explained that maybe, when his parents were dead, he would tell the world. 'I think even with all this freedom now, Beirut will stay an Arab city and homophobia will remain even if less than before. I don't like to put myself in these kinds of situation where I have to defend myself as gay. I'm just happy with what I am now.'[23] Abstaining from the required 'confession' and refraining from 'fixed identity categories, and public visibility' of the dominant lesbian, gay, bisexual, transgender, and queer (or questioning) (LGBTQ) discourse on the ontology of sexuality is what De Villiers describes as opaque tactics.[24] Opaque tactics question the opposition between silence and speech by keeping away from the closeted position. The tactics that the young men employed did not actively resist the closet and the confessional discourse associated with it. Although by using silence as a 'speech act', the young men made a queer space for their double life.

Just as being gay and religious is not something you just are but something that is constantly verified, managed, negotiated and played out, being 'closeted' is also something constantly negotiable and managed. Accepting a deviant position is already a way of coming out, since this acceptance craves a certain kind of self-awareness, being out to oneself. The second step, in order to reorient the religious orientation, is to be out to God. Being out is thus not only about revealing sexuality; it is also about coming out, as a practising Muslim.

'Being out' depends to some extent on 'being in', as it gains its meaning only by polarity, either by being 'out' and having to confess a private life and align it with a specific identity category, or being 'closeted' and thus presumed to be living in shame, secrecy or self-denial. The closet is thus a 'modern form of confessional discourse'.[25]

The closet metaphor is an object that the heteronormative straight line conjures up and that everyone will have to orient themselves in relation to. By keeping away from the closeted position or admitting to having been in it, thus proclaiming your deviant orientation, the narrative of the naturalness of heterosexuality is reproduced. Thus the metaphor of the closet, as a narrative belonging in a binary heteronormative game of suffering in silence or thriving through speech, was accidentally queered by the young men. These tactics do not render the closet meaningless; they just change the possible meaning(s) of the closet as well as its possible function(s). Consequently, the closet is not obsolete. Rather, the identified queer tactics create a new narrative of multiple closets, as the young men had come out of the closet many times. Through a consciously chosen opacity constructed for the purpose of being able to live a gay life parallel to the straight line, and through not addressing issues of sexuality in public, rocking the boat may be avoided. Silence becomes one of the most important tactics used by the young men. In relation to the straight line, the authorized discourse of what can and cannot be said is in close relation to the concept of 'being in' or 'being out' of 'the closet', as it also relates to the opposition between silence and speech, often juxtaposed with shame, guilt and pride. Being silent might therefore be seen as an unconsciously performed queer tactic leading to some kind of personal liberation. By not entering into 'the closeted position', which includes the way one is supposed to feel repressed and dream of being out, the young men challenged the discursively prescribed drama of 'outness' and 'closetedness', using silence as an empowering tool. Silence, and not outness or the sufferings of the closet, was a useful tactic for most of the young men, enabling a double life. The role of silence among the young men is to protect this double life. Thus silence has a triple nature; it is a way to escape from the classification according to the straight/gay binary; a tactic to pass as normal; and, at the same time, a sign of powerlessness of the deviant leading to the silencing of homosexuals by the majority of society.

Discussions about people's homosexuality may be less interesting than discussions about why some people feel it necessary to deny their sexual preferences and others to publicly announce them.[26] Rabīʿ's main reason for not being open about his sexuality was that he was afraid of losing his position in society, as he was now very successful in his field of work. He was not ashamed of his sexuality, but people would regard him as sick because they lacked education on this issue, he argued and added: 'I'm much more comfortable with my sexuality [in] that I'm much more clever how to enjoy my life, yet keeping it under the hat and avoiding situations that could be dramatic, all this with no stress no tension.'[27]

On the question of whether he would ever attend a pride festival in Beirut or any other public event that raises awareness about gays and lesbians in Lebanon, he answered that because of his family, he could not be exposed because 'this will hurt my family because it's against everything they believe'. 'Keeping it under the hat', as Rabīʿ called it, I presume is synonymous with 'being in the closet', as it involves a hidden unrevealed secret that is only kept in the mind of the hat's owner. Interestingly, another meaning of the phrase is 'think it, but don't say it', similar to the mentality of 'don't ask don't tell'.

Bilāl contended that being homosexual or bisexual had never hindered him in his career because he had chosen not to speak about his sexuality. He thought that there were too many misconceptions about homosexuals and he acknowledged that there was much discrimination against gay people in Lebanon, and therefore keeping silent was the only possible way to pursue his life. When I talked to Nabīl, he shared similar thoughts. Although he explained that his family were open minded about religion, he would never tell them about his gay life. He feared he would no longer be accepted by them and loved them too much to risk hurting them with this 'thing'. Still, at times, in certain settings, all of the young men had 'come out'.

Ghassān, who was the only one of the young men who was partially out to his family, planned his 'coming out' carefully, first by telling his sister (who had come out as a bisexual a year before) and then some close friends. It was eventually his sister who accidently 'outed' him to his mother. His mother had started to suspect that Ghassān was gay and had asked his sister, who said no at first, but then she gave in and explained that her brother was bisexual. Soon after, Ghassān told his mother himself with the words: 'Since I was fourteen I've been afraid that you and my father will reject me,' whereon his mother responded: 'You are my son and I will never reject you but this will always be a source of great sadness to me.'[28] Ghassān's sexuality was still a secret that the rest of the family kept from his father. The plan was to tell him later, when he had finished his degree and had become financially independent, Ghassān explained. The above examples show that silence could be defensive due to the homophobic society surrounding the young men. The strategies of everyday sexual self-management, the secrecy and double life, aimed to avoid the risks of unintended exposure and social risks. It also became clear that as the young men continued to manage their sexual and religious orientation in silence (in part because of shame, guilt or fear), these sin- or self-management practices were situational and context-dependent. The young men's narratives show that coming out of the closet is not a single act but is part of a continuous self-management, as they were forced to revisit the closet at times. By making the closet into a key metaphor of gay oppression, coming out and affirming a gay identity is often viewed as the supreme political act.

The narrative of the closet creates divisions between stigmatized and liberated individuals who are 'in' and 'out' of the closet. The concept of the closet indicates secretive (closeted) practices aimed at maintaining a norm of heterosexuality by excluding homosexuality from public life. While it is possible to see the young men's silence through this prism, it is equally relevant to understand their silence and secrecy as tactics enabling them to enjoy a secret gay life (referring to an unfixed understanding of the word). The problem is that these opaque and secretive practices both enable the double life (which makes possible a positive gay life) and reproduce the idea of the closet (representing a repressed gay life). The young men's tactics connect to an opaque queer position and to the closet that they have to revisit again and again, as they navigate between a straight and gay world. Consequently, there seem to be multiple closets.

Conclusion

As demonstrated in this chapter, speaking out loud was not always perceived as the best way to resist the heteronormative way of life and the criminalization of being gay by the young men in the study. As HELEM[29] activist Ghassan Makarem has identified, there are some crucial aspects of Lebanese society:

> People do not choose to identify with a criminal identity. Declaring a sexual preference that does not conform to imposed norms is an act of defiance against existing structures of oppression. We criminalize ourselves and reject the crime at the same time. This brings about a dual nature of such expression. One is used by the state and the ruling class to criminalize a section of society. The other is that of resistance and rebellion against criminalization and oppression.[30]

Many felt that it makes more sense to find ways of temporarily escaping the heteronormative for personal deliverance instead of publicly defying it. Due to power strategies of authoritative persons and organizations, in combination with familial pressure and other societal obligations, the possible resistance (and personal form of liberation) the young men performed was to constantly stretch the boundaries of what was lawful and permitted, in secrecy. Some of the young men did not interpret their sexual orientation as revealing their 'true selves'; instead they understood homosexuality as marginal in their psychic economies. Even those of the young men who did interpret their homosexuality as somewhat integral to their selves may have chosen to marginalize their sexual orientation without necessarily surrendering to an internalized homophobia or, as Massad suggests, imposed homophobia. Following Massad's line of argument, people who resist being part of the Gay International, refuse to adopt a gay identity, or merely do not have any association with such concepts, tend to be accused of being in denial by claiming that they suffer from internalized homophobia or false consciousness, and they are consequently put in the famous closet.[31]

Acting straight, which was something that all the young men engaged in, was a way of negotiating their place in heteronormative society without exposing a gay life. As secret deviants, the young men tried to transgress and circumvent norms. They were empowered by the cover that their alignment with 'the straight line' provided in public. Further, they found legitimacy in their lifestyles creating a homonormativity that did not disturb heteronormative views on sexuality such as monogamy, marriage and gender roles. Rather, homonormativity circumvents these values by establishing a new homonormative standard mimicking heteronormativity, legitimizing gay relations in the eyes of the young men but hardly, yet, in the opinion of the many. By viewing deviance as a position and a consequence, not as a quality that lies in the behaviour itself, then, 'acting straight' in public becomes less about hiding an ontological deviance and more about a tactical response to (a possibly life-threatening) labelling process, where the social interaction between people includes judging, stereotyping, violence and bullying when calling someone deviant. This oscillation between being extrovertly gay and being taken for straight in a generally homophobic society was a way of living for Ādam, who preludes this chapter, and the others interviewed for this study.

Notes

1 This chapter is based on fieldwork in Beirut, Lebanon between 2007 and 2013, which was conducted as part of my doctoral dissertation.

2 The reason for his death must remain untold because of privacy matters. Safety precautions related to the research subjects have been a constant issue when finalizing the text, as it has been of the utmost importance not to reveal the identity of anyone in the field, apart from those who have chosen to be public figures. Most of the people referred to in this study wanted to make sure that no names and photos were going to be used in the chapter and therefore, through informal verbal consent, all important features of the study were shared to make it clear to the subjects that it was not the purpose of my study, nor necessary to it, to use real names and photos. Anonymity was considered not only in regard to a potential reader but also in relation to the research subjects.

3 For more on Islamic funeral rituals and the topic of death, see Christine Schirrmacher, 'They Are Not All Martyrs: Islam on the Topics of Dying, Death, and Salvation in the Afterlife', *Evangelical Review of Theology*, 36 (3) (2012): 250–65.

4 Kecia Ali, *Sexual Ethics and Islam: Feminist Reflections on Qur'an, Hadith and Jurisprudence* (London: Oneworld Publications, 2006), 85.

5 Stephen O. Murray and Will Roscoe, *Islamic Homosexualities: Culture, History, and Literature* (New York: New York University Press, 1997).

6 Michel Foucault, *The History of Sexuality*, 3 vols (New York: Knopf Doubleday, 2012).

7 See, for example, Erving Goffman, *Stigma: Notes on the Management of Spoiled Identity* (New York: Simon & Schuster, 1986).

8 Judith Butler, *Gender Trouble: Feminism and the Subversion of Identity* (London: Routledge, 1990).

9 Sofian Merabet, *Queer Beirut* (Austin, TX: University of Texas Press, 2015).

10 Ibid.

11 Helma Lutz, Maria Teresa, Herrera Vivar and Linda Supik (eds), *Framing Intersectionality: Debates on a Multi-Faceted Concept in Gender Studies* (Farnham: Ashgate, 2011).

12 Article 534 of the Penal Code that criminalizes homosexuality is of Ottoman origin but was codified under the French mandate in 1943. To argue that the criminalization of homosexuality is solely a result of colonization, however, is a truth

with modification. Postcolonial Lebanon could have worked towards a change in its penal code. But it is still in use, although selectively. In Lebanon, despite its being a country with several influential religions, the condemnation and criminalization of homosexuality is not solely a product of religious traditions. Rather, legislation is a remnant of Lebanon's Ottoman and French colonial past, blended with religious morals concerning sexuality.

13 In June 2013, the Lebanese Psychological Society announced in a statement that homosexuality in itself does not cause any defect in judgement, stability, reliability or social and professional abilities: Dan Littauer, 'Being Gay is not a Disease and Needs No Treatment', LGBTQNation, 12 July 2013. Available online: https://www.lgbtqnation.com/2013/07/lebanon-being-gay-is-not-a-disease-and-needs-no-treatment/ (accessed 30 November 2017).

14 Sara Ahmed, *Queer Phenomenology: Orientations, Objects, Others* (Durham, NC: Duke University Press, 2006).

15 Men and women who die before they get married will be married in Paradise, according to local Muslim beliefs, and are therefore dressed in white as for a wedding before the funeral. The body is always buried in only a white sheet, however, without a coffin, on their side, facing Mecca.

16 Lisa Duggan, 'The New Homonormativity: The Sexual Politics of Neoliberalism', in Russ Castronovo and Dana Nelson (eds), *Materializing Democracy: Toward a Revitalized Cultural Politics*, 175–94 (Durham, NC: Duke University Press, 2002).

17 In Lebanon, people from different sects cannot get married unless one converts to the other's sect. According to the Lebanese Mattar Law Firm: 'Mixed marriages are permitted in Lebanon with the following remarks: A Sunni or Shi'a (Muslim) man can marry a Christian or Jewish woman without her having to convert herself, but a Muslim woman cannot marry a Christian or a Jew. Catholic men can marry a Muslim woman. In this case the couple receives the blessing at the sacristy, and the children must be baptized and raised as Catholics. Druze community only allows inter-Druze wedding […]. The same apply for the Israelite community. Orthodox church allows weddings with Muslims under the conversion condition. Under Muslim law, polygamy is permitted. However and nowadays it is regarded as being impractical and undesirable due to the additional economic burden and to the complications it brings into the family house.' Mattar Law Firm, 'Marriage Law/Lawyers in Lebanon', (n.d.). Available online: http://mattarlaw.com/marriage-in-lebanon/#mixed (accessed 30 November 2017).

18 Interview with ʿAlī, 1 May 2010.

19 Ahmed, *Queer Phenomenology*.

20 Email interview with Rabīʿ, 4 July 2013.

21 Bisexuality, or the claim to be bisexual, causes confusion in the discussion about binary constructed sexualities and evokes feelings of blurred boundaries when confronting both heterosexuals and gay men with sexual ambiguity. The subversiveness of bisexuality becomes even clearer in the light of family structures, since bisexuality seemingly challenges the concepts of sexuality, traditional relationships, monogamy, gender roles and identity. Hence, bisexuals do not conform to the morals of either the gay or the straight world. But since any kind of gay relations is forbidden and morally condemned in Lebanon, these views of temporary and situational orientations become part of a self-narrative that is sometimes described as internalized homophobia, only accepting certain types of homosexuality, as well as certain types of masculinity and religiosity.

22 Email interview with Rabīʿ, 4 July 2013.

23 Ibid.
24 Nicholas De Villiers, *Opacity and the Closet: Queer Tactics in Foucault, Barthes, and Warhol* (Minneapolis, MN: University of Minnesota Press, 2012).
25 Ibid., 5.
26 See, for example, Meem, *Bareed Mista3jil: True Stories* (*Express Mail/Mail in a Hurry*) (Beirut: Ciel, 2009), which contains the stories of forty-one individuals, mostly women, who identified as queer in Lebanon. The book is available in both English and Arabic versions.
27 Email interview with Rabīʿ, 4 July 2013.
28 Interview with Ghassān, 11 March 2011.
29 Founded in 2004, HELEM (which means 'dream' in Arabic but is also the acronym for Protection for Lesbians, Gays, Bisexuals and Transgenders, *himaya lubnaniyya lil-mithliyin*) was the first organization in the MENA region to set up a gay and lesbian community centre. HELEM was created out of an internet community called gaylebanon, launched in 1998. After a while, gaylebanon became an underground socializing group restricted to a few people who knew each other, called Club Free. In 2004, after years of empowerment and networking, Club Free became HELEM, and was officially registered at the Ministry of Interior and Municipalities in Lebanon. Shortly thereafter, it opened its centre in the area of Sanayeh in Beirut.
30 Ghassan Makarem, 'The Story of HELEM', *Journal of Middle East Women's Studies*, 7 (3) (2011): 98–112.
31 Joseph Massad, *Desiring Arabs* (Chicago, IL: University of Chicago Press), 100–60.

References

Ahmed, Sara (2006), *Queer Phenomenology: Orientations, Objects, Others*, Durham, NC: Duke University Press.

Ali, Kecia (2006), *Sexual Ethics and Islam: Feminist Reflections on Qur'an, Hadith and Jurisprudence*, London: Oneworld Publications.

Butler, Judith (1990), *Gender Trouble: Feminism and the Subversion of Identity*, London: Routledge.

De Villiers, Nicholas (2012), *Opacity and the Closet: Queer Tactics in Foucault, Barthes, and Warhol*, Minneapolis, MN: University of Minnesota Press.

Duggan, Lisa (2002), 'The New Homonormativity: The Sexual Politics of Neoliberalism', in Russ Castronovo and Dana Nelson (eds), *Materializing Democracy: Toward a Revitalized Cultural Politics*, 175–94, Durham, NC: Duke University Press.

Foucault, Michel (2012), *The History of Sexuality*, 3 vols, New York: Knopf Doubleday.

Goffman, Erving (1986), *Stigma: Notes on the Management of Spoiled Identity*, New York: Simon & Schuster.

Littauer, Dan (2013), 'Being Gay is not a Disease and Needs No Treatment', LGBTQNation, 12 July. Available online: https://www.lgbtqnation.com/2013/07/lebanon-being-gay-is-not-a-disease-and-needs-no-treatment/ (accessed 30 November 2017).

Lutz, Helma, Maria Teresa Herrera Vivar and Linda Supik (eds) (2011), *Framing Intersectionality: Debates on a Multi-Faceted Concept in Gender Studies*, Farnham: Ashgate.

Makarem, Gassan (2011), 'The Story of HELEM', *Journal of Middle East Women's Studies*, 7 (3): 98–112.

Massad, Joseph (2007), *Desiring Arabs*, Chicago, IL: University of Chicago Press.
Mattar Law Firm (n.d.), 'Marriage Law/Lawyers in Lebanon'. Available online: http://mattarlaw.com/marriage-in-lebanon/#mixed (accessed 30 November 2017).
Meem (2009), *Bareed Mista3jil: True Stories* (*Express Mail/Mail in a Hurry*), Beirut: Ciel.
Merabet, Sofian (2015), *Queer Beirut*, Austin, TX: University of Texas Press.
Murray, Stephen O. and Will Roscoe (1997), *Islamic Homosexualities: Culture, History, and Literature*, New York: New York University Press.
Schirrmacher, Christine (2012), 'They Are Not All Martyrs: Islam on the Topics of Dying, Death, and Salvation in the Afterlife', *Evangelical Review of Theology*, 36 (3): 250–65.

Chapter 11

PALESTINIAN QUEERS AND THE DEBATE ON SEXUAL IDENTITY AND RELIGIOUS NORMATIVITY

Nijmi Edres

Introduction

The debate on gender and sexuality in Palestine inevitably intersects the debate about the nation and relates to concepts such as religion, ethnicity and belonging. Looking at this debate, the chapter focuses on a specific case study: Palestinians with Israeli citizenship.[1] Palestinian Muslims with Israeli citizenship represent around 17.6 per cent of the total Israeli population, while Palestinian Christians with Israeli citizenship count for 1.54 per cent. Together, they represent a minority of around 1.6 million people.[2] Looking at how religion is configured and reconfigured by Palestinian queers in Israel is particularly interesting and can offer useful insights into the debate on the relationship between religious normativity and sexual identity.

Palestinian queers with Israeli citizenship find themselves in a context that is at the same time different from other Middle Eastern countries, as they represent an Arab minority in a non-Arab state and from the context of Arab minorities living in Western states, as their personal status and family issues are regulated by religious courts that are granted wide areas of jurisdiction and even exclusive authority in matters of marriage and divorce. Religious normativity has a central role in the life of Israeli citizens, and it is, for instance, impossible to celebrate a civil marriage in the country.[3]

Concurrently, Israel is the place in the Middle East where lesbian, gay, bisexual, transgender and queer (or questioning) (LGBTQ) rights are regarded as the most advanced by the international community. In a context where religious identity is so strongly addressed by the state, but where wide spaces of secularization are also open, one could expect the existence of a lively debate about the relationship between religious normativity and gender identity. Yet, and despite the growing number of religious LGBTQ movements in the Middle East, religious codes and individual adherence to them do not seem to stay at the core of the debate developed by Palestinian queers in Israel.

Indeed, if religion is marginal in the discourse developed by Palestinian Muslim and Christian queers, Israeli Jews in recent years have often and publicly explored the complexity of being religious queers. This chapter aims to describe how Palestinian queers configure their relation to religion differently than Jewish queers. In order to reach this aim, the chapter first contextualizes Palestinian debates into the Israeli framework, by underlining the role of religious courts and Islamic associations to shape the debate on gender issues among Palestinians, transforming it into an issue of resistance against 'Israelisation'. Then, the chapter discusses the history of Israeli and Palestinian LGBTQ organizations, showing the different approaches they have to religion. The avoidance of debating religious norms among Palestinian organizations is partly the result of the primacy they give to the national struggle over other debates. Yet it can also be explained by the fact that most of their members lack the religious education that would allow them to critically address such issues. Finally, relating the encounter to Palestinian queers, it shows examples of the ways they address religious debates while maintaining their affective bounds to Palestine by focusing on their private relation with God.

The historical connection between gender and nationality in Palestine

In continuity with British politics in Palestine during the mandate, the Israeli government decided after the foundation of the state to divide power and jurisdiction along subject-matter lines,[4] placing family law under the jurisdiction of religious communities. This decision was probably influenced by, among other factors, the desire to reduce dissent from Palestinian Muslims and Christians living inside the borders of the newly founded state, by granting them a space for autonomy in administering issues internal to the different religious communities and sensitive from the point of view of identity. That way, religious courts (be they Christian, Muslim, Druze or Jewish) were granted exclusive jurisdiction in almost all matters of family law and personal status.[5]

In the case of Palestinian Christians and Muslims, these courts represented the only Palestinian institutions remaining in power after the foundation of the State of Israel. As a result, judges working in religious courts in Israel – especially Muslim judges – could claim that religious courts represent the 'last bastion of Palestinian identity' in Israel.[6] They associate religious normativity as it is upheld in religious courts with resistance to the occupation and safeguarding the Palestinian identity in the Israeli context.

During recent decades, that strong relationship between gender norms and the Palestinian identity has been at the centre of the discourse of Muslim judges in Israel. Indeed, they have had to cope with the claims of feminist movements and the challenges imposed by Israeli civil law, including Israeli attempts to restrict the application of Muslim family regulations in specific areas. In cases of polygamy and male unilateral divorces (*ṭalāq*), for instance, the Knesset established a penal sanction as a deterrent.[7] In such cases, Muslim judges often reacted by rejecting external impositions, finding practical expedients such as avoiding the official registration of polygamous marriages and stressing the value of Sharia as a comprehensive, all-embracing and self-sufficient system.[8]

This connection between gender and national identity strongly affects the contemporary debate. In the specific context of Palestinians living in Israel, deviation from traditional gender roles is often seen as a form of Westernisation or, even worse, Israelisation. That is much more evident in the case of Muslims, due the strong historically rooted connections between Islam and the Arab identity.[9]

Further, studies on Palestinian religious associations in Israel have underlined the overwhelming prevalence of associations connected with the Israeli Islamic Movement (IIM).[10] Starting from the 1980s, the IIM had the potential to grow and widen its spaces of social and political influence.[11] The success of the IIM, which has some of its representatives sitting inside the Knesset, was possible thanks to the role played by its members in the area of education. The members of the movement indeed offered educational services, such as classes in the Arabic language and Muslim religion, that met the need of the Palestinian minority to protect and reinforce its identity roots in the Israeli context.[12] Today, the IIM is the main Palestinian religious force represented inside the Knesset. Despite its southern branch having opted for a more moderate position regarding Israel, from a religious point of view the movement still represents a conservative force that shows no intention of embarking on a religious theoretical reasoning that could seek an endorsement of LGBTQ claims.

A brief history of religious LGBTQ movements in Israel

In Israel, the first gay organizations were set up by secular Jews at the end of the 1970s, concomitant to the development of similar organizations in Europe and Northern America. Israel's pioneer national lesbian, gay, bisexual and transgender organization, now known as the Aguda, was founded in 1975.[13] Since then, the Israeli LGBTQ community operates on various fronts: in parliamentary and extra-parliamentary organizations; in the mass media; and in the juridical arena.

Another important organization for the Israeli LGBTQ community opened in Jerusalem in 1997, under the name of Jerusalem Open House for Pride and Tolerance.[14] The Open House is internationally known as the organizer of the Jerusalem March for Pride and Tolerance, the largest human rights demonstration in the city. It also provides numerous support services and social groups for LGBTQ youths, as well as a place where all LGBTQ Jerusalemites – including Orthodox Jews, Arabs and transgender individuals – can go for support.[15]

Since the second half of the 2000s, some LGBTQ organizations of religious Jews have been founded. In 2005, for instance, the Bat-Kol organization formed as a group for religious lesbians. Similarly in 2007 Havruta, an organization for religious gay men, was launched.[16] Despite the fact that major LGBTQ organizations such as the Open House used to provide support to Orthodox Jews, these organizations were independent, assisting Israeli Jews from religious backgrounds with the aim to push the 'religious public to fully accept LGBTQ individuals and families as equal partners of their community'.[17] It is no coincidence that in 2017 the Jerusalem March for Pride and Tolerance was held under the banner of 'LGBTQ and Religion'.

Through their activities, these organizations have gradually succeeded in the promotion of gay rights at a national level. Today, the rights of LGBTQ individuals in Israel are partially granted by the civil legislation. Same-sex sexual activity was legalized in 1988,[18] although the former law against sodomy had not been enforced since a court decision of 1963, when the Attorney General declared that sodomy laws established under the British mandate would not be enforced.[19] Although same-sex marriages are not performed in the country, Israel recognizes same-sex marriages performed elsewhere,[20] as well as unregistered cohabitation between same-sex couples (since 1994).[21] Discrimination on the grounds of sexual orientation was prohibited in 1992. Same-sex couples are allowed to jointly adopt after a court decision in 2008, having been previously allowed to adopt stepchildren and given limited co-guardianship rights for non-biological parents.[22]

Concerning religious debates, Israeli LGBTQ organizations can also register some success. In 2015, for instance, various Orthodox Jews, some of whom were active members of Yachad, an Orthodox Synagogue in Tel Aviv,[23] took part in an online campaign that reached more than 150,000 people in a few days, under the slogan 'Out, Proud and Religious'.[24] Likewise, in April 2016, the Beit Hillel association of religious Zionist rabbis released a position paper calling for religious communities to accept gays and lesbians and to let them fulfil congregational functions. Sure enough, such a statement was far from legitimizing same-sex acts, still defined as not permitted in the Torah.[25] Yet it was symptomatic of a process of public negotiation of religious norms and spaces of expression of sexual identities.

Nevertheless, acts like the stabbing of people at gay pride parades in 2005 and 2015, in both cases at the hand of the ultra-Orthodox Yishai Schlissel, prove that homophobia is still a current issue in Israeli society and that religion still has a primary importance in the discriminatory discourse against LGBTQ individuals. This is quite clear if we look at religious community leaders' declarations: just ten days before the Jerusalem Gay Pride event in 2016, Modern Orthodox[26] Rabbi Yigal Levenstein said that homosexuals were 'perverts' and 'deviants' devoid of 'the normalcy of life', and over three hundred rabbis from all over the country signed this statement.[27] The statement claimed that there was 'no room for legitimizing phenomena and behaviors that seek to glorify a way of life that contravenes human morality and the way of the Torah'.[28] Similarly, in summer 2015 Meir David Koperschmidt, of the anti-assimilation Lehava group, equated homosexuality with bank robbery, claiming 'we are the normal families [...] for sure they are not religious [...] they are supposed not to be proud of it [...] they are hurting every normal family'.[29]

Palestinian LGBTQ organizations and religious issues

Similar to what happens among Israeli Jews, there are quite a few known cases of homophobic declarations by relevant members of the Palestinian community.[30] Furthermore, as already mentioned, the rights of LGBTQ individuals are partially covered under the umbrella of civil legislation. Yet religious courts in Israel are the sole bodies that can marry and divorce.

The first groups to provide specific support to LGBTQ Palestinian peoples living within the borders of Israel, the Gaza Strip and the West Bank appeared in the early 2000s. The first official Palestinian LGBTQ organization, al-Qaws (al-Qaws for Sexual and Gender Diversity in Palestinian Society, 'Rainbow' in Arabic),[31] started in 2001 as an independent local project of the Jerusalem Open House, to specifically address the needs of Palestinian LGBTQs living in Jerusalem. After some years of activity in cooperation and under the umbrella of the Israeli Jerusalem Open House, al-Qaws expanded and became an independent national Palestinian organization. As we will see below, the separation from Jerusalem House was mainly on political grounds. Today al-Qaws hosts social activities in Jerusalem, Haifa, Jaffa and the West Bank as an arena for support for members of the LGBTQ Palestinian community.[32] It also operates a telephone support line.[33]

In 2002, a second group was formed to specifically address the needs of Palestinian lesbian women, Aṣwāt (Palestinian Lesbian Women, 'Voices' in Arabic).[34] Aṣwāt was founded as a project of the Palestinian Feminist non-governmental organization (NGO) Kayan, at the Haifa Feminist Center[35] and started as an anonymous email list to provide support to Palestinian lesbians. Since then it has developed into an established working group that hosts monthly meetings for its members and organizes lectures, events and educational opportunities. One of the most interesting activities promoted by Aṣwāt relates to the translation and publication in Arabic of texts related to sexuality and gender identity and to the editing of the first Arabic glossary of words related to homosexuality.[36]

Aṣwāt works to raise community awareness on the identities of 'Palestinian', 'gay' and 'female'. As is clear from the combination of these three words, the message developed by Aṣwāt (but also by al-Qaws) is focused on the intersection between gender, ethnic and national identity, as activists identify themselves as Palestinians in the first place when asked about where they belong. The same interconnection between sexual and gender diversity and the Palestinian struggle for freedom and equality is at the core of the discourse of the Palestinian Queers for BDS, a group that came together in 2005 to promote queer rights and stand for the Palestinian civil society call for boycott, divestment and sanctions against Israel.[37]

In the discourse developed by Palestinian activists, religion and religious identity are marginal. Contrary to what happens among Jewish queers, these groups have not actively engaged in the debate about the relationship between non-normative sexuality and religious normativity. Indeed, during the last decades the debate on gender and sexuality has been mainly shaped along lines of national belonging and identity politics rather than on religious morality and religious legal normativity.

That comes to light when considering the discourse developed by Palestinian LGBTQ activists gathered in associations such as Aṣwāt, al-Qaws and the Palestinian Queers for BDS. Their way of debating non-normative sexuality is clearly different from that developed in recent years by Jewish queers, who widened the space of debate, focusing on the relationship between religious normativity and sexual identity. On the contrary, they seem to avoid potentially divisive debates to emphasize their common Palestinian origins and their shared status as 'class B' citizens in Israel.

Being a Palestinian queer under Israeli occupation: The relevance of discriminative politics

As already mentioned, the first official Palestinian LGBTQ organization, al-Qaws, started in 2001 as an independent local project of the Jerusalem Open House. After a six-year period of cooperation between Palestinian and Jewish queers at the Open House, the activists of al-Qaws decided on a transition to an independent national Palestinian organization. After the transition, Haneen Maikey (al-Qaws' leader) declared to *The Guardian* that the desire to form an independent organization was based on the members' conviction that this was the only way to adequately address the specific and growing needs of Palestinian LGBTQs and provide a forum for internal dialogue about multiple identities and their relationship with Palestinian society at large.[38]

In the early 2000s, other Palestinian activists (Aṣwāt in 2002 and the Palestinian Queers for BDS in 2005) started to join independent national associations that tackled the specific needs of Palestinian LGBTQ individuals. Such organizations shared the will to address Palestinian rights and intersectional discrimination and to struggle not only against social injustice as a queer minority in Palestinian society but also against Israel's occupation.[39]

Moreover, Palestinian queers started to engage in campaigns against pinkwashing,[40] proclaiming their refusal to be exploited by the Israeli propaganda. The critique developed around the concept of pinkwashing, focused on the fact that by sponsoring the expansion of gay rights, Israeli authorities were diverting attention from other violations of human rights, such as mass incarceration of Palestinians, and depicting Middle Eastern states as gays' persecutors. This narrative ignored the existence of Palestinian gay rights organizations and the fact that homosexuality had been decriminalised in the West Bank since the 1950s, when anti-sodomy laws imposed under British colonial influence were removed from the Jordanian penal code.[41]

As a result of this debate, Jewish and Palestinian activists (both Muslim and Christian) separated and started developing a bilateral debate focused on national identity and the membership of LGBTQ activists to their respective communities. If such a separation succeeded in making homonationalism visible in Israel,[42] it also hindered the possibility of the two fronts sharing nation-crossing debates such as the one about the relationship between sexual identity and religious normativity.

In the light of the growing importance of religious normativity in identity debates among Palestinians in Israel, and considering the abovementioned constraints, Palestinian queers could try to develop their own discourse in the religious sphere. Yet, they do not engage with the religious framework. If, on the one hand, that has to be read as a conscious, active and strong refusal to engage in the non-secular sphere, on the other hand, it is possible to speculate on LGBTQ activists' perceived inability to deal with religious normativity.

In this regard, it is useful to look at the history of Islamic education in Israel. A government blockade was put on books and other cultural materials coming from the neighbouring Arab countries in the 1950s.[43] In the same way, Islamic education was inhibited and put under tight control until the first half of the 1960s.[44] In his work on Arabic education in Israel, Majid al-Haj convincingly claims that, for a long period of time, Palestinian students in Israel have been taught Jewish religion more than their own. Curricula and timetables from the 1960s show that the hours allocated to the teaching of Jewish religion in Arabic public schools in Israel were twice those that addressed the teaching of Islam. Moreover, curricula differed in terms of content: the Qur'an was presented as a literary text while the study of the Bible, *Mishna* and *Agada* was classified as a religious national subject.[45]

It was only in 1987 that a special committee composed by Sharia judges and Arab teachers was created. The committee paved the way for the drafting, during the 1990s, of new religious curricula for Arab education and for the availability of new textbooks to be used in secondary and high public schools (from tenth to twelfth grades).[46] Even then, students were given few means to actively discuss religious norms. Al-Haj specifies that the main educational goals for the subject study of 'Islamic religion' were: the development of the student's personality and love for the human race; respect for other religions; passion for work and science; development of a sense of social responsibility; and inner poise to be reached through the faith in God, his Prophet and the central figures in the history of Islam.[47] That is the opposite of what happened in the history of Jewish religious education in Israel, as during that time the country became the largest centre of *yeshivas* (Orthodox Jewish colleges or seminaries) in the world, with the highest number and most diverse types of institutes of Talmudic learning and students since the Talmudic era.[48]

As already mentioned, starting from the 1980s the associations connected with the Israeli Islamic Movement started to grow. The IIM associations focused their efforts in filling the omissions of the state towards the Palestinian-Muslim minority. Among other activities, they started to provide educational services centred on the promotion of Arab language, history and knowledge of Islam. This signified a promotion of Islamic education at the micro level (outside public institutions and schools). As highlighted by Shany Payes, this was possible thanks to the backing of the Israeli government, which during that time, decided to change its policy towards conservative Islamic forces in Israel. Indeed, the government started to consider the IIM as a counter power useful for limiting the influence and strength of the secular PLO (Palestine Liberation Organization) among Palestinians.[49] As a result, the growing attention on Islamic education after the 1980s was combined with a promotion of conservative tendencies rather that a liberalization of costumes.

'With my mother, [...] even what is ḥalāl *turns into* ḥarām*': Experiencing homosexuality as young Palestinians in Israel*

I met Līnā, Sūzān and Munā (pseudonyms) at the Jerusalem Open House on a winter afternoon.[50] Gender nonconforming gay men, they all referred to each other using female pronouns. They defined themselves as gay, and made it clear that at the time we met one of them was in the process of transition from male to female, while the others were seriously thinking about it and sometimes dressed in drag. My face-to-face interviews were limited to them and to their perception of religious identity. On account of this, many interesting questions remain open to investigation and would require further and more extended field work: how typical is it for Palestinian gay men to use female names and pronouns in such spaces (or elsewhere)? What do such practices signify for them, as well as for other Palestinian gay men? The narrow sample here considered obviously does not allow for generalization. Nevertheless, the interviews provided the opportunity to learn more about religious identity from the perspective of usually under-represented individuals. Līnā, Sūzān and Munā define themselves as Muslims. Yet there are slight differences between them: Līnā underlined that she prays every day; Sūzān described herself as secular and 'open minded'; Munā explained that she used to pray before the marriage of her last partner to another woman to form a standard heterosexual couple. Nevertheless, they all shared similar stories of violence and discrimination on the grounds of their sexual identity. Moreover, when asked about the reasons for such discrimination they all attributed a role to religion.

According to their own experience, people sometimes refer to the story of Lot and the episode of the Qur'an, where God destroyed the cities of Sodom and Gomorrah and killed their inhabitants by raining stones down on them.[51] The story of the destruction of the people of Lot is common to Judaism, Christianity and Islam. Indeed, as they underlined 'there is no big difference between Muslim and Christian gays, we are all discriminated inside our communities'. As explained by Sūzān, 'if being gay would be permitted by religion, maybe people would accept us as equal members of our communities'.[52]

When I explained to them my interest in the different way Israeli Jewish queers and Palestinian queers with Israeli citizenship configure religion, they proved to be aware of the questioning of religious normativity by part of their Jewish counterparts. Indeed, at the time of the interviews, they had been attending the activities of the Open House in Jerusalem for several months and they knew of past activities such as the march 'LGBTQ and Religion'.[53]

Yet these initiatives apparently had not influenced their attitude towards their own religion. As explained by Līnā, questions regarding the relationship between religious normativity and sexual identity are tackled at the individual level or in the restricted circle of intimates: 'I continuously ask myself and my mother if being gay is possible according to Islam, but she always says that it is prohibited, *ḥarām*. With my mother, everything is *ḥarām*. With her even what is *ḥalāl* turns into *ḥarām*.'[54] According to Sūzān, 'it makes no difference if I engage in debates about the possibility of being gay and Muslim. We know that it is not permitted by the Qur'an, that's what people always say. We will know the truth just in the end, after death, when everybody will be judged in front of God.'[55]

Nevertheless, Līnā, Sūzān and Munā tried to maintain a strong individual spirituality and connection to Islam. As explained by Līnā,

> I do believe in God. I can't stop thinking that I'm both gay and Muslim. I can't stop asking myself if it is OK to be a gay and to fulfil the ritual prayers at the same

> time. Anyway, I've never stopped fulfilling my praying duties as I am a Muslim, and that means that I must preserve a connection between me and God.[56]

In the case of Līnā, who was the most religiously committed of the three, such an intimate connection hasn't weakened over time, despite transformative changes, as at the time of the interview she had just started hormone therapy. However, it was configured as a form of individual spirituality around the bilateral relation between God and his creature.

Līnā, Sūzān and Munā's unwillingness to debate the relationship between their sexual and religious identity with other Muslims seemed to be due not to a lack of faith but more to the perception that there is no space for discussion. As Munā explained, while miming her normal way of walking, in her case even the simple act of moving around among people was a problem: 'If I simply walk, like this, people throw against me bad words, sometimes even fruits or garbage.'[57] In the case of Sūzān, the unwillingness to discuss seemed not to be due to the threat of physical harassment, but more to the perception of an impossibility of receiving any kind of approval from her surroundings:

> They just tell me that I am a man and that I have to behave like a man, I have to marry and to have children. I cry every day, asking myself why I don't manage to be like the others, but God made me the way I am. I don't know if they are right, we will see at the end of times.[58]

Such problems of communication with their surroundings are also reflected in the way Līnā, Sūzān and Munā become informed. When asked where and how they find answers to theoretical doubts about the relationship between religious and sexual identity, they all referred to their mothers or to individual searches on YouTube. Apparently, the same problem brought Līnā, Sūzān and Munā to the Jerusalem Open House, an organization led by Jewish Israelis.

In this regard, their approach is quite different from the approach of Palestinian LGBTQ activists, who refer to associations that specifically address the needs of Palestinians, such as the already mentioned Aṣwāt, al-Qaws and the Palestinian Queers for BDS, and the interconnection between gender identity and Palestinian struggles for freedom and equality. Despite such clearly different approaches, we can notice that both position themselves in the secular sphere and refuse to engage with the religious framework. Yet, in the case of activists of Palestinian organizations, such a position is ascribed to factors directly connected to the specific Israeli situation and the multifaceted discrimination it encompasses.

In our email exchange, Rīmā ʿAbūd from Aṣwāt pointed out that in its first years the organization tried to tackle the status of sexuality in religion, as some members considered themselves religious and needed to find some reconciliation with religion. At the same time, she didn't oppose the possibility that such an effort had been abandoned due to a perceived inability to engage in theoretical reasoning in the framework of religious normativity.[59] Such a question remains open. Nevertheless, in view of the historical framework described (and especially with reference to the strategies played by the government towards Islam in different historical periods), it is not possible to exclude the possibility that LGBTQ individuals of different generations were indeed prevented from having an informed approach towards their religion and that this is likely to have influenced their real possibilities of engaging in the debates on religion and sexuality, expressing themselves and negotiating their claims along the lines of religious identity and normativity. At the same time, this had the side effect of granting conservative forces the monopoly on the discourse.

Conclusion

The debate that LGBTQ Palestinians in Israel are shaping differs from the one recently developed by Israeli Jews. Israeli LGBTQ organizations are questioning religious normativity and even try to negotiate the spaces of their identity inside religious Orthodox communities. On the contrary, the Palestinian debate on sexuality does not engage with religious normativity. Rather, religion seems to be configured by Palestinian queers as a bilateral relation between God and each believer, and questions about the relationship between religious normativity and sexual identity are tackled at the individual level or in the restricted circle of intimates.

That self-exclusion from the arena of public debate about the relationship between religious normativity and sexual identity inside the different Muslim and Christian communities of believers is due to a complex interplay of different factors, which in some cases are tightly connected with the context of the Israeli-Palestinian conflict. As noted by Darren Rosenblum, 'queer identity is intersectional, since most queers face multiple aspects of discrimination, as women, as people of color, as poor people, as cross-gendered people, and as sexual subversives'.[60]

Looking at the portrayed framework leads us to some considerations. Two forces appear as particularly strong in affecting debates on LGBTQ rights; multifaceted discrimination of Palestinians as a whole (perceived as an ethnic and national community) by Israeli institutions, and subordination of gender issues to nationalism by Palestinians themselves. As a result of general discrimination, Palestinian LGBTQ organizations actively refuse to engage in nation-crossing debates such as that on religious normativity and sexual identity or to build intersecting alliances with the Israeli Jewish LGBTQ community. On the contrary, they focus instead on strategies to 'intersect' their claims for equality with those of the Palestinian minority as a whole. That implies facing ongoing subordination of gender issues to the urgencies imposed by the framework of the Israeli-Palestinian conflict and Palestinian national cause. At the same time, it is possible to speculate on LGBTQ activists' perceived inability to engage in theoretical reasoning in the frame of religious normativity and on the responsibility of Israeli policies in this regard, leaving the space open for conservative religious forces to shape the debate on LGBTQ rights in Israel.

Notes

1 These Palestinians are often referred to (especially in the Middle East) as '48's' as, during the tragic events that occurred between 1947 and 1949, they managed to stay in their homes, situated inside Israel after the founding of the state in 1948. In 1952 they obtained Israeli citizenship. Afterwards (although not automatically) Israeli citizenship was granted also to their descendants.

2 Central Bureau of Statistics (CBS), 'Statistical Abstract of Israel 2017', Table 2.3 (10 September 2017). Available online: http://www.cbs.gov.il/reader/shnaton/templ_shnaton_e.html?num_tab=st02_03&CYear=2017 (accessed 28 May 2018).

3 The juridical system of Israel is often classified as semi-confessional. For the classification of the Israeli Juridical system, see Serena Baldin (ed.), *Diritti tradizionali e religiosi in alcuni ordinamenti contemporanei* (Trieste: Edizioni Universitarie Trieste, 2005). For the interplay of common law and civil law in Israel, see Alfredo Rabello Mordechai, *Il sistema costituzionale dello Stato di Israele* (Torino: G. Giappichelli Editore, 2006) and Alfredo Rabello Mordechai, 'The Harmonization of Common Law and Civil Law in the Private Law of the State of Israel', in Celia Wasserstein Fassberg (ed.), *Israeli Reports to the XIII International Congress of Comparative Law*, 1–14 (Jerusalem: Harry Sacher Institute for Legislative Research and Comparative Law, 1990).

4 That means that jurisdiction is allocated according to subject (family matters such as marriage and divorce under the jurisdiction of religious courts and penal matters under the jurisdiction of civil courts, for example).

5 On the division of areas of jurisdiction during the first years after the foundation of the State of Israel, see Patricia Woods, *Judicial Power and National Politics: Courts and Gender in the Religious-Secular Conflict in Israel* (Haifa: University of Haifa, 2008) and Alisa Rubin Peled, *Debating Islam in the Jewish State: The Development of Policy toward Islamic Institutions in Israel* (Albany, NY: State University of New York Press, 2001).

6 Iyad Zahalka 'The Arab Public's View on the Status of the Shari'ah Courts', in Elie Rekhess and Arik Rudinitzky (eds), *Muslim Minorities in Non-Muslim Majority Countries: The Islamic Movement in Israel as a Test Case*, 79–94 (Tel Aviv: Tel Aviv University, 2013).

7 See Women's Equal Rights Law, Laws of the State of Israel, 5711–1951 and Penal Law Amendment (Bigamy) Law, 5719–1959.

8 For more details, see Aharon Layish, *Women and Islamic Law in a Non-Muslim State: A Study Based on Decisions of the Sharī'a Courts in Israel* (New York: Wiley, 1975), 72–90; Aharon Layish, 'Adaptation of Jurists' Law to Modern Times in an Alien Environment: The Case of Shari'a in Israel', *Die Welt des Islams*, 46 (2) (2006): 168–225; Moussa Abou Ramadan, 'The Shari'a in Israel: Islamization, Israelization and the Invented Islamic Law', *UCLA Journal of Islamic and Near Eastern Law*, 5 (2007): 81–129.

9 The strong bond between Islam and Arab Nationalism rests on the Qur'an as a vehicle for the transmission of Arabic language and history. For a comprehensive discussion about the relationship between Islam and Arab national identity, see the chapter 'Educating the Nation: Sati' al-Husri' in Youssef M. Choueri, *Arab Nationalism – A History: Nation and the State in the Arab World*, 101–24 (Oxford: Blackwell Publishing, 2000). About the growing role of Islamic associations in Israel and the relationship between Islam and Palestinian nationalism, see Nijmi Edres, 'La réaffirmation de l'identité palestinienne en Israël: le rôle du mouvement islamique israélien dans le cadre éducatif', *Maghreb-Machrek*, 220 (2014): 109–25, and Tilde

Rosmer, 'Resisting "Israelization": The Islamic Movement in Israel and the Realization of Islamization, Palestinization and Arabization', *Journal of Islamic Studies*, 23 (3) (2012): 325–58.

10 Dimitri Makarov, *Islam and Development at Micro Level: Community Activities of the Islamic Movement in Israel* (Moscow: Russian Center for Strategic Research and International Studies, 1997).

11 See Issam Aburaiya, 'Developmental Leadership: The Case of the Islamic Movement in Umm al-Fahim, Israel', MA thesis (Clark University, 1991).

12 See Edres, 'La réaffirmation de l'identité palestinienne en Israël'.

13 The Aguda, originally known as the Society for the Protection of Personal Rights (SPPR), was the first organization of gays and lesbians founded in Israel, in 1975. For more information see Association for LGBT Israel, 'Home', (n.d.). Available online: https://www.lgbt.org.il/ (accessed 21 December 2017).

14 Jerusalem Open House (JOH), "Our Vision', (n.d.). Available online:https://www.joh.org.il/ (accessed 21 December 2017).

15 See A Wider Bridge, 'Jerusalem Open House for Pride and Tolerance', (n.d.). Available online: http://awiderbridge.org/jerusalem-open-house-for-pride-and-tolerance/ (accessed 14 December 2017).

16 In 2008 Bat-Kol included more than 150 women between nineteen and sixty years old. For more information about the organization, see Bat-Kol, 'About Bat-Kol', (2014). Available online: http://www.bat-kol.org/english/. For details about Havruta, see Havruta, 'Friendship – Religious Gays', (n.d.). Available online: http://havruta.org.il/english (accessed 30 March 2017).

17 Quoted from Havruta, 'Friendship – Religious Gays', (n.d.). Available online: http://havruta.org.il/english (accessed 15 December 2017).

18 Employment (Equal Opportunities) Law, 1988. According to the provisions of this Law (section 2) as amended (on 2 January 1992), an employer shall not discriminate between his employees concerning work conditions 'on the basis of their sex, sexual orientation, personal status or their being parents'.

19 The Buggery Act 1533, was passed by the English Parliament during the reign of Henry VIII. It was the country's first civil sodomy law, as such offences were previously dealt with by the ecclesiastical courts. The Act defined buggery as an unnatural sexual act against the will of God and man. It remained in force until it was repealed and replaced by the Offences against the Person Act 1828. Buggery would remain a capital offence until 1861. The Attorney General decided in the early 1960s, and the Israeli Supreme Court ruled in 1963, that the law should not be applied to acts between consenting adults in private.

20 In a precedent-setting decision in response to a petition submitted by the Association for Civil Rights in Israel (ACRI), the Supreme Court ruled that the Population Registry must register the marriages of same-sex couples who were married abroad.

21 See the Supreme Court petition on behalf of El Al Airlines flight attendant, Jonathan Danilovich, who requested that his same-sex partner receive benefits from the company comparable to those received by heterosexual partners of employees. The revolutionary and precedent-setting ruling recognized the rights of same-sex partners for the first time. High Court of Justice case no. 721/94, 1994 ('High Court of Justice case no. 721/94', [Tel Aviv University, 4 May 1994]. Available online: http://www.tau.ac.il/law/aeyalgross/Danilowitz.htm [accessed 26 June 2020]).

22 For an overview, see Association for Civil Rights in Israel, 'Protecting and Promoting LGBT Rights in Israel', 15 February 2009. Available online: http://www.acri.org.il/en/2009/02/15/protecting-and-promoting-lgbt-rights-in-israel/.

23 For more information about LGBT-friendly synagogues, see LGBT Olim, 'LGBT-friendly Synagogues', (n.d.). Available online: https://lgbtolim.wordpress.com/synagogues/ (accessed 30 March 2017).

24 The campaign has been documented by *Haaretz*, see Judy Maltz, 'Out, Proud and Religious: LGBT Orthodox Jews Step Out of the Closet in Online Campaign', (*Haaretz*, 15 December 2015). Available online: http://www.haaretz.com/israel-news/.premium-1.692022 (accessed 30 March 2017).

25 For the full document, in Hebrew, see Beit Hillel, 'About Beit Hillel', (n.d.). Available online: http://www.beithillel.org.il/show.asp?id=71658#.W9r8CuJReUm (accessed 1 November 2018).

26 Modern Orthodox Judaism is a movement within Orthodox Judaism, also known as Zionist Orthodox Judaism.

27 Elie Leshem, 'Leading Rabbis Champion Peer Who Called LGBTs "Deviants"', (*Times of Israel*, 21 July 2016). Available online: http://www.timesofisrael.com/prominent-rabbis-back-peer-who-called-lgbts-deviants/ (accessed 30 March 2017).

28 Ibid.

29 Tamara Zieve, 'Ahead of Jerusalem Gay Pride Parade: Lehava Accuses Homosexuals of Harming Jewish Nation', (*Jerusalem Post*, 30 July 2015). Available online: http://www.jpost.com/Israel-News/Lehava-representative-equates-homosexuality-to-bank-robbery-ahead-of-Jerusalem-gay-pride-parade-410677 (accessed 30 March 2017).

30 In June 2015, for instance, Shaykh Kamāl Khaṭīb (a deputy belonging to the Israeli Islamic Movement) published a homophobic article commenting the same-sex marriage of Luxembourg premier Xavier Bettel. The article, titled 'You Make Me Sick', sparked a flurry of condemnations by Palestinian associations, shining a light on a usually suppressed debate on gay rights. Kamāl Khaṭīb, 'Qaraf yaqrifkū' (You Make Me Sick), (Yaffa48, 5 June 2015). Available online: https://www.yaffa48.com/?mod=articles&ID=19568 (accessed 2 July 2020).

31 alQaws, 'Index', (2014). Available online: http://alqaws.org/siteEn/index (accessed 30 March 2017).

32 alQaws, 'About Us', (2014). Available online:http://www.alqaws.org/about-us (accessed 30 March 2017).

33 Alkhat, 'Who We Are', (2018). Available online: http://www.alkhat.org/ (accessed 30 March 2017).

34 Aṣwāt, 'Mission and Vision', (n.d.). Available online: http://www.aswatgroup.org/en (accessed 30 March 2017).

35 Aṣwāt, 'Who We Are', (n.d.). Available online: http://www.aswatgroup.org/en/content/who-we-are (accessed 30 March 2017).

36 The full text can be downloaded, see Aṣwāt, 'Publications', (n.d.). Available online: http://www.aswatgroup.org/en/content/publications (accessed 30 March 2017).

37 For more information about the organization, see Palestinian Queers for BDS, 'Home', (n.d.). Available online: https://pqbds.wordpress.com/ (accessed 28 May 2018).

38 See Haneen Maikey, 'Rainbow over Palestine' (*Telegraph*, 10 March 2008). Available online: https://www.theguardian.com/commentisfree/2008/mar/10/rainbowoverpalestine (accessed 28 May 2018).

39 See Sarah Schulman, *Israel/Palestine and the Queer International* (Durham, NC: Duke University Press, 2012), Kindle edition, loc. 427.

40 In the context of LGBT rights, pinkwashing is used to describe a variety of marketing and political strategies aimed at promoting products, countries, people or entities through an appeal to gay-friendliness, in order to be perceived as progressive, modern and tolerant.

41 Ibid. For a comprehensive picture on pinkwashing strategies in Israel, see also Aeyal Gross, 'The Politics of LGBT Rights in Israel and Beyond: Nationality, Normativity and Queer Politics', *Columbia Human Rights Law Review*, 46 (2) (2015): 81–152; Ghaida Moussa, 'Narrative (Sub)Versions: How Queer Palestinian Women "Queer" Palestinian Identity', MA Thesis (Department of International Development and Global Studies Faculty of Social Sciences, University of Ottawa, 2011).
42 About pinkwashing and homonationalism, see Jason Ritchie, 'Pinkwashing, Homonationalism, and Israel–Palestine: The Conceits of Queer Theory and the Politics of the Ordinary', *Antipode*, 47 (3) (2015): 616–34.
43 Alisa Rubin Peled, *Debating Islam in the Jewish State*, 108–09.
44 Ibid.
45 Majid Al-Haj, *Education, Empowerment, and Control: The Case of the Arabs in Israel* (Albany, NY: State University of New York Press, 1995), 139.
46 Ibid., 151–52.
47 Ibid.
48 For the voice 'yeshiva', see Jewish Virtual Library, 'Orthodox Judaism: Yeshiva', (n.d.). Available online: http://www.jewishvirtuallibrary.org/yeshiva#8 (accessed 31 March 2017).
49 Shany Payes, *Palestinian NGOs in Israel – The Politics of Civil Society* (London: Bloomsbury Academic Studies, 2005), 87–101, 162.
50 Face-to-face personal interviews with semi-open questions in Arabic and English took place at the Jerusalem Open House on 6 December 2017. I am extremely grateful to Rīmā ʿAbūd, who dared to be involved in an email dialogue with me, and even more to Līnā, Sūzān and Monā (pseudonyms) who agreed to answer my questions, in face-to-face interviews, with patience and frankness.
51 Ibid.
52 Ibid.
53 Ibid.
54 Ibid.
55 Ibid.
56 Ibid.
57 Ibid.
58 Ibid.
59 Personal email exchange with Rīmā ʿAbūd, 22 January 2017. For ethnographic interviews with Palestinian activists, see Jason Ritchie, 'How Do You Say "Come Out of the Closet" in Arabic? Queer Activism and the Politics of Visibility in Israel-Palestine', *GLQ: A Journal of Lesbian and Gay Studies*, 16 (4) (2010): 557–76.
60 Darren Rosenblum, "Queer Intersectionality and the Failure of Recent Lesbian and Gay "Victories"', *Law and Sexuality*, 4 (1994): 83–122. Available online: http://digitalcommons.pace.edu/lawfaculty/210/(accessed 31 March 2017).

References

Abou Ramadan, Moussa (2007), 'The Shari'a in Israel: Islamization, Israelization and the Invented Islamic Law', *UCLA Journal of Islamic and Near Eastern Law*, 5: 81–129.

Aburaiya, Issam (1991), 'Developmental Leadership: The Case of the Islamic Movement in Umm al-Fahim, Israel', MA thesis, Clark University.

Al-Haj, Majid (1995), *Education, Empowerment, and Control: The Case of the Arabs in Israel*, Albany, NY: State University of New York Press.

Alkhat (2018), 'Who We Are'. Available online: http://www.alkhat.org/(accessed 30 March 2017).

alQaws (2014), 'About Us'. Available online: http://www.alqaws.org/about-us (accessed 30 March 2017).

alQaws (2014), 'Index'. Available online: http://alqaws.org/siteEn/index (accessed 30 March 2017).

Association for Civil Rights in Israel (2009), 'Protecting and Promoting LGBT Rights in Israel', 15 February. Available online: http://www.acri.org.il/en/2009/02/15/protecting-and-promoting-lgbt-rights-in-israel/ (accessed 26 June 2020).

Association for LGBT Israel (n.d.), 'Home'. Available online: https://www.lgbt.org.il/ (accessed 21 December 2017).

Aṣwāt (n.d.), 'Mission and Vision'. Available online: http://www.aswatgroup.org/en (accessed 30 March 2017).

Aṣwāt (n.d.), 'Publications'. Available online: http://www.aswatgroup.org/en/content/publications (accessed 30 March 2017).

Aṣwāt (n.d.), 'Who We Are'. Available online: http://www.aswatgroup.org/en/content/who-we-are (accessed 30 March 2017).

A Wider Bridge (n.d.), 'Jerusalem Open House for Pride and Tolerance'. Available online: http://awiderbridge.org/jerusalem-open-house-for-pride-and-tolerance/(accessed 14 December 2017).

Baldin, Serena (ed.) (2005), *Diritti tradizionali e religiosi in alcuni ordinamenti contemporanei*, Trieste: Edizioni Universitarie Trieste.

Bat-Kol (2014), 'About Bat-Kol'. Available online: http://www.bat-kol.org/english/ (accessed 26 June 2020).

Beit Hillel (n.d.), 'About Beit Hillel'. Available online: http://www.beithillel.org.il/show.asp?id=71658#.W9r8CuJReUm (accessed 1 November 2018).

Central Bureau of Statistics (CBS) (2017), 'Statistical Abstract of Israel 2017', Table 2.3, 10 September. Available online: http://www.cbs.gov.il/reader/shnaton/templ_shnaton_e.html?num_tab=st02_03&CYear=2017 (accessed 28 May 2018).

Choueri, Youssef M. (2000), *Arab Nationalism – A History: Nation and the State in the Arab World*, Oxford: Blackwell Publishing.

Edres, Nijmi (2014), 'La réaffirmation de l'identité palestinienne en Israël: le rôle du mouvement islamique israélien dans le cadre éducatif', *Maghreb-Machrek*, 220: 109–25.

Gross, Aeyal (2015), 'The Politics of LGBT Rights in Israel and Beyond: Nationality, Normativity and Queer Politics', *Columbia Human Rights Law Review*, 46 (2): 81–152.

Havruta (n.d.), 'Friendship – Religious Gays'. Available online: http://havruta.org.il/english (accessed 30 March 2017).

'High Court of Justice case no. 721/94' (1994), Tel Aviv University, 4 May. Available online: http://www.tau.ac.il/law/aeyalgross/Danilowitz.htm (accessed 26 June 2020).

Jerusalem Open House (JOH) (n.d.), 'Our Vision'. Available online: https://www.joh.org.il/(accessed 21 December 2017).

Jewish Virtual Library (n.d.), 'Orthodox Judaism: Yeshiva'. Available online: http://www.jewishvirtuallibrary.org/yeshiva#8 (accessed 31 March 2017).

Khaṭīb, Kamāl (2015), 'Qaraf yaqrifkū' (You Make Me Sick), Yaffa48, 5 June 2015. Available online: https://www.yaffa48.com/?mod=articles&ID=19568 (accessed 2 July 2020).

Layish, Aharon (1975), *Women and Islamic Law in a Non-Muslim State: A Study Based on Decisions of the Sharī'a Courts in Israel*, New York: Wiley.
Layish, Aharon (2006), 'Adaptation of Jurists' Law to Modern Times in an Alien Environment: The Case of Shari'a in Israel', *Die Welt des Islams*, 46 (2): 168–225.
Leshem, Elie (2016), 'Leading Rabbis Champion Peer Who Called LGBTs "Deviants"', *Times of Israel*, 21 July. Available online: http://www.timesofisrael.com/prominent-rabbis-back-peer-who-called-lgbts-deviants/ (accessed 30 March 2017).
LGBT Olim (n.d.), 'LGBT-friendly Synagogues'. Available online: https://lgbtolim.wordpress.com/synagogues/ (accessed 30 March 2017).
Maikey, Haneen (2008), 'Rainbow over Palestine', *Telegraph*, 10 March. Available online: https://www.theguardian.com/commentisfree/2008/mar/10/rainbowoverpalestine (accessed 28 May 2018).
Makarov, Dimitri (1997), *Islam and Development at Micro Level: Community Activities of the Islamic Movement in Israel*, Moscow: Russian Center for Strategic Research and International Studies.
Maltz, Judy (2015), 'Out, Proud and Religious: LGBT Orthodox Jews Step Out of the Closet in Online Campaign', *Haaretz*, 15 December. Available online: http://www.haaretz.com/israel-news/.premium-1.692022 (accessed 30 March 2017).
Moussa, Ghaida (2011), 'Narrative (Sub)Versions: How Queer Palestinian Women "Queer" Palestinian Identity', MA Thesis, Department of International Development and Global Studies Faculty of Social Sciences, University of Ottawa.
Palestinian Queers for BDS (n.d.), 'Home'. Available online: https://pqbds.wordpress.com/(accessed May 28 2018).
Payes, Shany (2005), *Palestinian NGOs in Israel – The Politics of Civil Society*, London: Bloomsbury Academic Studies.
Peled, Alisa Rubin (2001), *Debating Islam in the Jewish State: The Development of Policy toward Islamic Institutions in Israel*, Albany, NY: State University of New York Press.
Rabello, Alfredo Mordechai (1990), 'The Harmonization of Common Law and Civil Law in the Private Law of the State of Israel', in Celia Wasserstein Fassberg (ed.), *Israeli Reports to the XIII International Congress of Comparative Law*, 1–14, Jerusalem: Harry Sacher Institute for Legislative Research and Comparative Law.
Rabello, Alfredo Mordechai (2006), *Il sistema costituzionale dello Stato di Israele*, Torino: G. Giappichelli Editore.
Ritchie, Jason (2010), 'How Do You Say "Come Out of the Closet" in Arabic? Queer Activism and the Politics of Visibility in Israel-Palestine', *GLQ: A Journal of Lesbian and Gay Studies*, 16 (4): 557–76.
Ritchie, Jason (2015), 'Pinkwashing, Homonationalism, and Israel–Palestine: The Conceits of Queer Theory and the Politics of the Ordinary', *Antipode*, 47 (3): 616–34.
Rosenblum, Darren (1994), 'Queer Intersectionality and the Failure of Recent Lesbian and Gay "Victories"', *Law and Sexuality*, 4: 83–122. Available online: http://digitalcommons.pace.edu/lawfaculty/210/(accessed 31 March 2017).
Rosmer, Tilde (2012), 'Resisting "Israelization": The Islamic Movement in Israel and the Realization of Islamization, Palestinization and Arabization', *Journal of Islamic Studies*, 23 (3): 325–58.
Schulman, Sarah (2012), *Israel/Palestine and the Queer International*, Durham, NC: Duke University Press.
Woods, Patricia (2008), *Judicial Power and National Politics: Courts and Gender in the Religious-Secular Conflict in Israel*, Haifa: University of Haifa.

Zahalka, Iyad (2013), 'The Arab Public's View on the Status of the Shariʿah Courts', in Elie Rekhess and Arik Rudinitzky (eds), *Muslim Minorities in Non-Muslim Majority Countries: The Islamic Movement in Israel as a Test Case*, 79–94, Tel Aviv: Tel Aviv University.

Zieve, Tamara (2015), 'Ahead of Jerusalem Gay Pride Parade: Lehava Accuses Homosexuals of Harming Jewish Nation', *Jerusalem Post*, 30 July. Available online: http://www.jpost.com/Israel-News/Lehava-representative-equates-homosexuality-to-bank-robbery-ahead-of-Jerusalem-gay-pride-parade-410677 (accessed 30 March 2017).

INDEX

www.ingramcontent.com/pod-product-compliance
Lightning Source LLC
Chambersburg PA
CBHW050415280326
41932CB00013BA/1875
* 9 7 8 0 7 5 5 6 3 7 1 3 3 *